Applied History and
Contemporary Policymaking

Applied History and Contemporary Policymaking

School of Statecraft

Edited by
Robert Crowcroft

BLOOMSBURY ACADEMIC
LONDON • NEW YORK • OXFORD • NEW DELHI • SYDNEY

BLOOMSBURY ACADEMIC
Bloomsbury Publishing Plc
50 Bedford Square, London, WC1B 3DP, UK
1385 Broadway, New York, NY 10018, USA
29 Earlsfort Terrace, Dublin 2, Ireland

BLOOMSBURY, BLOOMSBURY ACADEMIC and the Diana logo are trademarks
of Bloomsbury Publishing Plc

First published in Great Britain 2023
This paperback edition published 2024

Copyright © Robert Crowcroft, 2023

Robert Crowcroft has asserted his right under the Copyright, Designs and
Patents Act, 1988, to be identified as Editor of this work.

For legal purposes the Acknowledgements on p. xi constitute an extension
of this copyright page.

Cover image © Mark Wilson/Getty Images

Bloomsbury Publishing Plc does not have any control over, or responsibility for, any
third-party websites referred to or in this book. All internet addresses given in this
book were correct at the time of going to press. The author and publisher regret any
inconvenience caused if addresses have changed or sites have ceased to exist,
but can accept no responsibility for any such changes.

A catalogue record for this book is available from the British Library.

A catalog record for this book is available from the Library of Congress.

ISBN: HB: 978-1-3501-7702-4
PB: 978-1-3503-4836-3
ePDF: 978-1-3501-7703-1
eBook: 978-1-3501-7704-8

Typeset by Deanta Global Publishing Services, Chennai, India

To find out more about our authors and books visit www.bloomsbury.com and
sign up for our newsletters.

In memory of Owen A. Hartley

Contents

Contributors

Jeremy Black is Emeritus Professor of History at the University of Exeter. The most prolific historian in the Western world, he is the author of more than 150 books. He lectures internationally and is a regular contributor to the media. Recent works include *Military Strategy: A Global History* (2020), *Tank Warfare* (2021) and *The French Revolutionary and Napoleonic War: Strategies for a World War* (2022).

Philip Bobbitt, KBE, FRHistS, is the Herbert Wechsler Professor of Federal Jurisprudence and director of the Center for National Security at Columbia University. He is the author of several works on statecraft, including *Tragic Choices* (with Guido Calabresi) (1980), *Constitutional Fate* (1983), *Constitutional Interpretation* (1991), *The Shield of Achilles: War, Peace and the Course of History* (2002) and *Terror and Consent* (2008). He has also served in various capacities in the US government.

Robert Crowcroft is senior lecturer in history at the University of Edinburgh. His most recent works include *The End Is Nigh: British Politics, Power, and the Road to the Second World War* (2019) and, as co-editor, *The Oxford Handbook of Modern British Political History, 1800-2000* (2018). He has held visiting posts at Oxford and Cambridge, and writes regularly for the media.

Giselle Donnelly is senior fellow in foreign and defence policy studies at the American Enterprise Institute. She is the author of *Operation Just Cause: The Storming of Panama* (1991), *Clash of Chariots: The Great Tank Battles* (1999), numerous defence policy studies and the forthcoming four-volume series on American strategic culture, *The Personality of Our Power*.

Andrew Ehrhardt is an Engelsberg Applied History Postdoctoral Fellow with the Centre for Grand Strategy at King's College London. He completed his PhD in the Department of War Studies, King's College London, where his research focused on the British Foreign Office and the creation of the United Nations Organization during the Second World War. Originally from New Orleans, Louisiana, he graduated from the University of Texas at Austin in 2012.

Steven F. Hayward is senior resident scholar at the Institute of Government Studies at UC Berkeley. He is the author of the two-volume *The Age of Reagan* (2001, 2010), *Greatness: Reagan, Churchill, and the Making of Extraordinary Leaders* (2005) and *The Politically Incorrect Guide to the Presidents* (2012). He was previously at the American Enterprise Institute and has held various visiting posts. He worked for the George W. Bush presidential campaign in 2004.

Charlie Laderman is senior lecturer in international history in the War Studies department at King's College, London, and a Research Fellow at the Hoover Institution, Stanford University. His most recent book is *Hitler's American Gamble: Pearl Harbor and Germany's March to Global War* (2021), co-authored with Brendan Simms. He is also author of *Sharing the Burden: The Armenian Question, Humanitarian Intervention and Anglo-American Visions of Global Order* (2019).

Margaret MacMillan is Emeritus Professor of International History at Oxford University. She was Warden of St Antony's College, Oxford, from 2007 to 2017. Her research specializes in British imperial history and the international history of the nineteenth and twentieth centuries. Publications include *The Peacemakers* (2003), *The Uses and Abuses of History* (2010) and *The War that Ended Peace* (2014). Her latest book is *War: How Conflict Shaped Us* (2020).

Francesca Morphakis is a historian of modern British politics. Her MSc thesis on special advisors was awarded the Jeremiah Dalziel Prize at the University of Edinburgh (2018). She is currently completing a doctorate on the power, networks and cultures of the British Civil Service elite (1919–56) at the University of Leeds, funded by the Arts and Humanities Research Council.

Paul A. Rahe holds The Charles O. Lee and Louise K. Lee Chair in the Western Heritage at Hillsdale College and is a visiting scholar at Stanford University's Hoover Institution. He is the author of *Republics Ancient and Modern* (1992), Against *Throne and Altar* (2008), *Montesquieu and the Logic of Liberty* (2009), *Soft Despotism, Democracy's Drift* (2009) and a series of books on the evolving grand strategy of ancient Sparta.

Lord Peter Ricketts was a British diplomat for forty years. From 2006, he was successively the permanent secretary of the Foreign and Commonwealth Office, the UK's first national security adviser and ambassador to France. He is now a cross-bench member of the House of Lords. His first book, *Hard Choices: What Britain Does Next*, was published in 2021.

Kori Schake leads foreign and defence policy studies at the American Enterprise Institute. She is the author of *Safe Passage: The Transition from British to American Hegemony* (2017) and, with Jim Mattis, the editor of *Warriors and Citizens: American Views of Our Military* (2016). Dr Schake has taught at Stanford, Johns Hopkins SAIS and West Point. She has also had a distinguished career in government, working at the US State Department, US Department of Defense and the National Security Council.

Jeremi Suri holds the Mack Brown Distinguished Chair for Leadership in Global Affairs at the University of Texas at Austin. He is a professor in the University's Department of History and the LBJ School of Public Affairs. Professor Suri is the author and editor of ten books on politics and foreign policy, most recently *The Impossible Presidency: The Rise and Fall of America's Highest Office* (2017). His writings appear in the *New York*

Times, *Washington Post*, *Atlantic*, *Foreign Policy* and other media outlets. He hosts a weekly podcast, 'This is Democracy'.

Graeme Thompson is an Ernest May Postdoctoral Fellow in History and Policy at the Harvard Kennedy School and a former policy advisor at Global Affairs Canada. He earned his DPhil in History at St. Antony's College, Oxford, and has held visiting academic positions at Harvard University's Weatherhead Initiative on Global History, the Bill Graham Centre for Contemporary International History and Massey College, University of Toronto.

Acknowledgements

I am much indebted to Abigail Lane and Emily Drewe at Bloomsbury for their support throughout the preparation of this volume. Their professionalism and efficiency made the task as painless as possible. It was a pleasure to work with them both.

Paul Lay, then the editor of *History Today*, generously published an essay on Applied History in his distinguished magazine in late 2018, which really got the ball rolling. Another piece was published by Ryan Evans for the brilliant website *War on the Rocks*. I am grateful to John Bew for inviting me to deliver a paper at King's College London in January 2019 which helped to spark this project into life. John has been particularly important in offering support, opportunities and contacts galore. The Royal Society of Arts, Scotland, facilitated an event on Applied History at the University of Edinburgh in early 2019, for which I am appreciative; Andrew Ehrhardt, David Kaufman, Julius Ruiz and Tereza Valny all offered rich contributions. Brendan Simms asked me to chair a discussion at Trinity College Cambridge in June 2019 that was probably the most stimulating academic dialogue I have been a part of. Many friends, particularly Jeremy Black, Lee Bruce, Harshan Kumarasingham and Richard Whiting, have provided helpful provocation in conversation.

One of my former doctoral supervisors, Dr Owen Hartley of the University of Leeds, sadly passed away in the summer of 2021. Owen was a wonderfully old-fashioned scholar: he published little and dedicated himself, wholly and with boundless enthusiasm, to teaching students. In doing so, he improved the critical thinking of literally thousands of us over a career that began in the late 1960s. His sense of intellectual mischief was infectious; the whole point of a university was to refine one's thinking and to have great fun in doing so. I can still hear a distinctive booming laugh echoing down the corridor outside his office as he floated his latest outrageous and counter-intuitive idea. Students new to university had never ever encountered anyone quite like this before. Frankly, neither had most of the academics. Owen was a genuine polymath, whose knowledge and insights were staggeringly broad. He possessed easily the most fertile and original mind I have ever encountered. Owen was always interested in the areas in which history and contemporary political problems collided. Hopefully he would have enjoyed this volume of essays, and it is to him that the book is dedicated.

Robert Crowcroft
University of Edinburgh
March 2022

1

Introduction

Robert Crowcroft

In 1614, the famed English adventurer and explorer Sir Walter Raleigh published *History of the World*.[1] The title page of this volume bore an engraving that remains visually striking more than four centuries later.[2] It depicts a woman identified as *magistra vitae*, the 'teacher of life', holding the Earth aloft while treading Death and Oblivion underfoot.[3] The phrase 'teacher of life' would have been instantly understood by readers in Renaissance Europe; it was an allusion to a famous declaration by the Roman statesman Marcus Tullius Cicero that *historia magistra vitae* (history is the teacher of life).[4] This woman holding up the Earth represented History itself. Nor was that all. On one side of the figure appears a beautiful young woman identified as Truth, while on the other she is flanked by a wizened old woman identified as Experience. The three are surrounded by columns: one representing the witness of time, another carved with books, a third indicating the messenger of antiquity and the fourth the life of memory. At the top of the frontispiece is the all-seeing eye of providence, looking out over the world.

Raleigh was making a specific, and far-reaching, claim. Few could have failed to grasp its import. Put simply, it was that history represented a powerful tool – practical and moral – for traversing the present and future alike. It was a source of sustenance for prudent rulers and their advisers: those who guided the affairs of states, declared war, forged peace and made laws. History constituted perhaps the surest means of equipping practitioners of statecraft with the knowledge, insights and character vital to their work. Nobody understood more keenly than Raleigh himself the fickleness of fortune in public life – he wrote the book while imprisoned in the Tower of London on charges of treason and was executed in 1618. Politics is a high-stakes affair.

Raleigh's book communicated a provocative idea, but not a novel one. The notion that history serves as a repository of 'usable' wisdom has been around for thousands of years. Leaders have taken comfort from it, in the hope that intuition gleaned from the trials of others might prepare them for the rigours of decision-making in their own times.

This volume of essays takes seriously the idea that studying the past can be a crucial aid for leaders and others involved in decision-making. That is particularly valuable in a context where the contemporary democratic world languishes in a severe crisis of governance. Policy competence has undoubtedly diminished in recent decades.[5]

That is visible at all levels, from the formulation of effective international strategies to failed attempts at reforming inflexible public services, from the weakening of national capabilities in a 'globalized' world to the regulation of capital. We detect the issue on virtually every front. Decision-makers visibly struggle to steer the ship of state. Their skills often seem to be located elsewhere, in attending to public relations, 'spin', 'optics' and control of the 'narrative'. They rely on glib phrases. The qualities of prudent, effective leadership are rarer now than at any time in living memory. The global pandemic that erupted in 2020 illuminated this in vivid colours, but the evidence has been there for two or three decades. A tendency towards wishful thinking in difficult areas of policy and a general incapacity in delivering desired outcomes have been the hallmarks of Western statecraft for a long time now. Domestically, the failures of recent decades eroded the legitimacy of institutions and damaged public trust in politics. Electorates do not feel that they are ruled effectively. Internationally, Western states have been complacent and overly optimistic since the end of the Cold War, enjoying a global environment temporarily devoid of overt competition between the great powers. That has now changed. With the growth in the means and ambitions of the Chinese Communist Party, and the determination of Vladimir Putin to restore Russia to former glories, improved statecraft is imperative.

Effective leadership is ultimately about *doing*. It is a matter of practice. Those who govern need to deliver things. Achieving this requires a grasp of detail, an ability to manage large and complex projects, and the skill of posing insightful questions. It demands a capacity to lead teams and get the best out of their members, as well as the judgement to take sound decisions in risky endeavours where lives and precious resources will often be on the line. There are no more taxing activities. To govern is to do, and to govern well is to deliver more often than fail. Yet this is where the problem lies. The culture of modern politics does not prize skills of doing. It does not cultivate or incentivize them. Far from it. It emphasizes skills of presentation. This has produced disaster. To announce that one intends to tackle a problem is a far cry from actually doing something effective about it. And many of the most acute challenges of statecraft mandate improvisation and adaptation. Pulling this off successfully requires insight into the heart of the matter and an ability to read the runes as to impending and future developments. It necessitates an ability to negotiate and persuade. It demands the steadfastness to hold to a course during moments of danger. Nor is the problem confined to elected politicians. The departments of state that serve decision-makers are mired in a crisis of competence every bit as acute. These large bureaucracies, staffed with full-time civil servants responsible for policy in a given area, are perpetually ineffectual and sluggish. There are few error correction mechanisms within the bureaucracies, or frameworks for evaluating success or identifying failure. Adverse professional consequences for poor performance are rare.

Statecraft necessitates the skills of the political. Upon them rests what Cicero described as 'the task of providing and maintaining those things on which the practical business of life depends'.[6] Yet it is precisely those skills which have eroded in recent decades, and which must now be reconstituted, and reasserted, in arduous domestic and global environments. The surging power of China – not only unchecked since the 1990s but also actively encouraged by the United States and many of its allies in the hope that a highly authoritarian state would become a good global citizen – poses grave risks to the security and values of liberal polities. Facilitating the rise of China may well be remembered as the gravest error in the history of American statecraft. In early 2022, Xi Jinping and Vladimir Putin expressed a joint ambition to reconfigure the balance of power across the vast Eurasian landmass and to upend the world order itself. In Britain, the inability (and unwillingness) of the governing apparatus to deliver on the electorate's decision to leave the European Union between 2016 and 2019 generated a political crisis unlike any for at least a century. This stretched the resources of the liberal democratic system to breaking point. Across Europe, the structures and ambitions of the European Union create perpetual conflict between the centre and the periphery. While the EU does not seem in danger of collapse, millions have been left unemployed and impoverished by its economic policies; its second-largest economy and leading internationalist power, the UK, opted to leave the bloc; any hope of the Union being a genuine weight in geopolitical affairs remains a pipe-dream; and the extent to which the EU may be fundamentally, and necessarily, anti-democratic bedevils the politics of many member states. Western military action in Iraq and Afghanistan generated rapid results on the battlefield, but political stability proved elusive; the humiliating withdrawal from the latter, and the rapid restoration of the Taliban, in August 2021, just weeks shy of the twentieth anniversary of the terrorist attacks of 11 September 2001, exemplified decades of sloppy statesmanship. Elites have failed time and again. Large parts of the Middle East and Africa are wracked by turmoil and nourish terrorist threats. And a worldwide, interconnected system of capital and industrial production generates stark challenges for jobs, wages and social solidarity. The economic policies favoured by political leaders increasingly fail to offer the security that citizenries crave. Cultural issues have bled into politics as well. In the United States, and increasingly elsewhere, the primacy of arguments about 'identity' – usually undergirded by a crude biological and sociological essentialism – poisoned the country's politics and is now America's leading cultural export to the world; yet for politicians it is a convenient means to organize their competition, ensuring that an ability to reflect (or manufacture) popular outrage is the key to electoral success, not the far more difficult task of actually leading. There are comparable examples aplenty across the liberal, parliamentary states. What is clear is that the political nous of leaders and officials has degraded at an alarming pace over the past three decades.

History may offer insights into this degradation. Let us briefly try one out. In 146 BC, the armies of the Roman Republic destroyed the North African city-state of Carthage, marking the end of a strategic rivalry that encompassed three wars stretching back 118 years. For the first two of these conflicts, Carthage had been a strategic peer competitor capable of posing an existential challenge to the Republic. Yet the final defeat of Carthage arguably permanently altered the psyche of Roman leaders, and, paradoxically, not for the better. The Roman polity enjoyed a new, previously unthinkable, degree of security. Romans were safe. Sallust, one of the greatest historians of antiquity, believed that this safety from acute external danger led to the erosion of Rome's 'fear-rooted' statecraft.[7] To state the argument simply, security turned the Romans self-indulgent and soft. Deprived of the unifying force, and clarification of mind, offered by an adversary powerful enough to destroy them, Romans lapsed into internal scheming and internecine rivalry. A new form of politics took root, Sallust believed, one that led, gradually but inexorably, to the collapse of the Republic.

The implications of this vision of statecraft were, and remain, stark. Sallust believed that nations needed a challenge – and a serious one – to keep themselves, and their people, sharp. An adversary helped to weld states together and give their citizens a common purpose. Enemies acted as a sort of political glue, providing clarity and focus. Domestic vitality and external strength were intimately connected. Sallust was not the only notable thinker of antiquity to appreciate the cold value of enmity. Plato, Aristotle, Thucydides, Polybius and Posidonius all did so too. This was a world in which power mattered, as did the ability to rouse oneself to confront it. In the Senate debates on the final obliteration of Carthage, Public Cornelius Scipio Nasica anticipated what might follow, asserting that 'fear was a necessary and suitable teacher for citizens' (and, one imagines, their leaders). Without it, political communities would become 'weak'.[8]

It does not require feats of imagination to wonder whether the collapse of the Soviet Union, a new era of geopolitical safety and unprecedented economic prosperity led to a slackening of political sharpness over the succeeding decades. There were fewer consequences for error. A favourable strategic environment for the West reduced the imperatives for hard thinking and prudent leadership. The good times were here, and many assumed they would be permanent, undergirded by enduring US strategic primacy and consistent economic expansion. Social stability – always a rare commodity – was arguably taken for granted as well, as politicians, intellectuals, public services, institutions and even the law itself began fixating on the areas of incompatibility and divergence between the populations of democratic states, rather than concentrating on what their people had in common. Henry Adams wrote that 'Politics, as a practice, whatever its professions, has always been the systematic organisation of hatreds'.[9] If politics requires enemies, in recent decades they were now to be found at home, perhaps even living next door.[10]

History always counselled against this hubristic self-indulgence, and so it has proved.[11] Nothing fails quite like success. By 2020, great power competition was back with a vengeance. Democratic states were gripped by toxic, perhaps irreconcilable, cultural divisions. Wishing away changes in the international balance of power, and setting citizens against one another, was never likely to turn out well. Yet, remarkably, politicians did it regardless. As the Scottish philosopher Adam Ferguson grasped, the danger is that a society accustomed to peace, security and prosperity will lack the public vigilance and political vigour necessary to rouse itself.[12]

In this climate, the imperative of sober leadership is pronounced. Fortunately, there is a source of inspiration that we might tap into. That is to look backwards, to the past. History is the richest, and arguably the only, manual available for the conduct of statecraft. It draws our attention to perpetual problems and animal truths. And it stands ready to be made use of in prolific ways. Mining the past serves to refine our thinking, hone our judgement and identify new frameworks for examining complex issues. History inculcates us against recency bias, deepens our understanding of contemporary problems and cultivates insight that might enable us to devise solutions. It teaches empathy and enables us to see matters from the perspective of others. For the great minds and political thinkers of antiquity, the highest virtue of statesmen was 'prudence', understood as the skill of giving the right answer at the right moment.[13] We might go further. Prudence, for the historian J. G. A. Pocock, should be understood as the ability to take decisions which 'stand the test of time'.[14] In other words, wisdom counts.[15] History is an invaluable tool for cultivating that wisdom.

Reflection on the past offers a proper, cooler and, indeed, more useful judgement on our present dispensations. The forms that politics has taken in the contemporary democratic world and the ways in which its institutions have evolved are not – with all due respect to national mythologies – a matter of social inevitabilities. Far from it. These things are best understood as *contingent* outcomes. They are fruits of decision. Alternative outcomes were possible, and often probable. Realization of that can be discomforting. Yet it can also open up the mind to a wider array of potentialities. At the same time, however, some aspects of reality are heavily deterministic – not least geography, but also the passions, the chain reactions unleashed by war and many others – in ways that are intimidating to ponder. Meanwhile, despite our psychological propensity to imagine otherwise, the present is not the *climax* of past events but, rather, merely one fleeting moment – though, of course, we may endeavour to purposefully enlarge it to good effect – in an unending sequence. History seethes with such revelations.

The decades since the Cold War have witnessed an alarming uncoupling of statecraft from history. That may well be at least a partial explanation for many of the failures that bedevil Western polities. Decision-makers across the West are increasingly unlikely to know much history, let alone cultivate insights into human behaviour that can only be acquired through sustained reflection on the past. Crucial bureaucracies retain sparse institutional memory. But the lack of historical temperament – even among those with degrees in history – also reflects changes within the historical profession itself, particularly at the university level, where 'traditional' subjects that were most relevant to statecraft and crucial in furnishing the tools for it – the study of politics, diplomacy and strategy – went into decline in favour of fields that often overlapped with crude political activism. Even the very concept of statecraft has fallen into disuse, as the intuition and judgement it prizes have been replaced with the more technocratic ethos taught on courses in 'Public Policy'.

Yet recent years have witnessed renewed and encouraging attempts by historians to assert the vitality of the relationship between history and statecraft. This movement, visible on both sides of the Atlantic and including some of the most prominent scholars and distinguished public intellectuals in the world, has been termed 'Applied History'. The book you are holding sits within that intellectual movement. It assembles a distinguished cast – of senior scholars, promising young researchers and some with practical experience at the highest levels of policy – to examine the ways in which historical insight might help to illuminate problems and enhance the quality of statecraft. It does not contend that studying history is a magic bullet. But it does maintain that the cultivation of a historical temperament serves to improve thinking and nourish the imagination. To be sure, there are several other modes of thinking, but thinking historically is a particularly crucial mode in that it attempts to draw upon, and render coherent, actual *experience* in such a way as to provide insight into the here and now. Political communities severed from the *mos maiorum*, or the way of ancestors, operate at a major disadvantage – not least because that experience was invariably hard-won.

The volume's core focus lies in the realm of political dilemmas, strategic challenges and world order, though it also ranges more widely, exploring institutional memory, the flow of ideas through bureaucracies and the constitutional order. It has no specific agenda – the editor himself would struggle to formulate one, much less impose it on contributors. Its purpose, rather, is to offer insights into the potentialities, and limitations, of history as a tool of statecraft. In the next chapter, I attempt to outline a case for why history can be a powerful resource for practitioners of statecraft. From there, a sequence of essays, by Giselle Donnelly, Paul Rahe and Graeme Thompson, ponder important questions of strategic culture, world order and great power rivalry, drawing on historical insights from the sixteenth century onwards. A pair of pieces by Kori Schake and Jeremi Suri examine some crucial contemporary challenges, the rising power of China and the problem of nation-building. Next, three essays by Francesca Morphakis, Andrew Ehrhardt and Peter Ricketts assess the ways in which significant figures within the twentieth-century British state attempted to 'do' Applied History, using insights derived from past experience in a bid to formulate sharper policy. Finally, contributions by Philip Bobbitt, Jeremy Black, Margaret MacMillan, Charlie Laderman and Steven F. Hayward dig into an array of fresh problems, from arguments about the US Constitution to military conflict, and from the uses of contemporary history to the withering of statesmanship as a concept.

There is no single, overarching hypothesis that runs through the volume; on the contrary, the authors each explore some of the ways in which historical insight and experience might be – or have been – tethered to the practice of political life. In doing so, they quite deliberately plough their own furrow. Chapters can be sampled in any order, and from a variety of perspectives. One thing readers will note is an argumentative, declarative quality to several of the essays. While some of the pieces ponder the ways in which past leaders sought to incorporate historical insight into their activities, others determinedly cast their gaze forward, challenging the reader by asking thoughtful and often world-renowned experts to translate a lifetime of knowledge into policy recommendations. Some will inevitably be uncomfortable with, and disapprove of, this reworking of the historians' task. Yet it is implicit within, and even fundamental to, the concept of Applied History. Indeed, it is probably the principal public selling point of the genre.

Applied History places historians in a difficult yet vital position: to try to turn their insights into policy advice. Making decisions in government, or recommending them, necessarily entails strident argumentation for x over y. This is the essence of policymaking. This is a theme that recurs throughout the book. Historians are instinctively uncomfortable with that, preferring to hedge and qualify, but policymakers must decide. To put it another way, those who govern have fewer places to hide. Several of the essays in the volume reflect that approach and the tensions which inevitably result. Some readers will agree with specific perspectives, others will not, but that is all to the good; well-written arguments invite disagreement and contestation. Given that political scientists and economists proffer advice as a matter of routine, historians might likewise aspire to become more relaxed about marshalling their insights and then sticking their head above the parapet. In short, allowing authors the scope to be declarative was both deliberate and necessary in a volume which seeks to bridge the gap between the radically different realms of historical study and practical policy advice. The very act of doing so will stimulate reflections and disagreement in readers. If we assume that Applied History is worth doing, or at least exploring, then this is at its core. Leaders and other decision-makers are always looking for 'answers' to their problems, or at least an edge – and if historians are to be even moderately useful in this space, they need to be willing to convert knowledge into advice in ways that can translate to conversations conducted in the world of policy. We should not shy away from this.

If there is something that unites the contributors, it is a plea for better politics. All of the essays touch on the practice of statesmanship. They argue for the imperative of effective policy, good governance and wise leadership. If the wielding of public authority across the democratic states is to be improved and the failures of this young century left behind, that requires rigorous study. It necessitates serious and sustained effort. It demands that leaders rise above short-termism, and that permanent officials reform to improve their track record of delivery. The essence of statesmanship is the fusion of word and deed, utterance and act. It is the art of choosing between alternatives. Statesmanship is characterized by an executive ethos – to put it another way, a temperament that enables one to take important decisions and to grapple with large, intimidating problems – as well as an ability to persuade, clarity in the formulation of goals, a capacity to connect ends and means, and the gift of adaptation. Leaders need to weigh the right and the expedient, the greater and the lesser good. These are the foundational skills of politics.

In recent decades, many in the West have essentially abandoned politics, in its truest sense, in favour of a cluster of misleading and idealistic soundbites. We are living through a major crisis of politics itself. We see this in the carelessness with which politicians engage in behaviour which makes it difficult for people of very different outlooks to live together in one society; we see it in their failure to grapple with an economic model that comes with acute costs; we see it in the inattention they pay towards the storm clouds brewing in East Asia, Europe and elsewhere. A reassertion of the political, and the skills that undergird it, is imperative.

The book proceeds from the assumption that statecraft is the highest of all human endeavours. As Cicero put it, 'The career of those who apply themselves to statecraft and to conduct in great enterprises is more profitable to mankind' than other pursuits.[16] Even at a distance of more than 2,000 years, it is difficult to disagree. No other activity runs such risks; no other activity can reap such rewards. And history offers one, potent, means to unlock knowledge of that way of life. As Kenneth Minogue perceived, 'political knowledge' – the knowledge of how to conduct politics – is a product of 'experience' – in other words, history.[17] Hopefully scholars and policy practitioners alike will find the volume a rewarding read.

Notes

1 Walter Raleigh, *History of the World* (1614).
2 Many copies of the image are locatable online, but one is: https://commons.wikimedia. org/wiki/File:Title_page_The_History_of_the_World_by_Walter_Ralegh.jpg.

3   For analysis, examine Lily Hawker-Yates, 'Sir Walter Raleigh's History of the World', https://www.canterbury-cathedral.org/heritage/archives/picture-this/sir-walter-raleighs-history-of-the-world/.

4   See Nicholas Popper, *Walter Ralegh's History of the World and the Historical Culture of the Late Renaissance* (Chicago, 2012).

5   Philip Zelikow, 'To Regain Policy Competence', *Texas National Security Review* 2, no. 4 (2019).

6   Cicero, *De Officiis* (Cambridge, MS, 1913), I, v, 19.

7   See Iskander Rehman, 'Why Applied History Matters', Engelsberg Ideas, 20 November 2020, https://engelsbergideas.com/essays/the-case-for-applied-history/.

8   Recounted by Plutarch in his account of Cato the Elder.

9   Henry Adams, *The Education of Henry Adams* (Oxford, 2009), 12.

10 Some of these issues were anticipated in Samuel P. Huntington, *Who Are We? The Challenges to America's National Identity* (New York, 2004).

11 Countless readers failed to grasp the real force of Francis Fukuyama, *The End of History and the Last Man* (New York, 1992). This is because, in many cases, they never went beyond the title.

12 Adam Ferguson, *An Essay on the History of Civil Society* (1767).

13 Bertrand de Jouvenel, *The Pure Theory of Politics* (Indianapolis, IN, 2000), 5.

14 J. G. A. Pocock, *The Machiavellian Moment: Florentine Political Thought and the Atlantic Republican Tradition* (Princeton, NJ, 1975), 24.

15 Consult Christopher Lynch and Jonathan Marks (eds), *Principle and Prudence in Western Political Thought* (Albany, NY, 2016).

16 Cicero, *De Officiis*, I, xxi, 73.

17 Kenneth Minogue, *Politics: A Very Short Introduction* (Oxford, 1995), 63.

2

For all time

History, statesmanship and the primacy of experience

Robert Crowcroft

During the late fifth century BC, the Athenian scholar and general Thucydides was hard at work composing an epic account of the contemporary war between Athens and Sparta that ran from 431 to 404. This massive conflict tore the Mediterranean world of antiquity apart and remains one of the most important wars ever waged. Conscious that he was living through momentous events, Thucydides was determined to record them for posterity. He was writing history in real time. Yet his was no mere chronicle. Thucydides subjected the crisis to rigorous and psychologically penetrating analysis that would shape how people assessed statecraft forever more. His work took the Peloponnesian War as its ostensible subject, but around this Thucydides wove perhaps the most sophisticated and compressed analysis of human political behaviour ever crafted.[1] The true subject was humanity itself – and, for Thucydides, the impulses that drive the human species do not change.

Read and reread over millennia, Thucydides has encouraged his audience to reflect on problems of power and leadership that are, quite literally, timeless. The text remains unsurpassed in its treatment of statesmanship. Those who wish to understand the origins of war, the practice of leadership, the difficulties of sustaining popular support, the execution of stratagems, the problems of maintaining alliances and the nature of power itself should begin with Thucydides. He proved far less interested in teaching his audience *what* to think, than in *how* to think. Thucydides offered few explicit conclusions, compelling the reader to instead arrive at their own. He was able to 'transmute' every political intrigue or military skirmish into a meditation on what it is to be human.[2] No one had written like this before. No one has done so since.[3]

There was, Thucydides argued, a direct connection between knowledge of the past and our successful navigation of the future. Given the rhythms of human nature, what happened in the past 'can be expected to happen again . . . in similar or much the same ways'. The work constitutes an inexhaustible source of wisdom about politics, one that has been mined by generations of leaders and those who serve them. His achievement was such that Thucydides remains the greatest historian to ever draw breath. And, crucially, he fully intended that his study of the Peloponnesian War would be 'a possession for all time'. It should remain useful, he hoped, 'so long as men are men'.[4]

This view of the practical utility of history was a common one in antiquity. Thucydides's predecessor Herodotus – the first true historian – conceptualized the past as an immense laboratory for studying 'human achievements' and *why* peoples did as they did, a task imperative lest this knowledge 'become forgotten in time'.[5] In his study of the struggle between the Persian Empire and the city-states of Greece during the fifth century BC, Herodotus ferreted out causation and consequence, and thus explanation. He posed questions and arrived at answers based upon the consideration of evidence. This act of asking questions was a crucial, indeed radical, innovation.[6] Herodotus framed what Arnold J. Toynbee later characterized as the historian's 'elemental question': 'How has this come out of that?'[7] And he did so in the service of contemplating great philosophical themes, not least the rise and fall of empires. Later, the Roman statesman and orator Marcus Tullius Cicero contended that *historia magistra vitae* (history is the teacher of life).[8] Cicero was fascinated by the character of political affairs and meditated on the resources that are available to the statesman, as well as the limitations of politics.[9] He reflected on history and philosophy to identify 'precepts' of 'the widest practical application' that might 'supply [us] with models'.[10] Few could match the Roman Tacitus in his feel for the psychology of political power and what the history of political conflict might teach.[11] Sallust, another Roman, is also noteworthy: for him, the past conveyed terrible warnings.[12]

This was a world in which the past was widely understood to constitute a repository of wisdom and instruction. And it was not just any kind of history that mattered. For the ancients, political history and the study of statecraft was nothing less than 'history itself'.[13] Man was, in the Aristotelian formulation, a 'political animal', first and foremost; and political history thus captured him 'engaged in his chief and predominant activity'.[14] That conviction of the primacy of the political to life was deeply embedded in the most iconic story of Hellenic culture – the account of the Trojan War offered in Homer's *The Iliad*, which saw man and god alike politicking and wrestling with the dilemmas of the human condition amid a titanic clash of arms.[15]

Let us fast-forward across the centuries to December 1513, and Niccolò Machiavelli, the Florentine diplomat, philosopher and historian, was penning a letter. The most famous – and unjustly maligned – thinker of the Renaissance, Machiavelli was a deeply patriotic man fixated with the stability of his beloved Florence. Machiavelli's world was shaped by the endless rivalry and warfare among the city-states of Italy. The peninsula was constantly beset by the forces of entropy and fragmentation. Machiavelli's life was thus consumed by a search for Florentine security. He grappled with these problems at length, most notoriously in his 1513 treatise *The Prince* which explored the ruthlessness and clarity about interests that statecraft demands. He followed this in 1517 with *Discourses on Livy*, outwardly a treatment of the classical history of Ancient Rome but really a guidebook as to how republics ought to be governed. In seeking out how Florence could stave off decay, Machiavelli looked to the past for inspiration. That was the intellectual context for the letter he wrote to a friend on 10 December 1513. In it, Machiavelli recounted that, every night after dinner, he would don his most 'regal and courtly garments' and retire to his study to read the great authors of antiquity, many of whom were historians. In his study he would, as he put it, 'enter into the ancient courts of the men of old, where they receive me with love, and where I feed upon that food which only is my own and for which I was born. I feel no shame in conversing with them and asking the reason of their actions'.[16] The fact that Machiavelli called those books 'food' was a telling remark. To dine with the ancients was the highest of educations.

When he wrote the letter, Machiavelli had just finished composing *The Prince*. That slim volume was essentially a distillation of historical experience. In commending it to Lorenzo di Piero de' Medici, the new ruler of Florence, Machiavelli wrote that he had 'nothing more dear or valuable' to offer 'than my knowledge of the conduct of great men'.[17] And he was concerned with knowledge which was 'effectual'. He argued that, as humans 'almost always tread the paths made by others', a 'prudent man' should study what the most skilful of leaders had done before.[18] Those who shouldered the burdens of leadership needed to look to the past in order to cultivate the ability to read situations and make sound decisions – even highly unpalatable ones – for the good of the polity and its citizens.[19]

We should dart forward again, this time to England in the late nineteenth century. Sir John Robert Seeley was one of the most distinguished scholars of the era.[20] Regius Professor of Modern History at the University of Cambridge, he is best known as the author of the 1883 masterwork on British imperialism, *The Expansion of England*.[21] Yet thirteen years prior to the publication of that justly famous book, in his 1870 inaugural lecture Seeley offered one of the most striking statements ever made about the benefits – and power – of reflecting deeply on the past. He asked his audience, 'Why should History be studied?' There was one reason above all others. 'History is the school of statesmanship', Seeley boldly declared.[22] In Seeley's mind, history was not about leafing through stacks of dusty documents and then assembling accounts that were of purely antiquarian interest. Just the opposite. History was something living and vital. It was nothing less than a master key for political leaders, one that unlocked both the present and the future. Those who engaged in statecraft were dabbling in the most arduous of all human endeavours. Intuition gleaned from the past might prepare them for these trials. If one knew history and cultivated its insights, one would be in a stronger position to navigate the currents of the present. It might even help us avoid coming to grief on the reefs of the future.

The young men gathered in that Cambridge lecture hall to listen to Seeley intone on the purpose of the past were the best and the brightest. Soon enough, they would take their place in governing the richest, most powerful nation on earth, one possessed of a vast empire and which had shaped the prevailing world order.[23] For these future policymakers and high officials to be informed that, in taking a degree in History, they were *actually* attending an advanced training centre for statecraft itself must have been extraordinarily exciting. And, indeed, many Cambridge History graduates of this era went on to be statesmen and administrators of the largest planetary empire humanity has ever seen.

Let us shift our focus once more, this time to Oxford and 1939. Professor Robin George Collingwood was only forty-nine years old but in rapidly failing health. A polymath whose expertise ranged from history to philosophy via archaeology, Collingwood was one of the most reflective thinkers on historical knowledge of the last hundred years. Conscious that he was living on borrowed time, Collingwood penned his snappy classic *An Autobiography*, an attempt to put on record his current thinking about the relationship between past and present. In it, he offered a wonderfully evocative description of the insight that can be derived from learning to think historically. Collingwood wrote that the difference between those who knew history, and those who did not, was akin to that between 'the trained woodsman' and 'the ignorant traveller' in a forest. While the latter casually marches along, unaware of their surroundings and thinking 'Nothing here but trees and grass', the woodsman, in contrast, sees what lurks ahead. 'Look', he will say, 'there is a tiger in that grass.'[24]

What Collingwood meant by this singularly arresting turn of phrase was that, through familiarity with peoples, places and ideas, those with a historical cast of mind are better equipped than others to see in advance how a situation might turn out – or at least to identify the key factors that will determine matters. They can spot dangers lurking ahead in the undergrowth; they discern alternative paths through the forest; and they know good spots in which to make camp. This was the reason why, for Collingwood, of all forms of human thought, history was a special one. There is something else, too. Historical knowledge allows us to place ourselves in the shoes of past actors and 're-enact' their choices. We can see the world as they saw it. Collingwood argued that history opened up the mind. It developed both sympathy and realism in equal measure. History can 'reveal the less obvious features' of a situation that are 'hidden from a careless eye'.[25] Moreover, 'What history can bring to moral and political life is a trained eye for the situation in which one has to act'.[26] To be sure, for Collingwood history did not offer ready-made rules and straightforward lessons, if only. Such knowledge had to be hard-won. What it did offer, however, was 'insight'.[27] Extending Seeley's metaphor of history as a 'school', for Collingwood it was 'a school of moral and political wisdom'.[28]

Like the other thinkers discussed earlier, Collingwood's musings implied an expansive vision of the relationship between historical knowledge and contemporary concerns. The understanding of long-term processes, the attention to the complexities of the sociopolitical order and, most of all, the deep grasp of human behaviour meant that those who possess historical 'insight' could be more than just a specialist in the past. By being able to identify the proverbial tiger in the grass, they might profitably advise on current and future challenges as well.

A few years later, in 1953, an eighteen-year-old American and future presidential speechwriter named James Humes was on an exchange visit in England organized by the charity The English Speaking Union. During his visit Humes was fortunate enough to receive some penetrating career advice from none other than the most famous person in the world. He met the seventy-nine-year-old prime minister Winston Churchill, the man who had led Britain through the Second World War and was then midway through his second premiership. And the most iconic statesman of the twentieth century was also one of its best historians. Churchill was steeped in historical knowledge. As a young man he consumed the six volumes of Edward Gibbon's masterpiece *The Decline and Fall of the Roman Empire*, published between 1776 and 1789, as well as the five volumes of Thomas Babington Macauley's seminal 1848 *The History of England*. Churchill himself was the author of multiple classic works of history, including his memoirs of the First and Second World Wars, a study of his ancestor the Duke of Marlborough and his *History of the English Speaking Peoples*. Few before or since have matched his turn of phrase. And few had reflected as deeply on the past as a source of ideas and inspiration. A reading of history underpinned Winston's entire worldview. It taught him that great nations fell when they lost the willpower that had driven them to success in the first place. And in Adolf Hitler, Churchill saw the latest in a long line of aspiring hegemons whose duty it was for Britain to resist and defeat. While others hoped that this 'tiger' could be appeased, Churchill saw the need to plunge into the forest and kill it. This conviction, and an ability to grasp that he was living through an epoch of world-historical significance, provided the wartime prime minister with the fortitude needed to wage the largest conflict humanity had ever experienced.

Encountering him eight years after the climax of that war, Humes asked the old man which academic subjects he should study to prepare for a career in public affairs. Churchill's answer was unhesitating. 'Study history. Study history. In history lies all the secrets of statecraft.'[29] The great war leader knew better than most that to mine the past is to prepare for the future, while some lessons transcend both time and space.

I

Envisage for a moment a school where one might converse with 'the men of old' and acquire knowledge of 'the secrets of statecraft'. Imagine an institution offering an education that will prove useful 'for all time' and hone an ability to spot 'tigers' waiting to ambush the unwary. Such a school would offer a unique education indeed. Fortunately, it exists, and there is no better foundation of knowledge for both political entrepreneurs and permanent officials. Crucially, ordinary citizens also stand to gain, not least in terms of holding their leaders to account and developing appropriate expectations of what statesmen may achieve. A political community with a developed sense of the connective tissues between past, present and future possesses vitality, adaptability and resilience. The rest of this chapter consists of an extended argument for the power of history as part of the statesman's toolkit. This entails reflection on the nature, and possibilities, of historical knowledge as well of the skills we might cultivate in leaning upon it.

If there is one thing that sustained immersion in the past consistently provides to us in the present, it is to nourish our *imagination*. A historical cast of mind opens up, and fertilizes, that faculty.[30] That, in turn, imbues us with a profound sense of possibility. Indeed, for many it is precisely this that sparks an interest in history in the first place. The past is a field of boundless extent and scope. The American historian Hayden White once remarked that the past is a realm which people can visit through their minds in order to 'dream'.[31] If by 'dream' we mean 'imagine', then this is an evocative metaphor. 'Historical thinking' is 'a special kind of thinking concerned with a special kind of object', called 'the past'.[32] And by pondering our own relationship to that object, we may unlock perspectives and insights hitherto concealed. Those who look to history possess an enviable intellectual freedom. They enjoy striking selectivity in terms of where, and when, they search for guidance; they boast the capacity for simultaneity, and can be in several times and places at once; and they enjoy a shifting scale that enables them to zoom in and out from a macroscopic to a microscopic analysis at a moment's notice.[33] Very few forms of analytical thought can match this range of possibilities.

Sadly, there are now professional historians – and lots of them – who are dubious about the practical value of historical knowledge and insight for the conduct of governance. In fact, they arguably make up the majority of the profession. This mindset has become the norm in the decades since the 1960s. Their argument is very simple: that we cannot identify useful 'lessons' from the past because the granular detail of one situation is not, and cannot be, replicated in another situation. Events and phenomena may outwardly seem to recur, but this is only on the surface, and, as we drill down, we find a bewildering array of factors and explanations which render comparisons problematic, if not downright distorting. To do so is to simplify that which rightly is complex. And because each event is an individual contingent circumstance, 'lessons', 'rules' or 'patterns' are difficult to divine and rarely applicable elsewhere. No two situations, the argument goes, will ever be the same and pretending otherwise is a sham. There is also the anxiety that those who search for lessons are really just looking for a shortcut: an ability to read the past in order to predict the future. And prediction is impossible.

Yet to conduct statecraft with this mindset would be absurd. Policymakers exist in an entirely different realm from professors authoring a scholarly monograph. Whereas historians are very wary of getting things wrong – and thus rely on qualification and hedging as a protective device to shield their reputations where certainty is impossible – those who take decisions that affect the lives of millions, in contrast, enjoy no such luxury. They must face the risk. By necessity they deal only in possibilities. Statesmen operate in a realm of unavoidable uncertainty – the fog of the real world – where decisions must be made immediately. They must choose before it is possible to know all of the facts, or to be sure of their ramifications. Policymakers are not, generally speaking, engaged in deep academic scholarship (though permanent officials producing weighty and authoritative policy briefings for their masters should immerse themselves in that kind of activity). What they are performing is a fundamentally different mental exercise; *they are not the same thing*. Statecraft is a practical activity, something that one must *do*. When informed leaders seek to use history, this is not principally an act of detail – it is, rather, an act of imagination. The precise sequence of events in a diplomatic crisis will not be replicable; that much is true. But examining a series of such crises might, for the statesman, highlight things to do and behaviours to shy away from. History fertilizes useful thinking about the conduct of leadership. That is where sceptics about the possibilities of employing history to illuminate statecraft are wrong.

To survey the past is, of course, to absorb details about what happened to particular individuals in a specific time and place. These details are fundamental. But, for those engaged in statecraft, the detail is ultimately secondary to the intellectual exercises that studying the fortune of past individuals open up. What did they do right? Where did they go wrong? How did a leader inspire their people? What might we be able to learn from, and avoid? To examine a biography of a famous leader is to ponder how they do what they did, how they shaped their world and the limits of individual agency. To read an account of a military campaign is to probe how humans function under extraordinary stress, how decisions are made and how we adjust to circumstances. In this sense, history is, first and foremost, a tool for thinking with. Using it stimulates the 'insight' that Collingwood so prized. History is 'the memory of things said and done', Carl Becker argued to the American Historical Association in 1931, 'running hand in hand with the anticipation of things to be said and done'.[34] As the thirteenth-century Italian theologian Thomas Aquinas put it, 'The knowledge of singulars pertains to the perfection of the intellective soul, not in speculative knowledge, but in practical knowledge, which is imperfect without the knowledge of singulars. . . . Hence for prudence are required the remembrance of past things, knowledge of present things, and foresight of future things'.[35]

Far from weighing us down with the sheer mass of information, then, this repository of collective human experience should encourage and empower. History conveys, first and foremost, the primacy of contingency. Indeed, the role of chance in public affairs is the most important lesson one can learn from the past. The course of life is not predetermined. Decisions matter and nudge us in different directions. Leo Tolstoy may have believed that history inexorably takes its own course and washes over the individual like a great tsunami, but he was simply wrong.[36] Human beings are overwhelmingly concerned with the short term – depending on the context, this may extend from a matter of hours to a few years – and we are conscious of the range of possibilities that lie before us. We weigh alternatives and select a course of action. A certain decision will create one reality; a different choice will create another reality.[37] We feel this in our bones. The future is present in our minds when we discuss it. And this endless activity of *deciding* between one thing and another is captured in the bulk of the historical evidence about the past that survives to us, no matter from which time and place it originated.

The cultivation of historical insight permits people to know the world around them, and thus – hopefully – to act wisely. 'We study history to see more clearly into the situation in which we are called upon to act', Collingwood argued.[38] If events were determined by impersonal national, international and economic structures, there would be no role for decision. Yet contingent decision-making is paramount. This, Collingwood maintained, is fundamentally what history is 'for'. 'History is for human self-knowledge', he concluded. 'Knowing yourself', Collingwood went on, 'means knowing what you can do; and since nobody knows what he can do until he tries, the only clue to what man can do is what man has done'.[39]

We ought to feel liberated by the provocations of sheer, naked possibility. While prediction is impossible, reasoning from history is nevertheless perfectly feasible and stresses the framing of pertinent questions. This is why, for Jacques Barzun, being a great *user* of history has much to recommend it.[40] It facilitates the rigorous testing of assumptions; seeks to discern the underlying, long-term dynamics of a given situation; identifies patterns; explores the history of relevant groups or institutions; probes the way in which actors think and formulate their goals; draws inferences; assesses what is known, what is presumed, and what is unknown; and hones our ability to react to the unexpected. The formulation and execution of policy is the exploration of possibilities; and a good working knowledge of the database of past human experience might help us to nudge possibilities into probabilities.

The insularity of the historical profession does no one any good (not least the university students who increasingly question whether what they are learning is of value to their future careers). And ever-smaller numbers of public officials have a strong familiarity with history, or the kind of temperament that such familiarity offers. Something has gone wrong. And those who wish to fix it should go back to basics and think seriously on what the past teaches us about public affairs. Crucially, we should also go about this in a mood of optimism. History *is* the one and only school of statesmanship.

II

Think of it like this. The human past constitutes a unique repository of information, a 'resource bank' in the words of the eminent student of strategy, Colin S. Gray.[41] It is a database, containing all recorded past events as related in innumerable texts, memories, legends and, in recent decades, modern media. This is, in the description of Isaiah Berlin, 'the sum of the concrete events in time and space – the sum of the actual experience of actual men and women in relation to one another and to an actual three-dimensional, empirically experienced, physical environment'.[42] Each of us draws upon this database, every day, in all aspects of our existence. In our personal and professional environments we constantly tap into memories of previous choices that worked well for us. We are cognisant of prior errors, and work to avoid similar outcomes in the future. We are able to do this because we access the database of our own individual experience. This, in turn, is one small branch of that vastly larger civilizational database which houses the accumulated experience of our species. There is more. This database of past activity is the *sole* repository of such information that will ever be available to us. There is, quite literally, nothing else to draw upon. We exist in the present; the future is a void; and the past, while astonishingly complex and often dispiriting, is, therefore, the only source of guidance we have.

'All knowledge', as Collingwood put it with his pithy profundity, is 'historical knowledge'.[43] Far from being 'useless as a guide to action' – as many professional historians in recent decades have depressingly concluded, much to the bewilderment of their students – historical experience is the one navigational tool we have at our disposal.[44] John Lewis Gaddis pointed out that while it is far from fool-proof, no alternative form of knowledge is better and most are decidedly inferior.[45] The great value of history for the conduct of statecraft is, then, that it is *a mode of thinking*, one that bears directly upon practice. Collingwood argued that it is 'precisely because history affords us something altogether different from rules, namely insight, that it could afford us the help we needed in diagnosing our moral and political problems'.[46] This is pressing because much of what we do is not explicable in terms of reason, as the thousands of pages of the Russian novelist Aleksander Solzhenitsyn convey in virtually tactile form; if anything, the force of *unreason* prevails in human affairs.[47]

In Collingwood's opinion, the very act of examining history served a didactic purpose. The concept he used to describe this phenomenon was 're-enactment'.[48] Collingwood asserted that the study of history is essentially the act of thinking through past decisions and actions in order to render them intelligible. He believed this is something that we all do, quite naturally, whenever we think about the past. When we read a history book – say a biography of a great leader – we place ourselves in the shoes of the subjects. We come to see things from their perspective. And through this, we develop a degree of empathy with them. We examine their choices, ask how they could (or should) have behaved differently, and what we might do in their place. We understand why they arrived at the conclusions that they did, for good or ill. By examining the past, we can – for a time – suspend our own worldviews and beliefs, and try out those of others. We see the world as others saw it, and quietly develop our own intuitions about it. 'Re-enactment' is essentially a process of intellectual osmosis.

Collingwood vividly illustrated how we can place ourselves in the shoes (or, in this case, the sandals) of past actors by reference to Julius Caesar's dilemma as he halted his army on the banks of the Rubicon in 49 BC. Caesar agonized over whether to march on Rome and plunge the Republic into civil war. While ever his forces remained in Cisalpine Gaul, there remained a chance of avoiding a confrontation. Yet he knew that once he crossed the river that marked the northern boundary of Italy, there could be no going back; the Senate would denounce him as a traitor guilty of insurrection. This was a crucial moment in the history of Europe. With good reason does the phrase 'crossing the Rubicon' still carry weight two millennia later. While very few of us have ever had to wrestle with decisions of such gravity, nevertheless we have all struggled with momentous choices that we were fully cognisant would alter our lives whichever path we took. Given that this is a common human experience it is fairly straightforward to at least imagine how Caesar must have felt. However imperfectly, we can reconstruct in our minds the emotions, doubts and anxieties that consumed him as he looked out across the Rubicon.

Re-enactment is thus a form of vicarious experience. For Collingwood, imaginative sympathy permits us to hone a richer appreciation of the past. And that is a practical tool as well. Philip Zelikow rightly observed that 'in the skills of statecraft, humans have not evolved very much'.[49] This might be thought depressing, but it is also reassuring. 'Politics has not changed since the beginning and is unlikely to change until the end', in the words of James Alexander.[50] And we can derive a certain usability from that realization. Saint Augustine framed the problem best in his *Confessions* – arguably the greatest autobiography ever written – when he noted that the past is an accumulation of previous presents.[51] Thus, while we cannot know the future, nevertheless we may detect in the present the 'causes or signs which are already in being' of what will be the future.[52] By re-thinking, or re-enacting, historical moments and deeds in our own minds, we acquire a deeper understanding of not merely specific individuals but the conduct of statecraft more broadly. From there, we cultivate intuition about what to do – and not do – in our own time. That is why, to Collingwood, 'history is thought'. 'History goes on in the mind of the historian: he thinks it, he enacts it within himself: he identifies himself with the history he is studying and actually lives it as he thinks it.'[53] And it is inevitable that in doing so we ask ourselves how the subjects of history succeeded, and where they went wrong. Pondering what we can glean from the past is crucial preparation for leaders and officials to take decisions in the daunting moments of uncertainty in their own lives.

Humans have always had a complex relationship with time, that 'ultimate conundrum'.[54] Whatever the acute scientific and philosophical problems associated with the phenomena – from its relationship with space to the role of memory in framing our understandings of its passage – nevertheless human beings are temporally oriented creatures.[55] And we are quite conscious of this fact. 'Time is the frame of all agency and the shifting horizon of hope and fear through which every conscious being moves', as John Dunn put it.[56] The urge to master time is as old as humanity itself.[57] We can detect this, perhaps most profoundly, in the civilization of ancient Egypt. So much of that culture revolved around a struggle to defy the effects of time. Here there was both an ambition that is difficult to grasp, such is its scope, and a painstaking regard for the future. It was doomed to fail, but that the attempt was made remains mindboggling. We see those aspirations expressed in the granite and basalt that give them physical form in the pyramids which dot the Valley of the Kings. These monuments have endured for thousands of years, and will likely endure for thousands more, a standing rejoinder to the conquering power of time. We detect the urge again, most poignantly, in the mummies of the pharaohs – faces still recognizable, despite the passage of millennia – that lie in museums across the world in a silent, yet unmistakeable, declaration of what Oswald Spengler described as 'the will to endure'.[58] And what a will it was. It is no coincidence Percy Bysshe Shelley chose Egypt as the setting for his reflection on the fleeting nature of greatness, 'Ozymandias'. Little of the titanic statue of the 'king of kings' may have remained visible above the desert sands, but there was still enough to impart a certain point.

This rootedness in time is why our species has invented many uses for history, from record-keeping to romance, and chronicle to antiquarianism.[59] It has been deployed to ruminate on the good and the wicked, the truthful and the inaccurate, and the wise and the foolish. We can render it variously as epic, tragedy and farce.[60] For Christians it frames the entirety of human existence, from the Fall to the Last Judgement. For peoples across the planet, it can be both a powerful patriotic glue and a brutally effective agent of disintegration.[61] Historical thinking boasts a range of shapes, textures and colours that remains quite bewildering.[62] In a very real sense, history is something deliberately *made* on the historian's desk, or – perhaps more often – in the mouth of the political leader.[63] In short, stemming from all manner of motives, humans have been impelled to endow the past with a degree of intelligibility. Herodotus aimed to ensure that knowledge was rescued 'from the oblivion of time'.[64] We may be condemned to remain 'baffled', as Augustine was, about time, but nevertheless we have a powerful psychological bond with it.[65] It is at least as important as our relationship with space. And, in *practical* terms, this makes historical experience something that, seemingly by nature, we look to in order to navigate the present and prepare for the future.

Despite the depressing recency bias and lack of perspective that characterizes contemporary culture, few occurrences under the sun are genuinely novel. Most of the problems that confront statesmen – be they political, economic, strategic or social – have recurred countless times. Almost any situation faced by a leader has been encountered by innumerable others before. The Hebrew scriptures, adopted by Christianity as the Old Testament, offer vivid political histories of the ancient world. Things have certainly changed since then, but perhaps not in their essentials. History is nothing more than experience and reflection on it. For this reason, there is no better learning tool. It helps us to make inferences, probe assumptions and take problems apart. It offers warnings aplenty, but it also instils a sense of possibility and optimism that challenges can be overcome and that which seems impossible may not be. As James Mattis, the former US Marine Corps general and secretary of defence – and himself a warrior-scholar – observed, history 'serves as a garden of the mind to which you can return again and again'.[66] Those who elect to study it are afforded an opportunity to stroll through that garden to their heart's content.

III

The problem, as alluded to earlier, is that even many political historians are now unlikely to share the Thucydidean vision of history as a manual for learning how to govern or for probing human psychology. In fact, this distinguished conception of the discipline has become an object of derision. A special distaste is reserved for those who try to use history to improve policymaking in the present and the future. Historians are expected to maintain a healthy distance from policy. Those who reject this pessimism, and adhere to the old Thucydidean paradigm, are outliers. Such individuals are charged with a variety of professional sins, from 'presentism' and 'going beyond the documents' to outright 'superficiality'. These are serious attacks on professional competence and personal ethics that betray genuine hostility. They have discouraged several generations of historians from raising their head above the parapet. The risks to one's career are too great. Scholars who have mounted public arguments for a return to the primacy of political history have been ridiculed, even by other political historians. That behaviour may reveal a degree of insecurity – that those who are bright enough to have something worthwhile to say beyond the confines of the academy will make the rest of the profession look bad, and thus ought to be silenced – but it is, sadly, common.

Then there is the fact that the primacy of political history within the academy has been aggressively attacked by newer sub-disciplines, most obviously cultural history. That field does have some merits, but preparing people to take decisions in high-stakes environments or contribute to governing their countries are perhaps not among them. Neither is the honing of judgement. Moreover, all too often cultural history is actually postmodernist political activism masquerading as serious scholarship.[67] Cultural historians are frequently dismissive of political history on the grounds that it is 'old-fashioned' (as if its persistence for millennia was a weakness rather than an indication of vitality and strength), studies the 'privileged' and prioritizes 'traditional power structures'. Histories of deeds are out. Histories of everything else are in. And perish the thought that Thomas Carlyle's 'Great Men' should be the focus of our attention.[68] Academic history is nowadays often little more than a 'distorting mirror' in which the past is assessed through a presentist (and deeply ideological) prism of contemporary liberal tropes – 'imperialism', 'patriarchy', 'racism', 'sexism', 'colonialism' and so on.[69] The field has thus become a part of the 'culture wars' that beset the contemporary West.[70] Those who work within it frequently adhere to the current liberal fixation with identity politics. Hard-won skills of critical thinking and the source-based interrogation of concrete historical episodes are increasingly downgraded in favour of attention to 'feelings' (and here there is usually a convenient overlap between the presumed emotions of past actors and the historians who write about them). When history is recast as 'a saga of oppression', the results may offer predictable and quasi-therapeutic 'sentimentalities', but they are of sparse intellectual value.[71]

Importantly, much of the historical profession has essentially given up on *causality* (trying to unravel why *x* occurred with reference to a series of preceding factors, and which used to be the intellectual core of the discipline) in favour of *description* (and often in a spirit of pity, or at least visible discontent).[72] This is doubly depressing because biology, mathematics and physics have made so many discoveries about causality that the range of intellectual stimulants which historians, supposed to be fixated on causality, might tap into is richer than ever. It is little wonder that in the United States, at least, fewer young people are choosing to study History. The discipline may be falling into a death spiral.[73] Many historians treat scholarship as an opportunity to stroll around the past expressing displeasure at the failure of previous societies (or European ones, at least – non-Europeans tend to be given a pass) to measure up to the cultural norms of twenty-first-century liberal European and Americans.[74] It borders on open contempt. None of this is terribly enlightening, or useful beyond reassuring historians of their own virtue. It is a fundamentally narcissistic endeavour.

All of this is hardly likely to encourage us to think highly of what the past might teach. As José Ortega y Gasset put it so movingly in 1941, 'Man's real treasure is the treasure of his mistakes, piled up stone by stone through thousands of years.. . . Breaking the continuity with the past, wanting to begin again, is a lowering of man and a plagiarism of the orangutan'.[75] The seminar room in the History department at John Hopkins University was once emblazoned with the words 'History is past politics and politics present history'. Such confidence seems unthinkable today.

All that this myopia has achieved is to drive historians from the public square. Academics from other fields – political science, economics, sociology and law – have proven perfectly happy to occupy it. Experts in these disciplines contribute to the public conversation, staff national and global institutions, and advise leaders to a degree that historians are deeply wary of. Historians' anxiety about their worth has impoverished public debate. The effects of contending that scholarship is antithetical to engaging with leaders have been calamitous. In choosing exile to the ivory tower, the contemporary historical profession has abrogated its responsibilities to wider society. Hal Brands and William Inboden have gone so far as to argue that those in the academy who wish to have nothing to do with policy are 'morally irresponsible'.[76] There is something here of Cicero's old warning that 'To be drawn by study away from active life is contrary to moral duty'.[77]

With scholars like this, it is little wonder that the standard of historical knowledge among elites is so bad, nor that leaders, officials and institutions lack the insights into human behaviour that only deep study of past politics can develop. Whatever objections could be mounted to Seeley's argument about 'the school of statesmanship', it did have one, singular, strength. It represented a view that History was a discipline of genuine public utility. Nowadays even many political historians no longer believe that.

Green shoots may, however, be visible. Over the past few years a growing number of scholars have begun fighting to reassert an old-fashioned conception of the utility of history. The term 'Applied History' first became part of the public consciousness in September 2016, when Niall Ferguson and Graham Allison advocated that American presidents should appoint a Council of Historical Advisers to sharpen analysis of pressing policy matters and consider useful precedents.[78] This idea generated much commentary, both positive and negative. Crucially, the concept of Applied History tills fertile public and political soil. Growing numbers of elites on both sides of the Atlantic are now acutely aware that the realm of government is deficient in basic historical knowledge, and eager to correct that. Senior political figures in Washington DC and London have shown they are open to working with historians, and asking what they need to do. Things are indeed changing, and for the better. Besides Ferguson and Allison, prominent scholars associated with Applied History include John Bew of King's College London, who took up a post as senior special advisor to the new British prime minister, Boris Johnson, in the summer of 2019; Kori Schake of the International Institute for Strategic Studies and then the American Enterprise Institute; Philip Bobbitt of Columbia; and Brendan Simms at Cambridge. Institutions such as the Belfer Center at Harvard, the Centre for Grand Strategy at King's College London and the Hoover Institution at Stanford are spearheading the effort to rebuild productive linkages between historians and policymakers. Scholars have endeavoured to use a historically grounded perspective to attack contemporary challenges.[79] *War on the Rocks*, a leading website for the US national security community, features regular articles making the case for Applied History. There are even brand-new peer-reviewed outlets, the *Journal of Applied History* and the *Texas National Security Review*, which are helping to bypass the more unimaginative and resistant gatekeepers of the academic world. In the UK, Alun Evans, the head of the British Academy, echoed Ferguson when he called for each Whitehall Department to appoint a historian who is expert in its area to whom it can turn for advice.[80]

This opportunity to actually engage with decision-makers is proving irresistible for many historians. It is perhaps a shame that what is now called 'Applied History' was once simply known as 'history' – one distinguished historian, who shall remain nameless, told the author that it ought to be called 'Proper History' – but what matters is that this energization is a welcome development.[81] It is one that signifies the reassertion of a humanistic culture of learning that was once regarded as fundamental to a liberal education. In many respects it is a case of putting old wine into new bottles. The way in which political leaders use history is a fundamentally different exercise from how professional historians do so, and the latter should not feel so threatened by acknowledging that fact. This is no time for academics to be haughty and aloof.

Clearly, then, Applied History has caught on, and rapidly. That it has done so indicates how strong the appetite for the old Thucydidean vision of the historian remains. It also underlines how desperate those tasked with steering the ship of state are for some cartographical guidance. To be sure, one cannot write a simple 'how-to' manual for statecraft. History can never be an infallible guide. Those seeking a shortcut through reality are destined to be disappointed. What history *can* do, however, as Thucydides discerned, is to teach us how to think. Michael Oakeshott framed the problem of the past in a quite wonderful phrase that James Alexander wrote 'has to be savoured slowly, like whisky': history is, for Oakeshott, 'an uncovenanted circumstantial confluence of vicissitudes'.[82] History may not be able to predict what is to come, but it can prepare us for it.

IV

Before we go any further, let us be clear about the limitations of historical knowledge. Those keen to sharpen their intuition through reflection on the past need to understand what can and cannot be achieved. Knowledge of the past cannot be leveraged in an easy and straightforward fashion to identify readily transferrable, neat 'answers' to current challenges. Such an expectation would be absurd. There is always the serious risk that we might make history into 'a dummy upon which to practise the skills of a ventriloquist'.[83] This we must be cognisant of in order to avoid. Moreover, history does not provide reliable 'rules' for action. This is often what decision-makers look for when mining the past. It is, of course, perfectly understandable that, when they look to history, they do so in the hope of finding accessible solutions. That is a very human thing to do. It is part of our species' conditioning to search for patterns in our response to situations (I find myself in circumstance x; I have experienced something like it before, and action y solved it; hence I will, in the first instance, attempt y again). The tendency to 'reduce the tangle and variety of experience to a set of principles' is particularly strong in the technocratic manner of governing that has come to dominate the West since the Second World War.[84] Officials invariably endeavour to convert experience into a formula. Yet history resists this conversion. And there are certainly no reliable, quasi-scientific 'laws'. Attempts to deduce causal laws of history have always failed.[85] Even those individuals who are possessed of masses of historical knowledge are not seers, able to reliably forecast future developments. To put the matter bluntly, it cannot be done. We are condemned to discern the future as did Saint Paul: 'through a glass, darkly'.[86] It would be wonderful if historical insight could be exploited to proffer hard-and-fast rules for action, but it cannot. Such knowledge must be hard-won. History is not a quick-fix.

What it *does* help us to develop is Collingwood's 'trained eye'. For that philosopher of history, the fetish for 'ready-made rules' was a phantasm imported from the natural sciences and useless in affairs where humans are the measure of things; what was *really* offered by history was *judgement*.[87] Armed with judgement, one can seek to improvise a way of dealing with a problem. And, crucially, it is judgement that enables us to identify precisely what type of situation we are in – many situations bear strong resemblances to others – as well as boosting our prospects of formulating a successful response. Prussian military theorist Carl von Clausewitz called this the coup d'oeil, the flash of insight, that comes from pondering prior experience.[88] Effective statecraft is less about devising extraordinarily sophisticated chess strategies than it is about grasping men's motivations, objectives and weaknesses. And if the study of history should prompt anything, it is reflection on these things. As the pioneering fourteenth-century Arab scholar Ibn Khaldun put it, reading history permits us to approach the 'inner meaning' of past events, decisions and actions.[89] It is a fundamentally deliberative activity.

The database of human experience serves another, related, function, too: it lends perspective. 'We are now accustomed to being told that crises are 'unprecedented'; that every political election is the most important 'ever' and so on. This barrage is exhausting. Conversations with history serve to anchor us against both the naivety of existential creativity and the anxiety that 'nothing like [whatever the crisis of the week is] has happened before'. It has almost certainly happened before – and often.

History thus helps us to take problems apart and pose better questions in weighing courses of action. Insights derived from the past illuminate pathways through the thickets of Collingwood's forest, as well as enhancing our appreciation of some of the deeper factors at work in human affairs. If we switch metaphors from the forest to the sea, we might say this helps leaders to recognize, and then react to, tidal currents that can be exploited and used.[90]

Decision-makers who study the past have always sought to do this. Those tasked with selecting courses of action that would shape the destiny of their nations looked frequently to past exemplars for counsel and inspiration. They digested the literature of Greece and Rome, and they pondered the great, and disastrous, leaders of history. Many of the most important thinkers of the Italian Renaissance stressed the importance of rulers doing precisely that.[91] Xenophon, Polybius, Tacitus and Livy were staples of such reading. Leading statesmen – including the dominant political figures of early-seventeenth-century Europe, Cardinal Richelieu and the Count-Duke of Olivares – amassed large collections of history books.[92] This was rooted in a 'monumental' conception of history, one in which the goal was 'to bring the past into the present for the sake of the future'; and it depended 'on the assumption that there is a direct connection of some kind between these different temporalities'.[93] It is not difficult to spot the – frequently unspoken, yet potent – assumption that time constituted a source of authority. As Gibbon, the most brilliant historian of the eighteenth century, saw matters, history might 'instruct the reader by sensible and profound reflections'.[94] The past housed such a huge repository of decisions – many among them being catastrophic errors and misjudgements – that there was no option but to study it for advice and warnings. Gibbon's contemporaries Sir William Robertson and David Hume of the University of Edinburgh similarly discerned the power of historical narrative as a pedagogical tool.

There is another reason too why statesmen have looked to the past. Leaders are tasked with intimidating responsibilities. They have often felt isolated and alone, unable to share their anxieties with another living soul. Many have felt that their only peers, the only ones who could understand the dilemmas they agonized over, were their long-dead counterparts – men (and occasionally women) who had been in the same position in ages past. Amid many sleepless nights, leaders have found encouragement in turning to their predecessors. As Livy put it:

What chiefly makes the study of history wholesome and profitable is this, that you behold the lessons of every kind of experience set forth as on a conspicuous monument; from this you may choose for yourself and for your own state what to imitate, from this mark for avoidance what is shameful in the conception or shameful in the result.[95]

This was why, for Seeley, history was not merely *a* school of statesmanship, but *the* school: it was the only route for high officials to acquire the insight into human behaviour, the moral capital and the habits of mind necessary for effective leadership. In other words, there is a concrete connection between history and political action. History was, Seeley told his students, 'the one important' thing, the 'indispensable' thing, that 'the legislator and ruler' must master. Studying it was 'a great seminary of politicians'.[96] Statesmen who have utilized history in this way – Churchill and Henry Kissinger being two prominent twentieth-century examples – did so as a means of intellectual provocation and moral counsel. The nineteenth-century British prime minister Benjamin Disraeli reflected that 'a statesman' is 'a practical character' whose role it is to assess situations and 'ascertain the needful and the beneficial, and the most feasible measure to be carried out'.[97] In other words, statecraft 'entails fusing insight with power' and is a 'union of the worlds of thought and action'. History is the best guide to that onerous task of high-stakes problem-solving.[98]

Let us return to Machiavelli. In grappling with the seemingly intractable problems of instability in early-modern Italy, Machiavelli believed that it was possible to erect a political order that might, in the judgement of one scholar, 'withstand the decay of time'.[99] This was an extraordinary ambition. History was the key to realizing it, precisely because 'History was essentially the scene of decay'. The nature of this decay had to be understood. The rise and fall of nations was not some inevitable, cyclical process, but instead rested on individual choices and their success or failure. It was, in Machiavelli's mind, a matter of contingency. How rulers played their hand was as important as the cards in the hand itself. As a result it could be plausible, if one cultivated a historical sensibility, to identify 'a recurrence of similar patterns and a set of examples' that might provoke creative thought about problems of statecraft. Historical insight, in other words, was artistry; and mastery of that art might enable the statesman to master *fortuna* itself. Those in the cockpit of politics struggled to escape the gravitational pull of the short term, but mining the past for what Machiavelli called 'effectual truth' might help statesmen to weaken that pull. Such was the dizzying scale of Machiavelli's objective, formulated in the pressure-cooker of permanent existential crisis. Few practitioners of statecraft have displayed such faith in the wisdom of the past as Machiavelli. Yet he knew that his recommendations on policy were possible because, if something had been done before, it could be done again.[100]

V

There are many powerful examples to draw from contemporary statecraft of what we might term 'the history deficit'. Perhaps the most notorious can be found in Allied planning for the occupation and rebuilding of Iraq following the overthrow of Saddam Hussein in 2003. Knowledge of the sectarian realities of the Middle East was disregarded for wishful thinking. Yet other instances abound, in both foreign and domestic policy.

The European Union is an attempt to transcend the past but does so by ignoring the historical reality that Germans, Poles, Spaniards and others possess distinctive national cultures. The results have been a corrosive weakening of democracy, and delegitimization of political institutions, that may terminate in disaster. Constitutional reform in Britain carried out under the government of Tony Blair was done with little regard for the historically successful nature of the previous practices. The country has been left with an unsatisfactory mess in the wake of their destruction, and no obvious route to cleaning it up (one answer, to revert the constitution to largely how it looked before, is so obvious that it will never happen). During the 1990s and early 2000s, Western governments and publics alike forgot what the world was like prior to the collapse of the Soviet Union and, without justification, complacently adopted the view that strategic competition between different nations – the most reliable political trend of human history – was now a relic of a barbarous age and of no account to the 'modern' world. In recent years, that competition has come roaring back with a vengeance – not least as regards China – leaving governments scrambling to react. Any decent historian could have predicted that a competition between Anglo-American and Chinese visions of world order would erupt sometime in the first quarter of the new century, and so it has proved. Meanwhile a generation of policymakers, accustomed to affluence and economic stability, showed remarkable naivete in assuming that serious financial crises were also a thing of the past. Their bewildered reaction to the crash of 2008 tells its own story.

Elected leaders and permanent officials in Western capitals often display alarming historical ignorance. There is frequently a striking lack of basic knowledge, both about the history of their own country and about the background of the policy problems being grappled with. Every bit as problematic, the deep insight into the permanent realities of the human condition – and the possibilities for wise action – that can only be honed through reflection on history is patently lacking. It has been replaced by a political culture of superficiality, sentimentality and soundbites suitable for the social media age. Public relations ability, or 'spin', has become visibly prized far more than policy competence. The massive bureaucracies which administer Western states possess little, if any, institutional memory. All too often, insiders' knowledge of what works and does not is shallow. I even know of senior figures at the State Department and the British Foreign Office who had never heard of Richelieu and had only the faintest idea about Otto von Bismarck. Such ignorance is dangerous.

There are other factors at work as well. It is a feature of human existence that we attempt to relate new, and puzzling, situations to those already familiar to us in order to make sense of them. The use of analogy can be a vital cognitive tool. Yet, in public affairs, the range of historical analogies employed to fertilize policy debate is depressingly limited. This is as true of private deliberation among elites as it is of public speech. The analogies are nearly all modern, and nearly all wrong. When the West is confronted by an international adversary causing trouble, one can be sure that the situation will be likened to the 1938 Munich crisis in which Britain and France chose to appease Hitler rather than confront him. So omnipresent is 'Munich' as a source of supposed strategic wisdom that we are essentially condemned to relive 1938 over and over again. The realities of the 1938 crisis, and its lessons, are so distorted by simplification and over-use that the analogy is positively unhelpful. The other analogy that crops up, particularly for Americans, is the Vietnam War. Any American activity abroad must, for decision-makers in Washington DC, be filtered through the experience of their predecessors being 'trapped' in south Asia. This memory, as distorted as that of Munich, has had baleful effects on US foreign policy. Contemporary leaders who display even a modicum of fight are hyperbolically compared to Churchill. Economic challenges are invariably seen through one of two lenses – either the Great Depression, or the inflation and instability of the 1970s.

Analogies are easy to misuse, then, and historians are right to be wary of ready transferability of 'lessons'. At the same time, however, analogy remains a valuable tool for thinking with. It is integral to human cognition. We are conscious of things that happened before the current moment, and thus navigate the present with the aid of the past. Equally, however, humans are also highly future-oriented. When we look ahead, we see a cluster of possibilities. One has no choice but to take the future into account, and to plan for it. Past, present and future are thus all simultaneously, and continually, at play in our minds. What historians can do is subject analogies to close scrutiny and judge whether or not they are appropriate given the differences and similarities between situations. Can we identify situations that are similar *enough* to current challenges to help us to frame provocative questions, test relevant assumptions and converse fruitfully about policy options? Like it or not, this is how the mind works.

Moreover, history enables us to go far beyond analogy. We can mine it for insights into good conduct that do not depend upon similarity between one situation and another. In other words, we might foreground not *analogy*, but *experience*. For example, the geopolitical rivalry between the United States and China is very different from the earlier rivalry between the United States and the Soviet Union, and will likely remain so. This is not a replication of the Cold War. Still, it would be very odd indeed if Americans did not probe their experience of the Cold War – when the United States authored one of the most impressive feats of statecraft in recorded history – for practical insights that can fulfil a 'How-To' function in other contexts, including when it comes to China. A political situation does not need to be exactly like another one, or even very similar to it, to be mined for examples of best practice that can be reconfigured and employed elsewhere. The commitment of the Truman administration to persuade Americans of the need to contain the Soviet Union remains a powerful exemplar of the potency of persuasion in political affairs. Truman and others, particularly Secretary of State Dean Acheson, were highly active in speaking to Congressional leaders, briefing journalists and delivering public speeches. This effort laid the foundation for an effective bipartisan, indeed national, consensus. The successor administration of Dwight D. Eisenhower offers enduring lessons about the value of considered strategic analysis, sober judgement and executive temperament. Eisenhower presided over an ongoing conversation about the Cold War within the national security apparatus; the constant familiarity with the issues meant that, when decisions had to be taken in moments of crisis, Eisenhower and his officials had been living with the problem for a long time. The wider applications of these facets of the Truman and Eisenhower administrations are obvious, and do not require a geopolitical situation comparable to that which confronted the United States in the mid-twentieth century.

Thinking seriously about the past experience of others, and pondering how we might adapt their successes and failures to enhance our own practice, is perhaps the single most valuable intellectual 'tool' offered by history for decision-makers, and has no necessary connection with straightforward analogy. By studying the prior practice of leadership, we can observe it in the round in ways that refine our own capabilities. Experience is king.

Those who know history are prudent, but they also recognize the power of human imagination and determination, properly applied, to transform things for the better. It is difficult to accept the excuses for failure that now offered so routinely by politicians, particularly after departing office, that some policy problems are intractable due to their 'complexity'. We are accustomed to hearing that something undesirable is 'just a fact of life'. Leaders grappling with them might do well to think about the supposedly 'impossible' problems overcome by their predecessors. As recently as within the span of a single human lifetime, governments conducted some of the most monumental feats of organization ever attempted, while faced with difficulties infinitely greater than virtually any that confront us today.

Anyone who has studied how the United States overcame the geographical distances and logistical challenges involved in waging the Pacific war against Imperial Japan will snort at the notion of 'complexity'. The Pacific is the largest space on earth, and the United States had to master it. As far as human endeavour goes, the American campaign to defeat Japan deserves a place at the forefront of our species' achievement.[101] So too do post-war American projects at the cutting edge of science and engineering, most notably the development of rocket technology that led to the intercontinental ballistic missile and the *Apollo* programme that put human beings on the moon. This required coordination, leadership and innovation. The programmes each involved hundreds of thousands of people, thousands of contractors and bewildering technical challenges; they necessitated effective project management, a meritocratic drive to tap into the best qualities of both the public and private sectors, and the trust to allow those tasked with solving problems to get on and do it. These were challenges of Olympian scope – and yet the fact that they were addressed successfully was no accident. It is little wonder that citizenries across the democratic world are dissatisfied with the competence of those who now compete to govern them, and have become impatient with their failures. They march through the forest resembling the 'ignorant traveller' identified by Collingwood.

To that small number of contemporary statesmen who continue to look to the past for insights, it remains just as potent as ever. Indeed, the response to one of the most significant public policy challenges of the twenty-first century – the financial crash of 2008 – bears the distinctive imprint of Applied History. Ben Bernanke, the chairman of the Federal Reserve Bank during the crisis, is a self-confessed 'Great Depression buff'.[102] He found himself responsible for preserving not merely the American, but the entire global, financial architecture. The crisis was on an extraordinary scale and policymakers found themselves overwhelmed by the pressure and the pace of developments. But as financial contagion and panic spread like wildfire following the downfall of Lehman Brothers, Bernanke saw echoes of the Wall Street Crash and the subsequent depression of the 1930s. He believed that in the interwar era, the mistakes of the Federal Reserve had helped to turn a stock market meltdown into a cataclysmic and protracted depression. The crisis was real and acute, but policy errors had compounded it. This could not happen again. In Bernanke's mind, the looming collapse of the banking sector threatened to wreck economies across the world, plunging America – and the globe – into a new Great Depression. He was privately convinced that, given the impact on so many financial institutions and its planetary scope, the 2008 crash was 'almost certainly' the most serious 'in human history'.[103] The chairman was therefore resolved that the central bank would avoid the errors it made after 1929 when it opted for a policy of money-supply contraction.[104] Bernanke held that this strategy, not the initial crash, was responsible for the prolonged depression.

Rather than battening down the financial hatches, Bernanke mobilized artillery of the trillion-dollar variety. The chairman slashed interest rates, turned on the printing presses and injected liquidity into the banking network. He refused to allow the financial ecosystem to fail and for credit, the lifeblood of the economy upon which ordinary Americans depended, to dry up. To this end banks were bailed out at mammoth cost, mortgages and bonds were purchased on an eye-watering scale, and the Fed's balance sheet ballooned. As the historian Adam Tooze argued, Bernanke turned the Fed into the liquidity provider of last resort to the whole global banking system.

> It provided dollars to all comers in New York, whether banks were American or not. . . . [T]he Fed licensed a hand-picked group of core central banks to issue dollar credits on demand. . . . Among technical experts it is generally agreed that [the way] in which the Fed pumped dollars into the world economy was perhaps the decisive innovation of the crisis.[105]

This response to the financial crash was a highly aggressive form of economic statecraft, and it flowed *directly* from the chairman's own historical sensibilities. Bernanke believed that the crisis closely paralleled the financial panics of the late nineteenth and early twentieth centuries and, in his memoir, remarked that this ability to place contemporary events in the 'context of history' was 'invaluable'.[106] The CBS television show *60 Minutes* remarked that as a scholar of the Great Depression, Bernanke had been 'preparing for this emergency his whole professional life'.[107] One can, inevitably, disagree with Bernanke's approach. The Federal Reserve's response to the 2008 crash will be debated for decades. That, however, is beside the point. What matters is that it constituted an undeniable application of historical insight to pressing contemporary problems.

Of course, it would be a misleading and one-dimensional exaggeration to reduce the crises of the last two decades to simply a lack of historical awareness among policymakers. The challenges of global financial crisis, a raging pandemic, the shifting balance of power, war-weariness and the doubtful future fiscal solvency of Western states would tax anyone. Meanwhile the currency that leaders are most lacking in is always, without exception, time. But statecraft is a brutal business – and, crucially, it was ever thus. Problems are always the norm; failures are legion, far more common than successes. Crises are not unusual. Indeed, they often erupt out of nowhere, like a squall at sea. Uncertainty is inescapable. Time is always short. What is conspicuously absent nowadays, however, are elites who can successfully address these problems. And one of the reasons for this is that many current leaders failed to attend classes at that 'school of statesmanship' conceptualized by Seeley. Those who lead are less likely than ever before to have immersed themselves fruitfully in the past. For Karl Schweizer and Jeremy Black, because of its fundamentally *human* focus, political history is a rich texture of insights, one that arms us against rigid and oversimplified explanatory formula. It illuminates the creative dimensions of statesmanship. And it provides us access to a rich deposit of accumulated wisdom that is essential to 'superior statecraft and sound governance'.[108]

VI

Time defines our existence. Humans not only pass *through* time, and are physically altered by its passage; our very psychology is oriented *around* it. Of course, our lives and consciousness exist purely in the present. Yet, through that strange feature of the brain called memory, we are cognisant of things that happened before the current moment, and thus navigate the present with the aid of the past. Equally, however, humans are always looking to the future. We are a unique species in our sustained and conscious interest in the future. We understand that the present is always in flux, and life a week from now, or a decade from now, might be rather different. When we stare ahead, we see a cluster of possibilities. One has no choice but to take the future into account, and to plan for it. Humans always look to the morrow. Past, present and future are thus all simultaneously, and continually, at play in our minds. And this is true not merely of the individual, but the broader social groups to which they belong. Families, tribes, nations, faiths and ideas all have a past, and they all have a future as well.

And thus we look backwards for sustenance and provocation. The ancients were the first to do so. To be sure, these impulses were not confined to the western extent of the Eurasian landmass.[109] The great Chinese scholar Sima Qian (*c.* 145–86 BC) peppered his *Records of the Grand Historian* – a staggering account of Chinese dynasties over some 2,000 years – with evaluations and judgements on the leaders he described.[110] The text sought out the moral truths that might be gleaned from the past. Here too, history served a fundamentally didactic purpose. Nor were the results simple; far from it. Complexity and contradiction abounded. Sima Qian embraced the multivalent character of historical reflection, and underlines that we should be wary of a narrow focus on Western conceptions.[111] Carefully selected anecdotes were the principal tool through which early Chinese historians imparted their message, most frequently highlighting the examples of wise leaders who exercised caution, understood the base motivations of men and disdained naivete.[112]

Let us end where we began. Though the civilizations of ancient Persia, Babylon and China had kept chronicles of historical events that were intended for subsequent information, the Greeks took this a critical step further.[113] Herodotus resolved that the past should not merely be recorded, but systematically interrogated for meaning. Engaging with it should constitute a form of stimulating intellectual activity, one that stretched the mind rather than a collection of names and dates. Indeed, the very word

Herodotus selected to describe his activity, *historia*, meant 'inquiry'. For Dionysius of Halicarnassus, a Greek scholar who lived at the time of Rome's ascendancy, history was conceptualized as 'philosophy teaching by examples', a means of taking ideas and measuring them against concrete experience. Then there was Polybius. A Greek who lived *c.* 200–118 BC, Polybius was a witness to Rome's rise to dominance. His forty-volume *Histories* – of which only five survive in their entirety – is comparable to Thucydides in its ambitions and analytical three-dimensionality.[114] He began his work by declaring that 'mankind possesses no better guide to conduct than the knowledge of the past'.[115] Polybius argued for what he called *pragmatike historia* – 'pragmatic history' – a mindset that would take a 'synoptical' view of the past, synthesize and interweave complex information, and tease out connections. Successful statesmen and military commanders are, he believed, like historians in that they require an imagination that can detect patterns in chaos, manage complexity and intuit cause and effect. Developing these abilities was essential.[116] Studying history thus had two, related, merits. First, it conferred *knowledge* of what had happened. Second, interpreting that knowledge honed the *analytical capabilities* integral to leadership. It was vital 'training' for any career in politics.[117] Polybius emphasized the role of human nature in explaining historical events.[118] And he was also a believer in education by example. As he explained, 'There are two ways by which all men can reform themselves, the one through their own mischances, and the other through those of others'.[119] The 'mental transference of similar circumstances to our own times' might provide us 'with the means of forming presentiments of what is about to happen', and acting accordingly.[120] History was thus 'the best education for the situations of actual life', for it relates the 'experience' of others.[121] Some ancient scholars foregrounded the experiential insights that history offered, while others emphasized moral teachings and a stimulus to virtue. But what mattered was that history *taught* something crucial about human life. There was a practical verisimilitude to the endeavour.

But nobody did this better than Thucydides. In the judgement of the superlative nineteenth-century historian Thomas Babington Macaulay, Thucydides 'surpassed all his rivals' throughout the ages.[122] His text did not offer anything so 'superficial' as 'lessons'.[123] Instead, as John Burrow concluded, 'We are taught by it indefinably – as we are taught by concentrated experience'.[124] 'Surely no more lucid, unillusioned intelligence has ever applied itself to the writing of history'.[125] The questions that he posed of the past could just as readily be posed of the present – at any time, and any place.[126] This was precisely why, in 1629, the English philosopher Thomas Hobbes asserted that Thucydides was 'the most politic historiographer that ever writ'.[127] His account of the war between Athens and Sparta 'doth secretly instruct the reader, and more effectually than can possibly be done by precept'.[128] Hobbes argued that 'the principal and proper work of history' is to 'enable men, by the knowledge of actions past, to bear themselves prudently in the present and providentially towards the future'.[129] Thucydides's text was thus 'a monument', one intended to 'instruct the ages to come'.[130] As Cicero put it millennia before, through Thucydides 'history hath roused herself, and adventured to speak'.[131]

Thucydides focused the attention of his audience on the eternal conundrum of the human. He made his readers into witnesses. He understood that people are invariably complex, contradictory creatures, moved more by emotion and circumstance than by reason. And he grasped the 'invisible forces' that impel us along.[132] He used these insights as tools to explore the limits of politics and the possibilities of statecraft. Human behaviour is the bedrock of politics, and studying history is how we acquire knowledge of that behaviour. The 'link between the past and the future is human nature, or the ways of human beings'.[133] At the risk of belabouring a point and exhausting the reader, history is not prophecy. Instead, it is about recognizing that there is an immediacy to the past that is of utility in the present, and for the future. Carl Becker felt that 'in a very real sense it is impossible to divorce history from life'.[134] Few articulated this more effectively than Collingwood. He proposed that 'the past lives on in the present', because it is 'incapsulated' within the present. Moreover, though it is 'at first sight hidden beneath the present's contradictory and more prominent features', nevertheless when one peels back the layers, one quickly realizes that the present *is* the past – specifically, an accumulation of decisions and actions. The past is, therefore, 'alive and active', and – precisely because it is so embedded within the present – history always stands 'in the closest possible relation to practical life'.[135]

Notes

1 Thucydides, *The War of the Peloponnesians and the Athenians*, ed. Jeremy Wynott (Cambridge, 2013). Unless otherwise indicated, this is the edition cited hereafter.

2 David M. Lewis, John Boardman, J. K. Davies, and M. Ostwald, 'Preface', in *The Cambridge Ancient History, V: The Fifth Century BC*, ed. Lewis et al. (Cambridge, 1992), xiii–xvi, at xiv.

3 Geoffrey Hawthorn, *Thucydides on Politics: Back to the Present* (Cambridge, 2014), ix.

4 Thucydides, *The War of the Peloponnesians and the Athenians*, 15–16.

5 Herodotus, *The Histories*, trans. Aubrey de Selincourt (London, 2003 edn.), 3.

6 R. G. Collingwood, *The Idea of History*, ed. Jan van der Dussen (Oxford, 1993), 18.

7 Arnold J. Toynbee, *A Study of History*, abridgement of vols. VII–X, ed. D. C. Somervell (Oxford, 1985), 353.

8 Cicero, *De Oratore*, II, 36.

9 Jed W. Atkins, *Cicero on Politics and the Limits of Reason* (Cambridge, 2013).

10 Cicero, *De Officiis* (Cambridge, MS, 1913), I, i, 3.

11 Tactitus, *The Annals*, trans. J. C. Yardley (Oxford, 2008).

12 For example, Sallust, *Caitline's War, The Jugurthine War, Histories*, trans. A. J. Woodman (London, 2007), 8–9.

13 Benedetto Croce, *History as the Story of Liberty*, trans. Sylvia Sprigge (London, 1941), 170.

14 Ibid., 170.

15 Homer, *The Iliad*, trans. Peter Green (Oakland, CA, 2015).

16 Niccolò Machiavelli to Francesco Vettori, 10 December 1513, https://courses .washington.edu/hsteu401/Letter%20%20to%20Vettori.pdf.

17 Niccolò Machiavelli, *The Prince*, ed. Peter Bondanella (Oxford, 1984), 3.

18 Ibid., 20.

19 For example, Niccolò Machiavelli, 'Description of the Methods Adopted by the Duke Valentino when Murdering Vitellozzo Vitelli, Oliverto da Fermo, the Signor Pagolo, and the Duke di Gravina Orsini' (1503).

20 Deborah Wormell, *Sir John Seeley and the Uses of History* (Cambridge, 1980).

21 J. R. Seeley, *The Expansion of England: Two Courses of Lectures* (Cambridge, 1883).

22 J. R. Seeley, *Lectures and Essays* (London, 1870), 296.

23 On perspectives at Oxford, see Reba Soffer, 'Duty, Character, and Confidence: History at Oxford, 1850–1914', *The Historical Journal* 30, no. 1 (1987): 77–104.

24 R. G. Collingwood, *An Autobiography* (Oxford, 1939), 100. I am grateful to Niall Ferguson for pointing me in the direction of this wonderful book.

25 Collingwood, *An Autobiography*, 100.

26 Ibid.

27 Ibid., 101–2, 105.

28 Ibid., 99.

29 John Plumpton, 'The Study of History and the Practice of Politics', address to the Churchill Society for the Advancement of Parliamentary Democracy, Toronto, November 2002, https://winstonchurchill.org/resources/speeches/speeches-about -winston-churchill/the-study-of-history-and-the-practice-of-politics/.

30 Herbert Butterfield, *The Historical Novel* (Cambridge, 1924) foregrounds the centrality of imagination in thinking about the past.

31 Michael Bentley, 'The West: Reflections on the Making of a Past', lecture at Ohio University, 26 September 2011, https://www.youtube.com/watch?v=LLY6NiNrxqw, 44, at 20.

32 Collingwood, *The Idea of History*, 2.

33 John Lewis Gaddis, *The Landscape of History: How Historians Map the Past* (Oxford, 2004), 22.

34 Carl L. Becker, 'Everyman His Own Historian', annual address of the President of the American Historical Association, Minneapolis, 29 December 1931, https://www .historians.org/about-aha-and-membership/aha-history-and-archives/presidential -addresses/carl-l-becker.

35 Thomas Aquinas, *Summa Theologica* (Raleigh, NC, 2006), 3790.

36 See, for example, Tolstoy's essay on historical determinism at the end of *War and Peace* (1869).

37 Isaiah Berlin, 'Historical Inevitability', in Berlin, *The Proper Study of Mankind: An Anthology of Essays*, ed. Henry Hardy and Roger Hausheer (London, 2013 edn.), 119–90.

38 Collingwood, *An Autobiography*, 114.

39 Collingwood, *The Idea of History*, 10.

40 Jacques Barzun, 'Bagehot as Historian', in *The Collected Works of Walter Bagehot, Volume Three: The Historical Essays*, ed. Norman St John-Stevas (London, 1968), 23–40, at 40.

41 Colin S. Gray, *Strategy and Defence Planning: Meeting the Challenge of Uncertainty* (Oxford, 2014), 115.

42 Isaiah Berlin, 'The Hedgehog and the Fox: An Essay on Tolstoy's View of History', in Berlin, *The Proper Study of Mankind*, 436–98, at 444.

43 R. G. Collingwood, 'Reality as History', in Collingwood, *The Principles of History: And Other Writings in Philosophy of History*, ed. W. H. Dray and W. J. van der Dussen (Oxford, 1999), 170–208, at 171.

44 Collingwood, *An Autobiography*, 99–100.

45 Gaddis, *The Landscape of History*.

46 Collingwood, *An Autobiography*, 101.

47 Aleksander Solzhenitsyn, *The Gulag Archipelago* (London, 1974).

48 See William H. Dray, *History as Re-Enactment: R. G. Collingwood's Idea of History* (Oxford, 1999).

49 Philip Zelikow, Ernest R. May, and the Harvard Suez Team, *Suez Deconstructed: An Interactive Study in Crisis, War, and Peacemaking* (Washington, DC, 2018), 1.

50 James Alexander, review of Martyn P. Thompson, *Michael Oakeshott and the Cambridge School on the History of Political Thought, Cosmos+Taxis: Studies in Emergent Order and Organisations* 8, no. 2&3 (2020): 66–83, at 80.

51 Saint Augustine, *Confessions*, trans. R. S. Pine-Coffin (London, 1961), 262–70.

52 Ibid., 268.

53 R. G. Collingwood, 'Croce's Philosophy of History', in Collingwood, *Essays in the Philosophy of History*, ed. William Debbins (Austin, TX, 1965), 3–22, at 6–7.

54 Geoffrey Thomas, 'Michael Oakeshott's Philosophy of History', in *A Companion to Michael Oakeshott*, ed. Paul Franco and Leslie Marsh (University Park, PA, 2012), 95–119, at 97.

55 A helpful starting point is Jimena Canales, *The Physicist and The Philosopher: Einstein, Bergson, and the Debate that Changed Our Understanding of Time* (Princeton, NJ, 2016).

56 John Dunn, 'Seeing in and through Time', in *The Western Time of Ancient History*, ed. Alexandra Lianeri (Cambridge, 2011), 307–14, at 307.

57 G. J. Whitrow, *Time in History: Views of Time from Prehistory to the Present Day* (Oxford, 1989).

58 Oswald Spengler, *The Decline of the West: An Abridged Edition*, ed. Helmut Werner (Oxford, 1991), 10.

59 See, for example, *The Oxford History of Historical Writing*, 5 vols (Oxford, 2011–2015).

60 Hayden White, *Metahistory: The Historical Imagination in 19th-Century Europe* (Baltimore, MD, 2014 edn.).

61 On the former, see *British Myths and Legends*, 3 vols, ed. Richard Barber (London, 1998). For a Middle Eastern sample, Ferdowsi, *The Shahnameh*.

62 For one perspective, consult Michael Bentley, *Modern Historiography: An Introduction* (London, 1999).

63 Michael Bentley, 'British Historical Writing', in *The Oxford History of Historical Writing, Volume 5: Historical Writing Since 1945*, ed. Alex Schneider and Daniel Woolf (Oxford, 2011), 292–309, at 309.

64 Collingwood, *The Idea of History*, 27.

65 Augustine, *Confessions*, 264.

66 Thomas E. Ricks, 'Best Defense', *Foreign Policy*, 28 March 2017, https://foreignpolicy.com/2017/03/28/book-excerpt-defense-secretary-mattis-discusses-his-favorite-books-and-why/.

67 For an almighty exception (and one of the best works of history written in the last half-century), see David Hackett Fischer, *Albion's Seed: Four British Folkways in America* (Oxford, 1989).

68 Thomas Carlyle, *On Heroes, Hero-Worship and the Heroic in History* (London, 1841).

69 J. C. D. Clark, *Our Shadowed Present: Modernism, Postmodernism, and History* (London, 2003), 22.

70   Jeremy Black, 'Why Historians Get It Wrong', *The New Criterion* 35 (February 2017): 37–9.

71   Kenneth Minogue, *The Liberal Mind* (Indianapolis, IN, 1999 edn.), xii.

72   On the decline of causality, see Mark Hewitson, *History and Causality* (Basingstoke, 2014).

73   Hal Brands and Francis J. Gavin, 'The Historical Profession Is Committing Slow-Motion Suicide', *War on the Rocks*, 10 December 2018, https://warontherocks.com /2018/12/the-historical-profession-is-committing-slow-motion-suicide/.

74   As demoralizing as it may be, this tendency is at least a good example of the fact that 'history' is generally constructed with more focus on the present than the past. Scholars intend that the past be 'usable', even (perhaps especially) when they deny that.

75   Jose Ortega y Gasset, *Toward a Philosophy of History* (New York, 1941), 81.

76   Hal Brands and William Inboden, 'Wisdom without Tears: Statecraft and the Uses of History', *Journal of Strategic Studies* 41, no. 7 (2018): 916–46, at 921.

77   Cicero, *De Officiis*, I, vi, 21.

78   Niall Ferguson and Graham Allison, 'Why the U.S. President Needs a Council of Historians', *The Atlantic*, September 2016, https://www.theatlantic.com/magazine/ archive/2016/09/dont-know-much-about-history/492746/.

79   Patrick Milton, Michael Axworthy, and Brendan Simms, *Towards a Westphalia for the Middle East* (Oxford, 2018).

80   *The Times*, 7 January 2019.

81   The term 'Applied History' was initially deployed in 1909 by Benjamin Franklin Shambaugh, a historian, political scientist and first Superintendent of the State Historical Society of Iowa. Shambaugh established a research group to investigate a wide variety of policy issues in state and local history. His belief was that this would assist lawmakers to address pressing political, social and economic problems. Over the next two decades, the group produced multiple specialist monographs that blended analysis of the historical background of an issue with concrete policy recommendations. Shambaugh saw history as a 'science' that could contribute to effective governance and social welfare. While we might dissent from his conviction that history is a science – it is an art – the impulse that animated Shambaugh was to link the past, the present and the future in profitable ways. I am grateful to Mattias Hesserus for delivering a fascinating paper on this at Gonville and Caius College, University of Cambridge, on 7 June 2019. I must also record my thanks to Brendan Simms for inviting me to chair a fruitful discussion over dinner at Trinity College that evening.

82   Michael Oakeshott, *On History and Other Essays* (Indianapolis, IN, 1999), 70; Alexander, review of Martyn P. Thompson, *Michael Oakeshott and the Cambridge School on the History of Political Thought*, *Cosmos+Taxis*, 80.

83   Michael Oakeshott, *The Politics of Faith and the Politics of Scepticism* (New Haven, CT, 1996), 67.

84   Michael Oakeshott, 'Rationalism in Politics', in Oakeshott, *Rationalism in Politics and Other Essays*, ed. Timothy Fuller (Indianapolis, IN, 1991), 5–42, at 6.

85   One prominent effort to identify 'laws' – and more sophisticated than Marx but equally wrong, albeit in different ways – can be found in Carl Hemper, 'The Function of General Laws in History', *Journal of Philosophy* 39, no. 2 (1942): 35–48.

86   1st Corinthians, 13:12.

87   Collingwood, *An Autobiography*, 101–2, 105.

88 Carl Von Clausewitz, *On War*, trans. Michael Howard and Peter Paret (Princeton, NJ, 1976), 102.

89 Ibn Khaldun, *The Muqaddimah: An Introduction to History*, 3 vols, trans. Franz Rosenthal (Princeton, NJ, 1967), Volume I, 6.

90 Hal Brands and Jeremy Suri, 'Introduction', in *The Power of the Past: History and Statecraft*, ed. Brands and Suri (Washington, DC, 2016), 1–24, at 6, 9.

91 James Hankins, *Virtue Politics: Soulcraft and Statecraft in Renaissance Italy* (Cambridge, MS, 2020).

92 John H. Elliott, *Richelieu and Olivares* (Cambridge, 1984), 24.

93 Neville Morley, 'Monumentality and the Meaning of the Past in Ancient and Modern Historiography', in *The Western Time of Ancient History*, ed. Lianeri, 210–26, at 219.

94 Edward Gibbon, *Essay on the Study of Literature* (1761).

95 Livy, *The History of Rome, Volume I: Books 1–2*, trans. R. G. Foster (Cambridge, MS, 2019), Book 1, 7.

96 Seeley, *Lectures and Essays*, 299.

97 Quoted in Robert Nisbet, *Conservatism: Dream and Reality* (Milton Keynes, 1986), viii.

98 Brands and Inboden, 'Wisdom without Tears', 917, 935.

99 John G. Gunnell, *Political Philosophy and Time* (Middletown, CT, 1968), 246.

100 See Catherine Zuckert, *Machiavelli's Politics* (Chicago, 2017), 9.

101 Paul Kennedy, *Engineers of Victory: The Problem Solvers Who Turned the Tide in the Second World War* (London, 2013), chapter four.

102 *Wall Street Journal*, 7 December 2005.

103 Ben S. Bernanke, *The Courage to Act: A Memoir of a Crisis and its Aftermath* (New York, 2015), 336. I am grateful to Andrew Ehrhardt for alerting me to this.

104 Ibid., 30.

105 Adam Tooze, *Crashed: How A Decade of Financial Crises Changed the World* (London, 2018), 9–11.

106 Bernanke, *The Courage to Act*, 398.

107 *60 Minutes*, 15 March 2009.

108 Karl Schweizer and Jeremy Black, 'The Value of Diplomatic History: A Case Study in the Historical Thought of Herbert Butterfield', *Diplomacy and Statecraft* 17, no. 3 (2006): 617–31, at 627.

109 Although Ancient India seems 'to have lacked much interest in history, at least as it is conceived in the West': David Morgan, 'The Evolution of Two Asian Historiographical Traditions', in *Companion to Historiography*, ed. Michael Bentley (London, 1997), 9–19, at 9.

110 Sima Qian, *Records of the Grand Historian*, 3 vols. (New York, 2017).

111 See Lei Yang, 'Building Blocks of Chinese Historiography: A Narratological Analysis of Shi Ji', unpublished PhD thesis, University of Pennsylvania (2016), and F. H. Mutschler, 'Sima Qian and his Western Colleagues: On Possible Categories of Description', *History and Theory* 46 (2007): 194–200.

112 David Schaberg, 'Chinese History and Philosophy', in *The Oxford History of Historical Writing, Volume 1: Beginnings to AD 600*, ed. Andrew Feldherr and Grant Hardy (Oxford, 2011), 394–414.

113 A rich and illuminating treatment can be found in Arnaldo Momigliano, *The Classical Foundations of Modern Historiography* (Berkeley, CA, 1990).

114 Polybius, *The Rise of the Roman Empire*, trans. Ian Scott-Kilvert (London, 1979).

115 Ibid., 41.

116 Iskander Rehman, 'Polybius, Applied History, and Grand Strategy in an Interstitial Age', *War on the Rocks*, 29 March 2019, https://warontherocks.com/2019/03/polybius -applied-history-and-grand-strategy-in-an-interstitial-age/.

117 Polybius, *The Rise of the Roman Empire*, 41.

118 Georgina Longley, 'Thucydides, Polybius, and Human Nature', in *Imperialism, Cultural Politics, and Polybius*, ed. Christopher Smith and Liv Mariah Yarrow (Oxford, 2012), 70–84.

119 Polybius, *The Rise of the Roman Empire*, 80.

120 Polybius, *The Histories, Books 9–15*, trans. W. R. Paton (Cambridge, MS, 2011), 12, 25b, 371.

121 Polybius, *The Rise of the Roman Empire*, 80.

122 Thomas Macaulay, 'The Romance of History by Henry Beele', in *The Miscellaneous Writings and Speeches of Lord Macaulay* (London, 1889), 138.

123 Burrow, *A History of Histories*, 48.

124 Ibid.

125 Ibid., 51.

126 Hawthorn, *Thucydides on Politics*, 12.

127 Thomas Hobbes, 'To the Readers', in Thucydides, *The Peloponnesian War: The Complete Translation*, ed. David Greene (Chicago, 1989), xxii.

128 Thomas Hobbes, 'On the Life and History of Thucydides', in Thucydides, *The Peloponnesian War*, 577.

129 Hobbes, 'To the Readers', xxi.

130 Hobbes, 'On the Life and History of Thucydides', 576.

131 Ibid., 577.

132 Thucydides, *The War of the Peloponnesians and the Athenians*, 190.

133 Ryan Balot, 'Was Thucydides a Political Philosopher?', in *The Oxford Handbook of Thucydides*, ed. Ryan Balot, Sara Forsdyke, and Edith Foster (Oxford, 2017), 320–38, at 321.

134 Becker, 'Everyman His Own Historian'.

135 Collingwood, *An Autobiography*, 100, 106.

3

The Whig way of war

The origins of Anglo-American strategy-making

Giselle Donnelly

Philip Yorke, 1st Baron Hardwicke and Lord High Chancellor of Great Britain, was among the grandest of the English oligarchs of the mid-eighteenth century. He might also be said to be a mastermind of Britain's rise to world power; in concert with Thomas Pelham-Holles, duke of Newcastle – twice prime minister and for decades a force to be reckoned with in Parliament – the two charted a course to an empire upon which the sun never set. They were equally the links between Robert Walpole, builder of a financially powerful and fully modern 'deep state' in the 1720s but ever cautious in matters of foreign policy, and William Pitt, who translated domestic power into a stunning series of global triumphs four decades later. And not only did these two grandees formulate a consistent strategic outlook, they institutionalized it into the doctrine of an all-powerful Whig party. And, most profoundly of all, they exported it across the Atlantic to Britain's American colonies, who have preserved and profited from the 'Whig way of war' ever since.

The essence of what international relations theorists would describe as a 'strategic culture' – a set of enduring habits towards the preparation, maintenance and use of military power – was, for Hardwicke, to balance Britain's strength as a maritime power with 'continental commitments'; that is, alliances and subsidies to European states and principalities, for the purpose of preventing any adversary from so dominating the balance of great powers as to challenge Britain's ability to 'rule the waves'. As the seminal American strategist Alfred Thayer Mahan later would argue in his magisterial *The Influence of Sea Power upon History,* the combination of a 'multi-ocean' navy and European alliances allowed Britain – in the early modern era a second-class 'bone for dogs' in the international system – to rise as a world-ordering political, military and economic power.

One could naturally infer, too, from Hardwicke that there would be a competing 'Tory' tradition, and indeed there was. This emphasized sea power to the exclusion of expensive and frustrating entanglements with the congeries of smaller European states and principalities whose political cultures were so uncongenial to a John Bull mentality and whose interests were intensely local, whereas Britain's were more naturally global. The Prussians were too militaristic and autocratic, while the Dutch were just the opposite: commercial and republican. These allies were also suspect in their Protestantism, as they were altogether lacking in the episcopal hierarchy of the English national church. Perhaps worst of all were the Hanoverians, who were thought to be 'Asiatic' in their political culture; sunshine soldiers had somehow become heirs to the British throne while proscribing the Tories from high office until 1760. The great prophet of Tory politics and strategy was Henry St. John, 1st Viscount Bolingbroke, whose 1738 pamphlet *The Idea of a Patriot King* succinctly summarizes the maritime alternative to the expansive – and expensive – Whig imperial strategy:

> Great Britain is an island: and whilst nations on the Continent are at immense charge in maintaining their barriers, and perpetually on their guard, and frequently embroiled, to extend or strengthen them, Great Britain may, if her governors please, accumulate wealth in maintaining hers. . . . Other nations must watch over every motion of their neighbors; in almost every conjuncture that arises. But as we cannot be easily nor suddenly attacked, and as we ought not to aim at any acquisition of territory on the continent, it may be in our interest to watch the secret workings of the several councils abroad; to advise, to warn; to abet, and oppose; but it can never be our true interest easily and officiously to enter into action, much less into engagements that imply action and expense.[1]

Taken together, Hardwicke and Bolingbroke represent a kind of baroque expression of strategic tonalities that originated in England's Elizabethan era and still provide an enduring framework for twenty-first-century Americans. This essay will argue that the Whig approach has been the most frequently dominant and successful strain in Anglo-American strategy-making, the key to the global primacy first of Great Britain, and now the United States. It will sketch the origins of this strategic culture in the sixteenth century through its first flowering in the eighteenth, its transmission to Britain's 'New World' colonies and its greatest expression in the period of America's rise to global power. Yet, it will also examine critical periods where the Tory, blue-water approach has gained favour, and conclude by asking whether the current moment is another 'Tory Time', and speculate as to the consequences if that is so.

I

While Americans see themselves as children of the Enlightenment, they are, more than they imagine, progeny of the Protestant Reformation and the way that shaped and shifted the English into the British, from a blood-and-soil nation (albeit with a Norman French nobility) into a more polyglot 'composite' imperial polity encompassing all the British isles and looking westward to expand into North America. And there was a de facto Whig way of war well before there was a political party which embraced that doctrine.

When Elizabeth came to the throne in 1558, England had fallen from the front-rank of powers. Her father, Henry VIII, despite the massive wealth appropriated from the church, largely had failed to subdue Scotland by his 'Rough Wooing' or to reclaim a toehold in France; Elizabeth's elder sister and predecessor Mary had been forced to sign away her rights to Calais. Even in England, the dukes and other major nobles of the north obeyed orders from London only when it pleased them, and the back-and-forth tides of Reformation and Counterreformation likewise divided Elizabeth's people. Scotland was, if anything, perhaps even more atomized. The 'lowlanders' were becoming aggressively Calvinistic but also Presbyterian and anti-episcopal; to Elizabeth, these potential allies also seemed potentially subversive. The border lords and Highlanders were a Gaelic law unto themselves, which to English eyes was no law at all. And France, by dynastic diplomacy and military deployments, threatened to restore the 'auld alliance'. Ireland was a kaleidoscope of provincial powers, some originally Norman and Catholic 'Old English', some Gaelic and Catholic if only to appeal to the pope and Spain for arms and support. The shortcomings of English colonial enterprise – state-sanctioned but privately organized and funded – and land power would be on repeated display until the very end of Elizabeth's forty-five years on the throne. Indeed, the final surrender of the Earl of Tyrone was accepted after the queen's demise; suppressing Hugh O'Neill's rebellion had taken nine years and was the most expensive English campaign of the Elizabethan era, far surpassing the costs of repelling Spanish armadas. In sum, the Tudor regime, its uniquely English approach towards Protestantism and its great-power ambitions frequently hung by a very thin thread, and the queen ruled a very Little England.

Yet this weakness made for clarity of strategic thought across the English political nation; competing personalities and favourites at court there might be, but there was a remarkable consensus about geopolitical ends, ways and means, and it was only in the Stuart years where the rift between maritime, 'blue-water' enthusiasts and continental engagers and alliance-makers solidified into the basis for partisan or factional advocacy. This Elizabethan strategic consensus provided – and still provides – the genetic material for the Whig way of war, leaving the Tory alternative as a reaction, an oppositional stance. The consensus was grounded in a set of priorities of power that formed a coherent and consistent view of both domestic and international politics, a 'security architecture'.[2]

The Elizabethans faced a complex puzzle. The core concern was the stability, durability and – importantly – legitimacy of the ruling regime, all of which was emphasized by the previous Tudor troubles and Elizabeth's sex. To be sure, the queen understood herself to be a divinely chosen monarch but was too astute a politician to push the point as her Stuart successors would. She knew that the English political nation and its parliaments, in particular, would not countenance flagrant absolutism or royal prerogative and had no qualms about using the power of the purse and taxation to get its way; even Elizabeth's most trusted and longest-serving adviser, William Cecil, viewed the crown as a semi-contractual arrangement, dependent upon a broad belief in its moral legitimacy.[3] The Privy Council and Parliament were particularly concerned and intrusive about the royal succession, to the queen's eternal annoyance. Nor could the English throne really be understood apart from the neighbouring kingdoms in Scotland and Ireland – or even Wales, though Henry VIII secured a union there in 1536. The English and Scots shared an island and, from a London perspective, Scottish independence itself was a latent threat and an invitation to mischief, especially French mischief; what to do about Mary, queen of Scots, a Stuart by birth but betrothed to the dauphin of France and niece of the brutally Catholic duke of Guise, was a decades-long plague to Elizabeth. Scotland was, in Cecil's view, a 'postern gate' into England and, if not safely bolted and guarded, an existential threat. Ireland was also seen as a potential staging ground for invaders – more likely to be Spanish than French – and Ireland's internal instability a petri dish for plots.

Beyond these close-to-home concerns, Elizabeth and her counsellors had a keen appreciation of the European and indeed global balance of power. It was not merely that the French or Spanish might meddle in British affairs but that the northwest coast of the continent provided an array of embarkation points for amphibious assault; Philip II's *Grande y Felicisima Armada* was but the prelude to a cross-Channel attack by the duke of Parma's armies from the Low Countries. And the famous victory at Gravelines was enabled by a blockade by Dutch flyboats of Medina Sidonia's fleet. It was Cecil's belief that this coastline should be viewed as a 'counterscarp' – in the fortification theory of the time, defences that sat outside the moat (in this case, the Channel) and the inner walls and keep. The 'wooden walls' of the Royal Navy were not the first guarantee of English security. Moreover, it was excruciatingly apparent to English strategists of the sixteenth century that Spain's colonization and exploitation of American resources – the plundered and mined ores of the Aztec and Inca empires – were the key to its bid for European hegemony and Counterreformation. Only by better competing in the global, imperial and colonial spheres did Elizabethans imagine they might begin to go toe-to-toe with such a powerful rival. Likewise, Henry VII's refusal to grant Bartolomo Colombo's request for support to his brother's voyages of to the 'New World' was regarded as a moment of English shame and strategic regret; the Elizabethans knew they were decades behind in the race with the Spanish. Thus, Sir Francis Drake, after crossing the Pacific during his three-year circumnavigation – which was really a scouting mission to find weak points in Spain's American empire – proposed an alliance to Babu, ruler of the Moluccas and chafing under Iberian dominance. As the Spanish agent reported to Philip:

> Captain Francis had said that he was a vassal of the Queen of England, if the Queen desired to favor and help him to expel the Portuguese from that region, he would concede to her the trade in cloves, which up to that time the Portuguese had had. Captain Francis, on the part of the Queen of England, promised that within two years he would decorate that sea with ships for whatever purpose might be necessary.[4]

This was far beyond the art of the militarily possible for an impoverished queen and a diminished power half a world away, but it was a serious statement of strategic ambition. Yet the Elizabethans not only had a world view; they had a plan for achieving world power. To begin with, they understood that Spain and the Counterreformation it championed transformed international politics into a confessional and ideological contest, a game they must play. Both at home and abroad, the English national and British imperial cause was inevitably entwined with the larger 'Protestant interest'; Reformation – particularly of the Anglican sort – in a single state was not enough.

This could be a burden as well as a blessing. International Protestantism was already a herd of cats, divided over matters of doctrine and, of more political import, church organization; Calvinists, and especially Dutch ones, seemed prone to an infectious republicanism, a virus among dissenting and non-conforming Englishmen as well. As they began their long revolt against the Hapsburgs, the Dutch several times offered Elizabeth their crown, an offer she stoutly would not accept. At the same time, she succumbed to a creeping military alliance and the deployment of land forces to the continent. She also gave troops to Henry Bourbon, the leader of the Protestant cause in France, before he decided that 'Paris was worth a Mass'. Then and later, the Protestant cause could accommodate Catholic allies in the struggle against 'universal monarchy'.

The Elizabethan strategic recipe also called for a mix of sea and land power, and saw how they could work together. The English and their Dutch allies were fortunate in that Philip II's navy had to divide its attention several ways: towards the carrying of large loads of treasure, spices and ores from its colonial outposts and towards repulsing the Ottoman galley fleets in the Mediterranean, which they successfully did at Lepanto in 1570. Galleys and small-sea maritime conflict made a test of prowess in close-in manoeuvring and boarding assaults, whereas, in the open waters of the Atlantic, longer-range gunnery and fleet tactics reigned supreme, and in these the English had a marked advantage, at least until Philip made 'the enterprise of England' his priority and, by adding the throne of Portugal to his titles, vastly increased his ocean-going naval power. The English army, by contrast, was no match for Philip's seasoned tercios in any significant battle. Nonetheless, by apprenticing themselves to the Dutch, English commanders began to catch up and, in Charles Blount, Lord Mountjoy, who finally did for Tyrone and the Irish, produced a very fine professional general, superb logistician and unforgiving counterinsurgent; his lieutenants were key to the later colonization not only of Ireland, but North America.

But the ability to continually influence events on the continent by direct military intervention of large-scale land forces would be a challenge, and thus – if reluctantly – Elizabeth accepted the need for a system of enduring and temporary alliances to achieve a stable balance of power and thus keep aspiring hegemons embroiled on land and unable to match Britain's multi-ocean naval capacity. What became a 'two-navy standard' – that the Royal Navy should be able to match its nearest two competitors – was attained not simply by superior shipbuilding capacity, but by preventing potential adversaries from likewise focusing their resources.

Finally, this strategic conception was also beyond the reach of Elizabeth's government and English finance. While her close advisers and small corps of clerks were enormously educated and intellectually sophisticated men, both culturally and politically, they were too few to accomplish much beyond the general conception of policy, although occasionally they would become more deeply involved in various projects, notably in Irish colonization. The parsimonious queen lacked the resources – both in specie and in loans – that Philip's American income provided, and it would be half a century before the Dutch innovations in banking and finance began to filter their way into London. One may see the signs of the 'Financial Revolution' to come in the colonial 'adventuring' joint-stock enterprises, but what would become a 'fiscal-military state' of the first order remained a distant dream. As, for example, in the 1589

'Counter-Armada' expedition to Portugal, the queen might find ways to leverage the patriotism and avarice of courtiers into 'public–private partnerships' in the British security interest, but in doing so she sacrificed coherence in command.[5]

II

That this fledgling strategic consensus, boiled down through forty-five years of trial and error, survived through the seventeenth century is a testament both to its innate strength and the incompetence of the Stuart monarchs, men who sought alternative approaches to the English security dilemma but proved themselves repeatedly out of synch with the political nation and flummoxed by external, European events. Yet paradoxically, by the time James II lost the throne for the final time, the Stuarts also presided over a string of North American colonies stretching from Maine to the Caribbean and providing the potential strategic depth for a British Empire. Between the Stuarts, the Roundheads of the Commonwealth made a kind of fetish of Elizabethan principles, and Cromwell's 'Western Design' expedition to the 'Indies' was meant to establish the permanent platform for threatening Spanish treasure fleets that had been Drake's dream and indeed the design of the Puritan grandees of the 1630s, who financed not only the settlement of 'New England' but 'Providence' Island off the coast of Nicaragua. Cromwell's plan for an assault on Hispaniola failed miserably, but Port Royal in Jamaica ended up serving the purpose. It was not until the coming of 'Dutch William' and the 'Glorious Revolution' of 1688 that the original strategic consensus was restored and brought to strategic maturity – or at least strategic adolescence.

Indeed, seen from a strategic perspective, traditional historiography inverts seventeenth-century revolutions and restorations. Measured by the yardstick of this essay, it was the Stuarts who were the champions of change, Cromwell and William advocated for a return to the 'Good Old Cause', the Elizabethan status quo, even though that was to be accomplished by revolutions in government, military affairs and finance. This pattern originated with James I's reaction to the outbreak of the Thirty Years' War, the climactic chapter in the wars of the Reformation, in 1618. For the previous fifteen years, James had been a very British king, proposing a formal union of England, Ireland and Scotland, the throne he had inherited from his executed mother, Mary Stuart, queen of Scots. He had also made a strong push for English colonization in Ulster, although his plans were based on the confiscation of property from Tyrone and other rebels, and investments on the part of courtiers and the livery companies of London, who were 'persuaded' by James to take on the development of Derry, which was henceforth denominated as 'Londonderry'. James also styled himself as 'Rex Pacificus'. This peacemaking king shied away from great-power competition, especially military confrontation in Europe, even when it meant defending the claims of his own daughter, Elizabeth, and her husband, Frederick, Elector Palatine to the crown of Bohemia, whose Protestant nobility had chosen him – Bohemia was an elective monarchy – in place of the Catholic nominee, Matthias, who they also feared was a stalking horse for absolutist Hapsburg rule.

Despite the family connection, James utterly refused to step up to the challenge of leading a Protestant coalition that soon became the defining confessional, ideological and geopolitical struggle of the era. This set him athwart the political nation and the Parliament. While it is questionable that this broader class much grasped the brutality or the emerging nature of the war, the king's reticence created a breach of trust. James then made it worse by proposing a dynastic and matrimonial 'Spanish match' between his son Charles and the Spanish *infanta* Anna Maria. It was shameful enough to see an English king try to split the difference between the forces of Reformation and Counterreformation, but it became a full-blown humiliation when Charles and the royal favourite, the duke of Buckingham, failed in their secretive mission to *el Escorial* to bring the girl back to England. During his final years, increasingly isolated and estranged from Parliament and his people, James retreated into strident assertions of his 'royal prerogative', especially insisting that commoners should not inquire into what the king claimed were the *arcana imperii* of strategy-making. James fulfilled his desire to keep the peace, but at the cost of retreating into weakness.

During his father's final years, Charles had attempted to uphold the family honour by a kind of populist posturing in advocating an amphibious assault on Cadiz and then a series of expeditions to protect French Huguenots from persecution by Louis XIII. This appeared, to the Parliament and the political nation, as a 'Blessed Revolution'.[6] But Charles quickly proved himself more prickly about royal prerogatives and, perhaps more importantly, on enforcing strict Anglican doctrine and episcopal order – and the political subservience they fostered. As the trials and atrocities of the Thirty Years' War made English Calvinists – who had been a majority of English church leadership from the beginning of the Stuart regime – more militant and puritan, Charles's attitudes likewise hardened and he withdrew his seeming support for engagement in Europe. To make matters worse, this coincided with the glory years of the great commander, Gustavus Adolphus; English Protestants found a champion, but he was a Swedish king, not a British one. The period marked by Gustavus Adolphus's consummate victory at Breitenfeld in 1631 to Charles's beheading before the Banqueting House at Whitehall in January 1649 – and the many 'Wars of the Three Kingdoms' across the British isles that intervened – can fairly be regarded as the first Stuart revolution. It was a catastrophic failure that also created a kind of imperial implosion.

This meant that, although the colonial project in North America continued – and in many cases, was propelled by refugees from Charles's persecutions in England and Scotland – it tended to detract from British power and purpose rather than add to it. This was true even in Virginia, the so-called Cavalier Colony that had remained loyal to the king. It had taken nearly four decades to wrest a secure enclave from the Atlantic to the fall line of the James River; the struggle against the Powhatan confederacy and disease had cost thousands of English lives and been marked by two brief 'massacres' that shocked London as well as the colonists. The Jamestown settlement had also struggled economically until it discovered that the tidewater soil was suitable for growing tobacco, which became the staple crop and export – and a vital source of revenue for the crown, despite James's loathing of the noxious weed. Yet by the late 1630s and 1640s, Virginia was more refuge for Royalists than source of royal strength. In 1645, colonial Governor William Berkeley, the second son of a prominent family, familiar face at the court of Charles I and solider in the 'Bishops' Wars' of the late 1630s, had come to England to seek additional military help to consolidate the colony and expand its growth, but scurried back across the Atlantic once he understood just how dire the Stuarts' situation had become. With the advent of the Commonwealth, Virginia's population grew from 8,000 to 40,000 at the time of the Stuart Restoration.

If Virginia proved no help to the Stuart cause, the other important English outposts in North America, the Massachusetts Bay and neighbouring Puritan colonies, were a central point of resistance. While Elizabeth I had failed to fulfil the desires of her most devout and aggressive Protestant counsellors and subjects, her *via media* carried enough prospect of further Reform to make them as warmly loyal as they were 'hot gospellers'. But as James soured on his meddlesome Parliaments and then Charles enforced increasingly strict obedience in both politics and religion, a substantial number of leading nobles began to look across the Atlantic, not just for refuge but as a potential base to preserve the pure church. Massachusetts founder John Cotton, later an adviser to Oliver Cromwell, saw the hand of providence at work: God had 'shut a dore' in England, but was 'opening a dore to us' in the New World.[7] The Puritans of 'new England' did not, like the Pilgrims of Plymouth, intend to separate from the world; they believed they were consummating the marriage between power and providence that had been at the heart of the Elizabethan imperial imagination. From the start, they drew a distinction between the 'profane men' of Virginia, who either had 'the vaine expectation of present profit', or were petty tyrants 'seeking only to make themselves great', and 'slaves of all that are under them', or incompetents 'not caring how they be qualified'. It was little surprise that the Powhatans had attacked them, since they 'have made Christ and Christianitie stinke in the nostrils of the poore infidels'.[8] Whether the Massachusetts men were purer than the Virginians, they were certainly luckier in that the coastal indigenous peoples of the region had been devastated by a pandemic that raged from 1617 to 1619. Rather than having to fight their way ashore and inland against a powerful confederation like the Powhatans, the New England settlers had but to marvel at 'this wondrous work of Jehovah' in 'wasting the natural Inhabitants with deaths' stroke', clearing the way for his chosen people.[9] The Puritans were also better organized and more socially cohesive than the Virginians, came in family groups and economically of the 'middle sort', neither 'gentleman adventurers' nor indentured servants. By the time the Puritan 'Great Migration' petered out in 1640 – and some colonists began to return eastward across the ocean to fulfil their providential mission – the population of the various New England enclaves had passed 20,000.

In sum, the first two Stuarts had, in a few decades, not merely squandered their Elizabethan imperial inheritance but turned the project upside down. The ebbing of Stuart power and influence was dramatic by every measure: the regime itself was embattled and widely viewed as illegitimate; rebellion was nigh in both Scotland and Ireland; London again a bone for European great-power dogs; the colonies grown but were a source of strategic instability rather than strategic depth. These multiple strategic failures were not only an essential element in the alienation of Puritans and the British political nation more broadly, but help to explain the behaviour of the Commonwealth state and in particular the actions of Oliver Cromwell as 'Lord Protector'. As a military commander, he was the instrumental figure in establishing an ideologically driven republican regime and its conquests of Scotland and Ireland, but he restored both the reputation of English arms – including, in the form of the New Model Army, as a leading land power – but the shape and direction of imperial strategy. While it is beyond the scope of this chapter to examine the record more fully, Cromwell's ambitious 'Western Design' was in fulfilment of the original Elizabethan desire for a permanent outpost in the Caribbean. Not only to be able to 'annoy' the Spanish who, despite the disasters of the Reformation wars of religion, remained an important power and retained the supply of wealth from their Peruvian silver mines but, as would become apparent in subsequent decades, to help secure the southern flank of Britain's North American possessions. And, tellingly, the seeming collapse of the Design did not just give Cromwell his first and only major military defeat but presaged the regime's collapsing domestic political legitimacy. The Lord Protector was sure that the Western Design was providential – 'We consider this attempt because we thinke God has not brought us hither where we are but to consider the worke that wee may doe in the world as well as at home.' When the bad news from the expedition was confirmed in London, Cromwell shut himself away, writing to Admiral William Goodsonn, the deputy commander of the Design fleet: 'It is not to be denied but the Lord hath greatly humbled us in that sad loss sustained at Hispaniola; and we doubt we have provoked the Lord; and it is good for us to know and to be abased for the same.'[10]

From a strategic perspective, then, it is better to think of the return of the Stuart dynasty as a second revolution, not a restoration. Charles II and James II took their father's precepts of royal absolutism, political obedience and reluctance to challenge the aspirations of would-be continental hegemons – in the late seventeenth century, the revived France of Louis XIV – to heart. Yet they went several steps farther, for they (especially James) were energetic empire-builders. In sum, they were willing to concede French domination in Europe while building a colonial network abroad that could extract resources and provide revenues that would leave the monarchy relatively free from parliamentary meddling. They were even willing to wage successive naval wars on the Dutch, traditionally regarded as the most natural Protestant ally and, as an emerging commercial and republican empire and tolerant society, a model for emulation. They hoped to split the spoils with Louis, but the otherwise fruitless conflicts did yield the Dutch trading colony of New Amsterdam, henceforth to be called 'New York', in honour of James, then duke of York. Indeed, the brothers made a complementary pair: Charles the wily fox, lover of political and other forms of human intrigue, James the hedgehog, single-minded and stiff-necked. It was only with Charles's death that the wheels finally came off: Charles had cleverly employed colonial charters to manipulate the ambitions of potential political opponents. Lord Anthony Ashley Cooper, who would become the driving force behind the effort to exclude the Catholic James from succession, had financed a 'Carolina' colony, his 'darling'; William Penn, the leading Quaker of the era – and son of the leading naval officer in the Western Design – was given a charter in the middle Atlantic region of North America and 'Pennsylvania' was purchased in return for Penn's support of Stuart policies in England.

III

Charles had left his brother with every prospect of success on the throne. The late king had successfully built a bloc of conservative Anglican 'Tory' support that had seen off the 'Whig' Exclusionists (the partisan names had become common through the early 1580s), and the matter of James's religion had been accommodated in the public mind, as James remained childless. And for most Englishmen, the prospect of renewed civil war was unthinkable; Charles's ne'er-do-well natural son, James Scott, the duke of Monmouth, made a poor Puritan champion, and the brief rebellion he led in 1685 collapsed in ignominy.

But James Stuart, past fifty when he inherited the throne in an age when average life expectancy was in the mid-thirties, was both a man with a mission – the eventual return of England to the Catholic Church – and a man in a hurry. And the defeat of the Monmouth uprising seems to have added a level of certainty and urgency to the king's programme. He appears to have calculated that a combination of royal fiat, the appeal of what he believed to be the undeniable truth of Catholicism, and an appeal to dissident Protestants (of which there were, as always, many) through a declaration of toleration would sweep aside Anglican objection. Similarly, the announcement that his queen, Mary of Modena, had borne a son meant that there could be a Catholic successor to the crown. In response, an alliance of leading nobles and churchmen 'invited' Prince Wilhelm Hendrik of Orange, the Dutch *stadholder* and husband of James's daughter (by his first, Protestant, wife, Anne Hyde) to intervene to defend the English church, English liberties and restore the British imperial project – and to assume the crown as William III. 'We have great reason to believe', they wrote,

> we shall be every day in a worse condition than we are, and less able to defend ourselves, and therefore we do earnestly wish we might be so happy as to find a remedy before it be too late for us to contribute to our own deliverance . . . the people are so generally dissatisfied with the present conduct of the government, in relation to their religion, liberties and properties (all which have been greatly invaded), and they are in such expectation of their prospects being daily worse, that your Highness may be assured, there are nineteen parts of twenty of the people throughout the kingdom, who are desirous of a change; and who, we believe, would willingly contribute to it, if they had such a protection to countenance their rising, as would secure them from being destroyed.[11]

Not entirely trusting that 95 per cent of Englishmen would support what was, 'invitation' notwithstanding, a foreign invasion, William – who had been planning for such an eventuality for the better part of a year – brought along 30,000 troops.

In turning to William and Mary, the English political nation was also pledging itself to what would be a decades-long war of containment against Louis XIV and France; William had been the 'saviour' of the Netherlands (despite his own absolutist tendencies and the Republic's mistrust) and, once he had secured the three crowns of Britain, engaged in a 'continental commitment' – measured not only in subsidies to European allies but the deployment of English forces – that far surpassed any

Elizabethan precedent. William's reign also saw the maturation of the British fiscal-military state; as Steve Pincus aptly put it, the British monarchy and its London financiers were 'going Dutch'.[12] And the king also, in his final years and after seeking a kind of 'bipartisanship' in Parliament, turned decisively towards the Whig party and its 'Junto' leadership in the face of suspicions of Tory dalliance with the exiled Stuart men. When the last of James's daughters, Anne, succeeded to the throne and the wars against France resumed, the duumvirate of Sidney Godolphin in London and the duke of Marlborough on European battlefields and capitals realized the kind of great-power leadership that Elizabeth's advisers might have dreamt of. Not until almost 1710 – and after great effusions of blood – did the mercurial and weakening queen turn to Tories, including the youthful Henry St John, the future Viscount Bolingbroke, scheming to return to power and end the seemingly endless war.

But this Tory revival was extremely brief and their signature achievement, the 1713 Treaty of Utrecht, became a byword for pusillanimity and a staple of Whig propaganda for decades after. Ironically for the Tories, the treaty also secured France's acquiescence to the 'Protestant succession', a previous act of Parliament that bestowed the British thrones on the niece of Charles I, the Electress Sophia of Hanover (a Dutchwoman by birth) and thence to her son, Georg Ludwig, one of the electors of the Holy Roman Empire. The British Empire was now yoked firmly to a continental European connection – and the new king promptly proscribed the Tories for their betrayal of Britain's European allies at Utrecht.

Through nearly fifty years of unbroken Whig ascendancy in government, the Whig way of war outlined at the beginning of this essay became not merely British strategic orthodoxy but a rigid doctrine. Under Hardwicke and Newcastle it became a 'system', an almost arithmetic formula. It also served to contain France in Europe, and then, under William Pitt's leadership of the ministry during the late 1750s and early 1760s, produced a stunning series of conquests that also threw France out of North America and stripped Spain of many of its possessions from the Mediterranean across the Atlantic and into the Pacific. The British Empire in 1763 enjoyed global reach and a kind of quasi-unipolar moment.

IV

Westward the course of Empire takes its way.
The four first acts already past,
A fifth shall close the drama with the day:
Time's noblest offspring is the last.[13]

George Berkeley – the Anglican bishop of Cloyne in Ireland, and thus a very imperial official as well as polymath philosopher – wrote these words, so redolent of apocalyptic Commonwealth 'Fifth Monarchy', in 1726, and they capture an enduring element in the Anglo-American colonial mind. The period from 1688 to 1763 also saw a step change in the size and wealth of Britain's North American 'string of pearls'. Colonial population increased more than eightfold, from approximately 250,000 in 1690 to more than two million by 1760; it had also become more diverse, including Scots, Irish, German, Scandinavian, Dutch and French, particularly Huguenot, immigrants as well as English. Sometime around 1750, trade with these 'New Englands' – settler societies with varied economies – became more valuable than the sugar and other extractive plantation economies of the British Caribbean. In 1747, the Royal Academy of Turku in Finland funded a survey of the colonies by the economist and natural historian Peter Kalm. 'It does not seem difficult to find out the reasons why the people multiply faster here than in Europe', he wrote. 'As soon as a person is old enough he may marry in these provinces without any fear of poverty. . . . The liberties he enjoys are so great that he considers himself as a prince in his own possessions.'[14] This rapid expansion inevitably created tension with New France, the French colony that stretched from Montreal and Quebec through the waterways of the Ohio Valley to the Mississippi and southward to La Nouvelle Orléans on the Gulf of Mexico. To Whig grandees like Newcastle and Hardwicke as well as to the colonists themselves, this engendered a fear of French encirclement; a new kind of 'backdoor' to Britain threatened to open in the trans-Appalachian west of North America. And, as much as the colonization and westward expansion of British rule across Ireland had been the objective of the Elizabethans, so did expansion appear as the objective of eighteenth-century British imperialists – especially in the colonies. 'Our North American colonies are to be considered as the frontier of the British Empire on that side', Benjamin Franklin argued in 1760, as English victories – and the costs – in the Seven Years War began to mount and there was a fear that London might trade advantage in North America for stability in Europe, as had happened at the Treaty of Aix la Chappelle in 1748, or possessions in the West Indies.[15] This was an argument Franklin had been pressing for a decade by then. It also carried an implied warning to London: the arc of history, demographics and empire was bending in an American direction. There would

> in another Century be more than the People of England, and the greatest Number of Englishmen will be on this Side the Water. What an Accession of Power to the British Empire by Sea as well as Land! What Increase of Trade and Navigation! What Numbers of Ships and Seamen! We have been here but little more than 100 Years, and yet the Force of our Privateers in the late War, united, was greater, both in Men and Guns, than that of the whole British Navy in Queen Elizabeth's Time.[16]

But after seventy years the old centre could no longer hold. When George III, who came to the throne in 1761, ended the proscription of Tories in the government, made peace with France (and, by that time, Spain) and embarked on a series of imperial reforms and economies, the long-dominant Whig strategic paradigm was swept aside in a torrent, as was the Pitt ministry. In Parliament, the aged Newcastle and Hardwicke could not hold back the growing tide of 'king's men' brought in by George III's patronage. The storm was felt immediately and most severely in North America. The new king's idea of retrenchment was to halt colonial expansion with a 'Proclamation Line' at the peak of the Appalachians in 1763 and the 'Quebec Act' of 1774. The first was couched as a concession to Britain's Indian allies against the French but infuriated Americans, for whom expansion was the purpose of the war, the second seemed to mollify the conquered French Canadians at their expense. The legislation for financial reforms were intended to help defray the costs of retaining a British army of 10,000 in North America; the colonists might have swallowed that, but not when it became a force for containment rather than expansion.

The Tory tide was likewise felt in Europe. Even before concluding a peace with France, George had directed his ministers to end the subsidies to Frederick the Great of Prussia, which had done so much to tie down French forces and finances in the long continental struggle. 'The more I consider the Prussian subsidy', the king wrote to John Stuart, once his tutor and now his closest adviser and Earl of Bute, 'the more objections arise in my mind against it, and as to the German war I am clear that if France is not willing for peace we must instantly know it on the head, and if men' – he was referring to the duke of Newcastle – 'will leave my country preferable to another; it will be they that are run at and not me'.[17] This was the popular language of Tory parsimony and xenophobia; it was as if Bolingbroke's 'Patriot King' had come to life.

Thus, among the many things it otherwise was, the revolt of the American colonies was a disagreement about imperial strategy. Ironically, many of the Revolutionary generation employed Bolingbroke-based rhetoric – indeed, referring to themselves as 'Patriots' and the Loyalists 'Tories' – in the pursuit of Whiggish geopolitical ends. This indicates how thoroughly embedded the Whig strategic paradigm had become; nor is it really surprising, for the Whig way of war had measured its security by looking beyond the metropolis to the farthest shores and frontiers and paying close attention to the nature of other regimes. This was a 'trans-oceanic' perspective, concerned to make the maritime domain safe and profitable by looking beyond the water's edges and keeping a global regard.

While even a cursory framing of the evolution of American strategic culture is beyond the scope of this essay, analogies abound. Just as 'Britain' was a construct to encompass many nationalities, so was 'America', likewise bound by an ideology – sometime flexible to the point of hypocrisy but nonetheless powerful – of liberty under law. While slavery endured, the legitimacy of the regime remained in doubt; to be whole, America must be free, resulting in the bloodiest of civil wars. The founding generations certainly viewed international great-power politics as a contest of empires, and thus were imbued with an expand-or-die impulse and a fear of exposure, and frontier paranoia. Even as they crossed a continent, Americans fretted about a lack of strategic depth; oceans were not moats but avenues of approach. The continuity is most apparent from the late nineteenth century onwards, once great-power status was achieved and assured. The pattern was particularly plain from 1941 to 2008. The great speeches of Theodore Roosevelt, the 'Four Freedoms' address by Franklin Roosevelt, the prologue sections of 'NSC 68' (the commonly used title of the Truman administration's definitions of 'United States Objectives and Programs for National Security' of 1950), and even George Bush's second inaugural speech of 2004 evince a 'personality of power' consonant with that of the Elizabethan Richard Hackluyt, James Harrington and the Commonwealthmen, William Temple, William III and William Pitt.[18] Yet it is also apparent that during the presidencies of Barack Obama and Donald Trump that a kind of strategic Toryism has overtaken the United States, a desire to stand back from the frustrations and costs of global military engagement, not only in the Middle East but also in Europe. The rhetoric of this current 'reform' – 'retrenchment' or 'retreat' might be more strategically accurate – mimics that of George III. Obama wished to do 'nation building at home', and Trump promised to put 'America First'.[19] Even Obama's trumpeted 'Pacific Pivot' was been something of an empty gesture, and the so-called European Reassurance Initiative temporarily slowed the pace of troops withdrawals. It is beyond the scope of this essay to predict what will come from the administration of President Joe Biden and beyond – although the withdrawal from Afghanistan, set to be complete on the twentieth anniversary of the 9/11 Al Qaeda attacks, continues the trend – but considering the failures of previous Tory interludes and the durability of the Whig way of war, there is perhaps reason to anticipate a future restoration. The current-day version of a Tory-like alternative future might look something like that forecast by the duke of Manchester in 1775:

> [The page of future history will tell how Britain planted, nourished, and for two centuries preserved a second British empire [in North America]; how strengthened by her sons, she rose to such a pitch of power, that this little island proved too mighty for the greatest efforts of the greatest nations. Within the space of twenty years, the world beheld her arms triumphant in every quarter of the globe, her fleets displayed victorious banners, her sails were spread and conquest graced the canvas. Historic truth must likewise relate, within the same little space of time, how Britain fell to half her greatness; how strangely lost, by misjudging ministers, by rash-advised councils, our gracious sovereign, George III, saw more than half his empire crumble beneath his sceptre.[20]

Notes

1 Henry St. John Bolingbroke, *The Idea of a Patriot King*, at https://socialsciences .mcmaster.ca/~econ/ugcm/3ll3/bolingbroke/king.html.
2 See Brendan Simms, *Three Victories and a Defeat: The Rise and Fall of the First British Empire* (London, 2007), xxii–xxiii.
3 See Stephen Alford, *William Cecil and the British Succession Crisis of the 1560s* (unpublished doctoral dissertation, St. Andrews Research Repository, 1997), viii, available at https://research-repository.st-andrews.ac.uk/handle/10023/641.
4 Quoted in John Sugden, *Sir Francis Drake* (London, 1990), 140.
5 See R. B. Wernham (ed.), *The Expedition of Sir John Norris and Sir Francis Drake to Spain and Portugal, 1589* (London, 1988), xiv–xv.
6 Thomas Cogswell, *The Blessed Revolution: English Politics and the Coming of War, 1621–1624* (Cambridge, 1989).
7 Quoted in Nicholas Guyatt, *Providence and the Invention of the United States, 1607–1876* (Cambridge, 2007), 26–7.
8 Quoted in Michael Leroy Oberg, *Dominion & Civility: English Imperialism & Native America, 1585–1685* (Ithaca, NY, 2003), 89.
9 Quoted in Alfred A. Cave, *The Pequot War* (Amherst, MA, 1996), 15–16.

10 Oliver Cromwell to William Goodson, 30 October 1655, at http://www.olivercromwell
    .org/Letters_and_speeches/letters/Letter_189.pdf.
11 See https://en.wikipedia.org/wiki/Invitation_to_William#cite_note-FOOTNOTEDal
    rymple1790appendix_to_book v,_pp. , 107–10.
12 See Steve Pincus, *1688: The First Modern Revolution* (New Haven, CT, 2011).
13 George Berkeley, 'Verses on the Prospect of Planting Arts and Learning in America',
    http://americainclass.org/wp-content/uploads/2014/02/2_BERKELEY-VERSES-ON
    -THE-PROSPECT-OF-PLANTING-ARTS-AND-LEARNING-IN-AMERICA.pdf.
14 See Peter Kalm, *Travels into North America,* at https://content.wisconsinhistory.org/
    digital/collection/aj/id/16932.
15 Benjamin Franklin, 'The Interest of Great Britain Considered', 17 April 1760, at
    https://founders.archives.gov/documents/Franklin/01-09-02-0029.
16 Benjamin Franklin, 'Observations Concerning the Increase of Mankind, 1751', at
    https://founders.archives.gov/documents/Franklin/01-04-02-0080.
17 Quoted in Simms, *Three Victories and a Defeat*, 490.
18 Theodore Roosevelt, especially 'The Strenuous Life', 10 April 1899 and 'the New
    Nationalism', 31 August 1910, at https://www.theodoreroosevelt.org/content.aspx
    ?page_id=22&club_id=991271&module_id=339335; Franklin Roosevelt, 'The
    Four Freedoms', 6 January 1941, at https://www.americanrhetoric.com/speeches/
    fdrthefourfreedoms.htm; National Security Council, 'United States Objectives and
    Programs for National Security', 14 April 1950, at https://digitalarchive.wilsoncenter
    .org/document/116191.pdf?v=2699956db534c1821edefa61b8c13ffe; George W. Bush,
    'Second Inaugural Address', 20 January 2005, at https://www.gutenberg.org/files
    /925/925-h/925-h.htm#link2H_4_0056; George F. Kennan, 'The Sources of Soviet
    Conduct', *Foreign Affairs*, July 1947, at https://www.foreignaffairs.com/authors/x
    -george-f-kennan; Richard Hackluyt, 'Discourse of Western Planting', 1584, at http://
    nationalhumanitiescenter.org/pds/amerbegin/exploration/text5/hakluyt.pdf; James
    Harrington, *Oceana and Other Works*, at https://oll.libertyfund.org/title/toland-the
    -oceana-and-other-works; for Sir William Temple, see Wouter Troost, *Sir William
    Temple, William III and the Balance of Power in Europe* (London, 2001); William
    III, 'The Declaration of His Highnes William Henry, By the Grace of God Prince of
    Orange, &c., Of the reasons inducing him, To Appear in Armes in the Kindome of
    England', 1688, at https://quod.lib.umich.edu/e/eebo/A66129.0001.001?rgn=main
    ;view=fulltext; see also Jeremy Black, *Parliament and Foreign Policy in the Eighteenth
    Century* (Cambridge, 2004), 100.
19 See https://www.voanews.com/archive/obama-focus-nation-building-home; and
    https://time.com/4309786/read-donald-trumps-america-first-foreign-policy-speech/.
20 Quoted in Simms, *Three Victories and a Defeat*, 579–80.

4

Carthage can now defeat Rome

Political order, seaborne commerce and the projection of power in Barbon and Montesquieu

Paul A. Rahe

In the summer of 1713, John Churchill, soon to be the duke of Marlborough, and Prince Eugene of Savoy conducted an army – supplied by Britain, the Dutch Republic and the Hapsburg monarchy – to the village of Blenheim on the Danube. There, on 13 August 1704, they annihilated a French army and captured its commander, which came as a terrible shock to everyone in France – not least, Charles-Louis de Secondat, baron de La Brède and de Montesquieu, the fifteen-year-old scion of an ancient aristocratic house.

This young man's fatherland had for centuries been the leading power on the European continent. It had sometimes been checked. But it had not decisively lost a major battle in a century and a half; and during the War of the League of Augsburg (1688–97) and the first few years of the War of the Spanish Succession (1701–14), it had looked as if Louis XIV, the Sun King of France, might put back together what had come asunder with the collapse of the Roman Empire and establish a universal dominion in Europe (and the New World) by uniting the crowns of France and Spain.

'Before the battle of Blenheim', Montesquieu remembered,

> France had risen to a time of greatness that one regarded as immutable, although the country was then on the verge of decline (*touche au moment de la décadence*). It is certain that the league [of those allied against Louis XIV] was in despair. That day at Blenheim, we lost the confidence that we had acquired by thirty years of victories. . . . Whole battalions gave themselves up as prisoners of war; we regretted their being alive, as we would have regretted their deaths.
>
> It seemed as if God, who wished to set limits to empires, had given to the French this capacity to acquire, along with this capacity to lose, this fire that nothing resists, along with this despondency that makes one ready to submit to anything. (*MP* 1306)[1]

Of course, as one would expect, the event was at first dismissed as a fluke. But when Marlborough managed in the years stretching from 1706 to 1709 to do the like thrice again – first, at Ramillies; then, at Oudenarde; and, finally, at Malplaquet – it became obvious, even to the unsuspecting glance, that there was something very much amiss and that the dream fostered by the Sun King regarding the destiny of France was unsustainable.[2]

The fact that the Treaty of Utrecht negotiated in 1713 and 1714 by that canny French monarch left his kingdom intact was a consolation – and for many this may have been all that mattered. But it did not radically alter the perceptions of those capable of seeing the implications of what had happened to Louis's armies on the field of the sword. Moreover, after the great king died at the beginning of September 1715, the extent of the fiscal crisis produced by his wars also became evident. When the Scottish financial wizard John Law, brought in a few years later to address the matter, managed by dint of financial legerdemain and an ill-advised paper money scheme to produce a financial bubble followed by an economic collapse that greatly increased the national debt and reduced the value of French bank notes to less than the paper on which they had been printed,[3] everyone was forced to concede that France was bankrupt – and the discerning in their number recognized that this was true in more ways than one. The monarchy did not command resources sufficient for the successful pursuit of the course set out for it by Louis, and it knew no other path. It was this gradually dawning realization that occasioned Montesquieu's interest in a diplomatic career; and it was, I believe, this that in 1731 finally gave the boundless curiosity evidenced by the man the focus that it had hitherto lacked. He would spend the next seventeen years reflecting on the circumstances that had put an end to the great ambition that had long animated his native land.

When, in 1731, Montesquieu finally settled down in the castle on his estate at La Brède to write, he had in mind a triptych, made up of three discrete essays. The first essay was to be a study of Rome's rise to imperial grandeur and its establishment of what his contemporaries called a 'universal monarchy'; the second was to be an exploration of the reasons why, after the fall of Rome, no one in Europe was able to duplicate this feat; and the third was to be a description of the peculiar form of government found in England and, we must presume, an account of its success in articulating an alternative grand strategy, suited to modern circumstances, that eschewed expansionism on the continent of Europe and aimed, instead, at promoting England's commerce, ruling the sea and defending the British isles.[4]

It was Marlborough's England that most interested Montesquieu. That country, which had been a French pawn in the time of its monarch Charles II, was responsible for France's decline. It had put together and, to a considerable degree, funded the coalition that had fought Louis XIV to a standstill in the War of the League of Augsburg, and it had done the like in the War of the Spanish Succession when France had suffered four successive defeats on the field of the sword. Above all else, Montesquieu wanted to know how and why such a catastrophe had been his country's fate. It is this aim that explains why he had spent in Britain nearly half of the time he devoted to the European tour he undertook at the end of the 1720s and the beginning of the subsequent decade. It is a great misfortune that his *Voyage en Angleterre* is lost almost in its entirety.[5] For it seems to have been in England that he discovered the 'principles' that underpinned the argument the future author of *The Spirit of the Laws* would advance in his mature writings (*EL* Préface),[6] and years later he would say, that – while 'Germany was made to travel in, Italy to sojourn in, . . . and France to live in' – it was 'England' that was made 'to think in'.[7]

During his extended sojourn in the UK, Montesquieu studied not only the regnant mores and manners but also the political regime, and this he did with consummate care. Having mastered the English tongue well enough to be able to read the language and follow conversations, he perused everything that he could get his hands on, and he questioned everyone he met. As far as we can tell, however, Montesquieu did not in these years acquire a copy of the little pamphlet, entitled *A Discourse of Trade*, published in London in 1690 by Nicholas Barbon, son of the Puritan firebrand Praise-God Barebones.[8] There is no entry for this slender volume in the catalogue of his library at La Brède.[9] In his published works and in what survives of his commonplace books Montesquieu nowhere cites the book, and in the pertinent secondary literature Barbon passes almost unmentioned. While in England, however, Montesquieu must have read it or have heard its argument rehearsed in detail – for the analysis that he set out to present in his triptych dovetails to a considerable degree quite closely both with Barbon's account of the obstacles he thought apt to prevent Louis XIV from establishing a universal dominion on the continent of Europe and with the Englishman's careful examination of the economic and institutional foundations of his own country's strength. What Montesquieu remarked on in retrospect Barbon had described in prospect.

I

Barbon's aim had been to elucidate the relationship between commerce, insularity and empire. To succeed, he had to persuade merchants to see beyond the particulars of the trade in which they were engaged and statesmen to recognize the political consequences of commerce when looked upon as a whole.

He began his argument with the Venetians and the Dutch, noting the degree to which these two commercial polities possessed a political weight far greater than the size of their territory would suggest possible. Then, he turned to the manner in which technology – the invention of gunpowder, in particular – had transformed the character of war and made commerce 'as necessary to Preserve Governments, as it is useful to make them Rich'. In his view, this rendered an anachronism what Livy and the other ancient writers had written concerning 'the Causes of the Rise and Fall of Governments', and the same criticism could be applied to the writings of Niccolò Machiavelli, who had inexcusably ignored the revolution being effected by the commerce carried on with great verve all around him in Florence. As Barbon put it, '*until* Trade *became necessary to provide Weapons of War, it was always thought Prejudicial to the Growth of Empire, as too much softening the People by Ease and Luxury, which made their Bodies unfit to Endure the Labour and Hardships of War*'. In antiquity, he added, this conviction had made good sense, for the fact that 'Trade *was not in those days useful to provide Magazines for Wars*' explains how it was that '*the* Romans . . . *in the almost Infancy of their State*, managed to

Conquer that Rich and Trading *City of* Carthage, *though Defended by* Hannibal *their General, one of the greatest Captains in the World.*'[10]

It was Barbon's opinion that commerce might also 'be Assistant to the Inlarging of Empire', and he argued – here also with explicit reference to Ancient Rome – that, 'if an Universal Empire, or Dominion of very Large Extent, can again be raised in the World, It seems more probable to be done by the Help of *Trade*; By the Increase of Ships at Sea, than by Arms at Land'. As for 'the *French* King's seeming Attempt to Raise Empire in *Europe*', he added, it was doomed. Thanks, at least in part, to the growth in trade; to the draining of lakes, bogs and fens; and the felling of forests, Europe had become, he explained, too populous for this to be workable. There were too many fortified cities and towns. The invention of the compass had promoted commerce, and printing had disseminated knowledge: 'the Countries and Languages are more understood, Knowledge more dispersed, and the Arts of War in all Places known'. No one was apt to gain a permanent advantage. And the '*Gothick*' form of government had taught men a love of liberty and a spirit of resistance to domination. In Europe, he observed, 'it is as difficult to keep a Country in Subjection, as to Conquer it'; and to massacre a country's inhabitants would not only be 'too Bloody and Inhuman', it would also be 'to lose the greatest share in Conquest; for the People are the Riches and the Strength of the Country'. Moreover, 'to Conquer, and leave them Free, only paying Tribute and Homage, Is the same as not to Conquer them: For there is no Reason to expect their Submission longer, than till they are able to Resist'.[11]

Barbon contended that there were no such 'Impediments' to 'inlarging Dominion at Sea'. The world's populousness did not matter. There were no fortified cities and towns in the way. Moreover, 'the Arts of Navigation being discover'd, hath added an Unlimited Compass to the Naval Power', and '*Gothick* Government . . . best Agrees with such an Empire'. Also, the English, residing, as they did, on an island, had a great advantage, which was not shared by the Dutch, who were subject to a 'Military Charge in defending themselves' against their neighbours on the European continent that the English did not have to pay. Moreover, if the latter were to pass 'an Act for a General Naturalization, that all Forreigners, purchasing Land in *England*, might Enjoy the Freedom of *Englishmen*', Barbon contended, those oppressed elsewhere would flock to their shores, increase their commerce and augment their power. Two centuries before Alfred Thayer Mahan published *The Influence of Seapower upon History*, Barbon had argued, along similar lines, that, as a naval, commercial power, England could enjoy 'an Empire, not less Glorious, & of a much larger Extent than either *Alexander's* or *Caesar's*'.[12]

II

In his triptych, Montesquieu sought to address the questions that Barbon had discussed and to do so in greater depth with greater insight. In his *Considerations on the Causes of the Greatness of the Romans and their Decline*, he pondered Rome's rise to what Europeans in his time and earlier called 'universal monarchy', and he considered the ultimate collapse of that dominion. Then, in his *Reflections on Universal Monarchy in*

Europe,[13] he examined the history of western Christendom and the situation in his own time. He brought to the latter task one advantage that Barbon had lacked: hindsight.

'It is a question worth raising', Montesquieu writes in the very first sentence of the latter work, 'whether, given the state in which Europe actually subsists, it is possible for a People to maintain over the other peoples an unceasing superiority, as the [ancient] Romans did'. Montesquieu thought this achievement 'morally impossible', and in support of this contention he gives two reasons: first, 'innovations in the art of war', such as the introduction of artillery and firearms, 'have equalized the strength of all men & consequently that of all Nations', and, second, 'the *Ius Gentium* has changed, & under today's Laws war is conducted in such a manner that by bankruptcy it ruins above all others those who [initially] possess the greatest advantages' (*RMU* 1.1-9).

The second reason offered needs explication. In Machiavelli's *Art of War*, when the dialogue's protagonist, Fabrizio Colonna, laments the decline of martial virtue in Europe, he traces its disappearance in part to 'the fact that the mode of living today, as a consequence of the Christian religion, does not impose the necessity for self-defence that existed in antiquity'. In pagan times, he observes,

> men conquered in war were either massacred or were consigned to perpetual enslavement where they led their lives in misery. Then, the towns conquered were either destroyed or the inhabitants were driven out, their goods seized, and, after being sent out, they were dispersed throughout the world. And so those overcome in war suffered every last misery. Frightened at this prospect, men kept military training alive and honoured those who were excellent in it. But today this fear is for the most part lost. Of the conquered, few are massacred; none are held for long in prison since they are easily freed. Cities, even if they have rebelled a thousand times, are not eliminated; men are left with their goods so that most of the time what is feared is a ransom. In consequence, men do not want to subject themselves to military orders.

This alteration in the rules of war had an additional consequence, of particular interest to Montesquieu, which Colonna is no less inclined to regret: 'That present wars impoverish the lords who are victorious as much as those who lose – for, if the one loses his state, the other loses his money and his possessions'. In ancient times, he explains, war was for the victors a source of enrichment. In modern times, the costs all too often exceed the gains.[14]

To the changes in outlook effected by Christianity Montesquieu was no less sensitive than his Florentine predecessor. But the developments within the *ius gentium* – which Machiavelli's interlocutor traces to Christianity, laments and evidently hopes to reverse – Montesquieu takes as a historic achievement, and it is on this basis also that he judges universal monarchy a moral impossibility. 'In earlier times', he explains, 'one would destroy the towns that one had captured, one would sell the lands and, far more important, the inhabitants as well.'

> The sacking of a town would pay the wages of an Army, & a successful Campaign would enrich a Conqueror. At present, we regard such barbarities with a horror

no more than just. We ruin ourselves [financially] in capturing places which capitulate, which we preserve intact, & which most of the time we return.

The Romans carried off to Rome in their Triumphs all the wealth of the Nations they conquered. Today victories confer none but sterile Laurels.

When a Monarch sends an Army into enemy country, he sends at the same time a part of his treasure so that the army can subsist; he enriches the country he has begun to conquer, & quite often he puts it in a condition to drive him out. (1.10-19)

Herein lies what Montesquieu regarded as a delightful paradox, for in modern times imperial expansion tends to eliminate the conditions prerequisite for the imperial venture's success.

Having listed two reasons why universal monarchy cannot be achieved, Montesquieu then adds a third – emphasizing that there are 'particular reasons responsible for the fact that in Europe prosperity cannot be permanent anywhere, & for the fact that there is a continual variation in [the distribution of] power, which, in the three other parts of the world, is, so to speak, fixed' (2.28-30). These arguments deserve closer scrutiny as well.

In Montesquieu's view, Europe differs from the rest of the world in one crucial particular: 'at present', it 'is responsible for all the Commerce in the Universe & for the Carrying Trade (*Navigation*) in its entirety'. Like Barbon, he is persuaded as well that in his own day, at least in Europe, Machiavelli's famous dictum has been proven wrong and that money really has become the sinews of war: that, 'to the extent to which a State takes a greater or lesser part in Commerce or in the Carrying Trade, its power necessarily grows or diminishes'. In consequence, he contends, since war gets in the way of trade, 'a State which appears to be victorious abroad ruins itself [financially] at home, while states which remain neutral augment their strength'. It can even happen that 'those conquered regain their strength'. In fact, 'decline (*décadence*) generally sets in at the time of the greatest successes, for these can neither be achieved nor sustained except by violent means' (2.31-39).[15]

Poverty was once an advantage in war. In antiquity, when citizen armies were predominant, those from wealthy communities 'were made up of men lost to flabbiness, idleness, & pleasure', and 'for that reason' these cities 'were often destroyed by the armies of neighbours accustomed to a life both painful & harsh, who were better suited to the war & military exercises of that time'. In his own day, however, 'the situation is not the same since no one group of Soldiers, the vilest part of every Nation, has a share in luxury greater than that of any other group, since in military exercises there is no longer need for the same strength & skill, and since it is now easier to form armies of regulars' (2.45-54).

In subsequent chapters, Montesquieu reinforces these claims, alluding, as had Barbon, to the shift in weaponry from arrows and spears to heavy artillery and firearms; touching on the motives that divide and paralyse modern monarchies; noting the relative stability that had taken hold in Europe; pointing to the depth of fortifications along France's border with Belgium; suggesting that the growth in communications attendant on trade denies anyone a lasting technological advantage; and contrasting the geography of Asia, which is favourable to empire, with that of Europe, which encourages the establishment of states of middling size. Along the way, he manages to remind his French readers of what had happened to their compatriots at Blenheim, Ramillies, Oudenarde and Lille. It is at this point that he begins a brief survey of the abortive attempts, from Charlemagne's day forward, to found a universal monarchy in Europe on the lines of Rome's great empire – ending with the projects undertaken by the Hapsburgs and then, in his own day, by the Bourbons – and he shows why each and every one of these enterprises failed (3.65-17.382).

Montesquieu's discourse was not without bite. In the seventeenth chapter of his *Universal Monarchy*, with his tongue firmly in cheek, he piously denies the charge levelled by his opponents that Louis XIV had aimed at universal monarchy, and then he discusses events in a manner suggesting that this had been Louis's aim after all. 'Had he succeeded', Montesquieu writes, in putative justification of his disclaimer, 'nothing would have been more fatal to Europe, to his Subjects of old, to himself, to his family. Heaven, which knows what is really advantageous, served him better in his defeats than it would have in Victories, & instead of making him the sole King of Europe, it favoured him more by making him the most powerful of them all.' Had Louis won the battle of Blenheim, 'the famous Battle in which he met his first defeat (*échec*)', Montesquieu tells us, 'the undertaking would have been quite far from achievement, it would have hardly begun. It would have required a great increase in forces & a great expansion in frontiers.' Moreover, he adds, the immediate prospect that the balance of power in Europe really would be overturned would have forced the lesser powers to enter the fray. 'Germany, which had hardly entered the war except through the sale of Soldiers, would have taken the lead: the North would have risen; the neutral Powers would have taken sides, & his Allies would have changed sides' (17.360-82).

What the Sun King had failed to recognize was that 'Europe is nothing more than one Nation composed of many' and that the rise of commerce had made his rivals for dominion his partners in trade. 'France & England have need of the opulence of Poland & Muscovy', Montesquieu argues, 'just as one of their Provinces has need of the others: & the State, which believes that it will increase its power as a consequence of [financial] ruin visited on another state on its border, ordinarily weakens itself along with its neighbour' (18.383-86).

The entire thrust of Montesquieu's argument throughout the *Universal Monarchy* is that in eighteenth-century Europe offensive war does much more harm than good to the aggressor. 'If conquest on a grand scale is so difficult, so fruitless (*vain*), so dangerous', he asks, 'what can one say of the malady of our own age which dictates that everywhere one maintain a number of troops disproportionate (*desordonné*)' to one's actual needs? We are not like 'the Romans', he notes, 'who managed to disarm others in the measure in which they armed themselves'. In modern Europe, instead, where this endeavour produces an 'Equilibrium' of sorts among 'the great Powers',

> this malady grows worse and worse (*a ses redoublemens*), & it is of necessity contagious, since as soon as one State augments what it calls its forces, the others of a sudden augment theirs, in such a fashion that one gains nothing thereby except the common ruin [attendant on insolvency]. Each Monarch keeps on foot

all the Armies that he would be able to field if the Peoples he governed were in danger of being exterminated, & we confer the name Peace on this effort of all against all. Thus Europe is ruined [by bankruptcy] in such a fashion that, if three private Individuals were in the situation in which the three most opulent Powers in this Part of the World find themselves, they would not have anything on which to live. Thus we are poor with all the wealth & commerce of the entire Universe. (24.432-52)

It is easy to see what Montesquieu had in mind when he sought to become a diplomat. Although at the end he denies that he 'had in view any particular Government in Europe' and insists that he is expressing 'reflections pertinent to them all' (25.468-69), it is perfectly clear that the work is an angry diatribe against Louis XIV and everything for which the Sun King of France had once stood as well as a call for a radical reorientation of French policy.

III

Montesquieu's triptych never appeared. For a variety of reasons particular to the reign of Louis XV, he came to think it impolitic to be so frank. So he set aside what he had already written on the English form of government; and, in 1734, he reluctantly suppressed his *Reflections on Universal Monarchy in Europe* and published his ruminations on Rome as a free-standing book entitled *Considerations on the Causes of the Greatness of the Romans and Their Decline*.[16]

Though checked, Montesquieu was undaunted; and soon thereafter he set out to compose a much larger work, entitled *The Spirit of the Laws*, wherein he laid out a comprehensive political science designed to provide his readers with an understanding of the range of political possibilities open to man; of the constraints imposed on human agency by geography, climate, religion, and inherited mores, manners and laws; and of the ways in which commerce, technological progress, and the liberation of women from domestic servitude can loosen such bonds. Therein, he discreetly inserted the argument of his *Universal Monarchy* and gave it a new twist, unanticipated in Barbon, by tracing the policy of France, which he thought suicidal, to imperatives inherent in the very nature of the monarchical form of government; and he also added a detailed discussion, in the two longest chapters of the work (*EL* 11.6, 19.27), of the English form of government and of the policy to which it naturally gives rise.

In this work, Montesquieu draws a sharp distinction between modern European monarchy and despotism. The difference follows from their differing structures – above all, from the existence of a landed aristocracy in the former, which does not derive its status or property from the passing whim of the ruler. What follows from this are intermediary powers, a quasi-independent judiciary, the rule of law, and an ethos of honour that serves as a check on everyone's conduct – above all, that of the king himself. That is the upside. There is a downside – part of which stems from the fact, wholly consistent with the manner in which the existence of a hierarchy of ranks transforms ordinary human vanity into a deep longing for honour, that monarchy's aim (*but*) is glory. This, Montesquieu makes clear, can be attained only in a deplorable fashion through success in war (5.19; 9.2, 7; 10.2; 11.5, 7; 13.1, 17; 20.22). In a sense, then, monarchy is at odds with itself. For success of the sort sought, were it to reach completion and eventuate in universal monarchy, would – as he had made clear in sections of his *Reflections on Universal Monarchy in Europe* that he later inserted into his *Spirit of the Laws* – be fatal to the monarchy as a monarchy by transforming it into an enormous polity governable only via despotism (*RMU* 17; *EL* 8.8, 15-17, 19-20; 9.6-7; 10.9, 16).

Of course, this may not have mattered. For, as we have seen, Montesquieu thought the establishment of a universal monarchy in Europe virtually impossible, and in his *Spirit of the Laws* he restates nearly everything from the argument of his *Universal Monarchy* that is pertinent to this particular claim.[17] To this, he adds another assertion not found therein: that, in a world gone commercial, monarchy is at a great disadvantage – since, given the nature of the government and the political psychology to which it gives rise, monarchy is incompatible with the commercial spirit and the institutions that enabled the Venetians, the Dutch and the English to succeed (5.9; 20.4-5, 7-8, 10-14, 21-22). In practice, then, the French monarchy is condemned to a pursuit of glory and conquest that the French economy cannot properly sustain.[18]

By way of contrast, the English polity suffers neither of the disadvantages attendant on monarchy. In a chapter of *The Spirit of the Laws* entitled 'How the Laws Can Contribute to the Formation of the Mores, Manners, & Character of a Nation', he demonstrates that the English form of government is – or, at least, ought to be – free from the 'malady' that threatens the powers on the continent with bankruptcy and ruin. In it, he allows us to comprehend that which had long occasioned on his part wonder: how it is that, in modern times, a well-ordered Carthage, such as England, 'whose principal strength consists in her credit and commerce', could 'render fictive wealth real', equip 'her Hannibal' with 'as many men as she could buy', and 'send them into combat', while Louis XIV's ill-ordered French Rome, 'in a spirit of vertigo', patiently awaited 'the blows' solely 'in order to receive them' and fielded 'great armies' only 'to see' her 'fortresses taken' and her 'garrisons deprived of courage, and to languish in a defensive war for which' she had 'no capacity at all' (*MP* 645).

Montesquieu does not attribute any special rationality to the English. Given the character of their constitution, he imagines, they would be 'always on fire' and 'would be more easily conducted by their passions than by reason', and, for this reason, he adds, 'it would be easy for those who govern the nation to make it undertake enterprises contrary to its real interests'. The chief passion of the English, the only one which Montesquieu sees fit to mention in this particular context, would appear to be their fondness for liberty, which, he says, they 'would love prodigiously because this liberty is genuine (*vraie*)'. In defending their freedom, Montesquieu intimates, this people would be no less resolute than were the citizens of classical Rome. This nation would 'sacrifice its goods, its ease, its interests; it would burden itself with imposts quite harsh, such as the most absolute prince would not dare make his subjects endure'. Moreover, possessing, as they would, 'a firm understanding of the necessity of submitting' to these taxes, the English 'would pay them in the well-founded expectation of not having to pay more; the burden would be heavier than the sense of burden' (*EL* 19.27).

In this chapter, Montesquieu refrains from intimating, as he does repeatedly elsewhere (13.17, 20.4-5, 10), that the monarchies on the European continent find it well-nigh impossible to inspire the confidence necessary to enable them to borrow the immense sums of money needed for the conduct of war in modern times. It suffices for him pointedly to remark that, given its laws, England should have little difficulty in sustaining the credit required. It could, after all,

> borrow from itself & pay itself as well. It would, then, undertake enterprises beyond its natural strength & deploy against its enemies immense fictional riches, which the confidence it would inspire & the nature of the government would render real.
>
> For the purpose of preserving its liberty, it would borrow from its subjects; & its subjects, seeing that its credit would be lost if it was conquered, would have yet another motive for exerting themselves in defense of its liberty. (19.27)[19]

England could borrow from its subjects because, under the constitution that Montesquieu has in mind, its subjects would not, in fact, be subjects at all. They would be citizens, as Montesquieu quickly acknowledges (19.27), in what he has already elsewhere described in *The Spirit of Laws* as 'a republic concealed under the form of a monarchy' (5.19). And, as such, they could see to the payment of the debts that they owed themselves.

Though inclined, like Rome, to defend itself with a resoluteness and a vigour that beggar the imagination, this England would by no means be a nation intent on conquest. If it occupied an island, as it might, it would recognize that 'conquests abroad' on the continent of Europe or elsewhere would serve only to 'weaken it'. If this island were blessed, as also it might be, with good soil, this nation 'would have no need for war as a means for enriching itself'. And since its laws would guarantee that 'no citizen would be dependent on another, each would take his liberty more seriously than the glory reserved for a few citizens or one'. In consequence, though the soldierly profession might be deemed useful and would no doubt often be dangerous, its members would be regarded as 'persons whose services are burdensome (*laborieux*) for the nation itself, & civil status would be accorded greater regard'.

The reason why the England imagined by Montesquieu would in this particular context be so unlike Rome is simple. Situated, as it would be, on an island and blessed with the farmland and constitution with which it would be blessed, it would quite naturally be a seat of 'peace & liberty'; and, when 'liberated from destructive prejudices' – such as those rooted in the otherworldliness to which the Christian religion gives rise – it 'would be inclined to become commercial' and to exploit to the limit the capacity of its 'workers' to fashion from its natural resources objects of 'great price'. It would be inclined to carry on a great trade with those nations to the South that require its commodities and have much to offer that the English could not provide for themselves; and in flight from the excessive taxes it would impose, many of its citizens, on the pretext of travel or health, would seek their fortunes abroad 'even in the lands of servitude itself' (19.27).

Commerce these Englishmen would conduct as other nations conduct war. This people would have 'a prodigious number of petty, particular interests'. There would be 'an infinity of ways' in which it could do and receive harm (*choquer et être choqué*). 'It would become sovereignly jealous, & it would be more distressed by the prosperity of others than it would rejoice at its own'. Its laws, 'in other respects gentle & easy, would be so rigid with regard to commerce & the carrying trade . . . that it would seem to do business with none but enemies' (19.27 with 20.12).

Commerce would, in fact, be dominant in every sphere. 'Other nations', Montesquieu remarks elsewhere, 'have made their commercial interests give way to their political interests: this one has always made its political interests give way to the interests of its commerce' (20.7). If England, he tells us, were to send out colonies far and wide, to places such as North America, 'it would do so', precisely as ancient Carthage had, 'more to extend the reach of its commerce than its sphere of domination' (19.27 with 21.21). With these colonies, in keeping with its aim, it would be generous, as the Carthaginians had been, conferring on them 'its own form of government', which would bring 'with it prosperity' so that 'one would see great peoples take shape in the forests which they were sent to inhabit' (19.27). Nearer home, to be sure, England would be less forthcoming. If it subjugated the populace of a neighbouring island, such as Ireland, it might 'confer on' this nation 'its laws' but then, out of jealousy regarding the island's location, the quality of its ports, and the nature of its resources, 'retain' this nation 'in great dependence in such a manner that the citizens there would be free while the state was itself a slave'. The neighbouring island's 'civil government' might be 'very good', but 'its prosperity would be rendered quite precarious', for it would be little more than a 'storeroom for its master' (19.27).

As an island-nation, possessed of 'a great commerce', Montesquieu's England 'would have every sort of facility for fielding maritime forces'. Safeguarding 'its liberty would not require that it possess strongholds (*places*), fortresses, & armies on land', but 'it would have need of an army at sea to guarantee it against invasion, & its navy would be superiour to that of all the other powers, which, needing to employ their finances for war on land, would not have enough for war at sea'.

England's supremacy at sea would not be without effect. 'The empire of the sea has always given those peoples who possessed it a natural pride. Sensing themselves capable of insulting anyone anywhere', the English 'would believe their power as unlimited as the ocean', and they would be inclined to exercise it when circumstances warranted. In consequence, 'this nation would have a great influence on the affairs of its neighbours. Because it would not employ its power for conquest, they would be more inclined to seek its friendship, & they would fear its hatred more than the inconstancy of its government and its internal agitation would appear to justify.' In consequence, although 'it would be the fate of its executive power almost always to be uneasy at home', it would nearly always be 'respected abroad' (19.27, with 20.8, 21.7). In short, thanks to the changes in the *ius gentium* that Christianity had inspired and to the great commercial revolution, the tables had been turned, and Carthage now had the advantage over Rome.

IV

Despite dramatic evidence suggesting the existence of a profound gap between the scope of French ambitions and the magnitude of the resources that the monarchy could bring to bear in time of war; despite the fact that, under Louis XV, France experienced repeated military defeats and was more than once brought to the brink of bankruptcy; and despite the fact that the cost of France's support for the American War of Independence under Louis XVI had consequences even more dire for the monarchy's exchequer, for its capacity to project power in Europe, and for the stability of the regime, Montesquieu failed fully to persuade his compatriots of the superiority of English policy.

Moreover, in no way did he succeed in persuading the French to abandon their fatal longing for primacy and dominion on the continent of Europe; and, in the wake of the Revolution and the radical reorganization of the administrative state that accompanied it, a reinvigorated France forcefully renewed its quest for predominance. In subsequent generations, as religious and dynastic loyalties lost purchase and nationalism and universalist ideology were promoted as alternatives, the most influential Frenchmen and those Germans and Russians who looked for inspiration to Paris, rather than London, failed to take heed. Napoleon Bonaparte tried to establish a universal monarchy in Europe on the Roman model, and, when opportunity knocked, Adolf Hitler and Joseph Stalin followed suit.

The simple fact that Great Britain withstood Napoleon proves the prescience of Montesquieu. Despite its diminutive size, its limited resources and population, Britain was able to put together, fund, and lead the various coalitions that ultimately inflicted on that would-be Caesar a defeat even more decisive than the one suffered by Louis XIV. Moreover, in 1940, Montesquieu's England stood up to Hitler, and for a time it did so alone. If, in the end, Great Britain did not put together, fund and lead the coalition that eventually defeated the Nazi colossus, if it did not put together, fund and lead the alliance that later contained, wore down and ultimately dismembered the Soviet empire, it was because the British came to be overshadowed by another commercial people, which took 'shape', just as Montesquieu had predicted, 'in the forests' of the New World, a great people endowed by Britain with a 'form of government, which brings with it prosperity'.

As Winston Churchill foresaw quite early in the twentieth century, this people was destined to be England's heir. For more than a century now, it has pursued a foreign policy modelled on the pattern of conduct pioneered by 'the republic concealed under the form of a monarchy' that Montesquieu discovered when he crossed the English Channel. This people has long enjoyed a supremacy not just on the sea but in the air, and, as a consequence, it has exercised 'a great influence on the affairs of its neighbours'. Moreover, because it does 'not employ its power for conquest' and never acquired a great empire, not even in a fit of absentmindedness, other peoples are 'inclined to seek its friendship', and they fear 'its hatred more than the inconstancy of its government and its internal agitation would appear to justify'. And while it is 'the fate of its executive power almost always to be uneasy at home', its executive is nearly always respected abroad. Even now, when once again there is occasion to fear 'the inconstancy of its government' and the 'internal agitation' to which, like its predecessor, it is prone, this people finds itself compelled to follow the path opened up in the wake of the Glorious Revolution by the nation that contained Louis XIV, defeated Napoleon, and stood up to Hitler.

In the Cold War with the Soviet Union, despite the propensity for 'inconstancy' and 'internal agitation' natural to a polity distinguished by a distribution of powers, and despite its inclination 'to make its political interests give way to the interests of its commerce', the United States proved steadfast. Whether today – in the face of a challenge posed by Xi Jinping's China that closely resembles the challenges posed by the France of Louis XIV and Napoleon, by the Germany of Hitler and by the Russia of Stalin and his successors – it still possesses the spiritual resources, the prudence and the resolve requisite if it is to play the role that circumstances have conspired to confer upon it remains an open question. In the last 300 years, Carthage has repeatedly defeated Rome, but this need not always be the case. After all, at the outset, it was not a foregone conclusion that Louis XIV, Napoleon, Hitler and Stalin would go down in defeat. On more than one occasion, what Montesquieu described as 'morally impossible' very nearly took place.

Such thoughts are sobering. They serve as a timely reminder that we have no grounds for the complacency that we so often evidence. They suggest, moreover, that the assessment of the English polity advanced by Barbon and refined by Montesquieu is a matter of more than mere antiquarian interest. It is in light of what the French *philosophe* stopped short of saying in 1734 that we should read and ruminate on what he actually said fourteen years thereafter in the masterpiece for which he is generally remembered today.

Notes

1 See Charles-Louis de Secondat, baron de La Brède et de Montesquieu, *Pensées, Le Spicilège,* ed. Louis Desgraves (Paris, 1991), from which I cite the notebooks that Montesquieu entitled *Mes pensées* by the entry number. All translations from this and Montesquieu's other works are my own.

2 See Winston S. Churchill, *Marlborough: His Life and Times,* Vol. I (Chicago, 2002), 711–868, and Vol. II, 95–627.

3 See Colin Jones, *The Great Nation: France from Louis XV to Napoleon* (New York, 2002), 1–72, and Antoin E. Murphy, *John Law: Economic Theorist and Policy-Maker* (Oxford, 1997).

4 In what follows, with the permission of the editor of *History of Political Thought* and of Yale University Press, I have drawn material from Paul A. Rahe, 'The Book That Never Was: Montesquieu's *Considerations on the Romans* in Historical Context', *History of Political Thought* 26, no. 1 (2005): 43–89, and *Montesquieu and the Logic of Liberty: War, Religion, Commerce, Climate, Terrain, Technology, Uneasiness of Mind, the Spirit of Political Vigilance, and the Foundations of the Modern Republic* (New Haven, CT, 2009), 1–60, where fuller annotation is provided than is possible here.

5 All that we have are the handful of pages making up what is called his *Notes sur L'Angleterre.* For a critical edition with an introduction and detailed notes, see Charles-Louis de Secondat, baron de La Brède et de Montesquieu, *Œuvres complètes de Montesquieu,* ed. Jean Ehrard, Catherine Volpilhac-Auger, et al. (Oxford, 1998–2008; Paris, 2010-), X 489–506. Hereinaftee, this editor will be referred to as *OC.*

6 I cite Montesquieu's *L'Esprit des lois* as *EL* by the divisions provided by the author (nearly always, book and chapter) from the second volume of Charles-Louis de Secondat, baron de La Brède et de Montesquieu, *Œuvres complètes de Montesquieu,* ed. Roger Caillois (Paris, 1949–1951).

7   See [Jean Le Rond d'Alembert], 'Éloge de M. le President de Montesquieu', in
     Encyclopédie, ou Dictionnaire raisonné des sciences, des arts, et des métiers, ed.
     Denis Diderot and Jean Le Rond d'Alembert (Paris, 1751–1772, viii–xviii (at vii);
     Neutochotel, 1765; Amsterdam, 1776–1777; Paris, 1777–1780).

8   See Nicholas Barbon, *A Discourse of Trade* (London, 1690), reprinted in *Commerce,
     Culture and Liberty: Readings on Capitalism before Adam Smith*, ed. Henry C. Clark
     (Indianapolis, IN, 2003), 66–99.

9   See Louis Desgraves and Catherine Volpilhac-Auger, *Catalogue de la bibliothèque de
     Montesquieu à La Brède* (Naples, 1999).

10 See Barbon, *A Discourse of Trade*, A1–4.

11 See ibid., 40–57.

12 See ibid., 57–61. Cf. Alfred Thayer Mahan, *The Influence of Seapower upon History,
     1660–1783* (Boston, 1890).

13 I cite Montesquieu's *Réflexions sur la monarchie universelle en Europe* as *RMU* by
     chapter and line from *OC*, II 339–64. An English edition in the translation of David
     W. Carrithers can now be found in Montesquieu, *Discourses, Dissertations, and
     Dialogues on Politics, Science, and Religion*, ed. and trans. David W. Carrithers and
     Philip Stewart (Cambridge, 2020), 170–87.

14 See Niccolò Machiavelli, *Dell'arte della guerra* 2, 5, in Machiavelli, *Tutte le opere*, ed.
     Mario Martelli (Florence, 1971), 332–3, 359–60. Note also *Istorie fiorentine* 5.1 and
     6.1, in ibid., 738–9, 765–6; note Machiavelli, *Discorsi sopra la prima deca di Tito Livio*
     2.6, in ibid., 155–6. The translations are my own.

15 Cf. Machiavelli, *Discorsi sopra la prima deca de Tito Livio* 2.10 and *Dell'arte della
     guerra* 7, in *Tutte le opere*, 159–60, 386.

16 For the details, see Rahe, 'The Book That Never Was', 43–89, and *Montesquieu and the
     Logic of Liberty*, 1–60.

17 Note Montesquieu, *EL* 9.1, 10.3, 24.3–4, and see 13.17, 20.23–21.23.

18 See Rahe, *Montesquieu and the Logic of Liberty*, 186–211 (with 31–45).

19 This passage should be read in light of Montesquieu, *EL* 22.17–18.

5

Globalization and world order

Economic integration and the implications for global power, 1846–1914 and 1989–2021

Graeme Thompson

In April 2021, Chinese president Xi Jinping told the Boao Forum for Asia that, 'In this age of economic globalisation, openness and integration is an unstoppable historical trend'.[1] Leaving aside objections about the openness practised by the People's Republic of China, what is striking about Xi's comments is that they could have been uttered by almost any Western political leader since the end of the Cold War. Former British prime minister Tony Blair, for instance, informed his Labour Party's conference in 2005 that questioning globalization was akin to debating 'whether autumn should follow summer'.[2] Though separated by sixteen years and a tectonic shift in world order – namely the rise of China as a geopolitical challenger to the United States – both leaders' remarks invoked the same narrative of historical progress. The arc of history, in their telling, bends inexorably towards global integration.

It is a cliché that we live in a globalized world. Globalization – a catch-all term for deepening economic and social integration and the accelerating movement of people, goods, capital and ideas around the world – has defined the late twentieth and early twenty-first centuries. In the heady days around the turn of the millennium, it was even a 'common assumption' that the transnational forces of globalization would undermine, perhaps fatally, the state itself.[3] But we should instinctively distrust whiggish claims of historical inevitability.[4] As every investment fund prospectus warns, 'Past performance is not indicative of future results.'

Indeed, recent events – from the 'Brexit' referendum in the UK to the election of Donald Trump as US president and the fallout from the Covid-19 pandemic – have called into question the seemingly unstoppable forces of globalization. Policymakers, increasingly aware of the 'dark side' of integration, are now confronted with debates over 'deglobalization', 're-globalization' and economic 'decoupling' amid growing tensions between the United States and China.[5] In light of the populist backlash apparent in many countries and the emergence of what some commentators have labelled a new cold war, it appears that globalization is undergoing a profound transformation. How can we make sense of these developments? And what might be their political, economic and foreign policy implications?

Thinking historically can help answer these questions. While economists are perhaps reluctant to allow political and strategic considerations to intrude on their models, international relations (IR) scholars have struggled to incorporate globalization into existing theoretical frameworks.[6] The latter are especially divided, as John Mearsheimer notes, between liberals and realists over the question of whether international 'institutions and economic interdependence . . . promote peace. Liberals believe they do; realists do not'.[7] Historians, however, are comparatively well positioned to help policymakers better understand the contemporary predicament. This is not to deny the valuable contributions of other disciplines, nor to assert that history is an infallible guide to the present or future. Yet historians – particularly imperial historians, focused on integrated economic and geopolitical systems – are familiar with the long-term evolution, vicissitudes and recurring crises of globalization, as well as their connection to shifts in world order.[8] They therefore have an important role to play in illuminating the powerful forces currently reshaping international politics and the global economy.

This chapter thus explores the relationship between globalization and world order from the perspective of imperial history. It aims to show, within the confines of a short essay, that periods of deepening economic integration over the past two centuries were facilitated by hegemonic or imperial states, but that globalization in turn contributed to political and geopolitical realignments that strained integration and shifted the global balance of power. Though some liberal IR theories credit economic interdependence with promoting geopolitical stability, recent history suggests that the causal arrow points in the other direction – that processes of globalization depend, in large part, upon favourable, and often fleeting, geopolitical conditions.[9]

The first section traces the development of contemporary globalization under American hegemony, an era recently punctured by the meteoric rise of China. The bulk of the chapter then turns to the analogous experience of the British Empire in the nineteenth and early twentieth centuries – the last time a world power presided over deepening globalization only to be challenged by the emergence of new geopolitical rivals. It concludes by reflecting on how 'applied history' can illuminate the future of globalization and world order.

I

Since it entered our vocabulary in the 1990s, globalization has become a foundational political and economic concept. A Google Ngram search reveals its exponential growth in usage since the end of the Cold War, peaking around 2005 – the same year that journalist Thomas Friedman published *The World Is Flat*, his *Zeitgeist*-capturing romp through the new global economy.[10] As Friedman then observed, globalization meant that 'we are now connecting all the knowledge centers on the planet together into a single global network, which – if politics and terrorism do not get in the way – could usher in an amazing era of prosperity and innovation'.[11]

Yet the central node in that global network was – and remains – the United States. It was American companies, culture and patterns of consumption that shaped global trends. Immigrants from around the world chased the 'American dream', as seen in the rapidly growing percentage of foreign-born US residents since the 1970s.[12] And Silicon Valley and Wall Street were the global seats of technological innovation and transnational finance. Globalization, it seemed to many, was near synonymous with Americanization.

To be sure, US-led globalization had a long pre-history. The American colonies and early republic were enmeshed in an Atlantic economy based on the triangular trade of commodities, manufactured goods and enslaved people between North America, Europe and Africa. Leading intellectuals like Benjamin Franklin, Thomas Paine and Thomas Jefferson participated in a transnational 'republic of letters' that shaped the Enlightenment,[13] and the US Declaration of Independence was itself subsequently 'globalized'.[14] From 1898, when the United States acquired an overseas empire, an integrated economic system linked the US mainland with colonial possessions in the Caribbean and the Pacific.[15] Though Henry R. Luce famously coined the phrase 'the American century' in *Life Magazine* in 1941, forty years earlier British journalist W. T. Stead already foresaw the 'Americanization of the world'.[16] And following the Second World War the Bretton Woods system resurrected international trade and finance with the US economy and the American dollar in overwhelmingly dominant positions. Even after 1971, when President Richard Nixon abolished the last vestige of the gold standard, the United States enjoyed the 'exorbitant privilege' of issuing the world's reserve currency and promoted economic integration between North America, Western Europe and Japan.[17]

But the extent of US-led globalization prior to the 1990s should not be exaggerated. From the second half of the eighteenth century to 1914, as we shall see, the British Empire was the world's most potent globalizing force. Continental expansion and the development of America's huge domestic market limited its exposure to international trade, and its Caribbean and Pacific empire was more regional than global.[18] Neither was the golden age of US economic dominance after 1945 especially globalized. The Cold War saw minimal economic exchange across the Iron Curtain, and import substitution limited the integration of the 'Third World' into the global economy. Moreover, inward migration to the United States hit its twentieth-century nadir in 1970, and despite the successes of Bretton Woods, the democratic 'free world' was nevertheless characterized by capital controls, non-tariff barriers and entrenched protectionism.[19]

With the end of the Cold War, however, globalization spread, deepened and accelerated. After 1989 the United States stood alone as the world's sole superpower and the vast extent of its supremacy, combined with a belief in American exceptionalism, made even history's greatest empires appear quaint.[20] During this 'unipolar moment', a 'liberal international order', previously confined to the industrialized West, expanded outward as US foreign policy actively pursued global economic integration.[21] Institutions like the International Monetary Fund (IMF), the World Bank and the World Trade Organization (WTO) promoted the US-led agenda of trade and financial liberalization, and according to this 'Washington Consensus', free trade and globalization would lead to democratization.[22] As imperial historian John Darwin put it, the

> American response to the end of the Cold War was to see it . . . as a metahistorical opportunity to shape the course of world history. This was the moment to complete the permanent transformation of the global economy, already under way in the 1970s and '80s . . . Freed from the tyranny of the command economy and . . . ideological warfare, hitherto subject peoples would naturally choose liberal democracy. The vital corollary for this global task was geostrategic . . . No state should be able to threaten its neighbours and carve out a regional 'empire' designed to exclude the global economy and its liberal culture.[23]

Unchallenged American power thus upheld a world order conducive to increasingly integrated patterns of trade, finance, communication and migration. In this respect, American hegemony was, after all, not so unlike the great empires of the past, whose power often facilitated connection, exchange and integration between disparate peoples and regions of the world.[24]

In many ways, then, American efforts vindicated Thomas Friedman's premonition of an 'amazing era of prosperity and innovation'. Over the past three decades more than a billion people escaped subsistence poverty, due in large measure to freer trade, rising productivity and improved health and educational outcomes; global trade in goods and services soared, with transnational value-chains producing more and cheaper consumer products; and powerful technologies revolutionized daily life, linking humanity in a worldwide network of instant communication.[25]

At the same time, however, the 'dark side' of globalization became impossible to ignore. As early as the 1990s protesters impugned the imperiousness of global capital, while some commentators worried that deepening interconnectedness would prompt – and, thanks to technology, even facilitate – violent defences of traditional cultures and beliefs.[26] In different ways, the terrorist attacks of 11 September 2001 and the global financial crisis sparked seven years later by the collapse of the investment bank Lehman Brothers starkly revealed the dangers of transnational integration.[27]

Unease with globalization has, if anything, only deepened over the past decade. One factor has been the rise of 'populism' in the industrialized West, often linked to large-scale immigration and growing economic inequality. The disappearance of stable manufacturing jobs, combined with the belief that a highly mobile, impeccably networked and possibly corrupt political and financial elite benefitted from globalization, helped to fuel the 'populist revolt'.[28] Thus the election of Donald Trump as US president in 2016 can be seen, in part, as a backlash against what Harvard economist Dani Rodrik has termed 'hyper-globalization'.[29] As Trump told a Pennsylvania audience during his first presidential campaign, 'Globalization has made the financial elite who donate to politicians very, very wealthy . . . but it has left millions of our workers with nothing but poverty and heartache.'[30]

A second and related factor is the dramatic rise of China. With Deng Xiaoping's economic opening in 1978, the People's Republic launched the largest and most rapid industrial revolution in world history. In 1980, China comprised just 2 per cent of the global economy compared to 22 per cent for the United States; measured in terms of purchasing power parity, China overtook the United States as the world's largest economy in 2014.[31] Though China's per capita income 'is still only around one-third that of the United States in purchasing-power-parity terms', it has nonetheless lifted hundreds of millions of people out of poverty and into the global labour market.[32]

For much of this period, American policymakers lauded China's economic liberalization as a precursor to political reform. As US president Bill Clinton argued in 2000 in favour of Beijing joining the WTO, 'The more China liberalizes its economy, the more fully it will liberate the potential of its people. . . . And when individuals have that power . . . they will demand a greater say.'[33] China, it was hoped, would move towards democracy and become a 'responsible stakeholder' in the US-led world order.[34] Over the next decade, the American and Chinese economies became deeply integrated in a near-symbiotic relationship that was a central feature of contemporary globalization. While China transformed into a manufacturing and export powerhouse, its profits and savings flowed into the US debt market, helping to lower global interest rates and fuel a debt-financed binge by American consumers on cheap Chinese goods.[35]

But even before the election of Donald Trump, the perception that China had 'stolen' US manufacturing jobs percolated through American opinion. In 2015, for instance, Democratic presidential candidate Bernie Sanders claimed that 'corporate America' had 'sold out American workers and essentially moved manufacturing to China'.[36] Following the 2008 financial crisis, which in some ways further accelerated China's rise, even more sober observers pointed to the distortionary effects of Chinese currency manipulation on international trade and financial flows.[37] And amid the American backlash against China, free trade and globalization in general, some measures of global economic integration had already peaked. As journalist Martin Wolf observed in 2016, 'Globalisation has at best stalled . . . as have the policies driving it.'[38]

Perhaps most significant, however, is that China's exponential growth has shifted the global balance of power. Indeed, since the ascent of Xi Jinping to China's presidency in 2012, the Chinese Communist Party has pursued an assertive grand strategy premised on the belief that its new economic clout should be matched by a commensurate role in a reformed world order. Its Belt and Road Initiative (BRI), which seeks to build an economic and infrastructure network centred on Beijing, combined with the rapid modernization of the People's Liberation Army and a vision for national supremacy in advanced 'dual-use' (i.e. civilian and military) technologies like artificial intelligence and quantum computing, reflects a transformative geopolitical ambition. And as political scientist Avery Goldstein observes, Beijing's burgeoning power 'accelerated a shift . . . away from the erstwhile bipartisan U.S. consensus favoring constructive engagement . . . [to] the newly dominant view that China was mounting a fundamental challenge to U.S. interests in Asia and perhaps to the United States' global leadership'.[39]

The fallout from the Trump presidency and the Covid-19 pandemic appear to have only reinforced this trend. In Washington, the new Biden administration has adopted a relatively hawkish stance towards Beijing and has yet to remove Trump-era tariffs on Chinese goods. President Biden himself described the geopolitical situation as 'extreme competition' between the United States and China, and his framing of that competition in terms of democracy versus authoritarianism has injected an ideological tenor to the rivalry that was previously lacking under Trump.[40] Though hope remains for Sino-American cooperation on global issues like climate change, growing calls to extricate strategic supply chains from China amid talk of an emerging cold war – heightened by Beijing's shrill 'wolf warrior' diplomacy and a frosty March 2021 Sino-American summit in Anchorage, Alaska – show just how far relations between the world's leading powers have fallen.[41]

It is therefore hard to escape the conclusion that American hegemony facilitated a process of globalization that in turn contributed to the rise of populism and the rapid emergence of new centres of economic and military power, most importantly China.[42] The United States is consequently grappling with domestic political realignments, based in part on opposition to free trade, and the relative decline of its global strategic position. But as history shows, this is hardly the first time that a world power presiding over an era of liberal globalization has been buffeted by political and geopolitical turmoil.

II

Today it is widely recognized that the 'long nineteenth century' that ended with the First World War in 1914 was an era of globalization – characterized by British imperial power, the industrial revolution and burgeoning global trade.[43] Yet British-led globalization, like its more recent American counterpart, had deep historical roots. Its origins lay in France's defeat of England in the Hundred Years' War in 1453, when English merchants, who lost access to a lucrative maritime trade with Bordeaux, sought out new markets in Iberia, where 'they learned of the new seafaring knowledge that carried Portuguese and Spanish navigators to the Caribbean and West Africa'.[44] Thus in the century following John Cabot's 1497 voyage to Newfoundland, Tudor England established itself as an oceanic power with a vision of an empire that was 'Protestant, commercial, maritime, and free'.[45]

By the seventeenth century, however, this 'empire of liberty', centred on the settler colonies of North America's Atlantic seaboard, rested on a mercantilist system comprising brutal sugar plantations in the Caribbean, trade in human beings between Africa and the Americas, and the corporate power of the East India Company.[46] With the Glorious Revolution of 1688 and the Union of England and Scotland in 1707, a *British* Empire, backed by a potent fiscal-military state, consolidated and expanded in an early form of globalization based on conquest, agriculture and extraction.[47]

The key advantage of Britain's fiscal-military state was its ability to finance, via debt and taxation, the naval power to meet its growing imperial commitments.[48] This proved critical to victories over France in the global Seven Years' War (1756–63) and the French Revolutionary and Napoleonic Wars (1792–1815). Although London's attempt to tax the American colonists to defray the cost of the former was met with rebellion and secession, the latter compensated their loss with the geopolitical prize of unchallenged British supremacy at sea.[49]

Yet after 1815 Britain overhauled its imperial system. Adam Smith's *The Wealth of Nations* (1776) laid the intellectual groundwork with its attack on mercantilism, and burgeoning British trade with the new United States soon vindicated his critique. As philosopher Jeremy Bentham observed in 1793: 'Turn to the United States. Before the separation, Britain had the monopoly of their trade; upon the separation of course she lost it. How much less is their trade with Britain now than then? On the contrary, it is much greater.'[50] By the early nineteenth century, then, a positive feedback loop, encompassing British textile production and slave-harvested US cotton exports, fuelled transatlantic trade.[51] And Britain's increasingly industrial economy, combined with an enormous debt burden and growing disaffection with elite corruption, prompted far-reaching political and economic reforms.[52]

As a result, by the 1840s, as in the 1990s, a recognizably modern system of liberal globalization emerged. The key date was 1846, when the campaign for free trade led by Richard Cobden and John Bright culminated with the repeal of Britain's protectionist Corn Laws and the onset of its 'liberal empire'. Partly, liberals sought cheaper food and raw materials for northern manufacturers and the new industrial working class, as well as to rein in the power of aristocratic landowners. Yet they also envisaged a world order 'based on free trade, peace, and progress in civilisation'.[53] As liberal philosopher John Stuart Mill argued in his *Principles of Political Economy* (1848):

> It is commerce which is rapidly rendering war obsolete, by strengthening and multiplying the personal interests which are opposed to it. And it may be said without exaggeration that the great extent and rapid increase of international trade, in being the principal guarantee of the peace of the world, is the great permanent security for the uninterrupted progress of the ideas, the institutions, and the character of the human race.[54]

And many European states followed the British lead. Across the continent, as economic historians Ronald Findlay and Kevin O'Rourke observe, 'average tariffs were falling throughout the 1850s' and in 1860 an Anglo-French commercial treaty 'established most-favored-nation relations between the two countries', laying the foundation for further liberalization.[55]

Furthermore, in Britain itself, Liberal chancellor of the exchequer, and later prime minister, William Ewart Gladstone transformed the state through low taxes, balanced budgets, sound money and laissez-faire. With the Royal Navy unmatched and Westminster committed to liberal fiscal and monetary policy, commercial, manufacturing and financial interests boomed. The city of London became the nerve-centre of a new global economy, with the pound sterling the world's reserve currency, the London Stock Exchange its primary marketplace and British banks and insurance companies its key financial institutions.[56] And while the British Empire proper – those areas coloured red on the map – served as a growing market for British goods, capital and labour, it was only part of a sprawling 'world-system' that included nominally independent states from Argentina to China.[57]

Of course, liberal free traders were often disabused of their utopianism as British statesmen intervened overseas to advance commercial and geopolitical interests. The

Opium Wars (1839–42, 1856–60) fought to pry open the Chinese market, the brutal suppression of the 1857 rebellion in British India and armed intervention in Egypt in 1882, not to mention countless wars waged from New Zealand to South Africa to Afghanistan, reflected the reality of military force that upheld the 'Pax Britannica'. In some respects, Britain's combination of global military power and liberal idealism at the height of the nineteenth century was reminiscent of post–Cold War America.

The economic results of British-led globalization, moreover, were extraordinary. From 1800 to 1850 global trade doubled, and from 1850 to 1914 it expanded another tenfold.[58] In Britain, the value of exports as a share of GDP rose from 14.6 per cent in 1856 to 25 per cent by 1913.[59] Nor was it only British manufactures that went overseas. From 1815 to 1930 approximately twelve million Britons emigrated to the British dominions and the United States.[60] British capital, too, boosted growth worldwide. Investments in imperial and foreign bonds, railways, utilities, banks and real estate increased British assets held abroad from £1 billion in the 1870s to £4 billion by 1913, comprising '44 percent of the world total of foreign investment'.[61]

British capital thus fuelled astonishing improvements in transportation and communications technologies, which were decisive in integrating the global economy. Railway mileage soared, opening continental interiors to settlement and commerce; telegraph cables allowed for near-instant communication across vast distances; and, with steamships and the opening of the Suez Canal in 1869, the cost of shipping declined precipitously.[62] Contemporaries were struck by the apparent compression of space and time by steam and electricity. In a justly famous passage, the economist John Maynard Keynes described the possibilities of daily life at the height of pre–First World War globalization:

> The inhabitant of London could order by telephone, sipping his morning tea in bed, the various products of the whole earth … and reasonably expect their early delivery upon his doorstep; he could at the same moment and by the same means adventure his wealth in the natural resources and new enterprises of any quarter of the world … He could secure forthwith, if he wished it, cheap and comfortable means of transit to any country or climate … But, most of all, he regarded this state of affairs as normal, certain, and permanent, except in the direction of further improvement[.][63]

At the same time, however, the liberal vision and Britain's position as a global power came under growing pressure as economic changes prompted opposition to free trade and the rise of new geopolitical rivals. After 1870, as historian Anthony Howe observes, the prevailing liberal order 'was rapidly dethroned by a new age of military conquest, imperial expansion, and neo-mercantilistic economic policies'.[64]

One contributing factor was the decline in the real cost of transportation and commodities. As cheap New World grain flooded Europe – where land and rents, and therefore agricultural production, were more expensive – powerful landed interests forced a reversion to protectionism. New World manufacturers, meanwhile, lobbied for high tariffs to protect against British industrial competition. Global economic integration, in short, led to the re-emergence of tariff politics, fought between the winners and losers of globalization.[65]

In Britain, opponents targeted the liberal vision as early as 1872, when Tory leader Benjamin Disraeli floated the idea of an imperial tariff and accused the governing Liberal Party of seeking to 'substitute cosmopolitan for national principles'.[66] This marked the onset of the 'new imperialism': a movement that combined an assertive foreign policy with protectionism, social reform and imperial consolidation. By the 1900s, 'imperialists' had become a force in British politics.[67] As imperial administrator Alfred Milner argued in 1908, imperialists appalled by 'overcrowded town populations, irregular employment, [and] sweated industries' sought 'to improve the condition of the people at home, and to improve it concurrently with strengthening the foundations of the empire . . . using duties either to increase employment . . . or to secure markets abroad'.[68]

For old-fashioned liberals, the political and intellectual assault on free trade seemed to show that 'sound economics have been sadly forgotten in England', while the imperialist programme as a whole smacked of 'a union of jingoism with a certain amount of socialistic radicalism'.[69] But the concurrent rise of 'new liberalism' or progressivism, as well as the nascent Labour Party, illustrated the extent of Edwardian disillusion with the Gladstonian state.[70] Although free trade remained entrenched, due largely to its popularity among workers and manufacturers, demands for social reform increasingly shaped British politics. This led to David Lloyd George's 'People's Budget' in 1909 – Britain's first explicitly redistributive fiscal policy with new taxes to fund social welfare.

The domestic political realignment was further catalysed by Britain's relative strategic decline. Though the value of its international trade and exports continued to rise in absolute terms, its 'share of world trade fell from 25% in 1860 to . . . 17% by 1913'.[71] Part of the explanation, as historians P. J. Cain and A. G. Hopkins observe, is that 'globalization included the rapid spread of industrialism in Western Europe and the United States', which 'increased the competitive element in world trade, promoted imperial ambitions, and threatened the *Pax Britannica*'.[72] Two states in particular seemed to embody the economic and geopolitical challenge to British power: the post–Civil War United States and the newly unified Imperial Germany.

While the United States became independent in 1783, it remained in effect a British economic colony for much of the nineteenth century. US exports to Britain, principally cotton, grew eightfold from 1820 to 1870 and accounted for roughly 50 per cent of all US exports from 1815 to 1860. In the same period, 40 per cent of US imports, predominantly manufactured goods, derived from the UK. US reliance on British capital investment was even more pronounced.[73] As late as 1890, as James Belich writes, 'there were more American stocks listed on the London stock market than on the New York stock market', and until about 1900 'Britain and the United States were in some respects a single economy'.[74]

British-led globalization, in other words, facilitated rapid US economic growth. The UK served as the key market for US exports and a primary source of manufactured goods and investment capital, even as high tariffs protected US manufacturers from the worst of British competition. By 1872 the US economy overtook the UK in terms of total GDP and by 1905 it surpassed British GDP per capita.[75] US protectionism appeared to have nurtured a powerful industrial sector, and American advocates of freer trade were constantly accused of serving British interests.[76]

The geopolitical implications of US growth were profound. Britain had tacitly supported the Confederacy in the Civil War, reflecting its dependence on southern cotton, but the Union victory in 1865 left the United States in a powerful position. The neighbouring British Dominion of Canada was sparsely populated and weakly defended, and Britain's key strategic interests lay in Europe, the Mediterranean and India. Thus in 1871, Prime Minister Gladstone and US president Ulysses S. Grant concluded the Treaty of Washington, which settled several outstanding Anglo-American disputes and effectively traded American recognition of Canada for Britain's de facto acknowledgement of US hegemony in the Americas.

Despite recurrent tensions, notably over Venezuela in 1895, Anglo-American rapprochement proceeded apace – thanks to an alignment of strategic interests, economic considerations and deep cultural and 'racial' affinities.[77] Gladstone himself celebrated the 'vast contribution' that each country made 'to the wealth and comfort of the other', and the United States, he admitted in 1878, 'at a coming time can, and probably will, wrest from us . . . commercial primacy'.[78] By 1898, many British commentators, notably the poet Rudyard Kipling in his poem 'The White Man's Burden' (1899), welcomed the American turn to overseas empire.[79] As George Parkin, the first secretary of the Rhodes Trust, wrote perceptively, the United States 'will be compelled to face European diplomacy . . . make themselves a great naval power . . . complete the canal through the Isthmus [of Panama] . . . and enter generally upon a new national course. . . . While there are great dangers . . . there are also considerable grounds for satisfaction'.[80]

While contemporaries lauded the nascent Anglo-American entente, however, relations between Britain and Germany soured. Like Britain and the United States, the two societies enjoyed long-standing connections, epitomized by the British royal family's Germanic origins. Both were majority-Protestant states and contemporary academic authorities maintained that English traditions of liberty and constitutional government derived from a shared Anglo-German 'Teutonic' heritage.[81]

Nor was it immediately clear that Berlin and London's strategic interests were opposed. 'Germany's interests lay mainly in Europe, Britain's overseas', as historian Margaret MacMillan observes, and '[w]hen Prussia . . . united the German states into the new Germany in 1870, Britain watched with benevolent neutrality'.[82] Indeed, Prime Minister Gladstone did not perceive the new German Empire as an imminent threat, so long as the integrity and neutrality of Belgium, with its ports on the English Channel, were upheld. But he was wary of the future. 'Growing military establishments, growing debt, growing dangers', he lamented during the Franco-Prussian War, 'such is the summary but true description . . . of the present crisis'.[83] Prussian militarism, he worried, would lead Germany to 'to abuse the power which she has undoubtedly acquired', and Britain would be called upon to sustain 'the rest of Europe against a disturber of the public peace'.[84]

Though Britain was geographically insulated from the continent, Gladstone recognized that it had 'constant relations both of personal and of commercial intercourse, which grow from year to year'.[85] At mid-century, British manufactured goods, as well as commodities like sugar, spices and cotton, either from the British colonies or re-exported via London, were in high demand in Germany. German exports of food and raw materials, moreover, found a steady market in the UK. As historian Paul Kennedy notes, not only was Anglo-German trade significant in volume, but patterns of exchange up to the late nineteenth century 'leave an overwhelming impression of the manner in which the two economies *complemented* each other'.[86] Parallels with Sino-American trade prior to the 2008 financial crisis, though inexact, hardly require emphasis.

In the 1870s, however, a prolonged economic slump shifted German politics towards protectionism. After 1879, Germany's industrialization advanced behind high tariff walls.[87] As the less developed country, moreover, it made rapid gains in 'steam, electric, and rail power . . . to achieve growth rates' substantially higher than Britain's.[88] Not only did Berlin specialize in comparatively advanced industries like chemicals and electrical equipment, but by 1914 it also produced significantly more steel and pig iron than the UK. Crucially, Britain remained Germany's leading export market while the British colonies provided a growing share of its imported raw materials. While London's commercial and financial clout compensated for its bilateral trade deficit, Germany had become the leading industrial power in Europe due, in part, to extensive trade with Britain and its empire.[89]

Initially, British statesmen sought to accommodate growing German power. In the 'Scramble for Africa', for instance, Britain acquiesced to German demands for increased influence on the continent, and Joseph Chamberlain, Colonial Secretary from 1895 to 1903, even sought to consecrate an alliance.[90] When imperialist mining magnate Cecil Rhodes died in 1902, the Oxford scholarships established in his name were open to British subjects, Americans and Germans.

But geopolitical tensions deepened as a 'new generation of German leaders dreamed of their country taking a larger role in international affairs . . . [and] transform[ing] the German Empire from a European continental state into a global sea power'.[91] This turn towards a world policy, or *Weltpolitik*, and Berlin's decision to challenge British naval supremacy in the North Sea was a redline that changed Britain's strategic calculus.[92] From 1908, fearing an invasion of the Home Islands that would strike at the source of British global power, London matched and exceeded the German naval build-up. It also repositioned its naval assets closer to home, thanks to ententes with Japan (1902), France (1904) and Russia (1907). For London, this constituted a 'strategic revolution . . . focused not on the defence of a far-flung empire, but on deterring a German bid for primacy in Europe'.[93]

In August 1914, however, it failed. With doubt over London's ability and determination to intervene in a continental land war, Germany invaded France through neutral Belgium, which Britain was treaty- and honour-bound to defend. The world's stock markets suspended trading, merchant ships stayed in port or risked being sunk, economies mobilized for military production and the integrated world of nineteenth-century globalization collapsed into a total war from which it never recovered.[94]

III

History, of course, does not exactly repeat itself. Historical change does not come in easily predicted cycles. And expecting historians to provide clear, unambiguous lessons for the present is a mistake. Nevertheless, knowledge of the past is essential to informed political analysis and decision-making. Observation and experience, argued the Scottish philosopher and historian David Hume, are fundamental in determining cause and effect, and history, by 'furnishing us with materials, from which we may form our observations', allows us to identify patterns and principles in human affairs.[95] Such is the invaluable contribution of 'applied history' to policymaking and statecraft. Abstract theories, as Hume concluded, disconnected from experience, 'can contain nothing but sophistry and illusion'.[96]

Much thinking about globalization since the nineteenth century has proved illusory. For those who believed, whether in the 1850s or 1990s, that economic integration would lead inexorably to a peaceful community of nations, the return of geopolitics and protectionism was an unwelcome shock. Comments like those quoted in the introduction of this essay further betray a self-interested and teleological view of globalization: that economic integration is inevitable and therefore not subject to politics, and that history itself is moving towards a predetermined destination. Historical analysis, on the contrary, suggests that globalization is a process like any other, shaped by political choices and 'subject to reversals, transitions, crises, and breakdowns'.[97]

There are, to be sure, important differences between the periods of British and American-led globalization. Britain, for instance, exported people, practised unilateral free trade, owned and earned income from a stupendous share of global foreign investment, upheld the gold standard and reduced its national debt. The United States, conversely, imports people, lowers tariffs on a reciprocal basis and has a negative net international investment position, a fiat monetary system and a rising national debt. In purely military terms, moreover, American power at its height, and the extent of its global alliance system, far exceeded that of Britain during the 'Pax Britannica'.[98]

Nevertheless, one pattern apparent across at least two centuries of imperial history is the dynamic relationship between globalization, economic and political change, and shifts in world order. Under the British Empire from 1846 to 1914 and American hegemony since at least the end of the Cold War, the world's leading power upheld a relatively liberal order conducive to burgeoning international trade, technological innovation and deepening interdependence. In both cases, however, economic changes unleashed by globalization prompted domestic political realignments, based in part on opposition to free trade, while facilitating the rise of new geopolitical rivals that shifted the global balance of power. Suddenly, states that appeared invulnerable for decades found themselves divided and overstretched, and the systems of globalization and world order that they upheld came under growing pressure.

Parallels between the Anglo-German antagonism after 1870 and today's escalating tensions between the United States and China are especially striking. China's rapid economic growth and military modernization amid extensive Sino-American trade recalls the rise of Germany in a context of economic integration with the British Empire. The Belt and Road Initiative, moreover, combined with Beijing's increasingly brash assertion of its new international power, might be seen as an expression of a Chinese *Weltpolitik* and a commensurate desire for its own moment in the sun. Continuing the analogy, China's challenge to US technological supremacy is reminiscent of the

Anglo-German naval arms race, while Taiwan looks disconcertingly like a twenty-first-century Belgium.

From another perspective, we might view the rapid development of China's internal market, its strategy to nurture high-tech manufacturing and the reorientation of regional and global trade towards Beijing as analogous to the US's own achievement of economic independence from the UK and its acquisition of an overseas empire in 1898. Yet the strategic and ideological limits of that comparison seem obvious. Whereas in the late nineteenth century Britain's geopolitical interests in North America were marginal and London saw the United States, its former colony, as a kindred 'Anglo-Saxon' democracy, today American interests in East Asia and the Pacific are substantial and Washington views China as a menacing and increasingly totalitarian state.

What conclusions for the future of globalization and world order can we draw from recent historical experience? Three observations seem reasonable. First, that liberal theories of international politics, for all their merits and attraction, place too much faith in the pacific tendencies of economic integration. The Anglo-German antagonism, as well as deepening US-China tensions, suggests that when economic and strategic interests collide, it is what imperial historian Ronald Hyam called 'the primacy of geopolitics' that tends to prevail.[99] Among imperial or great power rivals, economic interdependence can mean strategic vulnerability.

Second, and in line with that observation, it is clear that some degree of economic decoupling between the United States and China – a kind of strategic protectionism focused on critical supply chains and digital technologies with military applications – is already underway. Key questions are how far this process goes and what collateral damage the global economy suffers. Between China's Belt and Road Initiative and its unique digital and fintech ecosystems, furthermore, it is not difficult to imagine the emergence of a Sinocentric strategic and economic sphere challenging the United States.[100] This would not preclude Washington from deepening its ties in the Indo-Pacific or reforming and revitalizing the existing US-led system of multilateral 'rules-based globalization'.[101] It would, however, imply an increasingly divided and contested world order, not unlike the imperial rivalries of the late nineteenth century. As Margaret MacMillan recently mused, 'We thought the age of empires was over; maybe it has merely been resting.'[102]

And third, even if globalization evolves towards two (or more) imperial systems, international politics will remain indelibly globalized in the sense described by British geographer Halford Mackinder in 1904, contained within a 'political system . . . of worldwide scope'.[103] Transnational challenges like nuclear proliferation, climate change, environmental degradation and pandemic diseases acutely illustrate the globalized nature of the international system. This conjunction of geopolitical competition with the need for global coordination has led some experts to call for forms of 'cooperative rivalry' or 'managed strategic competition' between the United States and China.[104]

Here, however, history does offer a sobering lesson: peacefully navigating imperial rivalries is not easy. Prior to 1914, as John Darwin observes, 'the world's most powerful states . . . adopted a form of competitive coexistence', recognizing that global stability hinged on 'respect for their . . . uneasy balance of power'.[105] We know how that turned out. The catastrophe of the First World War must therefore serve as a warning amid the shifting world order of the early twenty-first century. History shows that there is nothing linear or inevitable about globalization, and failure by US and Chinese policymakers to manage their geopolitical tensions, to paraphrase former British foreign secretary Edward Grey, would mean the lamps going out all over the world. We would not see them lit again in our lifetimes.

Notes

1 Xi Jinping, 'Pulling Together through Adversity and Toward a Shared Future for All', *Boao Forum for Asia Annual Conference*, 20 April 2021, https://www.fmprc.gov.cn/mfa_eng/zxxx_662805/t1870296.shtml.
2 'Tony Blair's Conference Speech 2005', *The Guardian*, 27 September 2005, https://www.theguardian.com/uk/2005/sep/27/labourconference.speeches.
3 Martin Wolf, 'Will the Nation-State Survive Globalization?' *Foreign Affairs* 80, no. 1 (2001): 179.
4 Herbert Butterfield, *The Whig Interpretation of History* (London, 1931).
5 See for example Markus Kornprobst and T. V. Paul, 'Globalization, Deglobalization, and the Liberal International Order', *International Affairs* 97, no. 5 (2021): 1305–16; Henry Farrell and Abraham Newman, 'The Folly of Decoupling from China: It Isn't Just Perilous – It's Impossible', *Foreign Affairs*, 3 June 2020, https://www.foreignaffairs.com/articles/china/2020-06-03/folly-decoupling-china.
6 For an early critique of economists' views of globalization, see Dani Rodrik, *Has Globalization Gone Too Far?* (Washington, DC, 1997). On globalization and IR theory, see Arie M. Kacowicz and Mor Mitrani, 'Why Don't We Have Coherent Theories of International Relations About Globalization?' *Global Governance* 22 (2016): 189–208.
7 John Mearsheimer, *The Great Delusion: Liberal Dreams and International Realities* (New Haven, CT, 2018), 143.
8 John Darwin, *After Tamerlane: The Rise and Fall of Global Empires, 1400–2000* (London, 2007); A. G. Hopkins (ed.), *Globalization in World History* (London, 2002).
9 For the IR liberal contention that globalization promotes peace and geopolitical stability, see John Ikenberry, 'Globalization and the Stability of World Order', *Asia-Pacific Review* 5, no. 3 (1998): 1–13.
10 See Google Ngram, https://books.google.com/ngrams/graph?content=globalization%2Cglobalisation&year_start=1800&year_end=2019&corpus=26&smoothing=3&direct_url=t1%3B%2Cglobalization%3B%2Cc0%3B.t1%3B%2Cglobalisation%3B%2Cc0.
11 Thomas L. Friedman, *The World Is Flat: A Brief History of the Twenty-first Century* (New York, 2005), 8.
12 Abby Budiman, 'Key Findings about U.S. Immigrants', *Pew Research*, 20 August 2020, https://www.pewresearch.org/fact-tank/2020/08/20/key-findings-about-u-s-immigrants/.
13 James T. Kloppenberg, *Toward Democracy: The Struggle for Self-Rule in European and American Thought* (Oxford, 2016), 252–313.
14 David Armitage, *The Declaration of Independence: A Global History* (Cambridge, MA, 2007).
15 A. G. Hopkins, *American Empire: A Global History* (Princeton, NJ, 2018).

16 W. T. Stead, *The Americanization of the World; or The Trend of the Twentieth Century* (New York, 1901).

17 Barry Eichengreen, *Exorbitant Privilege: The Rise and Fall of the Dollar and the Future of the International Monetary System* (Oxford, 2011), 39–68. On the origins of modern globalization in the 1970s, see Niall Ferguson, Charles S. Maier, Erez Manela, and Daniel J. Sargent (eds), *The Shock of the Global: The 1970s in Perspective* (Cambridge, MA: The Belknap Press of Harvard University Press, 2010).

18 Hopkins, *American Empire*, 13.

19 Robert Gilpin, 'The Rise of American Hegemony', in *Two Hegemonies: Britain 1846–1914 and the United States 1941–2001*, ed. Patrick Karl O'Brien and Armand Clesse (Aldershot, 2002), 165–82; Budiman, 'Key Findings about U.S. Immigrants'.

20 Charles Krauthammer, 'The Unipolar Moment', *Foreign Affairs* 70, no. 1 (1990/91): 23–33. See also Michael Ignatieff, 'Empire Lite', *Prospect Magazine*, 20 February 2003, https://www.prospectmagazine.co.uk/magazine/empirelite.

21 G. John Ikenberry, *A World Safe For Democracy: Liberal Internationalism and the Crises of Global Order* (New Haven, CT, 2020), 276; Mearsheimer, *The Great Delusion*, 143.

22 Ngaire Woods, *The Globalizers: The IMF, the World Bank, and Their Borrowers* (Ithaca, NY, 2006).

23 Darwin, *After Tamerlane*, 480–1.

24 Hopkins, *American Empire*, 25–32.

25 Jeffrey D. Sachs, *The Ages of Globalization: Geography, Technology, and Institutions* (New York, 2020), 169–78.

26 Benjamin Barber, *Jihad vs. McWorld: Terrorism's Challenge to Democracy* (New York, 1995); Thomas L. Friedman, *The Lexus and the Olive Tree* (New York, 1999).

27 Niall Ferguson, *The Square and the Tower: Networks and Power, From the Freemasons to Facebook* (New York, 2017), 333–46.

28 David Goodhart, *The Road to Somewhere: The Populist Revolt and the Future of Politics* (London, 2017).

29 Dani Rodrik, 'Why Does Globalization Fuel Populism? Economics, Culture, and the Rise of Right-Wing Populism', *Annual Review of Economics* 13, no. 133 (2021): 133–70.

30 Quoted in David Jackson, 'Donald Trump Targets Globalization and Free Trade as Job-Killers', *USA Today*, 28 June 2016, https://www.usatoday.com/story/news/politics/elections/2016/06/28/donald-trump-globalization-trade-pennsylvania-ohio/86431376/.

31 Graham Allison, *Destined for War: Can America and China Escape Thucydides's Trap?* (Boston, 2017), xvi–xvii, 10.

32 Sachs, *The Ages of* Globalization, 180.

33 Bill Clinton, 'Speech on China Trade Bill', Paul H. Nitze School of Advanced International Studies, Washington, DC, 9 March 2000, https://www.iatp.org/sites/default/files/Full_Text_of_Clintons_Speech_on_China_Trade_Bi.htm.

34 Robert B. Zoellick, 'Whither China: From Membership to Responsibility? Remarks to National Committee on U.S.-China Relations', 21 September 2005, https://2001-2009.state.gov/s/d/former/zoellick/rem/53682.htm.

35 Niall Ferguson and Moritz Schularick, '"Chimerica" and the Global Asset Market Boom', *International Finance* 10, no. 3 (2007): 228.

36 Quoted in Ezra Klein, 'Bernie Sanders: The Vox conversation', *Vox*, 28 July 2015, https://www.vox.com/2015/7/28/9014491/bernie-sanders-vox-conversation.

37 Niall Ferguson and Moritz Schularick, 'The End of Chimerica', *International Finance* 14, no. 1 (2011): 1–26; Dani Rodrik, 'Making Room for China in the World Economy', *The American Economic Review* 100, no. 2 (2010): 89–93.

38 Martin Wolf, 'The Tide of Globalization is Turning', *Financial Times*, 6 September 2016, https://www.ft.com/content/87bb0eda-7364-11e6-bf48-b372cdb1043a.

39 Avery Goldstein, 'China's Grand Strategy Under Xi Jinping: Reassurance, Reform, and Resistance', *International Security* 45, no. 1 (2020): 193.

40 Demetri Sevastopulo, 'Biden Warns China will Face "extreme competition" from US', *Financial Times*, 7 February 2021, https://www.ft.com/content/c23a4e67-2052-4d2f-a844-e5c72a7de214.

41 Lara Jakes and Steven Lee Myers, 'Tense Talks With China Left U.S. "Cleareyed" About Beijing's Intensions, Officials Say', *New York Times*, 19 March 2021, https://www.nytimes.com/2021/03/19/world/asia/china-us-alaska.html.

42 For a version of this argument, see John J. Mearsheimer, 'Bound to Fail: The Rise and Fall of the Liberal International Order', *International Security* 43, no. 4 (2019): 7–50.

43 Dani Rodrik, *The Globalization Paradox: Democracy and the Future of the World Economy* (New York, 2012), 24–40.

44 John Darwin, *Unfinished Empire: The Global Expansion of Britain* (London, 2012), 17.

45 David Armitage, *The Ideological Origins of the British Empire* (Cambridge, 2000), 8.

46 Richard Drayton, 'The Collaboration of Labour: Slaves, Empires, and Globalizations in the Atlantic World, c. 1600–1850', in *Globalization in World History*, 98–114; Tirthankar Roy, *The East India Company: The World's Most Powerful Corporation* (Delhi, 2012).

47 P. J. Cain and A. G. Hopkins, 'Gentlemanly Capitalism and British Expansion Overseas I: The Old Colonial System, 1688–1850', *The Economic History Review* 39, no. 4 (1986): 501–25.

48 P. J. Cain and A. G. Hopkins, *British Imperialism, 1688–2000* (London, 2002), 668.

49 Darwin, *Unfinished Empire*, 131; Hopkins, *American Empire*, 95–141.

50 Jeremy Bentham, *Emancipate Your Colonies!* (London, 1830 [1793]), 25.

51 Sven Beckert, *Empire of Cotton: A New History of Global Capitalism* (London, 2015), 104.

52 Cain and Hopkins, *British Imperialism, 1688–2000*, 670.

53 Anthony Howe, 'Free Trade and Global Order: The Rise and Fall of a Victorian Vision', in *Victorian Visions of Global Order: Empire and International Relations in Nineteenth-Century Political Thought*, ed. Duncan Bell (Cambridge, 2007), 27.

54 John Stuart Mill, *Principles of Political Economy With Some of Their Applications to Social Philosophy* (London, 1909 [1848]), 582.

55 Ronald Findlay and Kevin H. O'Rourke, *Power and Plenty: Trade, War, and the World Economy in the Second Millennium* (Princeton, NJ, 2007), 396.

56 On the Victorian city of London, see Walter Bagehot, *Lombard Street: A Description of the Money Market* (London, 1873).

57 John Darwin, *The Empire Project: The Rise and Fall of the British World-System, 1830–1970* (Cambridge, 2009); John Gallagher and Ronald Robinson, 'The Imperialism of Free Trade', *The Economic History Review* 6, no. 1 (1953): 1–15.

58 Cain and Hopkins, *British Imperialism, 1688–2000*, 671.

59 Darwin, *The Empire Project*, 115; Cain and Hopkins, *British Imperialism, 1688–2000*, 153.

60 Gary B. Magee and Andrew S. Thompson, *Empire and Globalisation: Networks of People, Goods, and Capital in the British World, c. 1850–1914* (Cambridge, 2010), 111;

James Belich, *Replenishing the Earth: The Settler Revolution and the Rise of the Anglo-World, 1783–1939* (Oxford, 2009), 58.

61 Darwin, *The Empire Project*, 116. For British investment by region, see Magee and Thompson, *Empire and Globalisation*, 171–3.

62 See especially John Darwin, *Unlocking the World: Port Cities and Globalization in the Age of Steam, 1830–1930* (London, 2020).

63 John Maynard Keynes, *The Economic Consequences of the Peace* (New York, 2007 [1919]), 6.

64 Howe, 'Free Trade and Global Order', 27.

65 Findlay and O'Rourke, *Power and Plenty*, 378–407.

66 Benjamin Disraeli, 'Conservative and Liberal Principles: Speech at Crystal Palace, June 24, 1872', in *Selected Speeches of the Late Right Honourable the Earl of Beaconsfield, Vol. II*, ed. T. E. Kebbel (London, 1882), 524, 530.

67 Andrew S. Thompson, 'Tariff Reform: An Imperial Strategy, 1903–1913', *The Historical Journal* 40, no. 4 (1997): 1033–54.

68 Alfred Milner, 'Tariff Reform', in *Constructive Imperialism* (London, 1908), 10, 12.

69 Bodleian Library, Oxford, James Bryce to Goldwin Smith (copy), 23 December 1905, MSS Bryce 17/193, and Goldwin Smith to James Bryce, 27 November 1900, MSS Bryce 16/146.

70 Ben Jackson, 'Socialism and the New Liberalism', in *Liberalism as Ideology: Essays in Honour of Michael Freeden*, ed. Ben Jackson and Marc Stears (Oxford, 2012), 34–52.

71 Darwin, *The Empire Project*, 115.

72 Cain and Hopkins, *British Imperialism, 1688–2000*, 671.

73 A. G. Hopkins, 'The United States, 1783–1861: Britain's Honorary Dominion?' *Britain and the World* 4, no. 2 (2011): 239; David Reynolds, 'American Globalism: Mass, Motion and the Multiplier Effect', in *Globalization in World History*, 247.

74 Belich, *Replenishing the Earth*, 480.

75 Sachs, *The Ages of Globalization*, 154.

76 Marc-William Palen, *The 'Conspiracy' of Free Trade: The Anglo-American Struggle Over Empire and Economic Globalisation, 1846–1896* (Cambridge, 2016).

77 Duncan Bell, *Dreamworlds of Race: Empire and the Utopian Destiny of Anglo-America* (Princeton, NJ, 2020); Kori Schake, *Safe Passage: The Transition from British to American Hegemony* (Cambridge, MA, 2017).

78 W. E. Gladstone, 'Kin Beyond Sea', *North American Review* 264 (September–October 1878): 179, 180–1.

79 For British liberal opposition to American empire, see Goldwin Smith, *Commonwealth or Empire: A Bystander's View of the Question* (London, 1902).

80 Bodleian Library, Oxford, George Parkin to Alfred Milner, 10 May 1898, MSS Milner, 206/328.

81 William Stubbs, *The Constitutional History of England in its Origin and Development* (Oxford, 1880).

82 Margaret MacMillan, *The War That Ended Peace: The Road to 1914* (New York: Random House, 2013), 56.

83 W. E. Gladstone, 'Germany, France, and England', *The Edinburgh Review* 132, no. 270 (1870): 587.

84 Ibid., 587–8.

85 Ibid., 591.

86 Paul Kennedy, *The Rise of the Anglo-German Antagonism, 1860–1914* (London, 1980), 46 (emphasis in the original).

87 Ibid., 49. 56.

88 Ibid., 292.

89 Ibid., 293–5.

90 Darwin, *The Empire Project*, 80–1.

91 John H. Maurer, 'Imperial Germany's Naval Challenge and the Renewal of British Power', in *British World Policy and the Projection of Global Power, c. 1830–1960*, ed. T. G. Otte (Cambridge, 2019), 149–50.

92 See especially David Morgan-Owen, *The Fear of Invasion: Strategy, Politics, and British War Planning, 1880–1914* (Oxford, 2017), 131–54.

93 Darwin, *The Empire Project*, 261–2.

94 Adam Tooze, *The Deluge: The Great War and the Remaking of Global Order, 1916–1931* (London, 2014).

95 David Hume, *An Enquiry Concerning Human Understanding* (Oxford, 2007 [1748]), 60.

96 Ibid., 120.

97 John Darwin, 'Afterword: History on a Global Scale', in *The Prospect of Global History*, ed. James Belich, John Darwin, Margret Frenz, and Chris Wickham (Oxford, 2016), 180.

98 For an illuminating comparison, see O'Brien and Cleese (eds), *Two Hegemonies*.

99 Ronald Hyam, 'The Primacy of Geopolitics: The Dynamics of British Imperial Policy, 1763–1963', *The Journal of Imperial and Commonwealth History* 27, no. 2 (1999): 27–52.

100 Eyck Freymann, *One Belt One Road: Chinese Power Meets the World* (Cambridge, MA, 2021); James T. Areddy, 'China Creates Its Own Digital Currency, a First for a Major Economy', *The Wall Street Journal*, 5 April 2021, https://www.wsj.com/articles/china-creates-its-own-digital-currency-a-first-for-major-economy-11617634118.

101 Kori Schake, 'Building a More Globalized Order', in *COVID-19 and World Order*, ed. Hal Brands and Francis J. Gavin (Baltimore, 2020), 333.

102 Margaret MacMillan, 'The Big Idea: Is World Government Possible?' *The Guardian*, 22 November 2021, https://www.theguardian.com/books/2021/nov/22/the-big-idea-is-world-government-possible.

103 Halford Mackinder, 'The Geographical Pivot of History', *The Geographical Journal* 23, no. 4 (1904): 422.

104 Joseph S. Nye, Jr., 'America's New Great Power Strategy', *Project Syndicate*, 3 August 2021, https://www.project-syndicate.org/commentary/us-china-new-great-power-strategy-by-joseph-s-nye-2021-08; Kevin Rudd, 'Short of War: How to Keep U.S.-Chinese Confrontation From Ending in Calamity', *Foreign Affairs* 100, no. 2 (2021): 58–72.

105 Darwin, *After Tamerlane*, 329.

6

Applying history to an anomalous historical case

The rise of China

Kori Schake

In their book *Thinking in Time*, Ernest May and Richard Neustadt caution about the seductiveness of the wrong analogy: 'in the United States, to an extraordinary degree, the national political agenda is a product of careless comparisons.'[1] Four such comparisons are shaping thinking about the challenge a rising China poses for the United States as the dominant power and of the international order it created. The first is that 'history shows' the dominant power will choose conflict rather than cede primacy. The second is that the United States is a hegemon like any other, rather than the architect of a different kind of order, more stable and supportable because of the rules it established and enforces. The third is that the United States is a declining power, over-extended in its security commitments in ways that sap the vitality of its economy. And the fourth is that China is inexorably rising. These presumptions are faulty analyses in themselves, and lead to faulty policy prescriptions.

I

James Field writes that in histories of American foreign policy, predictably the worst chapter is the period of the 1880s and 1890s. In his view (from 1978) those chapters uniformly characterize Americans of the imperial period as a departure from the country's virtuous past: 'unlike their ancestors, they were all racists and wanted battleships and naval bases.'[2] Field condemns the practice for 'the same insistence on seeing the past through the prism of the present, the same perceptions of false continuities and imputations of sin, and the same tendentious impact on generalization and abridgment.' And he challenges historians to 'escape the conventional formulations so uncritically and tediously passed from article to article, book to book, and text to text'.

It is a perennial challenge not to project contemporary attitudes, to instead understand the past on the terms people of the time lived it. As David McCullough cautioned, the fundamental thing to remember about writing history is that the people living it didn't know how it turned out.[3] Conjuring the sense of uncertainty, an awareness of contingency, is essential to writing history. Evolutionary biologist Stephen J. Gould captured the parallel challenge for his discipline: that we believe evolution is a straight line because we know the starting point and its conclusion, but that ignores both outliers in the data and that data points are decision points – they could have shifted the trajectory. For Gould, history 'revels in the torturous crookedness of real paths destined only for interesting ends'.[4]

Field is correct that much of the scholarship on the Spanish-American War of 1898 treats it as the debutante ball of America as a rising power, with Alfred Thayer Mahan, William Randolph Hearst and Teddy Roosevelt's Rough Riders stampeding the country to war and empire.[5] In actuality, Spanish atrocities – we get the term 'concentration camp' from the Spanish practice of 'reconcentrating' Cubans off their farms into prison camps, resulting in the death of a fourth of the population – motivated American religious and human rights communities into activism.[6] American government hesitance is manifest in President McKinley's declaration in December of 1897 that annexation of Cuba would be 'criminal aggression', and Congressional passage of the Teller Amendment in 1898 precluding annexation.[7] What we call the Spanish-American War was an ongoing insurrection in which the United States, with British assistance, reluctantly intervened to assist the success of indigenous people against Spanish colonial rule backed by Germany.[8]

McKinley's war declaration established temporary US control of Cuba, outlining the terms for reversion to Cuban control, but the United States quickly came to consider independence 'impracticable'.[9] President McKinley questioned whether the Cuban insurgency 'possesses beyond dispute the attributes of statehood', and worried about European countries taking over the newly liberated territories of Cuba and the Philippines. But the ease of Dewey's success also tempted McKinley to expand the political and military aims of the war.[10] The Philippine-American War that continued until Philippine independence in 1945 would prove more costly to the United States than had the war and brinksmanship against two of Europe's great powers, Spain and Germany, in 1898.

Holding the Philippines at risk was a tactic that burgeoned into America's longest-lasting imperial commitment. The United States opened a Pacific theatre of operations as a feint to tie down Spain's fleet there and to hold at risk Spain's Philippine colony. This Commodore Dewey achieved six weeks before the first US forces arrived in Cuba, defeating the Spanish fleet in a single engagement without losing a ship.[11]

But the Spanish-American War in the Pacific became a German-American confrontation. Germany supported Spain and sought to prevent US control over the Philippines. A German squadron of 5 vessels and 1,400 infantry sounded the harbour, violated Dewey's blockade regulations, moved to resupply Spanish forces aground and attempted a naval base at Subic Bay.[12] US forces had intelligence from Philippine rebels and assistance from Great Britain, though, and those elements produced Dewey's success – which Dewey acknowledged in his memoirs.[13]

Britain was officially neutral, but kept France and Italy sidelined, provided consular services to Americans in Spanish territories and intermediary negotiators for Spain's surrender of Manila, allowed Commodore Dewey to use the sole Pacific telegraph cable to communicate with Washington, averted their eyes from American espionage in Gibraltar and denied Spanish ships coaling stations. The Royal Navy loaned Commodore Dewey landing craft, sold him fuel and coaling ships, allowed the United States to search its ships and even impress its sailors.[14] During land operations, the British reinforced American forces from gunboats, and, in one particularly tense German-American stand-off in Manila Bay, sailed British ships into position to prevent the German fleet firing on the Americans without also committing an act of war against Great Britain.

This more contingent, complicated story of the Spanish-American War gives much more insight into the hegemonic transition from Great Britain to the United States. Britain didn't stifle American ascension to hegemony; it overtly assisted it. Because what allows for a peaceful transition from Britain as the dominant international power to conceding that role to the United States was a burgeoning sense of sameness between the two countries. The United States because of westward expansion had come to think of itself in imperial terms, and Britain had democratized. They looked similar to each other and different from other great powers: democratic, free-trading, naval powers that established and upheld international principles.

The British government encouraged the expansion of American obligations beyond America's borders because they believed the two countries' interests aligned, that an internationally engaged United States would shed its republican principles and converge on British policies. When the United States annexed the Philippines, the *London Times* considered the US 'allies united with us in the Far East by the most powerful bonds of common interest, we should regard very differently the acquisition of the archipelago by any other power'.[15]

Action by governments was buttressed by a reciprocal public sympathy – what was strategy for governments was sentiment for publics. Similarities of language, culture and civil society made sympathetic portrayals accessible to publics. The two countries saw themselves as advancing humanitarian rights and commercial openness. The *New York Times* editorialized in 1898, 'they and we are the joint representatives and guardians of a principle of government that no other nation even fully understands – the principle of orderly freedom'.[16] British poet laureate Alfred Austin captured the sentiment during the Spanish-American War with his poem 'A Voice from the West':

Tis a proud free people calling loud
To a people proud and free.

Convergence between Great Britain and the United States at the end of the nineteenth century was an extraordinary event, unique in the annals of hegemonic transition. Faced with not just one but three rising challengers, Britain attempted to ally with all three; when that proved impossible, it chose to facilitate American success, enacting policies that catapulted the United States into becoming a great power. At the zenith of British power, and in anticipation of being surpassed by the United States, there was a convergence of perspective between the two countries, recognized both by government policymakers and citizens. Britain had seen an emerging deficit of relative power and responded by fostering a relationship that with the affectionate bonds of civil society made cumulative power possible.[17]

II

If what makes the 1890s the worst chapter of many an American history is seeing the past through the prism of the present, contemporary studies of hegemonic power transition burden analysis with seeing the present through the prism of the past. The international order constructed by the United States and its allies in the ashen aftermath of the Second World War is so markedly different from that undertaken by any previous hegemon that it abjures comparison.

Architects of the American order created a system in which enemies were made to surrender but were rehabilitated into allies. As the commander of Allied forces in Europe described the distinction, 'we come as conquerors but not oppressors.'[18] That departure from victors' punitive policies created the possibility of a very different sort of peace, more stable for defanging the cycle of resentments, mutually beneficial to an extraordinary degree. The American order was constructed on consensual rules that less powerful allies also could influence the development and enforcement of, giving them an important stake in upholding the order, since any alternative would likely reduce their influence. The American order is largely voluntary, its magnetism encouraging contributions from lesser powers and driving down the cost to the United States of sustaining it. American security 'guarantees' (for they are contingent) are widely extended to reduce regional arms races, constrain allies' choices and foster regional cooperation, further stabilizing the order.[19]

The American order extends beyond security, incorporating mutually reinforcing political, economic, diplomatic, intelligence and cultural benefits to participating states. American aid was dispensed to cajole governments away from communism, intelligence operations sustaining opposition parties and publications, democratic countries were preferenced for political attention, those with closest bonds were allowed to participate in deep intelligence sharing, stability was increased by embedding cooperation into international institutions.

And then there are nuclear weapons, which have made war so catastrophically damaging among great powers that it seems to have stabilized the relationships, preventing war between nuclear-armed states. Dwight Eisenhower, the first American president to grapple with the role of nuclear weapons in strategy, believed nuclear weapons would produce a 'stability of the stalemate' between the United States and Soviet Union, wherein neither would challenge each other's central security interests and wars would migrate to the periphery of their interests.[20] Granted, it took fifteen years of crises between the Soviet Union and United States to delineate the boundaries of each other's central security interests, and proxy wars shifted the burden of violence to states least able to shield themselves from great power interference. But nuclear weapons seem to engender among great powers what arborists term crown shyness – a reticence to grow into each other's space. 'Seem' because the data is still sparse, with only nine countries of 195 known to constitute possessor states.

These elements constitute what policy practitioners infelicitiously term the liberal international order or the rules-based international order. Rules-based is insufficiently descriptive, since illiberal orders also have rules; they are typically variants of might making right and to the victor go the spoils. The American order was conceived to be liberal in the philosophical rather than political sense: an order that creates free societies by dispensing the advantages of political attention from the dominant power to mediate disputes, giving the less powerful means to attain their interests by peaceful interaction, advancing prosperity through opening markets and establishing the transparent rule of law.

The order is built on the philosophy that states with governments representative of popular will are more peaceful and prosperous than the alternative, a Hegelian article of faith currently being tested by intolerant populism in many democratic countries, including the United States. Hegel believed that as people became more prosperous, they became more demanding political consumers, and that drove ineluctably towards democracy. Francis Fukuyama in his oft-derided but seldom read *The End of History and the Last Man* correctly anticipated the challenge of bored beneficiaries of the liberal order corroding it.[21] Nonetheless, advocates of the American-led order had previously considered democratic Serbia an outlier in its virulence rather than a challenge to the belief that democracies moderate aggression. As backsliding becomes more prevalent in both newly transitioned democracies (like Hungary and Poland) and long-established democracies like the United States, it poses a challenge to Hegel's notion of linear progress.

But it is the rise of a domestically repressive and internationally aggressive China that most challenges the existing order. Fukuyama was not ignorant of the potential problems of rising authoritarians, but believed 'the end-point of mankind's ideological evolution and the universalization of Western liberal democracy as the final form of human government'.[22] As Azar Gat argues, 'the current predominance of democracy could be far less secure', both because of the prosperity China has experienced since embracing capitalism, and the repressive ideology it is fostering internationally.[23]

The application of a 'Thucydides trap' to the risks of war between China and the United States are among the worst chapters of contemporary studies of hegemonic power transition. As Sir Lawrence Freedman summarized the application in a scorching review of the most popularized version, the framework relies on a faulty reading of Thucydides, unilluminating case studies, exclusion of the important regional dynamics and policy recommendations recycled from other contexts not because most applicable to this circumstance, but because simply preferential.[24]

Thucydides doesn't offer just one explanation for the Peloponnesian Wars. As Neustadt and May write, 'almost any reader sees his own period foreshadowed'.[25] While Thucydides does say, 'It was the rise of Athens and the fear that this instilled in Sparta that made war inevitable', the story he tells does not validate his conclusion. Thucydides describes the Spartans as 'always slow to go to war unless they were in necessity, and at that time they were also hampered by wars at home; until the Athenians' power grew considerably and started harming their alliance. They then felt that they could not postpone it'.[26]

In fact, a better reading of Thucydides's main argument is that preserving the freedom of its allies that were being threatened by Athens was the cause of war. Thucydides's Sparta is an unobtrusive hegemon, but Athens revels in the threats it poses to Spartan allies, rejecting any sense of justice in the actions of states. Rising Athens is the threat to the international order, not a declining Sparta. Sparta is not being directly threatened; it is weaker Spartan allies at risk, and therefore the international order disrupted by Athens's intimidation and demands. To the extent there is a Thucydides 'trap' consonant to the United States and China's circumstances, it is allies calling in a hegemon's security guarantees when threatened by an aggressive rising power. So when China embraces the notion of a Thucydides trap, they are embracing the Athenian claim that 'it has always been the law that the weaker should be subject to the stronger', a refutation of the consensual nature of American hegemony.

But as Donald Kagan has argued, the main thrust of Thucydides's argument in *The Peloponnesian Wars* is that wars result not from some mechanistic 'trap' but from human choice.[27] Thucydides writes that

> nobody is driven to war out of ignorance of its consequences and nobody is deterred by fear, if he believes he will gain more. [War] erupts when one considers that the expected gains are to be greater than the risks, and the other is determined to face the risks rather than tolerate any direct damage to its interests.[28]

Kagan is sympathetic to the policy difficulties posed by the circumstances facing both Athens and Sparta to war. But both Athens and Sparta are in thrall to the destructive rise of populists, and they choose war. In both polities, the ruling elites offer moderate counsels of restraint; both vibrant societies are brought to ruin by angry or enervated publics who ignore the moderating counsel of seasoned, educated elites.[29] Thucydides's Sparta is goaded into war by an elected leader, not their King; likewise Athens's Pericles, another elected official, who is the motive force in Athens's path to war, with an even more reckless set of demagogues coming to power after Pericles's death.

Graham Allison's characterization of a 'trap' conveys inevitability his own curated case studies do not bear out: of sixteen case studies of ostensible hegemonic transitions, only twelve resulted in war.[30] Moreover, the case selection is methodologically problematic; for example, it counts as a hegemonic transition the dissipation of German power by Britain and France in post–Second World War Europe, when all three were middle powers under the cooperation-inducing protection of the actual hegemon, the United States.

The idea of a Thucydides trap is a misreading of *The Peloponnesian Wars*. There is no mechanistic risk of war due to a rising power challenging the alliance commitments of a hegemon. There does appear to be a parallel between the aggressiveness of Athens challenging the international order Sparta had established and China challenging the current international order. And the ideological difference between China and the United States doesn't portend a peaceful assistance to common purpose the way Britain anticipated in ceding hegemony to the United States. But there are also so many important differences: the existence of nuclear weapons providing magnitudes of destruction that call into question whether purposes of war can be attained between nuclear powers, the depth of economic interconnectedness among all potential parties to the conflict, the stickiness of ideological commitment by democratic states making defection more difficult, the investiture smaller and middle powers have in the current order. Contorting Thucydides into a deterministic 'trap' obscures, rather than enlightens, the geopolitical dynamic at work in China's challenge to the American-dominated international order.

III

Another worst chapter of an excellent book is the conclusion from Paul Kennedy's *The Rise and Fall of Great Powers*. It is titled 'The United States: The Problem of Number One in Decline' and argues that the United States in 1989 suffered from 'overstretch', committing too large a share of its GDP to military obligations that would inevitably sap the vitality of its economy and cause its decline.[31] Kennedy considers differential economic growth rates, technological advances and military developments to demonstrate the oscillation of hegemony. His argument is powerfully descriptive but only calculable retrospectively. It is difficult using Kennedy's framework to determine when the hegemon will cease to be dominant. While Kennedy does a much more rigorous job of assessing differences from historical example than does Allison, there is an almost deterministic economics to his argument:

> It has been a common dilemma facing previous 'number-one' countries that even as their relative economic strength is ebbing the growing foreign challenges to their position have compelled them to allocate more and more of their resources into the military sector, which in turn squeezes out productive investment and, over time, leads to the downward spiral of slower growth, heavier taxes, deepening domestic splits over spending priorities, and a weakening capacity to bear the burdens of defense.[32]

Kennedy measures the decline of American economic power from 1945, but surely that artificially inflates US dominance, given the abject destruction of all other major powers. It also doesn't explain the stability of US share in global GDP for the past fifty years at about 20 per cent of global production. And his calculations of the insupportability of military spending don't anticipate the easily shoulderable roughly 4 per cent that has become the post–Cold War norm for US defence spending. The rates of defence spending and economic growth are not interactive as he suggests when the percentage of GDP allotted to defence is that low and the economy remains vibrantly dynamic.

Wars the United States elected to fight since 2001 give some credence to Kennedy's argument; the profligacy with which the United States chooses to use military force and the funding allocated to the range of foreign policy tools tilting so heavily towards military elements is consistent with the momentum of great powers towards decline. But the American economy has proven remarkably resilient compared to the competition; and as Kennedy himself argues, it's relative not absolute power that matters. Kennedy acknowledges that nuclear weapons may profoundly change the nature of conflict in the international order but does not credit their effect with producing stable great power relations; he considers just as likely catastrophically destructive wars among great powers utilizing only conventional weapons, which would sustain the connection between defence spending and economic drag. Kennedy may nonetheless prove right about the weakening capacity to bear the burdens of defence, as the result of domestic social welfare entitlements or challenges going unanswered to allies with lesser claims on American affinities and interests than have been European claims.

The major objection to Kennedy's 'The Problem of Number One in Decline' is less about Kennedy's strategic thinking and proof, than resentment at the burgeoning field of declinism his work unleashed among lesser scholars and political commentators.[33] The worst offenders lack a sense of historical perspective, imagining a mythical past in which US power was uncontested, other economies remained permanently hobbled by war or malevolent economic practices, allies were uncomplainingly compliant, America had no social divisions and was led by statesmen untainted and unimpinged by the grubbiness of domestic politics.

And yet, despite all its disputatiousness and difficulty, American power, and the American economy, are remarkably resilient. Seven of the ten most valuable companies in the world are American, as are twelve of the top twenty technology firms; US capital markets are extraordinarily deep, its universities world-leading, its innovation and investment ecosystems wildly dynamic, and its ability unmatched to draw the world's talent as immigrants.[34] American manufacturing, frequently cited as the harbinger of broader economic decline, is experiencing a renaissance.[35]

As tendentious as some of the arguments about decline are, they are an important antidote to the triumphalism of particularly the interregnum between the 1991 and the 2003 Gulf Wars and the vacuousness of political arguments about American exceptionalism. They spur a particular American insecurity that leads to revival. Journalist James Fallows perfectly captured the dynamic on the rise of China and American decline when returning to the United States after posted in China for five years. Fallows argues there is a peculiarly American cycle of crisis and renewal, 'the bracing "jeremiad" tradition of harsh warnings' that reveal a faith that America can be better than it is 'in spurring American improvement to both its domestic and international policies'.[36]

In light of Fallows's argument, declarations that the United States is more dominant than any hegemon in history or that the American military is the most powerful in the history of the world should be heard as worrisome indications of political and institutional dry rot. And the slow meshing of governmental gears to acknowledge China's threat, the beginning of a successful recalibration of American efforts to advantage.

American decline is a favourite theme of Chinese government officials. President Xi himself is fond of saying, 'the East is rising and the west is declining'.[37] It also seems to be a – and perhaps the – driving force behind China discarding its policy of biding its time and hiding its light, replacing it with a much more aggressive push to displace US dominance.[38] The theory tracks with China's increasingly assertive behaviour since the 2008 financial crisis, their increasing intimidation of countries in Asia and beyond, and their overt attempts to corrupt international institutions to their sole advantage.

IV

China's spectacular economic transformation since 1978 is one of the marvels of the modern world, something the World Bank has described as 'the fastest sustained expansion by a major economy in history'. Deng Xiaoping opening the economy to capitalism fostered an increase in per capita GDP from $184 in 1979 to $10,217 in 2019.[39] Within the span of less than two generations, China has increased its peoples' wealth by more than fifty-five times, lifting hundreds of millions of people out of poverty. It has become the world's second largest economy, its largest manufacturer, a major draw of foreign investment as well as source of outbound investment.[40] It has an ambitious 'Made in China 2025' plan to push progress in key sectors of the economy, and an ambitious Belt and Road Initiative to siphon excess domestic capital out of the banking system by investing in infrastructure development designed to shift the patterns of international trade China-centric. Its policymakers are often described in the West as ruthlessly brilliant, able to think in terms of centuries and make investments the messy politics of free societies would preclude.[41]

However, China is still a poor country by Western standards: its per capita GDP ranks only commensurate with Mexico's, and less than that of Malaysia, Russia, Romania or Chile. Chinese premier Li Kequiang stated recently that 600 million Chinese still live on $140 or less per month.[42] It is the world's manufacturing hub because of low wages and high tolerance for polluting industry. Its economy has now potentially caught in a pincer between reaching the stage of developed competition with German Mittlestand while being priced out of cheap manufacturing by Vietnam, Mexico and other low-cost workforces. Pollution, industrial overcapacity, an opaque and possibly unstable banking system, misallocation of capital in the financial system and conclusion of rural to urban migration are all pressures on continued growth. Elizabeth Economy concludes, 'as Xi seeks to bolster indigenous innovation and domestic consumption, his success depends on the intellectual and economic support of the very constituencies his policies are disenfranchising.'[43]

And that is even before attention to the potential for civil and political unrest due to collapse of the prosperity for docility Communist Party bargain, corruption, governmental cruelty or incompetence. China spends more on domestic security than it does on its military.[44] We in the West may no longer believe our values are universal, but Xi Jinping surely does, otherwise why construct so elaborate a social surveillance and control network? The creativity that fuels advanced economies is unlikely to survive such repression, as may already be evidenced by more than a third of China's millionaires seeking to emigrate (and the United States tops the list of preferred destinations).[45] So many more are attempting to move their money out of the country that the government instituted preventions.[46]

Navigating the middle-income trap stalls most developing economies, necessitating as it does generating domestic demand, finding new markets and developing innovations to increase productivity. China is still juicing its growth by investment. It has stopped and in many cases reversed the market reforms that generated its economic growth.[47] China's working-age population has been declining since 2012, and demography is becoming a tight constraint, one China's politics won't get around by immigration. Its government statistics on everything from GDP growth to Covid-19 infections are easily to repudiate.[48]

Its debt to GDP ratio is 280 per cent, leaping more than 25 per cent in the past year; surpassing 100 per cent is a generally accepted threshold for unrecoverability of economic solvency – beyond a debt to GDP ratio of one, debt becomes such a drag on growth that states cannot expand their way out of the debt problem.[49] Nor is China becoming more productive or raising its prospects for further prosperity, as the World Economic Forum Competitiveness Report shows (by comparison, the United States ranks first in prospects for additional growth).[50] Michael Beckley's research demonstrates that 'the United States is several times wealthier than China, and the gap appears to be growing by trillions of dollars every year.'[51]

China stalling portends a different and possibly even bigger problem than the problem posed by a rising China. The Chinese government has concocted a dangerous combination of stagnating economic success, centralized political control verging on cultish veneration, militarization of foreign policy and grievance of affronted cultural superiority. Frighteningly, the right historical parallel to contemporary China may well be Imperial Japan in the twentieth century.

If that is the China the world is looking at, the West doesn't have a 2035 China problem (which is the timeline most US policymakers are planning towards); it has a 2025 China problem. This, too, is consistent with China's increasingly aggressive behaviour: one theory is that China believes the United States is too weak to resist it and so is moving fast to change the order; a second theory is that China knows it is weakening and is attempting to secure gains while its chimera of dominance lasts. Mobilizing the West's own societies may be the biggest challenge, especially in the near term. Many of its leading countries are indulging solipsistic paroxysms.

V

China's patterns of behaviour in the past decade or so have grown increasingly repressive domestically and aggressive internationally. It has a million Uighur in 'reeducation' camps under implausible terrorism charges. It continues to attempt to erase Uighur and Tibetan culture. It violated its treaty obligations to respect for twenty-five years the autonomy of Hong Kong, and has arrested thousands of democracy protesters and journalists. It is forcing successful CEOs like Jack Ma and Simon Hu out of their companies, casting a pall over its most innovative champions.

The CCP undercuts its strategy of dominating international organizations by ignoring the Permanent Court of Arbitration finding against its incursions into Philippine waters, and kidnapping its own head of the Interpol policing agency. The

Belt and Road Initiative has made it the world's largest lender, of loans for fixed objects that are unlikely to ever be profitable, and already repossessed the Hambantota port in Sri Lanka.[52] It created monopoly control of rare earths and then used that advantage punitively in a minor fishing dispute with Japan in 2010. Its diplomacy is crudely threatening, and insensate to its negative consequences.

Its military is operationally provocative, wilfully endangering freedom of navigation and utilizing putatively civilian fishing fleets in violation of China's obligations under the UN Convention on the Law of the Sea. In 1989 Paul Kennedy commended China's approach to preserving its long-term growth prospects, but China is no longer 'struggling to avoid an excessive investment in military spending', instead is increasing its nuclear weapons stockpile, building the world's largest navy, deploying tens of thousands of missiles in the Taiwan Straits, developing 'carrier killer' missiles to target US ships and spending nearly what the United States does on its military.[53]

The worrisome changes in China's patterns of behaviour in the past decade do seem to have activated antibodies against its continued rise. American policy since the Clinton administration in the late 1990s had been to welcome China's rise as a 'responsible stakeholder' in the international order, allowing it preferential admission into the World Trade Organization and encouraging economic intermixing of supply chains, production and ownership.[54] Gradually, from the George W. Bush administration determining to equalize the Atlantic and Pacific fleets, through the Obama administration's 'pivot to the Pacific', to the Trump administration's trumpeting the return to great power competition, to the Biden administration describing China as 'the pacing threat', US policy has converged on a much more exclusionary policy.

Xi Jinping having committed to President Obama at their 2015 summit not to militarize the islands China was constructing in the South China Sea and then clearly doing so became widely accepted in Washington as a demonstration of both bad faith negotiation and damaging intent by China.[55] But while Washington has a hostile view, Wall Street does not – it views China as an investment bonanza, one of the few places for expanding sales of investment vehicles due to the weak government social welfare net and high propensity for personal savings.[56] Ray Dalio, the admired founder of investment firm Bridgewater, has argued that

> The US and China are also competing fiercely – some say warring – over trade, technology, geopolitics, capital markets and military power. No one can know how bad these wars will be, which country will win, or how. That is why I diversify and allocate money to both countries.[57]

Whether the US government continues to permit the free flow of capital into China is a risk Mr Dalio appears to be underweighting in his investment portfolio. Wall Street is already pretty unpopular among Americans; corporations publicly equivocating about which side of an ideological fight they are on is unlikely to be a political winner. Congress has already prohibited investments in companies with connections to the Chinese military, forbade investment by Chinese in American technology firms or purchase of components for US government computer networks from Chinese suppliers. American tech companies are also feeling pressure about complying with

Chinese surveillance laws, journalists digging out which companies sell components for it and boards of directors getting nervous about the public relations and profitability of doing business in China. Chinese espionage and cyberattacks are so pervasive in American networks that a 'splinternet' could soon replace the internet. Bifurcation of supply chains is likely for national security-related components, as well as redundancy in other national suppliers of all production.

Nor is the United States alone in those concerns. Debate over 5G networks is illustrative of the dynamic China has set off. Its clandestine attempts to mobilize Chinese Australians against the government, bribe legislators and infiltrate Australia's computer networks led Australia to be the first country to deny incorporation of Huawei components into its system. The Trump administration loudly demanded all America's allies forswear Huawei components, even threatening to exclude from intelligence sharing with the United States countries that did not. Britain initially insisted (over the objections of its national security cabinet members) it could manage the exposure, but as relations with China soured, it reconsidered and matched Australia's policy. Even Germany, the ally most pliant on commercial grounds, appears to be taking a neutral policy that will result in no Huawei components.

Needless to say, the realignment has less to do with Trump administration alliance management than with Chinese malevolent behaviour. India is a particularly interesting case of realignment. Traditionally non-aligned, sceptical of US intentions, China has shoved India into active defence cooperation with the United States, Japan and Australia in a Quadrilateral cooperative grouping. The United States cajoled ineffectively for years, but China's unrepentant attacks on Indian territory in the Himalayas and designs on the Sri Lankan Hambantota port have changed Indian policy.

Japan is the other particularly interesting case, dating back twenty years. Prime Minister Koizumi sought to reposition Japan as a security contributor internationally, participating in the war in Afghanistan (refuelling coalition ships) and relaxing defence spending constraints. As China has become more dangerous, Japanese governments have become incredibly creative, partnering with India on an investment fund to compete with China's Belt and Road by providing transparent contracts with ecological and labour protections, partnering with Australia to develop secure supply chains, cascading Coast Guard ships and training to regional countries like Malaysia so they can better patrol their national waters to prevent Chinese incursions. It's an elegant way to improve regional resistance to Chinese influence.

It will take an enormous amount of activism and cooperation by countries in Asia and beyond to prevent China from asserting its will to change the current patterns and structure of the international order. The United States is doing a reasonable job providing military security to bolster countries against Chinese influence. But as Paul Kennedy cautions in *The Rise and Fall of Great Powers*, 'the history of the past five hundred years of international rivalry demonstrates that military 'security' alone is never enough.'[58] Both the Trump and now the Biden administrations' doctrinal opposition to multilateral trade pacts severely limits their ability to align countries to US intentions, because for most countries, China is more an economic opportunity than a security threat.

The United States and other Western countries will need to dramatically improve their societal resilience against China co-opting elites, using ethnic and social cleavages to mobilize friction, luring Western investors and businesses into funding its repression and supporting Chinese standard-setting. But Western societies are capable of those things and appear to be slowly mobilizing towards the societal consensus that makes international commitments by democracies so durable.

The United States is a different kind of hegemon, and it created a different kind of international order. China, by contrast, is a much more traditional great power and wants to re-shape the international order as a macrocosm of its repressive domestic political order. The hegemonic transition from Britain to the United States was peaceful because of the ideological similarities between those countries at the end of the nineteenth century; China and the United States bear no such similarities. But the United States is not weakening, and China is not strengthening as much as advertised. And other beneficiaries of the current order are aligning to support it, constraining China's ability to continue rising without moderating its policies. Hegel may yet be proven right that a state cannot remain prosperous without political liberalization.

Notes

1 Richard E. Neustadt and Ernest R. May, *Thinking in Time: The Uses of History for Decision Makers* (New York, 1986), 58.

2 James A. Field, Jr., 'American Imperialism: The Worst Chapter in Almost Any Book', *The American Historical Review* 83, no. 3 (1978): 644.

3 David McCullough, Speech to the Hoover Institution Summer 1006 Board of Overseers Meeting (https://www.hoover.org/news/summer-2006-board-overseers -meeting).

4 Stephen J. Gould, *Wonderful Life: The Burgess Shale and the Nature of History* (New York, 1990), 15.

5 The simile is mine, *Safe Passage: the Transition from British to American Hegemony* (Cambridge, MA, 2016), 12. Goran Rystad, *Ambiguous Imperialism* (Lund, 1975) is an excellent guide to the literature.

6 John L. Offner, 'McKinley and the Spanish-American War', *Presidential Studies Quarterly* 34, no. 1 (2004): 51.

7 President William McKinley, *War Message, U.S., Department of State, Papers Relating to Foreign Affairs* (Washington, 1898), 750–60, https://www.mtholyoke.edu/acad/ intrel/mkinly2.htm.

8 Hugh DeSantis, 'The Imperialist Impulse and American Innocence, 1865–1900', in *American Foreign Relations: A Historiographical Review*, ed. Gerald K. Haines and J. Samuel Walker (Westport, CT, 1981), 65–90; Edward P. Crapol, 'Coming to Terms with Empire: The Historiography of Late-Nineteenth- Century American Foreign Relations', *Diplomatic History* 16 (1992): 573–97; Field, 'American Imperialism', 644–68.

9 McKinley, *War Message*.

10 Graham Cosmas, *An Army for Empire: The United States Army in the Spanish-American War* (New York, 1994), 110. Gardner, LaFeber and McCormick believe the McKinley administration having drawn up contingency plans for despatch of 20,000

troops to Manila in advance of the war constitutes an intention to have occupied the Philippines. LaFeber Gardner and Thomas J. McCormick, *The Creation of the American Empire: US Diplomatic History since 1883* (New York, 1976), 256.

11   Field, 'American Imperialism', 665.

12   Walter F. Bell, 'Great Britain: Policies and Reactions to the Spanish-American War', in *The Encyclopedia of the Spanish-American and Philippine-American Wars: A Political, Social, and Military History*, vol. 1, *A–L*, ed. Spencer Tucker (Santa Barbara, CA, 2009), 258. It should be noted that Bell believes Dewey and others overstate the importance of British assistance at Manila Bay.

13   George Dewey, *Autobiography of James Dewey* (New York, 1913), 266.

14   Donald M. Seekins, 'Historical Setting—Outbreak of War, 1898', in *Philippines: A Country Study*, ed. Ronald E. Dolan (Washington, DC, 1991), 22–7. Dino Buenviaje, 'Great Britain', in *The Encyclopedia of the Spanish-American and Philippine-American Wars* (New York, 2009), 255–6.

15   Charles A. Kupchan, *How Enemies Become Friends: The Sources of Stable Peace* (Princeton, NJ, 2010), 83.

16   *New York Times*, late September 1898, quoted in Bertha Ann Reuter, *Anglo-American Relations in the Spanish-American War* (New York, 1924), 113.

17   I'm grateful to Harvard University Press for allowing me permission to draw on chapter 8 of *Safe Passage* for this account.

18   General Dwight Eisenhower, photograph number 26311, U.S. Holocaust Museum, https://collections.ushmm.org/search/catalog/pa1086512.

19   G. John Ikenberry, *Liberal Leviathan* (Princeton, NJ, 2011).

20   Memorandum of Discussion at the 320th Meeting of the National Security Council, 17 April 1957, *Foreign Relations of the United States 1955–1957*, XIX, 482.

21   Francis Fukuyama, *The End of History and the Last Man* (New York, 1992), 328.

22   Francis Fukuyama, 'The End of History?' *The National Interest* 16 (1989): 3–18.

23   Azar Gat, 'The Return of Authoritarian Great Powers', *Foreign Affairs*, July/August 2007.

24   Sir Lawrence Freedman, book review, 'Destined for War: Can America and China Escape Thucydides's Trap?', *Prism* 7, no. 1 (2017).

25   Neustadt and May, *Thinking in Time*, 265.

26   Thucydides, *The Peloponnesian War*, trans. Ilias Kouskouvelis (Chicago, 1989), 1.118.2.

27   Donald Kagan, *The Outbreak of the Peloponnesian War* (London, 1969), 356.

28   Thucydides, *The Peloponnesian War*, 4.59.2. Ilias Kouskouvelis, 'The Thucydides Trap: A Distorted Compass', *E-International Relations*, 5 November 2017, https://www.e-ir.info/2017/11/05/the-thucydides-trap-a-distorted-compass/#_ednref10.

29   Kori Schake, 'The Summer of Misreading Thucydides', *The Atlantic*, 18 July 2017.

30   Belfer Center Special Initiative, Thucydides Trap, https://www.belfercenter.org/thucydides-trap/overview-thucydides-trap.

31   Paul Kennedy, *The Rise and Fall of the Great Powers: Economic Change and Military Conflict from 1500 to 2000* (New York, 1989), 532.

32   Ibid., 533.

33   See, for example, Charles Krauthammer, 'The Unipolar Moment', *Foreign Affairs* 70, no. 1 (1990/91): 23–33; Christopher Layne, 'The Unipolar Illusion: Why New Great Powers Will Rise', *International Security* 17, no. 4 (1993): 5–51; Kenneth N. Waltz, 'The Emerging Structure of International Politics', *International Security* 18, no. 2 (1993): 44–79; Kishore Mahbubani, *The New Asian Hemisphere: The Irresistible Shift*

of Global Power to the East (New York, 2009); Parag Khanna, *The Second World: How Emerging Powers Are Redefining Global Competition in the Twenty-First Century* (New York, 2009); Thomas L. Friedman and Michael Mandelbaum, *That Used to Be Us: How America Fell Behind in the World It Invented and How We Can Come Back* (New York, 2011); Arvind Subramanian, *Eclipse: Living in the Shadow of China's Economic Dominance* (Washington, DC, 2011); Edward Luce, *Time to Start Thinking: America in the Age of Descent* (New York, 2012); Amitav Acharya, *The End of American World Order* (New York, 2014); Gideon Rachman, *Easternization: Asia's Rise and America's Decline from Obama to Trump and Beyond* (New York, 2017); and Christopher Layne, 'The U.S.-Chinese Power Shift and the End of Pax Americana', *International Affairs* 94, no. 1 (2018): 89–111.

34 Martin Wolfe, 'China is Wrong to Think the US Faces Inevitable Decline', *Financial Times*, 27 April 2021.

35 Michael Prowse, 'Is America In Decline?' *Harvard Business Review*, July-August 1992.

36 James Fallows, 'How America Can Rise Again', *The Atlantic,* January/February 2010.

37 Chinese President Xi Jing Ping, quoted in Chris Buckley, '"The East Is Rising": Xi Maps Out China's Post-Covid Ascent', *New York Times*, 3 March 2021.

38 Jude Blanchette, *China's New Red Guards: The Return of Radicalism and the Rebirth of Mao Zedong* (Oxford, 2019).

39 World Bank national accounts data, and OECD National Accounts data files, https://data.worldbank.org/indicator/NY.GDP.PCAP.CD?locations=CN.

40 Congressional Research Service, *China's Economic Rise: History, Trends, Challenges, and Implications for the United States, 12 July 2006–25 June 2019* (RL33534).

41 Michael Pillsbury, *The Hundred-year Marathon: China's Secret Strategy to Replace America as the Global Superpower* (New York, 2016).

42 Sun Yu, 'China Faces Outcry after Premier Admits 40% of Population Struggles', *Financial Times*, 10 June 2020.

43 Elizabeth Economy, 'China's Inconvenient Truth: Official Triumphalism Conceals Societal Fragmentation', *Foreign Affairs*, 20 May 2021.

44 Josh Chin, 'China Spends More on Domestic Security as Xi's Powers Grow', *Wall Street Journal,* 6 March 2018.

45 Robert Frank, 'More Than a Third of Chinese Millionaires Want to Leave China, here's Where They Want to Go', *CNBC*, 5 July 2018.

46 Yusho Cho, 'China's Rich Seek Ways to Move Cash Abroad before Yuan Weakens', *Nikkei Asia*, 14 June 2020.

47 Derek Scissors, 'Now or Never for the Chinese Economy', *Policy* 34, no. 1 (Autumn 2018): 34–42.

48 Scott N. Romaniuk and Tobias Burgers, 'Can China's COVID-19 Statistics Be Trusted?' *The Diplomat*, 26 March 2020.

49 Bank of Finland Institute for Emerging Economies, Chinese debt-to-GDP ratio approaches 300 %, 29 January 2021, https://www.bofit.fi/en/monitoring/weekly/2021/vw202104_3/. For the 100% threshold, see Carmen Reinhardt and Kenneth Rogoff, *This Time Is Different: Eight Centuries of Financial Folly* (Princeton, NJ, 2009).

50 World Economic Forum, *The Global Competitiveness Report, 2016–2017*, September 2016.

51 Michael Beckley, 'China's Economy is Not Overtaking America's', *Journal of Applied Corporate Finance* 32 (Spring 2020): 10–23.

52 Bretton Woods lenders and other countries wouldn't issue loans for BRI projects because the economic calculations showing their eventual profitability were so

suspect. S. J. Vijay Kumar, 'TN Police on High Alert After Sri Lanka Passes Law on China-Backed Colombo Port City', *The Hindu*, 30 May 2021.

53 Kennedy, *The Rise and Fall of the Great Powers*, 539. For China's military build up, see *Military and Security Developments Involving the People's Republic of China* (U.S. Department of Defense, 2020). For calculations on Chinese defence spending, see William Greenwalt, 'China Already Outspends US Military? Discuss', *Breaking Defense*, 26 May 2021.

54 The term comes from Deputy Secretary of State Robert Zoellick's speech 'Whither China: From Membership to Responsibility?' 21 September 2005; but the policy predates the term by nearly a decade.

55 David Brunnstrom and Michael Martina, 'Xi Denies China Turning Artificial Islands into Military Bases', *Reuters*, 25 September 2018.

56 'Wall Street Keeps Pushing Into China as Washington Balks', *Bloomberg*, 20 December 2020.

57 Ray Dalio, 'Don't be Blind to China's Rise in a Changing World', *Financial Times*, 23 October 2020.

58 Kennedy, *The Rise and Fall of the Great Powers*, 539.

7

Nation-Building as Applied History

Lessons from the United States in Afghanistan

Jeremi Suri

For twenty years, the United States fought a ground war in Afghanistan – the longest war in American history. Few of the battles matched the traditional image of soldiers and armaments assembled on opposite sides of a battlefield. Few of the engagements ended in a clear victory or defeat for the United States, or its many adversaries.

The surprising part of the most recent Afghanistan War was not its length and indeterminate results, but how unexpected these phenomena were, especially for policy planners and political pundits. One of the most common misconceptions – rooted in a combination of historical ignorance and political hubris – is that strong powers can impose their will on weaker societies. The historical record clearly shows that local insurgencies often have deep and resilient reservoirs of resistance. They are very difficult to stamp out.[1] They are also too weak to achieve their aims against a powerful foreign force. Insurgencies tend to linger and bleed an occupying power, but they rarely take control of a conflict zone while foreign armies remain in place. More often than not, insurgent resistance undermines political order without replacing it. Insurgents are spoilers, not substitutes for the dominant force. Intervening foreign powers are not destined to fail; they are likely to exert important influence, but at enormous cost and with mixed results.[2]

Afghanistan is a revealing historical case. Warfare in this forbidding terrain was never about decisive 'victory' or 'success'. The mountainous and intemperate landscape, the complex mix of ethnicities and the surrounding presence of interfering groups make it almost impossible to achieve clear and consistent goals. Fragmentation and contradiction are the historical norm in Afghanistan and many other sites of foreign intervention. The experiences of the United States in Central Asia during the last two decades are instructive about what nation-building will continue to mean, in practice, when strong powers intervene abroad in coming years.[3]

I

Although often asserted by pundits, Afghanistan is not a 'graveyard' for foreign armies. The historical record shows that external actors – Islamic, Persian, British, Russian and

American – have been able to achieve limited aims in this territory. Each managed to police relatively secure borders in different time periods, and each conducted a series of profitable relationships with local tribal leaders. Tragedy for the external actors in Afghanistan came, time and again, when foreigners sought to turn access and influence into direct control. The costs of governing Afghanistan from afar are too great for any foreign power, including the United States, to bear.[4]

American policymakers appeared to have an instinctive understanding of this dynamic during the Cold War. Although Washington invested in a series of expensive development projects that produced very mixed results, the United States pursued modest objectives, including the maintenance of basic regional stability, peace between ethnic groups and protection of trade routes. The United States even accepted a large Soviet political and economic presence in the northern half of the country. Washington and Moscow pursued a balanced set of interests in Afghanistan, and they avoided the extended military conflict evident around Korea, Indochina and other Cold War battlefields.[5]

The communist-supported coup in Afghanistan in 1973, followed by another coup in 1978 and the Soviet invasion a year later, destroyed this balance. Fearing a loss of influence and ambitious to exert more direct control, Moscow sought to dominate its southern neighbour as it had not before. This effort united local groups and other regional powers, including the United States, to combat Soviet power. The Soviet Union quickly found itself fighting to defend a small and isolated regime, with a large, organized and popular international opposition. The problem was not the Soviet effort to exert influence, but Moscow's excessive ambitions, as well as its heavy-handed and unsustainable actions.[6]

After the 11 September 2001 attacks on the United States, President George W. Bush sought to expand American military and political influence in Afghanistan, for the purpose of defeating Al Qaeda, and overthrowing the Taliban regime that had given Al Qaeda support. This was a difficult, but feasible, agenda for the United States, given its technological capabilities and its unified public determination following the terror strikes on New York and Washington DC. Military operations in Afghanistan at the end of 2001 were effective because they matched American capabilities to a discrete set of challenges, and they drew on a firm domestic consensus. American operations also benefitted from strong international agreement and sympathy.[7]

This three-way match between *capabilities, challenges* and *domestic consensus* is essential for foreign military interventions. The three-way match also provides the foundation for the nation-building activities that frequently follow forced regime change. As a global power, the United States has consistently (and wisely) rejected the burdens of governing foreign societies directly, but it has found itself in the aftermath of an intervention seeking to empower an acceptable local alternative. This is the almost unavoidable pull of nation-building for presidents who send American soldiers abroad to eliminate a threat from a specific territory. The former 'failed state' that nurtured terrorism must become a functioning nation-state that can govern itself in stable and non-threatening ways. Democratic participation is preferable, but not necessary (at least in the short-run) for nation-building to allow for successful regime change, threat elimination and American military withdrawal.[8]

Even presidents, like George W. Bush, who wish to avoid the costs of nation-building, find this dynamic difficult to avoid. In Afghanistan, the overthrow of the Taliban in

November 2001 quickly created demands for American support of a new regime. There was no organic source of order or stability in the country that had been devastated by more than two decades of civil war and Islamic extremism. There was no ready and reliable successor to the Taliban. A new regime had to be created, and the United States had a direct interest, for its own post–11 September security, in making sure that happened. As chief destroyer of the old regime, the United States became the leading external influence on the new government.[9]

Nation-building, in this context, would have been difficult and prone to frustration for any set of American leaders. It was a necessary, but unwanted, task. The Bush administration, however, failed to recognize that it had entered this nation-building process, and it failed to recalibrate its capabilities and expectations accordingly. The president and his closest advisors were filled with fear of Al Qaeda and its Afghan allies, they were flush with their battlefield victory over the Taliban regime and they made policy with the wishful thinking that this battlefield victory would somehow produce lasting protections against the threats that originally motivated their intervention. Wishful thinking – or perhaps non-thinking – crippled American efforts.[10]

In early 2002 the United States faced an unavoidable choice between recalibrating its deployed forces for supporting a stable, self-governing Afghanistan, or departing without any assurance that the country would not return to its pre-war conditions. Like the decision to overthrow the Taliban, this was a strategic choice that required matching capabilities, challenges and a new consensus about what Americans (and their allies) were committed to support in Afghanistan. Nation-building after the Taliban might have failed even with the fullest of American efforts, but the Bush administration did not make a coherent choice to pursue this end or to abandon it. Instead, as I will show, the Bush administration advocated the benefits of nation-building without preparation for the American costs, commitments and sacrifices. The administration also allowed itself to become distracted with another incredibly costly, and unnecessary, war.

After a long process of review in 2009, President Barack Obama fell into a similar trap in Afghanistan. He refused to reject the need for a stable, self-governing Afghanistan, and he attempted to 'surge' American efforts temporarily. Nonetheless, he remained unwilling to prioritize the long-term commitment necessary for any chance of success. President Donald Trump repeated this cycle, with a smaller surge, and then a more precipitate effort to withdraw from the region.

Nation-building requires a deployment of diverse capabilities for decades, not just years. Presidents must recognize that fact and act to embrace long-term commitments, or they must abandon calls for nation-building in countries like Afghanistan. Halfway positions on this issue rarely work. The historical record screams that nation-building is simply not possible on the cheap.[11]

II

Witnessing the destruction wrought by a failing Afghan state, the United States embarked, with little debate in late 2001, on a war to kill the criminals who infested that regime. Americans knew little about Afghanistan and what might replace the Taliban, but they expected the people of the region to embrace representative government, territorial unity and popular sovereignty – especially after the domestic repression they had recently experienced. Almost instinctively, President George W. Bush encouraged this perception as American soldiers and bombs landed in Afghanistan to dislodge the Taliban's leadership.[12]

Speaking at the US Military Academy on 1 June 2002, Bush described 'an historic opportunity to preserve the peace'. 'We have our best chance since the rise of the nation state in the 17th century to build a world where the great powers compete in peace instead of prepare for war.' Referring to American nation-building in Germany and other countries after the Second World War, he affirmed that 'the tide of liberty is rising in many other nations'. As in the past, Bush pledged that the United States would continue to 'support and reward governments that make the right choices for their own people. In our development aid, in our diplomatic efforts, in our international broadcasting and in our educational assistance, the United States will promote moderation and tolerance and human rights. And we will defend the peace that makes all progress possible'.[13]

All of these values centred on the creation of strong, stable, secure nation-states, beginning in Afghanistan. All of these promises depended on American efforts to support this process, not by imposition, but through a combination of local partnerships, long-term investments and selective deployments of force. Bush and his closest advisors expected that Afghan citizens, liberated from oppressive rule, would embrace representative self-government in a single unified state. With American aid, Afghanistan would nurture new national leaders and institutions, according to Bush's vision. 'America has no empire', the president explained. 'We wish for others only what we wish for ourselves.'[14]

This striking universalism envisioned American-style nation-states sprouting from the ashes of extremism in the Middle East and other regions. Bush fused the progressive assumptions of the American nation-building creed with a global urgency born of the recent attacks. 'More and more civilized nations', Bush asserted, 'find themselves on the same side, united by common dangers of terrorist violence and chaos.'[15]

This analysis of Afghanistan and other 'failed states' was not new, but it gained priority attention in the United States after 11 September 2001. Throughout the country, observers focused on the problems of foreign development as they had not before – at least since the Vietnam War. The terrorist attacks made it clear that the absence of stable political order in distant societies, with little economic value to the United States, sent shocks far and wide. Failed states in faraway places threatened successful states close to home. With modern technology and communications, foreign turmoil that Americans had previously ignored now demanded immediate action.[16]

Action came through a combination of military and political intervention. On 26 September 2001, two weeks after the terrorist attacks, CIA agents began to land in Afghanistan. US Special Operations Forces soon followed. A ground-based American force of initially a few hundred soldiers and intelligence specialists attached itself to various warlord groups in the north-eastern part of the country – the remnants of the anti-Taliban 'Northern Alliance' – providing additional firepower, logistical support and, of course, money. Americans dispensed millions of dollars in cash to buy assistance from local leaders. They also adapted with great agility to the challenges of the terrain: riding on horses, living among nomadic groups and showing deference to local tribal and ethnic traditions.[17]

American soldiers accommodated the traditional nature of horse-born fighting, and they married that to the most modern elements of high technology combat. The United States supported, supplemented and often supplanted ground capabilities with the unprecedented speed, flexibility and accuracy of its air power. On 7 October 2001 US aircraft launched from Diego Garcia, countries around the Persian Gulf, and carriers in the Arabian Sea began pummelling Taliban positions in Afghanistan. While on horseback, American ground forces logged into their laptops, sending up-to-date targeting information to the planes overhead. B-1, B-2 and B-52 bombers – the workhorses of the American air arsenal – dropped their bombs, guided with precision navigation technology, on specified locations. They flew approximately 200 missions per day, and they hit as many targets with these flights as they did with 3,000 or more daily missions in the First Persian Gulf War, just a decade earlier. American bombs were lethal, they were ubiquitous and they frequently hit enemy forces, without warning, in difficult-to-reach caves and valleys.[18]

In the first weeks of combat, the United States fired 10,000 bombs and missiles into Afghanistan. These activities – termed 'Operation Enduring Freedom' by the US military – involved a vast web of aircraft and coordinating personnel, but very few Americans on the ground. The military campaign aimed to overthrow the Taliban and empower an alternative political system, dominated by figures with local legitimacy and new ties to Americans. The military campaign was also a new form of close ground–air force coordination with modern communications and precision guidance. The United States would extend its foreign reach and increase its lethality, while avoiding the perils of an intensive occupation. Firepower and accuracy would substitute for deployments of soldiers all across the countryside.

A heavy boot with a 'light footprint' – that combination of overwhelming air power and limited ground intrusion would, American policymakers hoped, allow more opportunities for the citizens of Afghanistan to assert their independence as Washington's allies. That was, of course, the lesson of the Vietnam War. For a generation of military and political figures who came of age in the shadow of America's failed efforts in Southeast Asia, and the domestic acrimony that accompanied those foreign policy failures, new wars required clear limits on the commitment of US soldiers abroad. The Bush administration began the 'War on Terror' with no draft, no calls for sacrifice at home and, most conspicuous, no plans for long-term occupation of Afghanistan or any other country. The goal was to defeat the Taliban, empower a new regime and build a stable nation-state from a distance. Partnerships with local anti-Taliban forces would cover for absent Americans in freed towns and villages.[19]

This was a revolution in warfare to dislodge a dug-in regime distant from American shores. This was also an ambitious effort to seed a new Afghanistan – independent, united and allied with the United States. The American planes dropped food, equipment and other assistance for the anti-Taliban groups. The president pledged that the 'oppressed people of Afghanistan will know the generosity of America and our allies'. The bombs from the air would help create openings for liberation on the ground. The tools for reconstruction would accompany the weapons of destruction.[20]

In late 2001 this plan looked brilliant. Operation Enduring Freedom produced a large number of devastating hits on Taliban and Al Qaeda targets, and it created very few civilian casualties – less than 400 confirmed deaths in three months of continuous bombing. Most remarkable, the United States lost only five aircraft in this intense period, without the death of a single American airman. Washington brought extraordinary power against its enemies with an efficiency no one had seen before. American planes hit enemy targets consistently and with very few collateral costs. Citizens of the United States and Afghanistan could contemplate a quick transition from Taliban rule to something much better.[21]

The Taliban fled the capital city of Kabul on the night of 12 November 2001. When a small group of Americans entered the former enemy stronghold the next day, along with a larger contingent of anti-Taliban Afghan soldiers, the residents greeted them with a joy unseen since allied troops liberated Nazi-occupied Paris in August 1944. The popular reaction showed a sincere desire for good government, reform and increased Western influence. Urban Afghan citizens looked like their American counterparts in their exuberant assertions of personal freedom, their embrace of foreign visitors and their demand for representative political voice. For all the superficiality in these images, I remember how deeply moving they were, especially among fearful Americans looking for a vindication of their basic ideals imperilled by terrorism.

This was not a delusion. Diverse observers saw similar things in liberated Kabul. The Pakistani newspaper *Dawn* reported that in defiance of Taliban prohibitions on music, people played patriotic songs and displayed public joy for the overthrow of their oppressors. They carried signs proclaiming, 'Death to Taliban', 'Death to Mulla Omar' and even 'Death to Pakistan'. *The Guardian* newspaper – a critic of Washington's war efforts – reported that children in Kabul chanted, 'Long Live America!' Television news around the world showed pictures of women removing their forced coverings, couples dancing in the streets and striking faces filled with smiles – an absent phenomenon in the dismal days of Taliban rule. The city and its citizens had apparently 'awakened' from a long nightmare. Many viewers far from Afghanistan felt a similar charge of optimism.[22]

III

Afghans from various ethnic and regional groups saw an opportunity for a new future in their country. The decades of violence and civil war since the Soviet invasion of 1979 and the emergence of the Taliban in the 1990s led many citizens to crave rest from the madness. During these decades, millions of Afghans had fled their rural homes for temporary refuge in urban communities and eventual exile in Pakistan, Iran and other foreign lands. With the defeat of the Taliban in late 2001, they began to return in large numbers – as many as three million refugees came home after the beginning of American military operations. These long-suffering Afghans had spent years living abroad, running foreign businesses and working with international aid groups. They were cosmopolitans of circumstance, still connected to their community roots, but also familiar with the possibilities of national and international institutions.[23] In many cases, global relief organizations had saved their lives. The returning refugees brought their international experiences back to their country, fused with a determination to end the violence that had forced them to flee. To many, a 'normal' nation-state looked like the most promising protector of local communities. Refugees observed effective nation-states abroad, and they recognized their own suffering in their decades of statelessness.

Despite their enduring differences, the people of Afghanistan had a broadly shared purpose after the defeat of the Taliban: to make their war-torn society into a stable nation-state, benefitting from American and other foreign support. Anthropologist Thomas Barfield, who spent more than a decade studying rural Afghan communities, observed that many local groups – at least in 2001 – viewed the United States as a potential ally, not as an invader. They also looked to Washington as a positive contributor to a united, independent Afghan governing system. As Barfield explains, and Afghans recognized, the United States was neither prepared nor willing to govern the region. There simply were not enough Americans in Afghanistan. Instead, Washington planned to help the Afghans rule themselves on terms compatible with the wishes of the people in the region and American interests as well. That was the kind of deal-making politics that pragmatic and war-weary Afghans could understand and embrace. It certainly improved upon the violent exploitation they had felt for so long at the hands of foreign invaders and domestic strongmen.[24]

The model of governance that seemed possible in late 2001 approximated the experience of the region in the middle years of the Cold War, especially 1964 to 1973 – a decade of great possibilities, in retrospect. During this period Afghanistan was a stable, predictable, even progressive place. It had a constitutional government that included a national legislature, a professional administrative class and protected rights for citizens, religions and ethnic groups. It had an expanding educational system (including a somewhat 'radical' university in Kabul), major infrastructural development projects and growing international appeal as a destination for tourists, particularly young adventure-seekers. Annual foreign aid from the Soviet Union and the United States – both sides in the Cold War – surpassed the country's domestic budget. In the early 1970s the future had looked bright for Afghanistan.[25]

Foreign observers and domestic citizens who remembered those years had good reason to look for their return after the removal of the Taliban, and the arrival of promised foreign assistance. This was the motivation behind the conference of Afghan notables assembled under UN auspices in Bonn, Germany from 27 November to 5 December 2001. In a series of meetings the four dominant anti-Taliban groups – the Tadjiks and Uzbeks from Northern Afghanistan (now in control of Kabul), the Afghan emigrés allied to Iran, the Pashtuns surrounding the exiled King Zahir Shah and the Pashtuns with strong ties to Pakistan – worked to create a shared government for Afghanistan. Their goal was to initiate a political process that would produce cooperation and stability in their war-torn country, and security against the return of the Taliban.

James Dobbins, the American diplomat who led Washington's delegation to the conference, recounts that the atmosphere among the participants approximated an 'extended family reunion'. Dobbins contrasts the amity of the Afghans with the mutual hatred of the former Yugoslav factions that the ambassador had addressed in prior years. Unlike the Serbs, Croats and Bosnians who looked back upon generations of conflict, the anti-Taliban groups assembled in Bonn 'recalled earlier eras', according to Dobbins, 'as times of ethnic harmony and national unity'. Afghanistan had a useful history that local and international leaders could invoke for nation-building. In the eyes of its own citizens, this was *not* a country doomed to stateless violence.[26]

The negotiations in Bonn were largely successful. The diverse group of Afghan elders who signed the final agreement at the conference – officially, the 'Agreement on Provisional Arrangements in Afghanistan Pending the Re-establishment of Permanent Government Institutions' – pledged 'to end the tragic conflict in Afghanistan and promote national reconciliation, lasting peace, stability and respect for human rights in the country'. They embraced a vision for 'the independence, national sovereignty and territorial integrity' of their country.[27] The Bonn Agreement was the clearest evidence of a shared commitment to a united, peaceful and representative future among a single Afghan people, under the protection of a functioning government. The agreement served as an initial constitution for a modern nation-state in Afghanistan. It provided a mandate for foreign countries, particularly the United States, to help the impoverished citizens of the region rebuild their society. This document was unthinkable before late 2001 and the overthrow of the Taliban.[28]

The dominant ethnic groups in Afghanistan agreed on three things. First, they affirmed the existence of a single Afghan state with limited powers to maintain country-wide security. They stipulated the creation of an Afghan national security force, trained and supported by the international community. They also included a recognition that the basic infrastructure of the country, especially the roads and tunnels, required central management. The Afghan state envisioned in Bonn was a protector of basic order, like its predecessor in the early 1970s. Second, the conference attendees pledged to cooperate in distributing the large expected infusions of foreign aid. The new government would receive the money from the donors and it would provide external accountability. Within Afghanistan, it would distribute aid to regional organizations, print currency, and float loans. The new government would become the central banker for Afghanistan. The new Supreme Court of Afghanistan would adjudicate disputes over law, property and contracts. Third, and perhaps most important, the rival groups in Bonn embraced a coalition of leaders who would share power. This was the most difficult part of the negotiations. Each group demanded greater representation in the government. In the end, the delegates found agreement around a rough balance of power that matched long-standing traditions. Uzbeks and Tadjiks occupied the key posts in the military and foreign affairs. Iranian-allied Pashtuns continued to dominate internal administration. Within this carefully calibrated framework, the Afghan groups chose a southern Pashtun, Hamid Karzai, for the position of head of state – 'Chairman' of the Interim Administration of Afghanistan.

This was a return to the pattern of Afghan governance from the prior century, before the coup against King Zahir Shah in 1973. Like the king, Karzai based his legitimacy on a regime composed of leaders from various regions and ethnicities around the country. Pashtun by background, Karzai represented the most numerous group in Afghanistan, and the one with an enduring tradition of country-wide authority. Like his Pashtun predecessors, especially Zahir Shah, he self-consciously tied his rule to the consent of the other ethnic stakeholders. Karzai's regime was a hierarchal coalition government, traditional to Afghanistan.[29]

Living in exile since his overthrow, King Zahir Shah had a vital role to play in this process. Due to his age, his distance from contemporary Afghanistan and his own hesitance to resume rule, the king did not join the new government. He granted it his support, however, affirming that it represented a unified collection of Afghan groups. He also opened the meeting of the Afghan tribal leaders in 2002 (the 'Emergency' Loya Jirga) that lent the new government-wide public support and confirmed Hamid Karzai's position as head of state. In early 2004 a second Loya Jirga met to approve a formal constitution. In October of that year, a country-wide election, with little evidence of cheating, elected Karzai president of Afghanistan. Thanks to the cooperation among the Afghan factions, including the king, James Dobbins recounts that 'all the benchmarks laid out in the Bonn Agreement were met more or less on schedule.'[30]

IV

The initial successes in Afghanistan encouraged a self-defeating strategic posture in the Bush administration. This was a prime example of 'victory disease', particularly among fearful, overconfident and historically ignorant Americans. The rapid defeat of the Taliban and the relatively smooth creation of a new regime led many observers to expect more for less in the near future. Despite the expert warnings about the fractious qualities of Afghan society, the United States had worked effectively with groups in the country to transform the government and create a representative political process. Despite the difficulties of conducting military operations in distant and forbidding terrain, a small American force had shown that it could seed local transformations. It seemed so easy, too easy.[31]

Secretary of Defense Donald Rumsfeld became a celebrity figure for his blunt advocacy of what he described as a rediscovered American flexibility in war, now married to the most precise and lethal modern technology. On 'the plains of Afghanistan', Rumsfeld wrote, 'the nineteenth century met the twenty-first century'. The United States and its allies combined capabilities 'from the most advanced (such as laser-guided weapons) to the antique (40-year-old B-52s updated with modern electronics) to the most rudimentary (a man with a gun on a horse)'. Strategic 'transformation', for the secretary of defence, meant a sophisticated return to basics – replacing the single enemy obsessions and excessive deployments of the Cold War with unique combinations of resources for maximum effects. A 'more entrepreneurial approach' to force and change would return Americans to what they always did best: political reform, at home and abroad.[32]

The United States would no longer need a large occupation army abroad, according to Rumsfeld. He argued that the United States was best suited to undertake targeted interventions, empowering positive local forces and dismantling their detractors. Washington would re-direct political processes, but then it would let local figures make the decisions, build the institutions and organize the investments. The United States would act as seed investor with early commitments and limited long-term obligations. The United States would initiate deep change from a careful distance.

This strategy promised grand achievements at bargain costs. It offered the possibility of global influence and security without the burdens of empire. Most of all, it promised that the world would become more like the United States as citizens in other societies made choices encouraged but not imposed by Washington. This superficial and self-serving promise of change on the cheap justified underinvestment of resources in Afghanistan. Rumsfeld and others in the Bush administration had a strong bias to reduce government interference in local decisions, best left to the market in their estimation. In addition, they believed that the United States had undermined its purposes when it became bogged down in the reconstruction of communities. This interpretation applied to poor regions at home and sites of violence abroad, America's inner cities and foreign countries like Afghanistan. For Bush, Rumsfeld and their closest advisors, the United States had to use its power more frequently against evil, but it also had to reject local efforts to tie down American capabilities.[33]

The quick defeat of the Taliban reinforced this neoconservative bias. In late 2001, as the post-Taliban government emerged from the negotiations in Bonn, the Bush administration made it clear that it intended to maintain a 'light footprint' in the region. The US State Department, the United Nations and much of the international community expected that the United States would deploy soldiers as peacekeepers throughout Afghanistan, but the White House rejected this option. 'We don't want to repeat the Soviets' mistakes', Rumsfeld explained. 'There's nothing to be gained by blundering around those mountains and gorges with armor battalions chasing a lightly armed enemy.'[34]

If the United States did not undertake this security role, other allies would not do so either. Policymakers in Washington understood that very well at the time. Bush administration officials had spent their early months in office lambasting their friends, particularly in Europe, for what they criticized as a self-defeating aversion to the use of force against threats. Washington's efforts to reduce its post-Taliban commitments in Afghanistan would only justify more of the same from other powerful societies. The United States led the early war and then it led the retreat.[35]

It deployed only 8,000 additional troops to Afghanistan in 2002. One scholar has pointed out that American troop commitments in the country were smaller, in relation to the size of the Afghan population, than in any major US reconstruction effort since the Second World War. In Germany, for example, Washington deployed 89.3 soldiers for every 1,000 inhabitants. In Afghanistan, the United States and other international contributors stationed only 1.6 soldiers for every 1,000 inhabitants.[36]

Rooting out insurgents, including Al Qaeda, and maintaining stability would have to fall on the shoulders of the new government's military and police units. The problem was that the Afghan military and police existed only on paper. The new government did not have the time, the resources or the expertise to create cohesive security forces during its first months in power. If anything, the chaos of the early days encouraged plundering and corruption, not coherent long-term planning. A light American footprint opened a power vacuum that armed militias – warlords, drug traffickers, Taliban loyalists and Al Qaeda operatives – quickly filled.

Without security, foreign donors turned away from Afghanistan. International pledges made to Karzai's government in the aftermath of the Bonn negotiations failed to materialize fully. Subsequent efforts to procure additional funding for infrastructure, industry and education met resistance from wealthy countries that were hesitant to enter a violent and unpredictable environment. During 2002 and 2003 the Afghan government received an average of only $60 in foreign assistance per citizen – less half of the per capita aid allocation for citizens in post-war Germany, adjusted for inflation. It was far less than the subsidies sent to other countries in transition: Haiti, Mozambique, East Timor and the Solomon Islands, among others.[37]

Inadequate aid to Afghanistan only increased the incentives for corruption among government leaders. They could not buy off all of the major groups, and they feared for their longevity in office. It made sense to hoard resources and invest them in self-protection, not broad social needs. In addition, the paltry international contributions to the country sent a discouraging message to citizens: the United States and its allies were not directly committed to the goals they articulated for Afghanistan. They had abandoned the country after the Soviet withdrawal in 1989. It looked like they would do the same again.

Under these circumstances, Afghan men and women had little reason to take risks for a new political future. They had little incentive to abandon the warlords and Taliban figures who promised local protection. An under-financed Afghan state devolved quickly into a collection of warring groups.[38]

V

The spiralling violence and disorder in Afghanistan after 2003 became Barack Obama's War in 2009. Like a prior Democrat four decades earlier, the new president entered the White House with a broad agenda for domestic reform, but also a lingering foreign conflict that he could not easily end. Thanks to the signs of limited recent success with the military 'Surge' in Iraq, Obama could withdraw soldiers from that conflict. In the case of Afghanistan, however, he confronted an immediate crisis that challenged American nation-building efforts throughout the region. The return of the Taliban also threatened to undermine order in neighbouring Pakistan, destabilize that country's nuclear arsenal and re-ignite terrorism near and far.

Echoing Lyndon Johnson's predicament in 1965, Obama in 2009 needed to salvage American goals in a distant country to fortify public confidence in his presidency. If he allowed the Taliban to re-establish power, he would appear weak and traitorous to American aims. If a major terrorist attack on American soil followed the return of the Taliban, his entire presidential agenda would unravel. After a long and acrimonious internal review, on 1 December 2009 the president announced his new strategy. It called for another 'Surge', like Iraq, combined with a regional diplomatic offensive. The United States and its NATO allies enlarged their military forces in Afghanistan from less than 65,000 at the start of Obama's presidency to almost 150,000 by the middle of 2010. American troop deployments increased from approximately 32,000 in January 2009 to more than 90,000 18 months later.[39]

Washington also increased its aid to the region, including Pakistan, and it pushed Afghanistan's neighbour to interdict and destroy Taliban sympathizers. Richard Holbrooke, an experienced negotiator in war-torn regions (including Vietnam and the former Yugoslavia), took the lead as the president's special envoy for this purpose. The US Departments of Defense and State and other civilian agencies also deployed more personnel to Afghanistan. They worked locally – as engineers, farmers, teachers and advisors – to address basic problems and build a sustainable foundation for coordinated national efforts. During Obama's first fifteen months in office the number of these diplomats on the ground more than doubled, deployed in all parts of Afghanistan.[40]

Despite frequent criticisms of President Hamid Karzai's corruption, Obama pledged to work closely with the Afghan leader, building more effective governing institutions and co-opting local groups that had become disaffected from the regime. Recognizing the importance of negotiations with diverse figures, Obama advocated cooperation with neighbouring Iran and even elements of the Taliban that appeared willing to join a national government. 'We will support efforts by the Afghan government', the president announced, 'to open the door to those Taliban who abandon violence and respect the human rights of their fellow citizens.'[41]

These redoubled American commitments in Afghanistan were promising, but they showed few immediate results. By all measures – insurgent attacks, assassinations of government officials, civilian deaths and troop fatalities – Afghanistan became a much more violent and chaotic place between 2010 and 2012. American aerial drone strikes showed some success in targeting Taliban and Al Qaeda figures, but the heavier American footprint on the ground did not increase daily security. Most frustrating, American support for Hamid Karzai and his Pakistani counterpart, Asif Ali Zardari, encouraged more corruption. Karzai and Zardari exploited Washington's dependence on their rule.[42]

President Obama recognized this problem. In response, the White House worked to nurture wider relationships in the region. The president wanted a partnership with local leaders in nation-building, not an American endowment for incompetence, corruption and double-dealing. This was a logical position, and it led the president to announce in December 2009: 'After 18 months, our troops will begin to come home. These are the resources that we need to seize the initiative, while building the Afghan capacity that can allow for a responsible transition of our forces out of Afghanistan.' 'This effort', Obama continued, 'must be based on performance. The days of providing a blank check are over.'[43]

During the 2012 presidential campaign Obama affirmed the continued potential for Afghan nation-building, but he also pledged to remove remaining American military forces from Afghanistan by the end of 2014. The American commitment was costly and, the president argued, the Afghan population should carry the direct burden for law enforcement and reconstruction. In this political context, a timetable for American withdrawal made sense. The 2014 deadline, however, was unrealistic for the achievement of stated aims. Yet again, an American leader was over-promising and under-committing.

At the end of Obama's presidency 8,400 American soldiers remained in Afghanistan – a small holding force providing security for the Afghan government in Kabul and training for the Afghan army. The United States had essentially abandoned its nation-building ambitions, although American aid continued to flow into the country. Washington authorized negotiations with Taliban forces, hoping to arrange for a stable government that would not again allow terrorist training on its territory.

Characterizing Obama as weak, President Donald Trump initiated his own mini-surge in US forces, bringing the total number to 14,000 during his first year in office, but that number soon fell again. Trump's strategic aims were incoherent. He promised more brute force against terrorists in Afghanistan: 'obliterating ISIS, crushing Al Qaeda, preventing the Taliban from taking over Afghanistan, and stopping mass terror attacks against America before they emerge.' At the same time, he abandoned any effort to improve the situation on the ground: 'we will no longer use American military might to construct democracies in faraway lands or try to rebuild other countries in our own image. Those days are now over.'[44]

How would the United States defeat its enemies in Afghanistan without helping to build a government that could secure itself against them? Trump never answered that question, and within months of surging American forces he returned to his deeper objections to the US military presence in Central Asia. He undercut his rhetoric of crushing the Taliban by accepting their presence in a new potential government, and demanding a complete withdrawal of all American forces while negotiations were still incomplete. If Obama surged and then cut back, Trump made big threats and then tried to run away. The arc of both strategies ended in the same place: disillusionment with the United States in Afghanistan and rising influence for the Taliban.

When President Joseph Biden announced that the last 3,500 American soldiers would leave Afghanistan by 11 September 2021 – twenty years since the 9/11 terrorist attacks that triggered the American intervention in the first place – he was bowing to an obvious reality. The American public, and most of the nation's leaders, no longer supported nation-building in Afghanistan. The US forces on the ground provided some limited security, but they lacked a clear strategic mission. They were not large enough to defeat the enemy or empower an alternative. They were, however, costly enough to drain American resources and distract from other priorities. For the soldiers, the experience of serving in dangerous terrain, without a clear purpose, was deeply demoralizing – part of a broader cynicism engulfing American politics at the time.[45]

VI

The frustrating twenty years of American intervention in Afghanistan teach many lessons. Foremost among them is that presidential leadership matters enormously. Successful military intervention requires an effective matching of *capabilities* to contemporary *challenges*. Presidents must also build a strong domestic and international *consensus* for their actions. They must persuade in order to lead.

Nation-building efforts after a successful military intervention are difficult to avoid. Destroying one regime raises the inevitable question of what will come next, and how the United States will insure that the successor government is not equally threatening to American interests. Nation-building also reflects the deep American aversion to direct imperial control of foreign possessions, and the desire to empower local leaders who share US interests and values. Nation-building has been and will remain an integral part of American foreign intervention.

Presidents must recognize this dynamic. They must make certain that war planning before a military intervention involves serious analysis of what the United States is prepared to do after regime change. What kind of government does the United States expect to take over? How will the United States contribute to a new stable, effective and representative regime? Most important: is the United States prepared to make the long-term contributions necessary for better political and social circumstances after completion of initial military operations, when the path to nation-building begins?

Americans have proven that they will rally behind their commander-in-chief to support foreign wars, even for two decades! Americans, however, require leaders who will invoke patriotism in battle only when the nation's core interests are at stake, and the benefits of intervention justify the long-term costs. Leaders must prepare the American government and the people to make the sacrifices necessary for intervention and nation-building if the United States is going to overturn a regime, like the Taliban in Afghanistan.

Presidents George W. Bush and Barack Obama made strong arguments for American interests in defeating Al Qaeda and the Taliban in Afghanistan. In the aftermath of the terrorist attacks launched from that region, they offered a persuasive case for American military intervention. They did not, however, prepare the country for the sacrifices necessary to nurture security and stability in Afghanistan. President Donald Trump made matters worse with an incoherent mix of threats and retreats. He confused allies, American military leaders and citizens. President Joseph Biden's decision to withdraw in 2021 was the most direct and honest response to the realities on the ground, after twenty years.

This history highlights the complexities of presidential leadership, foreign policy and nation-building. The initial military intervention in Afghanistan after the 11 September 2001 terrorist attacks was prudent, but it produced many new challenges that American leaders were unprepared to address. Successful presidential management of a foreign military intervention requires a rare combination of disciplined *focus*, analytical *rigour* and *luck*. Historical analysis does not offer a recipe but an indispensable source base for asking the right questions. After twenty years of war in Afghanistan, we can hope for a little more wisdom about what foreign nation-building really requires. Leaders should intervene abroad rarely, and with sober expectations.

Notes

1 See Jeremy Black, *Insurgency and Counterinsurgency: A Global History* (London, 2016); Seth G. Jones, *Waging Insurgent Warfare: Lessons from the Vietcong to the Islamic State* (New York, 2017).

2 See John A. Nagl, *Learning to Eat Soup with a Knife: Counterinsurgency Lessons from Malaya and Vietnam* (Chicago, 2002); David Kilcullen, *Counterinsurgency* (New York, 2010).

3   See, especially, Seth G. Jones, *In the Graveyard of Empires: America's War in Afghanistan* (New York, 2009).

4   See the superb book on this topic by Thomas Barfield: *Afghanistan: A Cultural and Political History* (Princeton, NJ, 2010).

5   See the old, but still valuable, account in Louis Dupree, *Afghanistan* (Princeton, NJ, 1973). See also Nick Cullather, *The Hungry World: America's Cold War Battle against Poverty in Asia* (Cambridge, MA, 2010), ch four.

6   Mohammed Kakar, *Afghanistan: The Soviet Invasion and the Afghan Response, 1979–1982* (Berkeley, CA, 1997); Larry P. Goodson, *Afghanistan's Endless War: State Failure, Regional Politics, and the Rise of the Taliban* (Seattle, 2001); Barnett R. Rubin, *The Fragmentation of Afghanistan: State Formation and Collapse in the International System*, 2nd edn (New Haven, CT, 2002).

7   See Dov S. Zakheim, *A Vulcan's Tale: How the Bush Administration Mismanaged the Reconstruction of Afghanistan* (Washington, DC, 2011), esp. 76–155.

8   This paragraph captures the main argument of my book: *Liberty's Surest Guardian: American Nation-Building from the Founders to Obama* (New York, 2011).

9   See Jones, *In the Graveyard of Empires*, ch 8.

10   See Fred Kaplan, *Daydream Believers: How a Few Grand Ideas Wrecked American Power* (Hoboken, NJ, 2008).

11   See Suri, *Liberty's Surest Guardian*, 266–83.

12   See Ronald E. Neumann, 'Washington Goes to War', in *Our Latest Longest War: Losing Hearts and Minds in Afghanistan*, ed. Aaron O'Connell (Chicago, 2017), ch 1.

13   President George W. Bush's Commencement Address at the United States Military Academy at West Point, New York, 1 June 2002. The text is available at: http://www.nytimes.com/2002/06/01/international/02PTEX-WEB.html.

14   Ibid.

15   Ibid.

16   For examples of newfound attention to development issues and nation-building within the US foreign policy community, see James Dobbins, John G. McGinn, Keith Crane, Seth G. Jones, Rollie Lal, Andrew Rathmell, Rachel Swanger, and Anga Timilsina, *America's Role in Nation-Building: From Germany to Iraq* (Santa Monica, CA, 2003); Francis Fukuyama, 'Nation-Building 101', *Atlantic Monthly*, January/February 2004; Esther Pan, 'United Nations: Nation-Building', Council on Foreign Relations Backgrounder, 2 October 2003, http://www.cfr.org/publication/7755/united_nations.html.

17   For an excellent overview of initial American military deployments in Afghanistan see: http://www.globalsecurity.org/military/ops/enduring-freedom_deploy.htm.

18   See President George W. Bush's speech to the nation, 7 October 2001. The text of the speech is available at: http://www.pbs.org/newshour/terrorism/combating/bush_10-7.html. See also http://www.globalsecurity.org/military/ops/enduring-freedom-ops-air.htm.

19   On the influence of the Vietnam War experience for the key policymakers in the Bush White House, see James Mann, *Rise of the Vulcans: The History of Bush's War Cabinet* (New York, 2004).

20   President George W. Bush's speech to the nation, 7 October 2001. See also http://www.globalsecurity.org/military/ops/enduring-freedom-ops-air.htm.

21   See Jones, *In the Graveyard of Empires*, 86–108; http://www.globalsecurity.org/military/ops/enduring-freedom-ops-aciv.htm; http://www.globalsecurity.org/military/ops/enduring-freedom-ops-aloss.htm.

22 See M. Ismail Khan and Danish Karokhel, 'Northern Alliance Troops Enter Kabul', *Dawn*, 14 November 2001, http://www.dawn.com/2001/11/14/top2.htm; James Meek, 'Freedom, Joy – and Fear', *The Guardian*, 14 November 2001, http://www.guardian .co.uk/world/2001/nov/14/afghanistan.terrorism12; Keith Richburg, '"Second Life" in Afghan Capital: Kabul Awakens to Find Taliban Gone, Harsh Rules Lifted', *Washington Post*, 14 November 2001.

23 See Barfield, *Afghanistan*, 280–2.

24 Barfield writes of a 'united people in a failed state', *Afghanistan*, 277–82. See also Barfield's discussion of the positive distinction many Afghan citizens drew between the American intervention and prior Soviet and British invasions. Based on interviews, Barfield reports that Afghan citizens looked to the United States for stability and reconstruction after civil war – for nation-building. See Barfield, *Afghanistan*, 275–7. See also Jones, *In the Graveyard of Empires*, 109–50.

25 Barnett Rubin argues that the influx of foreign aid in Afghanistan produced a 'rentier state' dominated by figures who lived off external capital and under-invested in domestic production. Recipients of foreign aid had an incentive to hoard that money for their personal uses, not the needs of the country. See Barnett Rubin, *The Fragmentation of Afghanistan: State Formation and Collapse in the International System* (New Haven, CT, 1995). Rubin is surely correct, but foreign aid also allowed central leaders to offer rival groups increased resources if they continued to work with the national government. The distribution of foreign aid among different groups encouraged inter-ethnic cooperation. This process broke down in the late 1970s because of poor central leadership and the Soviet invasion. See Barfield, *Afghanistan*, 195–225.

26 James F. Dobbins, *After the Taliban: Nation-Building in Afghanistan* (Washington, DC, 2008), 77–8.

27 See the text of the Bonn Agreement at: http://www.un.org/News/dh/latest/afghan/ afghan-agree.htm.

28 Ibid; Dobbins, *After the Taliban*, 77–116.

29 For background on Hamid Karzai and traditional Pashtun political authority in Afghanistan, see Ahmed Rashid, *Descent into Chaos: The U.S. and the Disaster in Pakistan, Afghanistan, and Central Asia* (New York, 2008), 3–23; Barfield, *Afghanistan*, 288–94.

30 Quotation from Dobbins, *After the Taliban*, 161.

31 On this point, see Rashid, *Descent into Chaos*, 61–83; Jones, *In the Graveyard of Empires*, 86–108.

32 Donald Rumsfeld, 'Transforming the Military', *Foreign Affairs* 81 (May/June 2002): 20–32.

33 For an excellent account of the political agenda behind the Bush administration's domestic and foreign policies, see Julian E. Zelizer, *Arsenal of Democracy: The Politics of National Security from World War II to the War on Terrorism* (New York, 2010), 431–503. See also Kaplan, *Daydream Believers*; Mann, *Rise of the Vulcans*.

34 Rumsfeld quoted in Jones, *In the Graveyard of Empires*, 117.

35 For an essay that powerfully articulated the neoconservative attacks on Europe's alleged military cowardice, see Robert Kagan, *Of Paradise and Power: America and Europe in the New World Order* (New York, 2002).

36 Data from Jones, *In the Graveyard of Empires*, 119–20. See also Rashid, *Descent into Chaos*, 171–218.

37 Data from Jones, *In the Graveyard of Empires*, 120–3.

38   David Kilcullen explains how foreign interventions, with insufficient security and inadequate partners on the ground, encourage local groups to join insurgencies for self-preservation – and sometimes profit. Kilcullen, *The Accidental Guerrilla: Fighting Small Wars in the Midst of a Big One* (New York, 2009), esp. 1–38.

39   For the data on foreign troops in Afghanistan, see the 'Afghanistan Index', updated every week, compiled by Ian S. Livingston, Heather L. Messera and Michael O'Hanlon at the Brookings Institution: http://usliberals.about.com/gi/o.htm?zi=1/XJ&zTi=1 &sdn=usliberals&cdn=newsissues&tm=85&gps=431_386_1276_852&f=00&tt=2&bt =0&bts=0&zu=http%3A//www.brookings.edu/iraqindex.

40   See the data on civilian personnel in the 'Afghanistan Index'.

41   Speech by President Barack Obama, United States Military Academy at West Point, New York, 1 December 2009, http://www.whitehouse.gov/the-press-office/remarks -president-address-nation-way-forward-afghanistan-and-pakistan.

42   The data on increased violence in Afghanistan is documented in detail in the 'Afghanistan Index'.

43   Speech by President Barack Obama, United States Military Academy at West Point, New York, 1 December 2009.

44   Speech by President Donald Trump, Fort Myer Military Base in Arlington, Virginia, 21 August 2017, https://www.nytimes.com/2017/08/21/world/asia/trump-speech -afghanistan.html.

45   For moving reflections on the cynicism induced by the wars in Afghanistan and Iraq, see veteran Phil Klay's collection of stories: *Redeployment* (New York, 2014.)

8

Applied history and contingency planning

Whitehall and the British War Book, *c.* 1911–39

Francesca Morphakis

This chapter illuminates the utility of Applied History in navigating a crisis, and there can be no more consequential crisis facing the state than war. Although one of the most important experiments with the machinery of government in the first half of the twentieth century, the War Book has hitherto been shrouded in considerable mystery. The War Book was an exercise in contingency planning in the civilian sphere. It was a blueprint that set out every decision and action to be taken during a period of rising international tension and was designed so that the state would immediately be placed on a war footing at the time that hostilities were formally declared. Unlike ministers, for whom government was a revolving door, civil servants' long departmental experience and expertise enabled them to cast their minds forward and devise solutions to administrative challenges. Far from being a 'beautifully designed and effective braking mechanism . . . against initiative and change', the Civil Service could innovate – when it so desired.[1] This process of innovation was not always smooth: the War Book project often progressed sluggishly, arrested by layers of slow bureaucracy, distractions and more urgent priorities. Furthermore, the creation of the War Book pointed to the development of a highly significant culture within Whitehall. This mindset was characterized above all by acute anxiety, particularly concerning Britain's changing position in the world and the disorienting pace of technological advance. Anxieties manifested in a belief in the value of contingency planning and drawing upon past experience to compensate for Britain's weaknesses. The War Book is thus a lens through which to examine the significance of historical thinking within Whitehall, with a particular focus on the generation of senior officials who devised, supported and implemented the War Book. This chapter begins by exploring the genesis and development of the War Book; it then examines questions of civil defence planning and the 'supreme control' in war. Finally, it briefly considers the longer-term impact of the War Book and how historically informed contingency planning became embedded within the fabric of the central state as both a useful and necessary exercise.

I

From its genesis in 1911 to its implementation on the outbreak of the Second World War in 1939, the War Book married senior officials who dominated Whitehall prior to the outbreak of the First World War with civil servants who rose to prominence in the interwar years. The project was rooted in a series of political, scientific and socio-economic events which were interpreted to spell the decline of the British Empire. After the heady days of Victorian confidence, British predominance confronted a series of acute challenges.[2] The Boer War demonstrated the limits of British power, while escalating fears of a major European war and the emergence of new economic and military powerhouses added to a growing sense of unease.[3] Complacency turned to anxiety. A series of reforms were instituted in the quest for 'national efficiency' and imperial security; although cast in Darwinian conceptions of the survival of the fittest, national confidence was undoubtedly shaken. Such pessimism was compounded by the potential applications of rapid and unparalleled technological advancement. For instance, the first cross-Channel flight in 1909 was an ominous warning that aviation might demolish British sea power. Within this environment, civil servants young and old struggled to accept the version of modernity confronting them. Despite Britain's victory in 1918, the First World War only amplified such worries.[4] The shaky peace settlement, the growing might of the United States, the spread of nationalist movements as well as economic frailty at home spurred further anxieties about the precarity of Britain's position. Moreover, the bloodiest and most mechanized war in history only magnified the threat of technological change. Technological innovations also increased the pace of activity and decision-making, creating a perception that the world was shrinking. Morbid thoughts were ever-present throughout the first decades of the twentieth century. The world became more disorienting as perceptions of space and time were distorted and the security of the British Empire was increasingly imperilled. In this context, officialdom sought a solution to British weaknesses. Armed with the power of organization and with a keen eye for lessons of the past, civil servants embraced notions of contingency planning as a legitimate and viable safeguard. These officials were historically minded; many had read History or Classics at university, or else were keenly interested in History, as evidenced by their reading choices and the use of historical allusions and metaphors in their writings. They thus firmly believed in the value of Applied History, where the lessons of the past were to be distilled and recorded to guide – but never to determine – actions and decisions in the future.

Established in 1904 as part of the reforms following the Boer War, the Committee of Imperial Defence (CID) was responsible for advising on national and imperial security.[5] It became the focal point of small-scale contingency planning, including censorship and the treatment of aliens in wartime.[6] The Naval Assistant Secretary to the CID, Maurice Hankey (who was to become the first Cabinet Secretary[7] in 1916), possessed a keen eye for organization and coordination.[8] He circulated a memorandum to the CID, calling for the creation of a sub-committee 'to elaborate a system for coordinating . . . action . . . on the occurrence of strained relations and on the outbreak of war'.[9] He stressed that such preparations would have a considerable impact on mobilization and the success of operations. Hankey's memorandum stirred the CID to create a sub-committee for the Coordination of Departmental Action on the Outbreak of War in April 1911. It comprised almost entirely permanent secretaries, who were the heads of the Whitehall departments. As chairman, Arthur Nicolson (Permanent Under-Secretary of the Foreign Office) successfully encouraged his colleagues to outline the actions which their departments should take, as well as the support they would require from other departments in an emergency.[10] Against the backdrop of the Agadir crisis and turmoil in the Balkans between 1911 and 1914, senior civil servants discussed principles and schemes, while it fell to junior officials to elaborate the details. This was sometimes a difficult struggle against 'official inertia' and rivalrous departmentalism.[11] Nevertheless, the Coordination Committee was made a standing sub-committee in 1913 and charged with keeping the War Book continually under review; this marked the first step towards inculcating a culture of contingency planning within Whitehall. The War Book was finally completed on the eve of war.[12] Running to 318 pages, it dealt with a wide range of issues, including the protection of vulnerable points, censorship and the control of enemy shipping. Each chapter laid down departmental responsibilities, with long lists of decisions which had been coordinated and cross-referenced. The necessary bills, proclamations, telegrams and letters were all pre-printed and classified in order of priority to avoid flooding lines of communication. The volume was divided into two stages. The 'precautionary stage' characterized strained relations; during this time, preparations were to be made to start the national engine and put it into gear. Approximately forty-eight hours later, the 'war stage' would follow – when the machine would spring, fully formed, into action. The War Book was opened in the last days of July 1914 and proved to be a very effective mechanism for coordination.[13] Naturally, there were omissions. Officials could not anticipate the ultimate scale of war: total war was a hitherto unknown phenomenon.[14] Omissions included the transfer of industry to wartime production, the mobilization of industrial manpower and the question of executive direction in war. These issues were improvised extemporarily and impacted the effective prosecution of the conflict.

Maurice Hankey was a central figure in embedding contingency planning into the fabric of Whitehall culture. He never doubted that it was of such value that it should continue postbellum; nor did he doubt that the conflict represented a learning experience. During the war, he convinced the Reconstruction Committee to direct departments to record their experiences of 'the practical working of all war administrative machinery' and was particularly interested in 'imperfections' and 'suggestions as to remedies'.[15] To expedite this sluggish process, just ten days after the armistice, Hankey pressed the War Cabinet to recognize that it was a 'matter of the first importance that the experience of the present war should be available in practical form for any future war'.[16] Departments duly submitted their reports, detailing the omissions in the first War Book and describing innovations and remedies.[17] Some thought that Hankey, now Secretary to the Cabinet and the CID, was obsessed with war-readiness.[18] He was, and nor was this entirely altruistic. He privately confessed to his deputy, Tom Jones, that 'the Department that has the War Book has the key of the whole defence organisation in its hands'.[19] An ambitious man with a keen eye for power, Hankey wished to consolidate the newly-created Cabinet Office as a predominant organ of the central state and to secure his own position. In the midst of post-war turmoil, contingency planning was a low priority. However, it was the responsibility of the CID to overcome this war-weariness, look ahead, learn from the past and recast defensive preparations.[20] The Coordination Committee was reconstituted in February 1920 and tasked with investigating 'the machinery set up during the war, the powers exercised, and the steps probably necessary to re-establish the [machine] in another war'.[21]

Key principles and assumptions governed interwar planning. The metaphorical 'concert in sight' was assumed to be a large-scale war against either Germany or Germany and Russia in combination. Preparations always centred on a 'worst-case' total war scenario as it would be more straightforward to scale down plans for a smaller conflict than to scale up measures for a larger-than-anticipated war. A crucial aspect of the War Book's rationale was a belief in 'institutional memory', embodied in a written record. It was deemed likely that those who had been closely involved with the First World War volume would have retired by the outbreak of the next war, and thus recording experiences and reflections while these were fresh was invaluable. However, planners always kept in mind the very real danger that War Book plans – if misinterpreted, misapplied or inappropriate – could be a greater obstacle than a 'clear sheet and a clear mind' in a crisis. Elaborating on this concern, Hastings Ismay (at this point, Assistant Secretary to the CID) cogently argued that 'younger and fresher minds . . . may see further and more clearly. . . . It is not for us to be confident that, because we know more of the past, we can . . . see more clearly than they do into the future. What we can do is to record for them our experience, and our reflections upon it'.[22] Similarly, Warren Fisher (Permanent Secretary to the Treasury) reminded his colleagues that the War Book 'did not pretend to be comprehensive' or infallible and urged them not to restrict their minds to what had been previously devised.[23]

Senior civil servants played a leading role in the compilation of the War Book, often through the activities of the Coordination Committee, which was responsible for compiling and revising chapters related to each department's sphere of activity and for constructing the necessary apparatus of government. A wide circle of officials was therefore drawn into preparations and became familiar with War Book arrangements. Fisher, for example, played an important role in preparing Whitehall for the descent into war through his work on manpower and broadcasting arrangements. Hankey was an even more active participant and took personal responsibility for devising the Cabinet Office's War Book chapter.[24] John Anderson of the Home Office was also active and keenly interested in preparations, not least because many of the issues under discussion came under the direct purview of his department, including policing, security, civil defence, emergency services and communication. Moreover, as Cabinet Secretary from 1938, Edward Bridges was a vital driving force in reforming and implementing the War Book in the dying months of peace. Nevertheless, the project struggled against inertia and competing priorities throughout the interwar period.[25] The Treasury was particularly sluggish; a decade in the making, its chapter amounted to three pages.[26] The department was responsible for staffing new wartime departments, consulting with the Board of Trade on blockade matters, consulting with the governor of the Bank of England on credit facilities and preparing a war loan bill. In the 1930s, more thorough planners expanded the scope for the Treasury's activities in wartime.[27] In contrast, departments, including the Foreign, Cabinet and Home Offices, possessed complex and wide-ranging responsibilities, from sounding the alarm at the international situation to a wide array of civil defence issues. The second War Book was more 'ambitious' and more comprehensive.[28] In this way, and as the machinery became more complex, the War Book shifted from a template of departmental chapters to thematic chapters in order to better capture the cooperative, cross-Whitehall nature of preparations. War Book planning accelerated from 1935 as the international situation grew steadily darker and preparations assumed a new urgency, yet many of the schemes contained within the volume remained nebulous until 1938.[29]

By the summer of 1938, officials were acutely anxious about the international situation and the readiness of preparations.[30] The Munich crisis in the autumn of 1938 simultaneously provoked greater urgency in preparations and exposed numerous shortcomings. It spurred a thorough post-crisis stocktaking as officials reflected on the immediate past, distilled vital lessons and ultimately treated the Munich crisis as a wargaming exercise.[31] When the Coordination Committee convened on 23 September 1938 to consider the situation, officials were frustrated with timid ministers' concerns that opening the War Book prematurely might further strain international relations and thus precipitate a conflict. While civil servants had enjoyed considerable latitude in devising preparations and constructing the necessary machinery, the authority to institute plans rested with the Cabinet, and so the psychological war-readiness of ministers was a potentially fatal complication. Permanent secretaries began to discuss the notion of a 'preparatory period' to precede the 'precautionary stage'. This would permit the engine of war to be ignited more than forty-eight hours before the declaration of hostilities to further ready the machine and to overcome timidity.[32] The 'preparatory period' comprised hushed and entirely non-aggressive manoeuvres such as the manning of coastal defences, the protection of vulnerable points and censorship. From his new position as Secretary to the CID, Hastings Ismay successfully spearheaded attempts to secure ministerial approval for this reform. He was eager to use the momentum generated by the crisis to 'strike while the iron . . . is hot' and found much support from his fellow officials as Munich had 'brought to light the hesitancy which (so strangely) exists to institute a Precautionary Stage' and how 'these War Book things, though they can be done quickly, not always are'.[33]

By August 1939, peace, as John Anderson confessed to his father, hung 'by a very slender thread'.[34] On 23 August, the CID authorized the institution of the 'preparatory period' and the apparatus of war was placed into first gear.[35] Three days later, on 26 August, the Coordination Committee convened at the prime minister's request.[36] Edward Bridges explained that officials had to recommend which actions within the 'precautionary stage' could no longer be safely delayed and which were neither provocative nor would attract undue publicity. Civil servants laboured over the War Book, scouring chapter by chapter for such measures. The procedure should have been far simpler: a single telegram – 'Institute Precautionary Stage' – to set in motion a chain of measures across the world. However, a Cabinet later the same day delayed instituting either the 'precautionary stage' or the list of preparations recommended by permanent secretaries.[37] This was the Cabinet's first substantial deviation from the War Book. Ministerial hesitancy was not the sole obstacle to the smooth functioning of the War Book. When Home Office officials attempted to despatch the batches of pre-printed telegrams which ordered the promulgation of Defence Regulations, the incompetence of their Permanent Under-Secretary, Alexander Maxwell, became apparent. The code word authorizing synchronizing at the BBC – to prevent enemy aircraft from tapping into the wavelengths – had been stored in Maxwell's safe. Yet, 'in a fit of absentmindedness which sometimes overcame him, he had picked it up . . . could not make head or tail of it and had thrown it into his wastepaper-basket'. There followed an unhelpful dash to rearrange matters with the BBC.[38] As storm clouds gathered overhead, Bridges became concerned that the Cabinet was delaying the institution of the 'precautionary stage' beyond what was wise. He grasped the inherent danger in delaying; only some of the measures included in the 'precautionary stage' had been actioned, and as the stages and measures were interdependent, further delay risked the entire machine missing a gear as the cogs began to move discordantly and grinding to a halt. Bridges wrote to Horace Wilson, the premier's right-hand man, urging him to address the issue with Neville Chamberlain.[39] This warning – along with others – went unheeded. Ministers were reluctant to take the necessary decisions. Quite apart from concerns of provoking Adolf Hitler when the French were unwilling to formally commit to war, the prime minister was also hopeful of accommodation with Germany.[40] Senior officials were therefore forced to bow to political hesitancy. They met daily and spent hours determining the minimum measures which could no longer be safely postponed; each evening the Cabinet authorized a series of further preparations. It was an untidy process, but ultimately effective. By 31 August, almost all the measures in the 'precautionary stage' had been actioned, although the stage was only formally instituted on 1 September when the German army crossed the Polish frontier.[41] By the end of the day, telegram boxes once stuffed with thousands of messages lay almost empty.[42] Senior officials expected the Cabinet to approve the 'war stage' on 2 September, but this was not so. The Coordination Committee convened for the final time on 3 September. Officials sat in conclave as the 11.00 am ultimatum to Germany expired; at 11.13, Bridges returned from the Cabinet room to inform his colleagues that the time had come to despatch the telegrams which instituted the 'war stage' around the world.[43] Whitehall was once more at war.

II

The 'supreme control' – executive direction in war – is of paramount importance. Arrangements had been beyond the scope of planners prior to the First World War. H. H. Asquith's 'business as usual' approach soon proved inadequate, and his gradual reform of the Cabinet system between 1914 and 1916 was insufficient. Upon becoming prime minister in December 1916, David Lloyd George established a small, executive War Cabinet, including ministers without portfolio who were unburdened by departmental duties. This body of six was served by the secretariat. These innovations taken in combination – a dynamic premier, a small executive and a secretariat – eased strains in the state apparatus, facilitated greater coordination and offered stronger executive direction.[44] After the war, having witnessed first-hand the strengths and deficiencies of Asquith and Lloyd George's contrasting systems, Hankey drafted a document which detailed the organization of the War Cabinet and the secretariat to guide future generations.[45] The Cabinet Secretary detailed the various experiments with the executive direction of war and outlined the capabilities of each to cope with the demands of total war. Reflecting on his experience, he recommended that in total war, only a small War Cabinet, supplemented by smaller non-executive committees, would suffice.[46] The Chiefs of Staff concurred and supported the principle that the lessons of past wars and emergencies 'should be on record for the benefit of future Governments which may find themselves confronted with similar situations'.[47] Hankey's memorandum was thus included in the War Book. It was laid down that in a crisis, the Cabinet Secretary was responsible for placing in the hands of the prime minister a memorandum explaining the evolution of the system during the First World War and presenting options to suit a range of scenarios, although the decision as to which system would be adopted rested with the prime minister of the day.

Questions of executive control subsequently received very little attention until the summer of 1938. One of Edward Bridges's first actions upon succeeding Hankey was to comb over the War Book and familiarize himself with his responsibilities as Cabinet Secretary.[48] Bridges also sought Hasting Ismay's guidance given the man's past intimacy with War Book preparations.[49] Bridges's actions emphasized that institutional memory was embodied in people as much as in dry documents; there was a performative dimension to the transmission of Whitehall's memory. As the Munich crisis developed, Bridges fulfilled his duty and placed into Chamberlain's hands Hankey's memorandum on the 'supreme control'. He advised Chamberlain that 'in the event of . . . a war of unlimited character . . . the War Cabinet system would be immediately essential'.[50] There was no margin for error in a world where the enemy could strike with great force at short notice – in essence, where time was accelerating as the world shrank. Chamberlain also consulted with Hankey during the Munich crisis, hoping to learn from his personal experience and long expertise.[51] The prime minister, however, remained undecided on the question of executive control should war break out.[52] His reluctance to be drawn on the matter is easily explained by his fervent belief that war could be avoided. Nevertheless, Bridges sought to 'harvest the experience' of Munich to devise solutions to problems which the crisis had highlighted.[53] He wished the prime minister to place on record which decision he would have taken had war broken out, as a guide in future crises.[54] Fellow officials agreed with Bridges that on the matter of the 'supreme control', it would be beneficial for the premier of the day to be presented with a clear plan of action to approve, rather than a series of options. Rupert Howarth (Deputy Cabinet Secretary) admitted that the issue was so significant 'because the time factor is so much more important now than in 1914'.[55] Horace Wilson broadly agreed on the recommendation of a small War Cabinet with executive responsibility in the event of a large-scale war and concurred that the 'time factor' was increasingly important.[56] Like so many of his generation, Wilson was acutely anxious about time.[57] He confided to an intimate acquaintance his fears of the dangerous 'competition in speed' gripping the world and confessed that operating the machinery of government had become impossible as 'the speed of life today [is] beyond the power of the intelligence and nervous system of the human being. Sound judgement could not be exercised under the conditions now ruling. Decisions had to be given . . . without time for reflections'.[58]

Senior civil servants induced Chamberlain to contribute to the communal store of experience; the prime minister duly placed in the War Book an addendum that he would have formed a small, executive War Cabinet in the autumn of 1938.

The issue of executive direction arose once more as the international scene darkened in the summer of 1939. On 23 August, as the Nazi-Soviet agreement was signed, Chamberlain sought Hankey's advice on establishing a War Cabinet.[59] They discussed the innovations and strengths of Lloyd George's system, and Hankey emphasized the importance of a small group of ministers, largely free from departmental responsibilities.[60] The premier valued Hankey as an official who had been down the proverbial mine before and who might know the way out. Similarly to Bridges's consultations with Ismay, Chamberlain's reliance on Hankey during informal consultations further suggests a performative dimension to the transmission of institutional memory. On the outbreak of war, Chamberlain appointed a War Cabinet of nine members, one of whom was Hankey himself. The bloated, ageing body raised eyebrows; it was perceived as a War Cabinet in name only which could not effectively direct the war effort.[61] It was not what senior civil servants throughout the interwar period had recommended. Bridges admitted to Wilson that he felt 'a good deal perturbed' by the size and composition of the War Cabinet, while other officials agreed that it violated the 'soundest' principles established by Lloyd George – and even agreed by Chamberlain months prior.[62] Civil servants had laid careful plans and drawn on past experiences. Yet even though officials had learned the lessons of the past, politicians had not and failed to grasp the importance of a small, executive War Cabinet.

Chamberlain was ultimately a poor wartime premier; he was more Asquithian than Lloyd Georgian.[63] It was only in May 1940 when Winston Churchill replaced Chamberlain that 'Whitehall was galvanised. . . . We realised we were at war'.[64] Churchill, who had served in bloated cabinets in the First and Second World Wars, understood the lessons of his experiences and instituted the smaller, more dynamic War Cabinet. Moreover, Bridges recalled that the apparatus of government also began to operate at a pace and with an intensity of purpose unlike anything which had gone before: 'the machine . . . overnight acquired one or two new gears, capable of far higher speeds than had ever been thought possible'.[65] Under Churchill, the apparatus of government and the strength of the core executive were extemporarily reformed far beyond Lloyd George's system of 1916. This was the result of the prime minister's personality, in combination with more imaginative reforms in the machinery of government. The former was not in the hands of War Book planners, but the latter were. The measures outlined in the War Book were important – and even with Chamberlain's deviation, far better than the situation in 1914. However, there was one clear failing in preparations. Contingency planners suffered from hubris and overconfidence. They took too much comfort in the past. They were united in the belief that they could map the experience of the 'supreme control' during the First World War directly onto a second total war without further imagination or innovation. Confident that they had discovered the perfect state of administration, officials did not countenance altering the system beyond that established in 1916. It was therefore once more necessary to improvise in the midst of war, at one of the most acute moments of crisis. Such was the danger of looking only to the lessons of the past rather than simultaneously casting minds forward.

III

Civil defence planning was designed to protect the population from enemy attacks such as strategic bombing and was integral to War Book preparations. Air Raid Precautions (ARP) were a form of passive defence against air attack, stemming from the fear that active defences were imperfect and so the bomber would always get through. Profound anxieties surrounded aerial warfare. The frantic pace of technological advancement in the interwar years was disorienting to those who could only compare it to the relatively slow progress of the Victorian and Edwardian eras. By 1938, the record flight speed was 2.7 times faster and the record flight distance was 3.6 times further than it had been at the end of the First World War.[66] The world appeared to be shrinking as distances could be covered faster and easier; as a result, the length of warnings and the margins of error shrank. There existed pervasive fears of a 'knock-out' blow – a pre-emptive aerial strike preceding the declaration of war, where the enemy would rapidly target industrial and urban areas – in order to break morale and destroy military-industrial capacity. The Air Staff continually increased estimates of the tonnage likely to be dropped on British cities as the trajectory of air power capabilities rocketed. However, the chief of the air staff conceded that any estimate was 'pure guesswork'.[67] As the prime minister, Stanley Baldwin, admitted, the 'potentialities' were 'incalculable and inconceivable'.[68] Whitehall and the world beyond were terrorized by increasingly apocalyptic visions of death and destruction as aerial warfare became synonymous with Armageddon.[69] This trope was found in books as well as films during the period, and such dramatizations of futurological thought were reinforced by newsreels of the bombing of Guernica during the Spanish Civil War.[70] Harold Macmillan was not exaggerating when he confessed that he 'thought of air warfare in 1938 rather as people think of nuclear war today'.[71] Deep anxieties gripped the Whitehall elite. Fisher never forgot the haunting experience of 'watching with trepidation German aeroplanes following the course of the Thames'.[72] Hankey questioned the value of preparations which educated Britons 'not to get in a panic when they are being blown to bits'; similarly, John Anderson was highly pessimistic and his mind was clouded with apocalyptic outcomes.[73] Although always of a nervous disposition, Robert Vansittart of the Foreign Office was terrified of how 'the speed and ease with which new types [of air power] are being developed makes it a far more formidable danger than anything in the way of naval or military armaments'.[74] At the heart of this anxiety was the realization that the Channel and the Royal Navy no longer guaranteed the inviolability of the British Isles.

The War Book of 1914 had omitted provisions for civil defence and so the response to Zeppelin raids had been improvised, largely by Arthur Dixon.[75] The experience of raids during the First World War demonstrated the vulnerability of the civilian population and the importance of 'proper organisation and protection'.[76] The addition of civilian defence to the War Book was one of the key recommendations in post-war stocktaking.[77] However, little could be learned from the First World War as attacks had been so limited and air power developed so rapidly in the interwar period. Contingency planners therefore had to 'marry the lessons of the past to a future hypothetical experience'.[78] In contrast to the question of the 'supreme control', officials engaged in civil defence planning frequently looked beyond the lessons of war and were more imaginative; they also sought to learn from German and French defence preparations and harnessed their experiences of planning for contingencies such as strikes.[79]

Much of the work on civil defence in the interwar years was sluggish and hampered by obstructions. The burden of planning in the 1920s fell largely on John Anderson's shoulders, although the detail of schemes was usually elucidated by juniors within the Home Office, including Frank Newsam and Norman Brook, two future permanent secretaries in the making and who both supported post–Second World War contingency planning. Anderson was one of the most skilled administrators to inhabit Whitehall, and he brought his talents to bear on preparations. He identified those who were more expert in their fields and empowered them to reform the machinery as required; Arthur Dixon used the knowledge he had accumulated during the First World War to improve the coordination and effectiveness of the emergency services.[80] Anderson also chaired the ARP sub-committee, which was the central coordinating body for ARP preparations, responsible for devising principles and translating these into detailed plans. He handled the sub-committee with great skill and was both methodical and meticulous in examining a range of issues, including shelters, poison gas, evacuation, lighting restrictions, warning signals, treating casualties, moving the seat of government and repairing damage. Anderson's efforts were crucial in laying the foundations of ARP schemes. However, the sub-committee's consultations with experts in industry and infrastructure were hampered by the need for secrecy and especially after the signing of the Locarno Agreements in 1925, optimism for peace. Anderson repeatedly pressed for greater freedoms of inquiry and tested the limits of how far cautious ministers would permit schemes to be developed.[81] He also worked to draw ministers more closely into preparations, bringing to their attention numerous issues for decision – such as whether evacuation would be government policy, and if so, who was to be evacuated.[82] He hoped to spur more meaningful progress, yet politicians' timidity and competition for their attention undercut his efforts.[83] After a decade's work, the ARP sub-committee had made satisfactory progress in examining the issues and collecting information, although there existed no detailed plans or schemes.[84] Moreover, Anderson's successor at the Home Office, Robert Russell Scott, was much more passive and never as assertive or as knowledgeable.

Matters were somewhat improved in 1935 – the year of the Abyssinian crisis. It was only then that significantly wider freedoms were bestowed on planners, although certain sensitive consultations were still forbidden, as was educating the public. The creation of an ARP department to coordinate inter-departmental efforts and turn vague proposals into firm plans did not greatly advance progress; local authorities were obstructive, finances were short and civil defence planning was 'political dynamite'.[85] Greater progress was made in 1937 as international tensions mounted and the devastating aerial bombardments during the Spanish Civil War re-ignited anxieties. Preparations were made to convert the basement of the Office of Works into the reinforced seat of government; it ultimately grew into a sprawling subterranean network of tunnels and bedrooms, offices, map rooms, meeting rooms and a mess, with a power station and water supply. This 'Hole in the Ground' became the 'nerve centre of British war direction'.[86] At the same time, Warren Fisher, Hankey, Russell Scott, Edward Bridges, Horace Wilson and other senior officials successfully recommended that the Exchequer should provide technical, administrative and especially financial assistance to local authorities, upon whom rested the responsibility for ensuring adequate civil defence measures, to encourage further progress.[87]

Despite nearly two decades of planning, civil defence preparations were at an embryonic stage by 1938, lacking in both coordination and detail.[88] Fisher later correctly criticized that it 'dragged on in a typically English amateurish fashion until a scare . . . accelerated and methodised preparations'.[89] In May 1938, Hankey and Fisher recommended that the country should be divided into regional units under the charge of controllers, who were to be responsible to a minister for home security. They stressed that only limited lessons could be learned from past wars as aerial bombardment was 'inherently different from anything which it has hitherto been necessary to contemplate'. They therefore turned to other emergencies, namely the General Strike of 1926, to guide them.[90] The transport and supply apparatus, as well as the lines of regional administration, had long since been recognized as a valuable template in contingency planning; Anderson had set about distilling the lessons for wartime emergencies immediately after the strike.[91] Indeed, it was also in the spring of 1938 that Anderson returned to Whitehall. He had kept a close eye on lamentably inadequate preparations and was chosen to chair the backbench Committee on Evacuation given his expertise.[92] His committee's recommendations became the key elements in the evacuation scheme instituted in September 1939. Home Office staff worked furiously to translate these recommendations into schemes and completely revised the 'obsolete' War Book in the summer of 1938.[93] However, as plans were still incomplete at the time of the Munich crisis, the Coordination Committee reanimated the Civil Emergency Organisation which had been so successful during the General Strike and renamed it 'Scheme Y'.[94] Anderson was promoted from the backbenches and used his new position of executive responsibility to coordinate all aspects of civil defence, facilitating inter-departmental cooperation and devolving responsibility.[95] Following the crisis, there was a thorough overhaul of civil defence procedures and machinery.[96] It was decided, for example, that greater responsibility should be given to the Ministry of Health and Board of Education in evacuation matters.[97] It was also agreed that 'Scheme Y' – a short-term expedient – was to be included in the War Book as an integral part of civil defence.[98] By September 1939, an elaborate air raid defence scheme had been created, with wardens, firemen, rescuers, ambulances, messengers and a complex but efficient system of organization with local, regional and national layers. There were undoubtedly omissions and difficulties in the implementation and operation of civil defence measures, including confusion over evacuation orders and the lack of deep shelter provision, although preparations were more successful than had officials not engaged in planning.[99]

IV

Copies of the War Book were entrusted to Chief Constables in leafy Devon and Pembrokeshire for safekeeping in the winter of 1940, because: 'If and when the present war comes to an end, we – or our successors – will . . . have to do the same thing again, and it would be rather a tragedy if they had to start from scratch'.[100] This demonstrated the belief that the War Book was an immensely valuable store of institutional memory and that contingency planning was both necessary and beneficial. In preserving and subsequently revising the volume, officials wove a culture of contingency planning into the fabric of the British state. The War Book returned to Whitehall in 1944, and throughout the 1940s, planners attempted to distil the lessons of the Second World War, while also adapting measures to new developments, such as the nuclear age, modern communications, the creation of new departments and obligations arising from membership of the United Nations.[101] Official Histories of the Second World War were another means by which civil servants reflected on, investigated and distilled the lessons of the past.[102] Edward Bridges was a great supporter of the Official Histories, which were originally to be 'for Government use'.[103] One of the first volumes acknowledged that as the aim of the project was primarily 'to fund experience for Government use', the volumes were therefore to be critical and to reveal trials and errors, as it would be futile and dangerous to tell only the stories of success.[104] Norman Brook agreed that the past must not be whitewashed if future governments were to learn from mistakes.[105] This culture persists. Today, contingency planning remains a central responsibility of the Cabinet Office, although officials' capacity to perform this function has been subjected to serious scrutiny in recent years.

Senior officials in the first half of the twentieth century shared a dominant mindset. They regarded the world they inhabited with anxiousness and pessimism; they thus sought to compile an historically informed guide to gain advantage in times of crisis and to mitigate against what they perceived to be Britain's weaknesses. Officials had simultaneously to glance in the rear-view mirror, to adapt to contemporary transformations and to engage in a spot of crystal ball gazing. To a considerable extent, they succeeded, helped in no small part by the blessing that was the Munich crisis. While the second War Book was not perfect – there remained a number of omissions and oversights – the result of decades of historically informed planning was far superior to extemporary scrambling. Furthermore, the revision of the War Book in the interwar years offers several wider insights into Applied History and contingency planning. Naturally, learning from the past can be dangerous if the wrong lessons are learned or if the mistakes of the past are repeated; it can also lull planners into a false sense of security in which overconfidence prevents them from being imaginative or innovative. Fundamentally, learning from the past requires unflinching honesty in self-reflection; human nature is often averse to such self-criticism, especially when it is a public activity. Yet most significantly, learning from the past and harnessing the power of organization matter very little if competence in its many guises is lacking at the heart of state.

Notes

1 Shirley Williams, 'The Decision Makers', in *Policy and Practice: The Experience of Government* (London, 1980), 79–102, at 81.
2 David Reynolds, *Britannia Overruled: British Policy and World Power in the Twentieth Century* (London, 1991), 66–72.

3 Simon Heffer, *The Age of Decadence* (London, 2017).

4 Richard Overy, *The Morbid Age: Britain Between the Wars* (London, 2009).

5 Hastings Ismay, *The Memoirs of General the Lord Ismay* (London, 1960), 45–7.

6 Franklyn Johnson, *Defence by Committee: The British Committee of Imperial Defence, 1885–1959* (London, 1960), 95–6.

7 The Cabinet Secretary was responsible for drafting an authoritative record of Cabinet proceedings, circulating agenda, memoranda and the minutes of meetings to Cabinet ministers, and ensuring the smooth operation of the Cabinet Office. As the first Cabinet Secretary, Hankey made the role his own and often ranged into policy advice.

8 Stephen Roskill, *Hankey: Man of Secrets. Volume I, 1877–1918* (London, 1970), 78–86.

9 The National Archives [hereafter TNA], CAB 38/16/21, 121B, 'Coordination of Departmental Action on the Outbreak of War', 4 November 1910.

10 TNA, CAB 15/2, K5, Note by the Home Office, 24 April 1911; K10, 'Note of Action to be Taken by the Foreign Office', 4 July 1911.

11 Churchill Archives Centre [hereafter CAC], HNKY 8/29, 'Talk between Aston and Hankey', 3 March 1931.

12 TNA, CAB 15/5, War Book, 1914 edition.

13 CAC, BRGS 1/1, Memoir, ff. 36–7; Johnson, *Defence by Committee*, 131–3.

14 David Bell disagrees, *The First Total War: Napoleon's Europe and the Birth of Warfare as We Know It* (Boston, 2007).

15 TNA, T 1/11950, Hankey to Treasury, 25 July 1916.

16 TNA, CAB 24/70, GT6338, Memorandum, Hankey, 21 November 1918.

17 TNA, CAB 15/6/18, 'Home Office Memorandum on the Revision of the War Book', June 1919.

18 CAC, BRGS 1/1, Memoir, ff. 36–7.

19 Keith Middlemas (ed.), *Thomas Jones, Whitehall Diary. Volume I: 1916–1925* (London, 1969), 11 February 1919, 76–7.

20 Ismay, *The Memoirs of General the Lord Ismay*, 50.

21 TNA, CAB 15/1, K8, 11 February 1920.

22 Liddell Hart Military Archives, ISMAY 1/3, 'Principles of Preparation for War'.

23 TNA, CAB 15/1, K27, 18 March 1939.

24 TNA, CAB 21/2577, 'Cabinet Office Internal War Book', 15 November 1930.

25 TNA, CAB 15/22, K165, Anderson to Hankey, 3 December 1929.

26 Richard Hopkins eventually took the matter in hand, TNA T 199/98, Hopkins to Hawtrey, September 1928; Hopkins's minute, 28 May 1929; Hopkins to Fisher, 6 June 1929; CAB 21/2579, 'Entries Recommended in a Treasury Chapter', 5 July 1929.

27 Largely the work of James Rae and Edward Bridges, TNA, CAB 15/24, K294, 'Progress Report on the Treasury War Book', 10 February 1938.

28 TNA, CAB 15/1, W8, Coordination Committee, Eighth Report, 20 November 1925.

29 TNA, CAB 15/24, K263, 'Home Office Progress Report', 18 November 1936; K287, 'Home Office Progress Report', 12 November 1937.

30 TNA, CAB 15/33, K(WB)240, 8 June; K(WB)242, Cadogan to Hankey, 10 June 1938.

31 TNA, CAB 3/8, 301A, 12 November 1938.

32 TNA, CAB 15/1, K26, 23 September 1938; CAB 15/24, K298, 24 September 1938.

33 TNA, CAB 104/93, Pownall to Ismay, 7 December 1938.

34 British Library [hereafter BL], MSS Eur F 207/34, Anderson to father, 29 August 1939.
35 CAC, WELL, Memoir.
36 TNA, CAB 15/1, K28, 26 August 1939, 5.15pm.
37 TNA, CAB 15/1, K29, 26 August 1939, 9pm.
38 CAC, WELL, Memoir.
39 TNA, CAB 104/94, Bridges to Wilson, 25 August 1939.
40 Brian Bond (ed.), *Chief of Staff: The Diaries of General Sir Henry Pownall. Volume I, 1933–1940* (London, 1972), 23 August 1939, 218–20.
41 Ismay, *The Memoirs of General the Lord Ismay*, 97.
42 CAC, WELL, Memoir.
43 TNA, CAB 15/24, K323, 3 September 1939, 10.30am; HO 45/19760, Burgis to miscellaneous officials, 3 September 1939, 11.15.
44 Johnson, *Defence by Committee*, 144–7.
45 TNA, CAB 15/39, 'Memorandum on the Organisation of the War Cabinet Secretariat'.
46 TNA, CAB 175/7, 'Memorandum on the System of Government Control during the War of 1914–1918'; 882B, 'Supreme Control in War'.
47 TNA, CAB 175/5, 883B, 'Supreme Control in War', Trenchard, Madden and Milne, 23 May 1928.
48 CAC, HNKY 4/30, Bridges to Hankey, 7 August 1938.
49 TNA, CAB 104/123, Bridges to Ismay, 11 September 1938.
50 TNA, CAB 104/123, Bridges to Chamberlain, 17 September 1938.
51 CAC, HNKY 4/30, Inskip to Hankey, 12 September 1938.
52 CAC, HNKY 1/7, 27 September 1938.
53 TNA, CAB 104/124, 'The Supreme Control in War: Summary of Papers'.
54 TNA, CAB 175/7, Bridges to Wilson, 5 November 1938.
55 TNA, CAB 104/123, Memorandum, Howarth, 7 November 1938.
56 TNA, CAB 175/7, Wilson to Fisher, 2 December 1938.
57 TNA, CAB 175/7, Fisher to Chamberlain, 7 December 1938.
58 Marguerite Dupree (ed.), *Lancashire and Whitehall: The Diary of Sir Raymond Streat. Volume I: 1931–1939* (Manchester, 1987), 28 June 1938, 576–8.
59 CAC, HNKY 1/7, 23 August 1939.
60 TNA, PREM 1/384, 'War Cabinet', Hankey, 24 August 1939.
61 N. J. Crowson (ed.), *Fleet Street, Press Barons and Politics: The Journals of Collin Brooks, 1932–1940* (London, 1998), 3 September 1939, 253–4.
62 TNA, PREM 1/384, Bridges to Wilson, 3 September 1939; Yates to Rucker, 3 September 1939; Wilson to Bridges, 4 September 1939.
63 John Colville, *Footprints in Time* (London, 1976), 71–2.
64 Ibid., 75–6.
65 Bridges in John Wheeler-Bennett (ed.), *Action This Day: Working with Churchill* (London, 1968), 220.
66 Uri Bialer, *The Shadow of the Bomber: The Fear of Air Attack and British Politics, 1932–1939* (London, 1980), 153.
67 TNA, CAB 3/4, 143A, 'Note by the Air Staff', 24 October 1925.
68 Hansard, Commons, 10 November 1932, Fifth Series, vol. 270, c. 632.
69 Overy, *The Morbid Age*, especially chapter 5.
70 Bialer, *Shadow of the Bomber,* 153; Robert Mackay, *Half the Battle: Civilian Morale in Britain During the Second World War* (Manchester, 2002), 39–40.

71 Harold Macmillan, *Winds of Change, 1914–1939* (London, 1966), 522.
72 Warren Fisher, 'The Beginnings of Civil Defence', *Public Administration* 26 (1948): 211–16, at 213.
73 CAC, HNKY 3/43, Hankey to Robin, 3 April 1938; TNA, CAB 46/1, 2 June 1924 and 23 June 1924.
74 TNA, CAB 63/46, Vansittart to Hankey, 18 January 1933.
75 An Assistant Secretary in the Home Office, who became the greatest authority on coordinating the emergency services.
76 CAC, HDSL 4/11, 'Early Bombing Experiences (1914–1918) and their Lessons'.
77 TNA, CAB 15/6/18, 'Home Office Memorandum on the Revision of the War Book', June 1919.
78 Terence O'Brien, *Civil Defence* (London, 1955), 4–5.
79 TNA, CAB 46/11, ARP(O) Committee.
80 CAC, WELL, Memoir.
81 TNA, CAB 3/4, 133A, John Anderson, 24 January 1925; CAB 3/5, 14 July 1927; CAB 46/4, ARP 57, 'Authority for Consultation and Cooperation', 27 May 1927.
82 TNA, CAB 46/12, ARP(O) 132, 'Note by the Chairman', Anderson, 4 April 1932.
83 TNA, CAB 47/6, ARP(P), 17 October 1932, and 2 February 1933.
84 O'Brien, *Civil Defence*, 33–5.
85 CAC, ROSK 7/87, 'Notes on Disarmament and Re-Armament in the 1930s', Hodsoll; HDSL, 4/15, Review of ARP Department Work, May 1936, Hodsoll; BRGS 1/1, Memoir, f. 36; Fisher, 'The Beginnings of Civil Defence', 214.
86 James Leasor (ed.), *War at the Top: The Experiences of General Sir Leslie Hollis* (London, 1959) 9.
87 TNA, CAB 16/141, DPR 181, 'Financial Aspects of Air Raid Precautions', Simon, 23 March 1937; CAB 16/172, ARPS meeting, 7 May; ARPS 15, 'Report', 30 June 1937; O'Brien, *Civil Defence*, 62; 95.
88 Liddell Hart Military Archives, ISMAY 1/14/66, Hodsoll to Ismay, 19 June 1958.
89 Fisher, 'The Beginnings of Civil Defence', 215.
90 TNA, CAB 3/7, 289A, 'The Coordination and Control of Passive Defence Measures in Time of War', Fisher and Hankey, 23 May 1938.
91 John Wheeler-Bennett, *John Anderson: Viscount Waverley* (London, 1962), 102–7; TNA, CAB 46/2, 31 May 1926.
92 BL, MSS Eur F 207/34, Anderson to father, 26 April 1938.
93 TNA, CAB 2/8, 15 September 1938; CAB 15/1, 1415B, Coordination Committee, Twentieth Report, 17 June 1938; Richard Titmuss, *Problems of Social Policy* (London, 1950), 28–9.
94 TNA, CAB 15/1, K-26, Minutes, 23 September 1938.
95 O'Brien, *Civil Defence*, 166–73; Edward Bridges (1958), 'John Anderson, Viscount Waverley, 1882–1958', *Biographical Memoirs of Fellow of the Royal Society* 4 (1958): 306–25, at 313.
96 TNA, HO 144/21266, Bunker to Gwynn, 13 March 1939.
97 TNA, CAB 3/8, 301A, 'Report of Conference', 12 November 1938.
98 TNA, CAB 15/1, K27, 18 March 1939.
99 TNA, HO 45/19760, Anderson to Brook, 30 August; 'Evacuation', Brook; Wilson to Anderson, 31 August 1939.
100 TNA, HO 45/19760/700050, Wells to Morris and Evans, 20 February 1940.
101 TNA, CAB 175/9, 'Government War Book', November 1948; HO 205/374, Home Office War Book memorandum, July 1950.

102 Their utility as such had long since been recognized; see Robert Horne in Hansard, House of Commons, 13 June 1922, Fifth Series, vol. 155, col. 283.

103 TNA, CAB 21/1084, 'Functions of the Cabinet Secretariat', Bridges, 14 September 1944.

104 Readers can judge for themselves the success of this; see W. K. Hancock and M. M. Gowing, *British War Economy* (London, 1949), xi.

105 Margaret Macmillan, *The Uses and Abuses of History* (London, 2010), 40–1.

9

'Longhaired theoreticians' and long-term thinkers

The use of history within the British Foreign Office during the Second World War

Andrew Ehrhardt

During a conversation in December 1943, the British Foreign Secretary Anthony Eden remarked to Orme Sargent, an under-secretary of state in the Foreign Office, that at the end of the current war the great powers would occupy similar positions to those they held at the conclusion of the Napoleonic Wars in 1815. Stalin, Eden suggested, might even take the place of Tsar Alexander. Though a playful exchange on the margins of official business, a stimulated Sargent furthered explored the historical parallel, delivering a letter to Eden days later. On reflection, Sargent thought that the 'dramatis personae' might be the same, but their roles would be different. The United States would take the place of Great Britain in 1815, the victorious power outside of continental Europe whose strength in industry and foreign trade would leave it wary of continental commitments but open to worldwide connections. Russia might play the same role as in 1815 – the victorious power ambivalent about its future role, while France would assume the part of Prussia, the power which had been defeated early on before rejoining the side of the victorious powers prior to the end of the war. Germany, on the other hand, would take the place of France in 1815, the 'tyrant state which has been defeated'.

As for Britain, after the end of the war, Sargent suggested that it might take the place of Austria in 1815. At the end of the Napoleonic Wars, he wrote, Austria suspected the intentions of Russia and was uncertain as to Britain's willingness to assume its continental role. In the present day, Britain suspected Russia just the same, while it remained sceptical of American involvement in Europe. Austria in 1815 sought to have all matters 'settled and secured' by the end of the war, and it desired a return to a 'pre-war system of European States restored and stabilised under some system which it will be able to control and which will prevent any one Great Power from dominating Europe'. In this way, Austria – like Britain in the current period – became the 'champion of the smaller European states'. 'What is clear', he wrote to Eden, 'is that if our analogy is correct you yourself are destined to be the British Metternich.'[1]

While Sargent noted that this was a broad outline and more 'food for thought', his historical thinking reflected a characteristic of many in the Foreign Office in this period. In moments when the international order was changing – or indeed, in moments when it needed to be reconstructed – Foreign Office officials and others associated with the department looked to history for insight.

This essay explores the extent to which conceptions of a post-war world were conditioned by historical study and experience, both among civil servants and historians themselves. The period marked a highpoint, at least until that stage, of an institutionalization of what scholars today refer to as 'Applied History'.[2] Indeed, the case of the Foreign Office and its planning for the post-war international organization, in particular, is one of the great examples of historians and policymakers applying historical knowledge in the service of diplomatic ends. It also reveals two fundamental characteristics of such historical application – namely, that conceptions of international order, while often visionary and future-focused, are almost entirely conditioned by historical precedent; and second, that competent individuals derive different, sometimes opposing, insights from historical experience.

I

The Second World War marked the second great mobilization of historians into the Foreign Office. It built on a precedent set towards the end of the First World War, when a number of British historians were brought into government service.[3] In that period, both the Foreign Office's Political Intelligence Department and the Directorate of Military Intelligence had historians in their ranks, with J. W. Headlam-Morley serving in the former and Harold Temperley and Charles Webster brought into the latter.[4] More notable, however, was the decision to attach historians to the British delegation attending the Paris Peace Conference. The initiative was led by the young classicists Arnold Toynbee and Alfred Zimmern, both teaching at Oxford at the time, who wrote to members of the War Cabinet Secretariat that those governments which could mobilize relevant historical knowledge would be at an advantage during the forthcoming peace negotiations: 'Whichever party is in possession of the most detailed knowledge regarding the economic and political facts, the plans of the enemy, and the bearing of these facts upon their own, will have a formidable advantage over its opponents in making peace.'[5]

From this, the Historical Section was created in 1917 under the direction of the Cambridge historian George W. Prothero. Originally based in the Admiralty, the Historical Section soon moved to the Foreign Office, where it went on to produce over 170 'handbooks' which addressed questions for the British delegation travelling to Paris.[6] Generally speaking, these historical papers were more supplementary rather than essential reading, although some diplomats, including a young Harold Nicholson, considered these 'peace books', as they were known, to be invaluable.[7] After perusing a study on the Congress of Vienna written by Charles Webster, Nicholson later reflected somewhat harshly that 'I knew exactly what mistakes had been committed by the misguided, the reactionary, the after all pathetic aristocrats who had represented Great Britain in 1814'.[8]

In the years after the war, a number of these historians returned to their university postings, while others set out on new projects which would transform the relationship between historical study and policymaking in the UK.[9] James Headlam-Morley, the assistant director of the Political Intelligence Department during the war, went on to become the historical advisor to the Foreign Office, a position he took over from Prothero. Though his responsibility centred on producing historical memorandum for officials, one of Headlam-Morley's principal preoccupations was to make British foreign policy more accessible to the British public – an initiative which required more access to the archives as well as historians who could write and teach in sober and intelligible terms. Charles Webster, by then the Woodrow Wilson Chair in International Relations at the University College of Wales, Aberystwyth, felt similarly, though he spared no critique of a Foreign Office still hesitant to release old documents. 'If we cannot know the secrets of today's diplomacy, at least we might be allowed to know those of yesterday. . . . It is vital for the understanding of present-day problems that we should know more of the diplomatic history of the nineteenth century.'[10] In a remark which would foreshadow some of the tension between academics and officials in the Foreign Office, Permanent Under-Secretary Eyre Crowe, who had earlier described the academics around the Foreign Office to be 'meddlesome busy bodies', now labelled Webster a 'terror'.[11]

Other historians associated with the wartime work of the Foreign Office and other government departments were also involved in the establishment of the British Institute of International Affairs in July 1920.[12] Led by Lionel Curtis in its early years, the institute eventually hired Toynbee as its Director of Research in 1924. In December of that year, Toynbee published the first *Survey of International Affairs*, a volume of contemporary history which would become one of the hallmarks of Chatham House's work during the interwar period. At the heart of this initiative was a desire, shared by a number of these historians, to make the conduct and practice of diplomacy more accessible to the public.[13] In other words, history was not just useful for those concerned with high policy, but it was seen as essential to an educated public. In the preface of the first edition, Toynbee included a quote from Polybius which read: 'The study of general contacts and relations and of general resemblances and differences is the only avenue to a general perspective, without which neither profit nor pleasure can be extracted from historical research.'[14]

Into the 1930s, historians and political scientists associated with Chatham House were contributing to policy debates through their own writing as well as through debates held at the institute. It was not uncommon in these years for prominent political leaders to engage with intellectuals on the great questions of British foreign policy and international order.[15] On a more substantive level, there were also a series of study groups convened in the latter half of the decade which would lay the groundwork for a new, more formalized relationship with the Foreign Office. Former official-turned-professor E. H. Carr led a group focusing on nationalism, while in early 1939, months before the outbreak of war, a study group dedicated to 'world order' had been designed on the back of recommendations by Curtis, one of Chatham House's original founders.[16]

More so than British statesmen and diplomats who had become consumed by crises in East Asia and Europe, the academics associated with Chatham House in the late 1930s were focusing their attention and ambitions on the construction of a future international system. The World Order Study Group, in particular, turned to outlining new schemes for regional and international order. And in this pursuit, the use of history was deemed indispensable. As Toynbee wrote in 1939,

> The time has now come to try to obtain all the light possible on our own symptoms by studying the symptoms of other societies that unquestionably have fallen in the past. If we can identify the more important symptoms, diagnose the maladies to which they point, and then trace these maladies back to their causes, this may help us to deal with our own case.[17]

Many of the historians associated with this World Order Study Group would go on to form the leadership of the Foreign Research and Press Service (FRPS) when it was established in August 1939.[18] Made up predominantly of academics associated with Chatham House prior to the war, the FRPS came to serve as a principal research body for a host of government departments, work which Toynbee considered to be of 'first class national importance.'[19] By December 1941, Toynbee and his staff in the FRPS were drawing up a provisional scheme for the production of handbooks, ones which would be modelled on those produced for the British delegation to the Paris Peace Conference. These 'historical chapters', they wrote, 'are planned with an eye to the light they throw on current problems.'[20]

In addition to their primary research function, a number of academics working within the FRPS established themselves as thinkers grappling with the big questions of future world order. Toynbee's effort to create a 'peace aims' section within the FRPS led a number of ministers to think that these 'learned men' were covering a certain void when it came to thinking about the future.[21] By the autumn of 1940, the FRPS began working directly with the Cabinet Committee on War Aims – the first concerted effort by the government to outline the nature and parameters of a post-war world.[22] Toynbee himself was brought into the committee as one of the only non-ministerial attendees, even helping to shape the grouping's principal objectives.[23]

The Cabinet committee was largely futile in its efforts, however. By the New Year 1941, there had been no agreement among its members and its original brief was transferred to a smaller sub-committee. Despite the setback, a small group of FRPS academics, including Toynbee, Zimmern and Webster continued to draft ambitious documents related to the post-war world.[24] One in particular, titled 'British-American World Order', described, through a historical lens, the reality facing the future international system.

> The tendency to increasing interdependence, and likewise the tendency to an increasing concentration of armed power, must not be thought of as impersonal forces altogether independent of human volition, though it is not likely that any

effort of statesmanship can arrest them. In the end they are simply the outcome of certain persistent and widespread human desires in the changed circumstances of today.

The solution, the paper proposed, centred on the 'English-speaking peoples' to 'take the lead in the setting up of a world-order on constitutional lines'.[25]

The willingness and ability of FRPS members to address big questions related to the post-war world, at times, ran up against the wishes of the Foreign Office. Despite their reluctance to go too far in the way of post-war planning at this stage –'We are so much in the thick of the battle that we should feel this too great a responsibility', one official wrote – the Foreign Office worried that the work of these professors might be misconstrued by those inside and outside of Whitehall as official policy.[26] The result was an FRPS which was now more closely tied to, and bound by, the Foreign Office hierarchy.[27] Yet on a another level, the Foreign Office approach in this regard stemmed from a common dilemma when academic expertise and policy interact – namely, that officials are not only protective of their own briefs but deem the work of academics, and particularly historians, to be disconnected from practical possibilities. 'I hope it is clearly understood that the Research Centre is to be a Research Centre and not an auxiliary Foreign Office', one official warned.[28]

II

Until 1941, the Foreign Office itself lacked an overarching strategy for the post-war period. The day-to-day demands of carrying out the war preoccupied both officials and their foreign secretary. Although there was no shortage of proposals from those on the fringes of government, at the centre, there was resistance to big and bold ideas for the future, at least at this stage of the war. Officials in the Foreign Office, Orme Sargent, wrote, 'shall do best to stick to simple, short-term ideas, based on certain fundamental, permanent principles . . . and to eschew, however alluring and plausible they may be, far-reaching and all-embracing Utopias'.[29]

But as time went on, certain core pillars of a post-war strategy were developed. Sargent himself took up the issue in September 1940, writing that European countries, during the years which preceded the war, had suffered from a 'moral collapse' and had lost the 'will to self-preservation'. The UK itself had consistently failed to stand up for these smaller European powers. In the future, he wrote, much would depend on three factors: Britain remaining involved in facilitating order on the continent; its own ability to maintain the necessary armaments required for the task; and the willingness of the United States to share some of this burden. Crucially, however, support from Washington, Sargent warned, would only come if Britain was willing to be involved on the continent. 'They will wish Great Britain to play Sparta to their Athens, and if we show any tendency to imitate Sybaris instead, we must not be surprised if they quickly wash their hands of us and make other plans for their own defence which might well prove fatal to this country'.[30]

Though the signing of the Atlantic Charter in August 1941, the United Nations Declaration in January 1942 and the Anglo Soviet Treaty in May 1942 marked what British officials came to see as the 'fixed points' of their post-war policy, the government still lacked an overarching strategy. The Parliamentary Under-Secretary of State at the Foreign Office, Richard Law, warned that without this strategic vision, the UK ran the risk of repeating the same mistakes as the interwar period. 'It was in our strategical thinking, in the strategy of peace, that we made our mistakes. It was because our strategy was wrong that our tactics, whatever they were – and they were various – never worked out.'[31]

Months later, the first attempt at such a strategy was put forward by the newly formed Economic and Reconstruction Department within the Foreign Office. The author of that document, and the head of that department, was Gladwyn Jebb, a mid-career official with ambition and a propensity for frustrating superiors. Having read modern history at Magdalen College, Oxford, Jebb was raised on the works and deeds of famous European leaders. Of Cardinal Richelieu, he had once written that the seventeenth-century statesmen was 'unquestionably the greatest that France ever produced'.[32] As Jebb rose through the ranks of the Foreign Office, he rarely shied away from addressing central questions of British foreign policy, even when such considerations exceeded his brief. In June 1936, Jebb wrote with confidence that 'The "Grand Design" of the League of Nations is over', and that it was time to revamp British foreign policy with 'an astute and lively pursuit of "Realpolitik"'.[33]

Years later, as he set out to address the post-war international order, Jebb's recommendations were rooted firmly in opposition to historians such as Toynbee and Zimmern who the government had, rather mistakenly in his view, turned to for ideas in the years prior. These 'sentimentalists and idealists', as he unfairly labelled them, put forward proposals which were divorced from diplomatic and political practicality.[34] Despite these differences in outlook, Jebb shared with these classicists a respect for and grounding in historical study, a characteristic which would colour his proposals for the post-war world.

In what became his first substantial memorandum aimed at the post-war period, Jebb's entire recommendation was framed by what he viewed as a successful precedent from the preceding century. By bringing together the United States, the United Kingdom, the Soviet Union and China into a working agreement to maintain peace and security across the world, Jebb suggested that they might arrive at a 'Concert of the World' which, Jebb predicted, might keep the peace as the Concert of Europe had stabilized the continent between the Battle of Waterloo and the First World War.[35]

The debate that this memorandum sparked within the Foreign Office was contentious, and senior officials differed over a range of propositions, from the dismemberment of Germany to Jebb's initial recommendation for the great powers to take on spheres of influence. But importantly, many of the arguments put forward, whether in the affirmative or negative, sought to 'apply' the lessons from particular readings of history. Christopher Warner, Head of the Northern Department, took exception to Jebb's idea of the great powers maintaining pre-eminence in specific regions. Instead, he suggested that the concert – or 'supreme council' – emphasize 'the conception that the world is an indivisible whole and that all three powers of the

Concert, as trustees for the other United Nations, have an equal interest in every area'. This arrangement, Warner believed, would represent a system more akin to that which was instituted at the Congress of Vienna in 1815.[36]

After several changes, the Foreign Office advanced Jebb's paper to the Cabinet, this time under the title of the 'Four Power Plan'. Spanning well over twenty pages, the memorandum laid out a comprehensive vision for the political and security architecture of the post-war world. At the heart of the recommendation, however, remained Jebb's idea of a Concert of great powers operating at the centre of a wider grouping of United Nations. Though it would not be formally approved by the Cabinet, it was lauded by officials across various government departments and became the de facto grand strategy for the post-war world. The famed economist Lionel Robbins, then working in the Economic Section of the Treasury, admired its scope and ambition, writing that 'as a piece of draftsmanship it reminded me of the great State papers of pre-1914'.[37]

III

When Britain declared war on Germany in September 1939, Charles Webster was professor of International History at the London School of Economics. A historian of nineteenth-century British diplomatic history, Webster had earned his reputation as one of the first scholars to examine the Congress of Vienna in 1814–15.[38] After writing a dissertation on the subject at Cambridge in 1909, Webster began what was a meteoric rise, securing his first professorship at the University of Liverpool in 1914 and soon after, publishing a monograph which built on his dissertation. In the early years of the First World War, Webster served as junior officer in the Army Service Corps, but by the end of the conflict he was brought to Paris as one of the historians attached to the British peace delegation. This was not without some concerted effort on his part. Given his historical scholarship on what was, until that time, the most profound peace settlement, Webster was determined to be involved in the conference which would inevitably conclude the war.[39] Moreover, he believed that his own expertise would be of some value. The Congress of Vienna, he wrote for the Foreign Office, was the 'only assembly which can furnish even a shadowy precedent for the great task that lies before the statesmen and peoples of the world'.[40]

Though his influence at Paris was marginal, Webster continued to distinguish himself as a historian capable of combining rigorous diplomatic history with commentary on contemporary affairs, particularly issues related to the League of Nations.[41] In these years, his history of the Congress of Vienna and his studies of Lord Castlereagh's foreign policy were balanced with writing for the *Nation and Athenaeum* and *The Times*.[42] A leading figure in the elite Chatham House milieu, Webster was brought into the FRPS in 1939, where he served as one of the senior figures among a group of talented historians, economists and political scientists.

As Gladwyn Jebb and the Economic and Reconstruction Department continued to work on their proposals for the post-war world, they began to consult with Webster, then considered by Foreign Office officials to be the resident expert on international organizations. Jebb's disdain for certain historians associated with the

FRPS – particularly Toynbee who he wrote off as a 'longhaired theoretician' – did not extend to Webster, who he considered to be a 'great power man'.[43] In January 1943, as officials in the Economic and Reconstruction Department continued to plan for the immediate post-war period and beyond, Jebb had asked Webster to draw up a series of papers on the armistices and peace settlements which had been initiated in the period between 1918 and 1919.[44] This historical knowledge, most of which examined aspects of peacemaking and the intricacies of international organization, came to be seen by Jebb and others within the Economic and Reconstruction Department as invaluable to their own work. Webster, Jebb wrote to a colleague, was 'frightfully good' at producing 'short and snappy documents' which could feed into policy development.[45]

Beyond the historical research which Webster delivered to the department, he was also asked to review the latest iteration of Jebb's 'Four Power Plan', the document which advocated a 'Concert of the World' and had, by that time, become a major Foreign Office memorandum. Webster's comments proved useful, but a few in particular stand out for the way in which they brought history to bear on the question. First and foremost, Webster advocated the need for the smaller powers to be brought closer, and more formally, into the larger system. Instead of being a great power dictatorship, the future international order would need to involve the smaller powers. Attuned to Jebb's preference for the nineteenth-century Concert of Europe, Webster noted that the inclusion of smaller powers in disputes relevant to them was a principle which dated back to the Conference of Aix la Chapelle in 1818.[46] A second recommendation involved the location and frequency of meetings between the great powers. Where Jebb had recommended peripatetic council meetings, Webster warned that this arrangement would lead to 'a return to the "Concert" system which, in fact, often means "crisis" meetings and the reluctance or even refusal to be present on the part of one of the powers'. Drawing on more recent historical experience, Webster noted that one of the great successes of the League system, at least after Austen Chamberlain's initiative in the years after the Locarno Treaties, was the 'the regularity of the meetings of the principal statesmen'.[47]

Perhaps most important was the way in which Webster couched his recommendations as being in line with what he called the 'great tradition of British policy'. Negotiation between the great powers and respect for smaller states, he argued on a number of occasions, were distinct legacies of British statecraft and approaches which officials in the post-war period would do well to emulate. Concerning the former, the need for the great powers to ensure frequent and substantive discussion between themselves, Webster spoke of this being in the mould of certain statesmen he admired, namely Lord Castlereagh, Lord Palmerston, Lord Salisbury and, more recently, Lord Balfour and Sir Austen Chamberlain.[48] In a similar fashion, Webster characterized British policy in the years after the Napoleonic Wars as one which sought to respect the rights and interests of smaller powers. He considered Lord Castlereagh, one of his political heroes, as a statesman who not only 'did more than any other man of his period to try and work out a feasible scheme for the co-operation of the Great Powers', but Webster also saw him as 'the greatest defender of the small powers, seeing quite clearly that the two objects were not incompatible but complementary'.[49]

IV

By January 1944, planning within the Economic and Reconstruction Department entered a new, more concerted phase. The Americans, British and Soviets had agreed at the Moscow Conference in October 1943 to establish a post-war organization. In the months that followed this meeting, officials in Moscow, Washington and London set out on their own plans for such an institution.

The Economic and Reconstruction Department remained the principal nucleus of planning for the post-war organization. But as the planning moved into a new, more detailed phase, Jebb's fondness for the nineteenth-century Concert of Europe gave way to more recent historical precedents. The League of Nations, in particular, became the key historical reference point for these British planners. Despite years of disparaging remarks about the institution, when it came to basic structures and functioning of an international organization, the Foreign Office began to look to the League as an indispensable blueprint.

In mid-February 1944, Webster met with Lord Robert Cecil, the principal architect of the League on the British side. Though a steadfast supporter of the institution since its inception, Cecil admitted that the 'essential failure' of the organization was an inability to gather and mobilize a collective force to resist violations of its Covenant. A post-war organization was essential, he believed, but this time it would need the requisite force behind it from the start.[50] It was an opinion shared by Webster. A year prior, he and his colleagues in the FRPS had begun a study outlining the failures of the League of Nations. Though there were notable successes, the organization's shortcomings were catastrophic. But this did not mean that the pursuit of a future organization was futile. As the authors concluded, 'None of the defects in the Covenant was so important as to make it impossible for the League to succeed. Success or failure depended upon the manner in which the Great-Power members of the League would interpret and develop their Covenant obligations.'[51]

Indeed, officials in the Economic and Reconstruction Department recommended that a number of key League structures – in particular, the Economic and Financial Sections, the Health Section and the International Labour Organisation – might be carried over into the new organization.[52] But Jebb was clear that, for the post-war organization to succeed, certain mistakes would need to be avoided. 'The reason why [the League] wouldn't work was in the first place because the existing Great Powers could not agree as among themselves on certain essential things. And until we do get agreement between the World Powers on these essential things no international machine however perfect will ever work.' The Permanent Under-Secretary at the Foreign Office, Alexander Cadogan, also weighed into these planning discussions. His own experience working in – and then leading – the League of Nations section in the Foreign Office between 1924 and 1934 gave him first-hand insight into some of the early successes and later failures of the organization. 'The "machine" of the League became the golden calf', he wrote, and in the future, it would be necessary to avoid a similar 'idolatry'. In line with Jebb's (and the FRPS's) feeling about the need to usher the will of the great powers behind the organization, he added that 'I don't think it's difficult to construct a perfectly good machine. But it's useless without the power and dangerous without the steering gear'.[53]

V

It is clear from even a basic reading of this history of Foreign Office planning that officials were aiming to 'apply' historical knowledge to the questions of policy before them. But on a deeper level, these officials, as well as their counterparts in Moscow and Washington, drew very different insights from their historical references. This reality can be seen in one of the great debates among Foreign Office officials of the time.

In the summer of 1943, the Economic and Reconstruction Department received a paper from the Institute of International Studies at Yale entitled 'The Small Powers and the Enforcement of Peace.' Among other points, the principal author, Professor Arnold Wolfers, had written of the great powers needing to maintain a balance of power between them in order to 'serve as a check on each other'.[54] The conception was somewhat of an aberration, at least in the view of Foreign Office officials, many of whom considered American thinking to be fundamentally opposed to such crude considerations of power. Indeed, Woodrow Wilson had once disparaged such an approach to international politics, while more recently, the US Secretary of State Cordell Hull spoke confidently that there would 'no longer be need for spheres of influence, for alliances, for balance of power'.[55]

For Jebb, Wolfers's paper struck a harmonious chord. The balance of power, he had written elsewhere, was an inescapable reality of power politics. The history of the nineteenth century, in his opinion, had revealed the benefits of this balance operating and adjusting properly, whereas the interwar period had revealed the futility of those attempts which sought to transcend it. 'There are those who seem to think that the balance of power is an old and discredited notion, bearing no relation to modern conditions', he wrote. But to say that this was an outmoded form of statecraft, Jebb believed, was to indulge in baseless idealism. 'In all human affairs what is inevitable is some state of tension. That tension must be maintained evenly, and not be too great or too small. When either of these phenomena occurs, a war seems to follow.' The solution, timeless in the context of modern politics, was a balance of power.[56]

His primary partner in the planning process saw it differently, however. Webster himself understood the significance – and indeed the present importance – of the balance of power.[57] But crucially, he did not view it, like Jebb, as a kind of immovable reality of international politics. Instead, Webster drew from his own historical mind and research a conception of a progressively evolving international system, one which had moved from an anarchic state of nature to a more civilized internationalist order. In this historical framework, the Congress of Vienna was not so much the ideal international order (as Jebb tended to see it) but was instead the first great modern iteration of an internationalist structure. This conception, while far from perfect, had been reinforced and advanced by later conventions and organizations, among them The Hague Conventions of 1899 and 1907 and the League of Nations in 1919. The structures and mechanisms of international order were, in other words, evolving in a certain direction – one which would culminate in a robust world government (and perhaps even a world state).[58]

VI

With the signing of the United Nations Charter on 26 June 1945, both Jebb and Webster took to celebrating. Not only had victory over Germany been secured, but their own work had also laid a foundation for future peace. In the weeks that followed, however, both men returned to London from San Francisco to find a British public somewhat indifferent to their recent accomplishment.[59] It was in this context of dampened enthusiasm for the new organization that the new prime minister, Clement Attlee, prepared to present the United Nations Charter to the House of Commons. As a way of encouraging support for the nascent organization, Webster was asked to prepare a briefing on whether, and to what extent, the UK should claim credit for the production of the Charter.

Naturally, Webster framed the recommendation in the context of the British precedents in the first half of the nineteenth century. Lord Castlereagh, he wrote, was the wise statesmen who, more so than any other delegate at Vienna, had shaped the subsequent Concert system. Yet rather tragically, the humble Castlereagh did little to sell this policy to the British public. The result was a citizenry who, Webster argued, 'associated [the system] with the absurd Holy Alliance which was . . . solely the work of the Tsar'. Canning, on the other hand, had essentially done the opposite. Having done little to protect the smaller states of Latin America, the foreign secretary nonetheless claimed credit in his oft repeated phrase about 'calling the New World into existence to redress the balance of the Old'. Taking these precedents into account, Webster turned to the present question at hand, and argued that

> Neither Castlereagh or [sic] Canning are the right guide at the moment. What we need is something between the two. We must, of course, tell nothing but the truth. But the truth should be told in such a manner as not to offend others who have worked with us. . . . [And] if we are to arouse the interest of the people of this country in the Charter we should be able to show them that their own country has played a not unworthy part in creating it. They are likely to take a far more lively interest in it if they realise that it is founded to a large extent on British conventions many of which date right back in our history.[60]

Though only a fraction of Webster's writing here made it into the prime minister's speech to the House on 22 August 1945, there remained an essential point – one Webster had been championing for years prior – which held that the creation of the organization was in the tradition of British statecraft dating back to 1815.[61]

That Webster placed this development in the time-stream of British diplomatic history was hardly an aberration. Indeed, to a great extent, the approach of British officials to the post-war world was stimulated and shaped by their reading of both distant historical precedent as well as their experience of more recent history. The perceived mistakes of the interwar period and the inadequacies of the League of Nations drove officials into articulating certain aims – among them that the victorious great powers should, working together, take on the primary responsibility for the maintenance of peace and security; and second, that an international organization, while necessary, should not inhibit an effective functioning of that great power responsibility.

On perhaps a deeper and more intellectual level, however, the work of the Foreign Office and its principal planners also reveals important insights into the way in which historical events can yield different conceptions related to the nature and evolution of international politics. Jebb and Webster, though both students and admirers of certain aspects of nineteenth-century British diplomacy, nevertheless harboured very different frameworks which shaped their practical recommendations. For Jebb, history had revealed certain timeless elements of statecraft, chief among them the balance of power, which, in turn, led him to think that the stability provided by the Concert of Europe should be emulated. Webster, on the other hand, saw value in both the balance of power and the Concert system, but crucially, he viewed these as precedents which could, and eventually would, be transcended. The Concert, to Webster, was the first modern stage in a progressive internationalism – one which might eventually arrive at an ever-more robust and extensive form of world government.

Importantly, when it came to the subject of a post-war international order, the historians tied to the Foreign Office – Webster included – played a central role in stimulating and shaping the wider discourse. The academics associated with Chatham House, in particular, had taken up these questions well before the outbreak of war, and once fighting began, they were called upon as both the experts on past precedents and the generators of ideas for the future. Thus, somewhat ironically, historians in the early years of the war were ahead of their counterparts in government when it came to thinking about 'long distance schemes'.[62] But why exactly was this the case? One can point to the obvious fact that these professors simply had more time and less pressure to reflect, ponder and plan. Though true to some extent, a fuller explanation lies in a fundamental but overlooked reality – namely, that knowledge of ancient and modern international history equipped these scholars with a distinct conception of the phenomena, processes and institutions which comprise world order.

Notes

1 The National Archives, Kew, Foreign Office records (FO) 800/277/Mis/43, Orme Sargent to Anthony Eden, 20 December 1943.

2 Graham Allison and Niall Ferguson, *Applied History Manifesto* (Cambridge, MA, 2016); Robert Crowcroft, 'The Case for Applied History', *History Today* 68, no. 9 (2018): 36–41.

3 Keith Hamilton has written of even earlier efforts by Foreign Office officials, namely Eyre Crowe, to establish a research section of the Foreign Office library. The idea here was to have the Foreign Office release documents publicly from the period prior to and including 1837, and to give permitted scholars access to documents through

the year 1860. Keith Hamilton, 'The Pursuit of "Enlightened Patriotism": The British Foreign Office and Historical Researchers during the Great War and its Aftermath', *Historical Research* 61, no. 146 (1988): 316–44, at 317–18.

4   Erik Goldstein, 'Historians Outside the Academy: G. W. Prothero and the Experience of the Foreign Office Historical Section, 1917–1920', *Historical Research* 63, no. 151 (1990), 195–211, at 203. Arnold Toynbee, Alfred Zimmern and Lewis Namier were also brought into the Political Intelligence Department when it was created in April 1918. Hamilton, 'The Pursuit of "Enlightened Patriotism"', 322.

5   Quoted in Goldstein, 'Historians Outside the Academy', 195.

6   Goldstein, 'Historians Outside the Academy'. At the conference itself, there was, Charles Webster later reflected, an 'immense conglomeration of historical talent'. Charles Webster, 'The Study of International Politics', Inaugural Lecture Delivered Before the University College of Wales Aberystwyth, 23 February 1923 (Cardiff, 1923), 11.

7   T. G. Otte has written of the peace books that 'their real value lay in establishing the nature of the problems likely to be settled at the Peace Conference rather than in producing blue prints for their solution'. See T. G. Otte, '"The Light of History": Scholarship and Officialdom in the Era of the First World War', *Diplomacy & Statecraft* 30, no. 2 (2019): 253–87, at 264.

8   Quoted in Goldstein, 'Historians Outside the Academy', 203.

9   T. G. Otte has written of the ways in which many of these historians' experience in government during the war shaped their academic approaches in the decades that followed. See Otte, 'The Light of History'.

10 Charles Webster, 'The Labour Government and Secret Diplomacy', *The Nation & The Athenaeum*, 21 June 1924, copy of this article is in London School of Economics archives, Charles Webster papers, Webster 5/5. This initiative of Webster – and the pushback it received in the Foreign Office – has been covered in Hamilton, 'The Pursuit of "Enlightened Patriotism"', 339–40.

11 For Crowe on 'meddlesome busy bodies', see Sir Alan Campbell, 'Sir Eyre Crowe, 1864–1925', FCO Historical Branch, Occasional Papers, no. 8 (1994): 43. Webster described as a 'terror' is quoted in Hamilton, 'The Pursuit of "Enlightened Patriotism"', 340.

12 As a number of historians have written, the idea for such an institute was originally negotiated in May 1919, on the side lines of the ongoing Paris Peace Conference. Though some proposed a bi-national institute, it was eventually decided that Americans would develop their own institute (the Council on Foreign Relations), and the British would set up a new organization, called the British Institute for International Affairs. The name was later changed to the Royal Institute for International Affairs. William McNeill, *Arnold J Toynbee: A Life* (New York, 1989), 121.

13 There were undoubtedly other political motivations – among them versions of federalism and internationalism – which permeated the ranks of Chatham House in the interwar period. See Gerald Studdert-Kennedy, 'Christianity, Statecraft and Chatham House: Lionel Curtis and World Order', *Diplomacy & Statecraft* 6, no. 2 (1995): 470–89, at 470–1; Inderjeet Parmar, *Think Tanks and Power in Foreign Policy: A Comparative Study of the Role and Influence of the Council on Foreign Relations and the Royal Institute of International Affairs* (New York, 2004), 70–4.

14 Polybius, *The Histories*, Book I, Chapter 4, quoted in Arnold Toynbee, *Survey of International Affairs, 1920–1923* [1924] (Oxford, 1927), x.

15 To take one example, Ernest Bevin chaired a lecture delivered by Lionel Curtis in February 1939 entitled 'World Order'. Then still serving as the General Secretary of

the Transport and General Workers Union, Bevin complained that 'the trouble with the League of Nations had been that it had been given a political head, a Labour tail, but no economic body'. Bevin remarks are cited in Lionel Curtis, 'World Order', *International Affairs* 18, no. 3 (1939): 301–20, at 318.

16   Michael Cox, 'Review essay: E. H. Carr, Chatham House and Nationalism', *International Affairs* 97, no. 1 (2021): 219–28; Curtis, 'World Order', 301–20.

17   Arnold Toynbee, 'The Downfalls of Civilisations', Hobhouse Memorial Lecture at the LSE, 1939, copy in Toynbee 3, the Papers of Arnold Toynbee, Bodleian Library Archives, University of Oxford.

18   For some background on the establishment of the Foreign Research and Press Service, see Andrea Bosco, *Federal Union and the Origins of the 'Churchill Proposal'* (London, 1992), 144, 154–8; Robert Keyserlingk, 'Arnold Toynbee's Foreign Research and Press Service, 1939–1943 and Its Post-War Plans for South-East Europe', *Journal of Contemporary History* 21, no. 4 (1986): 539–58, at 542–46.

19   Quoted in McNeill, *Arnold J. Toynbee*, 180.

20   FO 371/28909/W14445, Note on the Provisional Scheme for Foreign Office Handbooks, 23 December 1941.

21   CAB 21/1582, Duff Cooper to Lord Halifax, 9 September 1940. For 'peace aims' section of the FRPS, see McNeill, *Arnold J. Toynbee*, 182.

22   CAB 21/1582, Minutes of the War Cabinet Committee on War Aims, WA(4) 1st Meeting, 4 October 1940; Duff Cooper to Neville Chamberlain, 12 September 1940; Keyserlingk, 'Arnold Toynbee's Foreign Research and Press Service', 548–9. See also Raymond Douglas, *The Labour Party, Nationalism and Internationalism, 1939–1951* (London, 2004), 103–10.

23   For an account of the committee and its work, see Christopher Hill, *Cabinet Decisions on Foreign Policy, October 1938–June 1941* (Cambridge, 1991), 188–215.

24   See for example memoranda by Arnold Toynbee, 'The Oceanic versus the Continental Road to World Organisation: The Two Roads and their History' and 'Why Great Britain Cannot Cut Herself off from the Continent', 30 June 1941, FO 371/28902/W9336.

25   The paper was authored by Toynbee although Zimmern, Webster and other leading members of the FRPS contributed. Memorandum by Arnold Toynbee, 'British-American World Order', 25 July 1941, FO 371/28902/W9336.

26   FO 371/28899/W4533, R. A. Butler to Arthur Greenwood, 10 April 1941.

27   FO 371/28899/W5327, Frank Ashton-Gwatkin to Arnold Toynbee, 2 May 1941.

28   FO 371/28899/W6547, Foreign Office minute from 20 June 1941.

29   FO 371/25207/W9699, Sargent minute on paper by Julian Huxley, 10 August 1940.

30   FO 371/25208/W11399, Memorandum by Sargent, 'Some Observations on Peace Plans', 28 October 1940.

31   FO 371/35363/U830, Richard Law, 'Speech to Cambridge Society for International Affairs, 18 March 1942', *Time and Tide*, 21 March 1942.

32   Papers of Gladwyn Jebb, Churchill College, University of Cambridge, GLAD 9/1/7, Essay by Jebb, 'How far is it true that Richelieu was as great a failure as a home minister as he was successful as a politician?', undated.

33   FCO 73/262/It/36/8, Memorandum by Jebb, 'Probable consequences of closing or failing to close the Suez Canal to Italy', undated, 1936.

34   FCO 73/264/Pwp/42/48, Jebb minute, 4 November 1942. Quoted in Sean Greenwood, *Titan at the Foreign Office: Gladwyn Jebb and the Shaping of the Modern World* (Leiden, 2008), 164.

35 FCO 73/264/Pwp/42/8, Draft memorandum by Jebb, 'Relief Machinery: The Political Background', August 1942, 2.

36 FCO 73/264/Pwp/42/18, Warner minute, 18 August 1942.

37 FCO 73/258/Eu/43/1, Lionel Robbins to Nigel Ronald, 25 February 1943.

38 T. G. Otte, '"The Confederation of Europe"? British Views of the Congress of Vienna in the nineteenth and twentieth centuries', in *Der Wiener Kongress 1814/1815, Vol. II* (Vienna, 2019), 321–30.

39 Papers of Charles Webster, LSE Archives, Webster 23/6, Webster, unpublished autobiography, 1.

40 Charles Webster, *Congress of Vienna, 1814–1815* (New York, 1963), iii.

41 At Paris, Webster produced an admirable paper on the lessons of the Congress of Vienna, though US president Woodrow Wilson was said to have scoffed at what he deemed to be a form of 'old diplomacy'. According to Webster, Wilson remarked that there would be 'no odour of Vienna . . . brought into the proceedings'. Webster mentioned this anecdote in the preface of the 1934 edition of his book *The Congress of Vienna*. For a copy of this preface, see Webster, *Congress of Vienna, 1814–1815*, 15.

42 Webster, *The Congress of Vienna, 1814–1815*; Webster, *The Foreign Policy of Castlereagh, 1812–1815*, Volume I (London, 1931) and *The Foreign Policy of Castlereagh, 1815–1822*, Volume II (London, 1934).

43 On Webster as a 'great power man', see Gladwyn Jebb, *The Memoirs of Lord Gladwyn* (New York, 1972), 120. Jebb wrote of Toynbee and Chatham House that 'So long as Chatham House endeavors to exercise a sort of droit de regard over F.R.P.S., the Foreign Office will be open in Parliament to the accusation that its policy is being influenced by longhaired theoreticians. Once the F.O. form their own Research Section such criticisms will have no foundation'. FCO73/264/Pwp/42/57, Jebb to Richard Law, 7 December 1942.

44 As a part of his work for the Foreign Research and Press Service, Webster had been drafting documents related to the armistice and peace settlements between 1918 and 1919. Copies of these papers, along with other memoranda, can be found in Webster 11/1 and 11/2, the Papers of Charles Webster, LSE Archives. These historical accounts were, in turn, circulated to British diplomats. See FCO 73/264/Pwp/43/4A, Jebb to Clark Kerr, 11 February 1943.

45 FCO 73/266/UN/43/1, Jebb to Michael Wright, 7 June 1943.

46 Webster's understanding of the Conference of Aix la Chapelle went back to his doctoral thesis at Cambridge. See Papers of Charles Webster, King's College, University of Cambridge, KCAC/4/11/1/Webster, Webster, Introduction, 'Studies in Foreign Policy, 1814–1818', Dissertation, 1909.

47 FO 371/35396/U2066, Note by Webster, 'Some Considerations on a United Nations Organisation', 6 May 1943.

48 Webster drafted the covering brief for the memoranda which was presented by the Minister of State. See FO 371/40689/U3128, Richard Law, Covering brief for 'Future World Organisation: Forthcoming Conversations at Washington', 16 April 1944.

49 Papers of Charles Webster, LSE Archives, Webster 15/2, Webster, Castlereagh or Canning, undated.

50 Webster diary, 15 February 1944, P. A. Reynolds and E. J. Hughes, *The Historian as Diplomat: Charles Kingsley Webster and the United Nations, 1939–1946* (London, 1976), 26–7.

51 Papers of Charles Webster, LSE Archives, Webster 11/6, Memorandum by the Foreign Research and Press Service, 'Memorandum on the Causes of the Failure of the League', 11 January 1943.

52 FO 371/40685/U350, Jebb minute, 19 January 1944.

53 FO 371/40686/U2198, Cadogan minute, 4 February 1944.

54 FO 371/35397/U3814, Arnold Wolfers, 'The Small Powers and the Enforcement of Peace', 1 August 1943, Yale Institute of International Studies.

55 For Hull's comments, see 'Allies on the Offensive', *The Times*, 19 November 1943. President Roosevelt made similar remarks in the aftermath of the Yalta Conference held in February 1945. See David Reynolds, 'The Diplomacy of the Grand Alliance', in *The Cambridge History of the Second World War*, ed. Richard Bosworth and Joe Maiolo (Cambridge, 2015), 301–23, at 319–20.

56 FCO 73/263/Mis/44/1, Gladwyn Jebb, Lecture on 'The Balance of Power' delivered to the Canning Club, Oxford University, 21 February 1944.

57 Papers of Charles Webster, LSE Archives, Webster 1/23, Letter from Charles Webster to Sir Stafford Cripps, 23 September 1942; Webster, 'Review of *Europe's Classical Balance of Power* by Edward Vose Gulick', *The English Historical Review* 72, no. 282 (1957): 131–2.

58 In 1908, as a graduate student at Cambridge, Webster wrote a paper entitled 'The Evolution of a World State.' Decades later, it was clear through a number of editorials in *The Times* that Webster held on to these seemingly radical views. Papers of Charles Webster, LSE Archives, Webster 21/1, Webster, 'The Evolution of a World State', unpublished paper, 3; Webster, 'A Matter of Gradual Evolution', *The Times*, 16 July 1938.

59 FO 371/50732/U5998, Memorandum by Jebb, 'Reflections on San Francisco', 25 July 1945.

60 Papers of Charles Webster, LSE Archives, Webster 15/2, Memorandum by Webster, 'Castlereagh or Canning', 24 July 1945.

61 *Hansard*, House of Commons Debate, Vol. 413, cols. 659–755, 22 August 1945.

62 This phrase was used by Jebb to describe what he believed the officials in the Economic and Reconstruction Department should be focused on. FCO 73/263/Misc/42/1, Gladwyn Jebb to Orme Sargent, 20 June 1942.

10

Problems left over from history

British officials and three diplomatic challenges

Peter Ricketts

Old nations carry a lot of history around with them. It lurks just below the surface of their relations with other countries, a danger to the unprepared. I found in forty years as a member of the Foreign and Commonwealth Office (FCO) that the past was never far away. The Gibraltar desk officer needs a working knowledge of the 1713 Treaty of Utrecht, still the basis of Britain's claim to the Rock. Handling the Argentina/Falklands dossier means delving even further back – to 1690, when Captain Strong staked a claim to the islands and tactfully named them after the First Lord of the Admiralty of the time. When working on the Arab–Israel dispute in 1981, I was involved at the edges of the negotiations between Israel and Egypt about the former's withdrawal from the Sinai Peninsula. The two sides could not agree where the border between them would run. There was a dispute in particular as to which side of the line the beach resort at Taba fell. When it went to international arbitration, we in the FCO were able to dig up from the archives a crucial piece of evidence – the 1906 border delimitation survey report, with a map agreed between Mr W Jennings-Bramley, the British Frontier Administration Officer in Sinai and Rushdi Bey, the Ottoman Commandant of Aqaba. It pointed the way to some stone markers in the desert, which were still in place. As a result, if you spend a holiday there, you are in Egypt.

Since history has played such a part in its work, the FCO is the most historically aware Whitehall Department. For more than a century, it has had its own in-house historical capability. In 1918, ministers realized that they would need historical expertise from outside the civil service as they grappled with re-drawing the map of Europe at the coming Versailles peace conference. The Admiralty's Naval Intelligence Department and the Department of Information had already stolen a march on them by setting up their own historical sections. The War Cabinet decided that both should be moved into the FO to form the Political Intelligence Department (the forerunner of the present-day Research Analysts) and a separate Historical Section. They have been there ever since, in different shapes and sizes.

The aim of this chapter is to consider three case studies from my own experience to illustrate some of the factors which influence whether history can be successfully applied to the practical business of making foreign policy. The first concerns the

UK-China negotiations over Hong Kong in 1982–4, the last great diplomatic set-piece of the decolonization era. The second examines the efforts to inject historical expertise into Mrs Thatcher's approach to German unification in 1989–90. The third marks the only occasion during my career when the FCO's own professional historians emerged from the shadows to take centre stage, at the London Conference on Nazi gold in 1997.

I

No problem during my career was more suffused with history than Britain's negotiation with China over the future of Hong Kong, which began with Mrs Thatcher's visit to Beijing in 1982.[1] The phrase *problems left over from history* was often used by Chinese premier Zhou Enlai to refer to territorial disputes – for example, the Sino-Indian border and Taiwan. It applied with a vengeance to Hong Kong since, in Chinese eyes, the territory had been ceded to Britain under 'unequal treaties' imposed by imperial force on the nineteenth-century Qing rulers. But Zhou had been in no hurry to deal with the problem. The UK-China negotiations only happened when they did because the 1898 Convention of Peking – which gave Britain an extension to the Crown Colony amounting to some 92 per cent of modern Hong Kong – defined a leasehold period of 99 years. That period seems to have been chosen because the British negotiator, the British minister to China, Sir Claude MacDonald, thought that it was 'as good as forever'. But leaseholds eventually fall due. Hong Kong land leases normally run for fifteen years, and by the late 1970s the uncertainties about post-1997 were weighing on the property market.

Deng Xiaoping's emergence as paramount leader of China in late 1978 prompted hopes in Hong Kong that he would put economic interests ahead of politics, particularly when he launched his 'open door' policies, inviting inward investment into China and creating special economic zones. Governor Sir Murray MacLehose went to Beijing in 1979 to sound out the ground and Deng told him that Hong Kong people could 'set their hearts at ease'. But in April 1982, while Mrs Thatcher was busy recapturing the Falklands Islands from Argentine occupation, Deng took advantage of a visit by the former prime minister Edward Heath to pass a clear message to London. China would take back sovereignty over Hong Kong, but maintain its status as a free port and international financial centre. From then on, it was clear that Britain would have to conduct a full-blown negotiation with China over the future of Hong Kong.

Yet this negotiation so steeped in history happened without the benefit of professional historical expertise. There were three main reasons for that. First, this was a negotiation with a very different China. Deng had only recently triumphed over the Gang of Four and swept aside Hua Guofeng to become the unchallenged leader. Deng was a largely unknown quantity in the West, and his policies were only just taking shape. Previous diplomatic negotiations, of which the most high-profile had been Kissinger's in 1971–2 to establish relations between the United States and China, had taken place with Mao Zedong and Zhou Enlai.

Second, it was a negotiation unlike any other. It was not an independence negotiation, nor a bilateral deal on trade or diplomatic relations which had been the stock-in-trade of dealings with Communist China at that point. In those cases, both sides had something to gain. As Kissinger described his negotiation

> What the Chinese leaders wanted was reassurance that America would not cooperate with the Kremlin in the implementation of the Brezhnev doctrine; what Nixon needed to know was whether China might cooperate with America in thwarting the Soviet geo-political offensive.[2]

In the Hong Kong negotiation, the Chinese side held most of the cards.

The third reason was that the whole process was carried out in great secrecy. On the British side, Mrs Thatcher decreed that very few people were to be involved in London and Hong Kong. This was partly because of the acute anxieties in Hong Kong. The six million residents, many of them refugees from the successive upheavals on the mainland, had to watch as their fate was decided above their heads between London and Beijing, with only the (British) governor and a small team around him fully involved at the Hong Kong end. Once the period of negotiations began following Mrs Thatcher's visit to Beijing in September 1982, confidence in Hong Kong was fragile. It would have been even more so if Hong Kong people had been told about Deng's confirmation to Mrs Thatcher in those September talks that China would certainly recover Hong Kong in 1997, otherwise 'new China would be like the Qing dynasty and present leaders like Li Hongzhang' (a Qing Minister in the late nineteenth century regarded by the Chinese Communist Party as the archetypal traitor). Deng said that this decision would be announced after 'one or two years', setting a deadline for the negotiations of September 1984. The secrecy surrounding the negotiations meant that the Hong Kong media watched for the slightest sign of how the negotiations were going. When they reached a deadlock in September 1983, the Hang Seng index dropped by 15 per cent.

These conditions made it difficult to consult anyone outside the magic circle. The content and tempo of the negotiations added to that. The heart of the negotiations was a document (which became the annex to the Joint Declaration signed by the two sides in December 1984) spelling out the details which underpinned China's undertaking that after 1997

> the current social and economic systems in Hong Kong will remain unchanged, and so will the life-style Rights and freedoms, including those of the person, of speech, of the press, of assembly, of association, of travel, of movement, of correspondence, of strike, of choice of occupation, of academic research and of religious belief will be ensured by law in the Hong Kong Special Administrative Region.[3]

The expertise on this mass of highly complex material, from the legal, taxation and financial system to land leases, shipping and air services, was held by the Hong Kong government. The negotiations themselves took place in Beijing, at an increasingly frantic pace as Deng's deadline of September 1984 for agreement drew nearer. English and Chinese texts were discussed in parallel. For the British side, this involved an intense three-way, two-language consultation. The team in Beijing would report by telegram each evening the evolving text and its problems. The governor and the small team involved in Hong Kong would comment. London would take any necessary decisions and respond with instructions. Geoffrey Howe records in his memoirs that, in the first nine months of 1984, the FCO sent 2,400 telegrams to Hong Kong and Beijing, and received 2,300 and 1,700 from them respectively. I was involved as private secretary to Geoffrey Howe from late 1983, and vividly recall the piles of telegrams on the table of the Head of Hong Kong Department, Tony Galsworthy, as he worked through the various instructions needed for the start of the new working day in Beijing. I also waited late in the office for the nightly submissions to the foreign secretary on tricky points from Percy Cradock, the former ambassador to China, at that time the master strategist and the closest adviser to both Geoffrey Howe and Margaret Thatcher on the whole Hong Kong issue.

This was not a process on which external historical expertise could hope to get any purchase. There was another reason as well why Mrs Thatcher was determined to keep the whole process secret. The decisions involved were agonizingly difficult for her. Charles Moore, in his biography, notes evidence that as early as January 1982 Mrs Thatcher accepted that sovereignty would have to be conceded.[4] But the more she immersed herself in the issue, the more she recoiled from the idea, and the more determined she became to reach an agreement that would be acceptable to the people of Hong Kong. During her September 1982 visit, she pressed Deng Xiaoping and his premier Zhao Ziyang hard on the idea of continued British administration after 1997. But they bluntly rejected that. After testing all the other options to destruction, Mrs Thatcher moved by slow, painful steps to accepting that the British administrative link would have to be broken in 1997. This was the most compelling reason for keeping the strategic decisions about handling the negotiations to a small inner group.

Mrs Thatcher did, however, make herself the conduit for views from Hong Kong. In the absence of any elected representatives, these were mainly the Unofficial Members of the Governor's Executive Council (ExCo), who were in the extremely uncomfortable position of being closely linked to the British administration of Hong Kong, but excluded from the magic circle of knowledge as to what was going on in the negotiations. They also had very little experience of Chinese political leaders, who were unwilling to engage with them. Their knowledge of China was mainly through business dealings, and as a result they often took an over-optimistic view on whether China would allow its economic interest in Hong Kong to take precedence over the politics of control. As Charles Moore put it, Mrs Thatcher

> understood more clearly than colleagues that the confidence in capitalist Hong Kong which everyone, even the Chinese communists, wished to maintain, depended much more on whether Hong Kong people believed in the future than on whether China and Britain could get all the sub-clauses right.[5]

Mrs Thatcher did, however, seek advice from one exponent of the art of Applied History – Henry Kissinger. She invited him to dinner at No 10 Downing Street in November 1982 after his visit to China the previous month. He told Charles Moore that 'the whole evening was her fighting the idea of giving up Hong Kong at all, and then seeing various levels of retreat'.[6] Her side of the conversation is airbrushed out of the No 10 account.[7] This records Kissinger's impressions of China and Deng, and on Hong Kong reports him as saying that although he had not discussed the subject much, 'they were groping for a legal framework which gave them sovereignty but enabled Hong Kong to remain more or less what it is'. That is recognizable as a summary of Deng's thinking as he put it to Mrs Thatcher. But his surmise about where the Chinese bottom line would lie sounded more like Mrs Thatcher than Deng

> He believed they would accept titular sovereignty with British administration continuing . . . Chinese history showed they were used to the concept of vague suzerainty without actual control.

If Kissinger so misjudged Deng's intentions having just talked to him, there was little prospect that China scholars would have been able to add much value.

The downside of a policy devised and implemented in conditions of great secrecy is the risk of group-think and the absence of challenge. The FCO's China hands who masterminded the policymaking were something of a cadre apart in the Foreign Office. They had all followed a similar path which began with Chinese language training and led to postings in Hong Kong and Beijing. Those destined for the top were seconded to Hong Kong in mid-career as the governor's political adviser and would expect to finish their careers either as ambassador in Peking or in gubernatorial splendour in Hong Kong, or – in the case of the governor during the 1982–4 negotiations Sir Edward Youde – both. As a result, they knew each other well and had a lot of shared experience of Hong Kong and China. Sir Percy Cradock was the dominant intellectual force within this group. The governor Sir Edward Youde and Tony Galsworthy, who had been Cradock's political counsellor in Beijing before returning as head of Hong Kong Department in 1984, also had both a deep knowledge of China and recent experience of Deng's regime. That group, at that time, had more relevant expertise among them than any external China scholar could hope to have. So the historical expertise was supplied from within the home team – with the strengths and weaknesses of that.

Cradock was clear at the very first meeting Mrs Thatcher held on the issue – in July 1982 – that it would be necessary to concede sovereignty to avoid confrontation.[8] The FCO team had little doubt that this would mean ceding effective British control as well. But there *was* challenge in the system, and it came largely from one person – Mrs Thatcher herself. She kept up a sustained barrage of doubts and questions as she searched for a way of safeguarding the interests of Hong Kong people and finding a solution which was politically saleable to her party and Parliament. In the process, she tested Chinese bottom lines hard. The combination of her obduracy and the negotiating skills of the FCO team achieved the remarkable commitment by Communist China in an international treaty to keep the rights and freedoms and the way of life of capitalist Hong Kong intact for fifty years.

There is, however, one area where an external challenge at an earlier stage to the traditional British approach to Hong Kong could have paid dividends. This is the development of a more democratic system of local government in Hong Kong. The main weakness in the Joint Declaration with hindsight was that it contained only a passing reference to this. After 150 years of British rule, the Legislative Council (LegCo) was in 1984 still wholly appointed by the governor. The last concession Geoffrey Howe squeezed out of his Chinese counterpart before the deal was sealed in September 1984 was that LegCo would after 1997 be 'constituted by elections'. It now seems paradoxical, but this had not been a big issue during the negotiations. Mrs Thatcher was much more preoccupied with achieving some form of continuing British say in the affairs of Hong Kong after 1997. The Unofficial members of the Executive and Legislative Councils were mainly preoccupied with Hong Kong's economic interests and had no great wish to see the arrival of elected politicians.

After 1984, Governor Sir Edward Youde began very cautiously to introduce the vote, first with a process of indirect election by small functional constituencies and, from 1991, the first direct election for eighteen out of the sixty seats in the legislature. By then, the Chinese crackdown on popular protests in Tiananmen Square in Beijing in 1989 had politicized debate in Hong Kong, and the pro-democracy party headed by Martin Lee won fourteen of the directly elected seats. The last governor Chris Patten arrived in 1992 determined to leave Hong Kong with a stronger legacy of local elected government. I was part of the negotiating team that laboured through seventeen rounds of negotiations in Beijing during 1993 trying to secure Chinese agreement that the last election under British rule in 1995 should take place with a modestly increased franchise and that the LegCo elected then should continue beyond the 1997 handover, creating useful continuity. This was all too late. The Chinese leadership were more determined than ever to avoid Hong Kong infecting China with the virus of democracy. After the handover, they replaced the 1995 LegCo with one of their own design.

After the 1997 handover, the development of local democracy was essentially frozen, until the changes to the electoral system imposed by the Chinese authorities in 2021 marked a major step away from genuine democracy. Many LegCo Members stood up with great courage to the encroachment by the Chinese authorities on the rights and freedoms promised to the people of Hong Kong in the Joint Declaration since 2019. But they would have been in a stronger position if local democracy had put down deeper roots. It would have given Hong Kong greater resilience if governors of the 1970s and 1980s had been challenged to give the people of Hong Kong more of a voice in local issues through elections to LegCo. That would have created a local political culture. It would also have enabled British negotiators in the 1980s and 1990s to argue that local democracy was an essential part of Hong Kong's way of life.

II

One way of viewing British policymaking on Hong Kong in the 1980s was that an inner group of officials used their knowledge of Chinese history, politics and tactics to help Mrs Thatcher discard an unachievable objective (continued British administration) in favour of a just achievable one (pinning the Chinese side to a detailed undertaking to preserve Hong Kong's way of life for fifty years).

The debates in Whitehall about the issue of German reunification in the months after the fall of the Berlin Wall in late 1989 bore some resemblance to this, but they were played out in a much wider and more public setting, as part of the hectic diplomacy as Chancellor Kohl bulldozed his way towards reunification. They essentially involved challenging the instinctive historical analogies leaders like Mrs Thatcher reach for in reacting to a crisis. In this case, a group of external historians were brought in to conduct this challenge at a second Chequers seminar in March 1990. It was a discreet occasion – until the frank record by the prime minister's private secretary Charles Powell was leaked to the media three months later, just when German worries about Mrs Thatcher were beginning to ease.

The prime minister had played a key role in making the outbreak of freedom in Eastern Europe possible. She had been the first Western leader to establish a rapport with Gorbachev – indeed her first meeting with him, at which she decided he was a man she could do business with, came on the eve of her departure to sign the Hong Kong agreement in December 1984. But instead of seeing the fall of the Berlin Wall in November 1989 as an unalloyed triumph, she was immediately worried about the prospect of a reunified Germany. She was concerned that, if this happened fast, it could destabilize Gorbachev and therefore the prospect of a new relationship with Russia. But her central fear was of a revival of a powerful nationalist Germany at the heart of Europe. Here, she reached for what American historians Richard Neustadt and Ernest May called in their book on the uses of history by decision-makers[9] an 'irresistible analogy' drawn from her personal experience. Charles Moore commented:

> As a child of the 'home front' in the Second World War, she had a visceral dislike of German power.[10]

He also quoted comments from Condoleezza Rice, then the Russia expert on the US National Security Council staff, that the perception of the prime minister's approach in the White House at that time was that

> Whenever she would talk about German unification, Thatcher would bristle, recalling how the Germans had sent her family scurrying into bomb shelters as a child.[11]

Mrs Thatcher drew an instinctive analogy between the Germany of her childhood and the likely behaviour of a reunited Germany in the 1990s. She was not alone in worrying about the implications of a strong Germany for European institutions. President Mitterrand seems to have been just as uneasy in private, but he was not nicknamed The Sphinx for nothing. Mrs Thatcher was anything but sphinx-like. Even before the Wall came down, she was remarkably frank with Gorbachev during a visit to Moscow on 22 September

> Although NATO traditionally made statements supporting Germany's aspiration to be reunited, in practice we would not welcome it at all.[12]

She spoke in similarly forthright terms to a wide range of leaders. Mrs Thatcher's emotional response trapped her in the contradiction of welcoming victory in the Cold War and freedom for the countries of Eastern Europe while opposing the direction which the East Germans inevitably sought to take – a single, united Germany. She was slower than other Western leaders to see that reunification was going to happen, and more public than anyone else in expressing her worries. George Bush moved fast to support Kohl's accelerating drive for reunification. Mitterrand kept his anxieties largely to himself and put the Franco-German relationship above all else. Even Gorbachev came to terms with the inevitability of unification before Mrs Thatcher.

The Foreign Office advised from the outset that the focus should not be on trying to stop reunification but on handling the implications for the EU and NATO. A first attempt to persuade the prime minister to take this line was made at a Chequers seminar in late January confined to ministers and officials. It made some tactical progress, concluding that British policy should be to slow down reunification for a 'transition period' but not as a covert attempt to prevent the process. It did not, however, make any headway in contesting Mrs Thatcher's irresistible analogy, or the conclusion she drew from it that a reunified Germany was not in Britain's interests because it could once again become a nationalist power threatening the balance of power in Europe.

That amounted to a fundamental difference of view between the prime minister and other Western leaders about the nature of modern Germany. It was to address this that Charles Powell arranged for the application of external historical expertise at a second Chequers seminar in March 1990. Six eminent historians[13] with a range of different specializations and political views participated. The official team were excluded on the grounds as Powell put it that the PM would not take this kind of advice from the Foreign Office.

Powell prepared the agenda carefully with Mrs Thatcher in advance (all the documents are published in the volume on German Unification in the Documents on British Policy Overseas series[14]). He proposed a series of questions for participants to answer, starting with 'what does history tell us about the character and behaviour of the German-speaking people of Europe? Are there such things as enduring national characteristics? Have the Germans changed over the last 40 years . . . or are we really dealing with the same old huns?' The questions also probed what the tendencies of a united Germany would be – towards territorial dominance, or could they find satisfaction in something broader than Germany? They rounded off with how to handle the Germans – stand up to them or the honeyed approach? Mrs Thatcher's reaction was to widen the focus and consider as well the future of the USSR/Russia and 'whether we pursue spheres of influence, or alliances of democracy or geographical alliances.' Her mind was ranging very widely:

> It seems to me that, while in the past, history was determined largely by the personalities and ambitions of the rulers of the people, in future it will be decided much more by the character of the people.

The Powell record did not attribute comments to individuals, so it is impossible to know how much of Mrs Thatcher was reflected in the list of unflattering attributes which Powell noted had been

> mentioned as an abiding part of the German character in alphabetical order, angst, aggressiveness, assertiveness, bullying, egotism, inferiority complex, sentimentality.

But it is clear from the record that the bulk of the discussion was made up of the historians disputing the prime minister's basic analogy:

> There was a strong school of thought among those present that today's Germans were very different from their predecessors. It was argued that our basic perception of Germans related to a period of German history running from Bismarck until 1945. . . . There was no longer a sense of historic mission, no ambitions for physical conquest, no more militarism . . . we should have no real worries about them.

Mrs Thatcher evidently tested her worries about how unification could change Germany in the medium term:

> Could some of the unhappy characteristics of the past re-emerge with just as destructive consequences? . . . There was already evident a kind of triumphalism in German thinking and attitudes which would be uncomfortable for the rest of us . . . at worst the extremes at both ends of the political spectrum could grow in influence, leading to a return to Weimar politics (although no-one argued this with any great conviction).

The trend of the discussion about German influence in Eastern Europe seems to have been reassuring, and to have dealt with another part of the prime minister's instinctive analogizing:

> More widely, it was likely that Germany would indeed dominate Eastern and Central Europe economically. But that did not necessarily equate to subjugation. Nor did it mean that a united Germany would achieve by economic means what Hitler had failed to achieve militarily.

The record suggests that the prime minister found more support for her concerns about the impact of reunification on East–West relations. But the seminar pointed the way to the policy which would soon be adopted by the Western Allies:

> All that would suggest that an accommodation could be found which would enable a united Germany to remain in NATO with transitional arrangements to enable the Soviet Union to help keep forces in East Germany.

One dog which did not appear to bark was the EU, although there is distinctively Thatcherian growl audible:

The European Community was surprisingly not much mentioned. German behaviour in the EC 'we pay so we must have our way' was seen by some as the harbinger of Germany's economic dominance over Eastern Europe.

Overall, the Thatcher analogy seems to have been successfully challenged, with a nice flourish of the grand sweep of history:

We were reminded that in 1945 our aim had been a united Germany shorn of its eastern provinces but under democratic and non-communist government, with the states of Eastern Europe free to choose their own governments. We had failed to get that in 1945 but had won it now. Far from being agitated, we ought to be pleased.

Charles Moore quotes one participant, Timothy Garton Ash, as recalling that Mrs Thatcher's own summing up was, 'All right, I'll be very nice to the Germans'.[15] That conclusion duly appeared in the Powell record, but with a prudent hedging of bets for the longer term:

The overall message was unmistakeable: we should be nice to the Germans. But even the optimists had some unease, not for the present and immediate future, but for what might lie further down the road that we can yet see.

Did this exercise in Applied History really cause Mrs Thatcher to reconsider her instinctive worry that history might repeat itself with the arrival of a united Germany? The seminar coincided with a period where some of her most immediate concerns were easing, with a victory for Kohl's party in the elections in East Germany on 18 March reducing the risk of political instability and the emergence of a framework for Allied coordination on the security implications of reunification in the shape of the 2 plus 4 process – the two Germanies plus the four powers with Berlin responsibilities – the United States, the USSR, France and the United Kingdom (although Mrs Thatcher insisted on calling it the 4 plus 2). After the seminar she stopped publicly disobliging remarks about German reunification (although the beneficial effect of this on her and Britain's standing in Germany was undermined briefly by the leaking of the Powell record to the press in July 1990). The application of historical expertise seems at least to have helped her recognize that there was another side to the argument, a more optimistic scenario than the one she had instinctively reached for, and that her public presentation should reflect that.

Perhaps that is as much as Applied History can achieve when faced with as deep and visceral an instinct as Mrs Thatcher's about Germany. It may have influenced her tactics for handling the German question, but it didn't change her conviction that she had been right to try to slow reunification while encouraging a democratic system in East Germany. In the closing pages of her memoirs, the tone is unrepentant. She accepts that the policy failed but will not agree that it was wrong. She regards reunification as 'economically disastrous' which 'created a German state so large and dominant that it cannot easily be fitted into a new architecture in Europe'. The old stereotype is still there. She had tried but failed to create a breathing space in which a new architecture in Europe could be devised where a united Germany would not be a destabilising influence/over-mighty subject/bull in a China shop.[16]

Some Eurozone members, having been on the receiving end of German economic policy during and after the financial crisis, might well agree with her sentiments. And she foresaw more clearly than any of her peers how profoundly the rapid enlargement of the EU and NATO would change Russian attitudes to the West. But her dark forebodings about the behaviour of a united Germany based on her irresistible analogy with the Germany of the past have proved unfounded. Mrs Thatcher undoubtedly listened hard at her Applied History seminar. But how much did she really hear about how fundamentally modern Germany had changed?

III

My last case study concerns another thorny problem left over from history – what to do with the looted Nazi gold that was still in the vaults of Central Banks in Western capitals after the end of the Cold War. Resolving it relied heavily on historical research to open up a dark period in Europe's recent past.

Unlike other assets, gold from many sources can be melted down and made anonymous without losing its value. It is therefore peculiarly difficult to establish the provenance of any given bar of gold. This characteristic greatly complicated the task of the Allies in the years after 1945 in working out where all the gold the Nazis had stashed away in Germany actually came from. Some of it could have been the remains of German pre-war reserves. Much of it was certainly gold bars looted from the central banks of countries the Nazis occupied (known as monetary gold). But there was also a third category which was particularly distressing – gold taken from victims of the Holocaust, which came to be known as 'victim gold'. This included personal possessions and even dental fillings recovered from those murdered in the concentration camps.

What to do with the looted gold found by the Occupying Powers was already an issue at the 1945 Potsdam Summit. The Western Allies persuaded Stalin that they should take responsibility for dealing with it (along with other stolen assets found outside the Soviet sector). The Reparations conference of eighteen Allied nations in Paris in 1946 agreed that looted monetary gold discovered by the allies should be pooled under the auspices of a Tripartite Gold Commission (TGC, made up of the United States, Britain and France) and distributed on a pro rata basis to countries that could show their gold reserves had been looted during the war. By 1948, the TGC's pool of looted monetary gold amounted to around 336 tonnes. Most of this was distributed to the claimant countries in the following years. But the last claim, from Albania, was not settled until the 1990s. That left the TGC holding around 5.5 tonnes for a final distribution to claimants.

The 1946 conference also agreed that it would not be feasible in the circumstances of the time to return victim gold to individual claimants and their families. But given its terrible provenance, the Allies decided that it should be kept separate from the monetary gold, and form part of a $25m fund for the benefit of refugees in Germany who could not be repatriated – mainly stateless Jewish survivors of the Holocaust.

Suspicions lingered, however, that some gold taken from victims of the Holocaust had inadvertently found its way into the monetary gold returned to central banks around Europe. By the 1990s, Jewish organizations were arguing strenuously on moral as well as humanitarian grounds that the residual gold being held by the TGC should not be distributed to the claimant countries but used to compensate the victims of Nazi persecution and their descendants. The British Member of Parliament Greville Janner was also campaigning for an International Conference to decide this approach. In 1996, he produced some British wartime documents marked top secret about the movement of gold and laundering of the proceeds by neutral nations. They had been found in US archives and Mr Janner accused the UK government of a cover-up. The foreign secretary Malcolm Rifkind turned to the FCO official historian, Gill Bennett, to get to the bottom of it and publish a report based on access to open and closed archives. Gill recognized the documents as having been open in the British National Archives since 1972. Having been through all the documents held by the government, she published a ground-breaking report, 'Nazi Gold: Information from the British Archives'[17] in September 1996. Mr Rifkind was attracted to the idea of an International Conference, but he postponed decisions until after the general election on 1 May 1997.

With the victory of Tony Blair's Labour government that day, Robin Cook became foreign secretary. One of his first decisions was that Britain would indeed hold an international conference on Nazi gold in London before the end of the year. He announced this on 6 May. The following day, the sensitivity of the whole issue was highlighted with the publication of the 'Eizenstat Report'[18] in Washington. Stuart Eizenstat was the State Department under secretary for international commerce. He took a close interest in the Nazi gold issue, was nonplussed to find that the Brits had got a report out first and pressed the State Department Historian, William Slany, to come up with a bigger and better US equivalent.[19] The report made difficult reading for a number of countries which had maintained business dealings with Nazi Germany, particularly Switzerland. The Swiss authorities were accused of knowingly handling vast sums of looted gold through their banking system, and then dragging their feet over an agreement to transfer part of this gold to the TGC. Other countries which had been neutral during the war also came in for criticism.

This was a diplomatic minefield. Switzerland was unwilling to face another round of public criticism for its dealings with Nazi Germany. The German government were concerned that the conference could become a lever to extract further compensation for victims of the Holocaust, to whom they had already given over 100 billion deutschmarks. The Jewish groups were pressing strongly that all the remaining TGC gold should go to individuals, most of it to Jewish organizations representing victims. The claimant countries were expecting the TGC to respect its legal obligation under the Paris Agreement to distribute the remaining gold to them. This was a political and moral minefield for a new foreign secretary to venture into.

Nonetheless, Robin Cook was determined to tackle the problem and convinced that the way through was to establish the historical facts. The truth about the provenance of the gold originally recovered by the TGC, and particularly the extent to which victim gold had found its way into the bars distributed by the Commission, was buried in the archives of many countries. So the official historians would be central to the process. Gill Bennett even gave formal testimony ahead of the conference to the Banking and Finance Committee of the US House of Representatives.

All this stimulated archival research in many capitals. Some of the claimant countries worked up detailed descriptions of how the Nazis laid hands on their gold. The countries which had been neutral during the war and had therefore maintained business relations with the Third Reich were particularly in the spotlight. The criticism tended to focus on Switzerland. They set up an Independent Historical Commission under Professor Bergier, to document their case that Switzerland had been in an extremely difficult position as the only neutral country entirely surrounded by Axis powers and had no choice but to have close dealings with Berlin. Argentina, Portugal and Turkey also undertook new research into their wartime dealings with Nazi Germany.

The story emerging from the archives was that a small amount of victim gold was likely to have found its way into the bars distributed to claimant governments – as Jewish groups had suspected. The tripartite countries used this conclusion to urge the claimants to make a voluntary donation of some of the final distribution of TGC gold to a fund for victims and their descendants. This was a middle way between expectations of Jewish groups that the whole 5.5 tonnes would go to victims and their families, and the need to avoid legal challenges if the rights of claimant countries under the 1946 Paris Agreement were not honoured.

The claimant countries were reassured that their entitlement to the residual gold was not to be questioned, and one by one they accepted the compromise of a voluntary contribution. The Americans also undertook to make a contribution to the fund. At the conference, the British did as well. The French made their contribution direct to victims' groups in France. Switzerland and others who had been worried that the conference could be used to mobilize further pressure on them were reassured that its purpose, as Robin Cook put it, was to establish historical facts not take policy decisions, and to provide a moral impetus in favour of individual restitution rather than an obligation.

The conference brought together forty countries, plus the Holy See as a silent observer, together with six organizations representing surviving victims of Nazi persecution, various financial institutions and the TGC. Robin Cook in opening the conference described its purpose as to piece together the 'incomplete jigsaw' of knowledge spread around many countries about the gold stolen by the Nazis, and to shine a light into corners that had stayed dark too long.

The neutrals were not the only countries which had to face up to the uncomfortable truth that their wartime practices had contributed to the problem. The Allied record was not unblemished either. The conference paper from the delegation of the Czech Republic recounted that as the threat of Nazi occupation loomed in 1938, the Central Bank in Prague moved almost all its gold out of the country to what it thought was safety abroad. A large part went to the Bank of England. But when the Germans arrived in Prague they forced the Czech central bank officials at gunpoint to instruct the Bank of England to transfer 23 tonnes of the Czech gold via the Bank of International

Settlements to the Deutsche Reichsbank. The Bank of England promptly carried out this request despite protests from the Czech government in Exile. This drew a withering response from Winston Churchill from his position on the backbenches of the House of Commons. Noting that the British people were being asked to pay gigantic taxes as the country mobilized for war, he added:

> If at the same time our mechanism is so butter-fingered that this six million pounds of gold can be transferred to the Nazi Government of Germany . . . it stultifies altogether the efforts our people are making in every class and in every party to secure national defence and rally the whole forces of the country.[20]

The Allies also accepted that their procedures for collection and restitution of looted German gold in the chaos of 1945 had contributed to the problem. This level of honesty was a distinctive aspect of the proceedings. The conference chairman, Lord Mackay, paid tribute in his conclusions to a 'concerted international effort to shed light on a tragic episode in our past'. He added that the search for truth had been a theme running through the conference and quoted the comment from Edgar Bronfman of the World Jewish Council that the accurate writing of history constituted a 'moral restitution'.

How successful was the London conference as a policy initiative? It certainly ensured that the moral case for compensating victims of Nazi persecution and their descendants was taken into account in the final distribution of gold by the TGC, which happened in 1998. The International Fund launched at the conference received over $50m in voluntary donations, mainly as a result of twelve of the claimant countries agreeing to contribute their share of the final payout from the TGC to the Fund. The United States contributed $5m and the UK £1m, even though neither had received any gold from the TGC.

The conference also had a wider impact. It seemed to break a taboo and to make possible a whole series of further initiatives to compensate the victims of Nazi persecution. Some had been under way before the conference, but were given added impetus by the publicity it generated. The Swiss government for example appointed an international committee in 1997 headed by Paul Volcker, former head of the US Federal Reserve Board, to audit dormant bank accounts to determine which belonged to victims of the Holocaust.

Other initiatives flowed directly from the London conference. The United States held a follow-on Washington conference on Holocaust-Era Assets in 1998, which focused on looted art and cultural property, triggering a hunt for works of art stolen by the Nazis which continues to this day. The Swiss government also established a fund for Holocaust survivors, and in 1998 Swiss Banks reached an out-of-court settlement worth $1.25bn with claimants who alleged that they had blocked efforts by survivors to reclaim money owed to them. In 1999, the German government reversed a previous policy and agreed to pay compensation to Holocaust survivors in the former Soviet bloc. A total of $4.8bn, half of it from German companies, was paid to former forced and slave labourers.[21]

What lessons can be drawn from the experience of the Nazi gold initiative? Deft diplomacy building on a solid basis of fact was important. Robin Cook was a politician with a keen sense of the power of historical research to support policymaking. He and the FCO team built confidence among the participants that no one would be put in the dock, and no claimant put under pressure to give up their entitlement. The representatives of the victims were given full opportunity to make their case, reinforced by the jigsaw of information assembled from the official archives. The government historians were an integral part of the policymaking process. The network of personal links among this group of professionals with a reputation for integrity helped smooth the way to wider cooperation in an area which remained highly sensitive for many governments. The successful resolution of this issue created a momentum for other equally dark corners of Europe's wartime history to be exposed to the daylight. The Nazi gold initiative showed that transparency and honesty about the past can help to heal even the most painful problems left over from history.

Notes

1 Most of the British archives on the Hong Kong negotiations are still closed. The following account draws on published sources, my own recollections as Geoffrey Howe's private secretary from the autumn of 1983 and private information from a number of my former colleagues who were at the heart of the negotiations.
2 Henry Kissinger, *Diplomacy* (New York, 1994), 727.
3 Cmnd. 9543, *Sino-British Joint declaration on the Question of Hong Kong*, signed 19 December 1984.
4 Charles Moore, *Margaret Thatcher. The Authorised Biography, Volume Two: Everything She Wants* (London, 2015), 11.
5 Ibid., 97.
6 Ibid., 16.
7 TNA, FCO 21/2069, Letter from John Coles No 10 to John Holmes FCO 15 November 1982.
8 Moore, *Margaret Thatcher, Volume Two*, 12.
9 This is a central theme in Richard E. Neustadt and Ernest R. May, *Thinking in Time: The Uses of History for Decision Makers* (New York, 1986).
10 Charles Moore, *Margaret Thatcher. The Authorised Biography, Volume Three: Herself Alone* (London, 2019), 471.
11 Ibid., 488.
12 Ibid., 478.
13 The participants were Lord Dacre (formerly Hugh Trevor-Roper), Professors Gordon Craig, Fritz Stern, Norman Stone and Timothy Garton-Ash and George Urban.
14 *German Unification 1989–1990. Documents on British Policy Overseas, Series III, Volume VII* (London, 2010), Appendix. The quotations in the following paragraphs are all taken from the documents printed there.
15 Moore, *Margaret Thatcher, Volume Three*, 529.
16 Margaret Thatcher, *The Downing Street Years* (London, 1993), 814.
17 *History Notes*, Foreign and Commonwealth Office, Issue 11, September 1996, at https://issuu.com/fcohistorians/docs/history_notes_cover_hphn_11.
18 See *US and Allied Efforts to Recover and Restore Gold and Other Assets Stolen or Hidden by Germany During World War II: Preliminary Study* (Washington, DC, 1997).

19 Gill Bennett gives a personal account of her dealings with Slany and her
    Congressional appearance in her recollections for the British Diplomatic Oral History
    Programme at https//www.chu.cam.ac.uk/media/uploads/files/Bennett_UGtTWdM
    .pdf.
20 House of Commons debates (Hansard), Fifth Series, 24 May 1939, Volume 347,
    column 2760.
21 There is a useful summary of the many different initiatives on restitution which
    followed after the London conference in Greg Brasher, *Turning History into Justice:
    Holocaust-Era Assets Records, Research and Restitution* (Washington, DC, 2001),
    https//www.archives.gov/research/holocaust/articles-and-papers/turning-history-into
    -justice.html.

11

Clio's role in construing the US Constitution

Philip Bobbitt

I can think of no more consequential use of history in public affairs than the construction of the US Constitution on the basis of determining the intentions of the framers and ratifiers of its text. And yet no aspect of American jurisprudence, perhaps even of American governments, is as baffling to foreigners or strikes many Americans themselves as so absurd as the practice of using history to construe the Constitution.

Why would we want to return to the understandings of the late eighteenth century when so much has changed? As the legal commentator Jeffrey Toobin put it,

> It's often noted that the United States is governed by the world's oldest written constitution that is still in use. This is usually stated as praise, though most other products of the eighteenth century, like horse-borne travel and leech-based medical treatment, have been replaced by improved models.[1]

Moreover, putting aside the desirability of resurrecting the sensibilities of an eighteenth-century agrarian society – racist, patriarchal, imperialist – there are considerable difficulties in the attempt to do so. Professor Jonathan Macey has observed,

> it generally is assumed that [the use of historical argument in constitutional construction] is impossible because the original document, either standing alone or supplemented by contemporaneous historical sources, simply does not generate answers to modern legal questions of constitutional interpretation.[2]

And yet the centrality of historical argument to the operation of judicial review, that is, the review of government actions by courts – has never wavered in the 218 years since *Marbury* v. *Madison,* the case that confirmed but did not establish American judicial review. Why did this happen? How did this devotion to, even obsession with, historical argument happen? Why does it continue? Should it continue?

In this chapter I will attempt to show how historical argument in constitutional law is done according to the parameters of a particular convention in Anglo-American legal reasoning, and I will give examples of how very modern problems have been resolved according to this sort of reasoning. But we ought to begin with a different historical question: How did we get here in the first place, how did a pragmatic, future loving people tie themselves to the intentions of people of the past, in some cases, the long distant past?

I

'Thus, in the beginning all the World was America', wrote John Locke in the *Two Treatises of Government.* Of this famous and evocative passage, one historian wrote,

> Steeped in the colonial zeal of his patron, the Earl of Shaftesbury, John Locke saw America as the second Garden of Eden; a new beginning for England should she manage to defend her claims In the American continent against those of the Indians and other European powers. America, like the world described in the original Genesis, is England's second chance at paradise, providing the colonial masters of the old world with a land full of all the promise known in that first Idyllic state. America thus represents for Locke and his readers a two-sided Genesis, a place to find both the origins of their past and the promise of their future.[3]

The colonial Americans themselves didn't disagree. Nor were they entirely mistaken to think so. For after the revolution they found themselves in a wondrous situation: before them lay a continent unspoiled and vast with riches which they could exploit undisturbed by the corruption of the old order, while at the same time they inherited a centuries-old set of legal practices developed by English common law. Their genius – beyond that of John Locke – was to do something the common law had never contemplated. This was to put the state itself under law. Thus, they had a fantastically endowed future to which they could apply the methods of adaptation and rationality that were accepted by consensus. Before establishing the new state, colonial Americans did not have to forge a political and social consensus; they were free to develop the economy and the society because they had inherited a consensus with respect to legal methods. As Grant Gilmore put it,

> It is entirely clear that the men who guided our affairs from the 1770s or 1780s . . . understood their unique and privileged historical situation: it does not fall to the lot of every generation to make such a fresh start and a vigorous, literate, and sophisticated society already in full flood of economic and social development, conscious of its immense potential for ever-growing power and wealth.[4]

In the following pages I will attempt to show how the common law method of interpreting an agreement according to the intentions of its parties is applied to construing the provisions of the Constitution. The consequences of this development have been profound: it has allowed the Americans, with one fateful breakdown that itself ushered in a rebirth of the principles of the Declaration of Independence and brought into being a new constitutional order, to achieve a broad fidelity and adherence to the Constitution even when there was deep division as to its proper meaning.

As Akhil Amar has recently stressed,[5] it was the novel adoption of the proposed Constitution by an unprecedented series of popular votes – up and down a continent over the course of an entire year – that gave the US Constitution an entirely different basis than other written charters of the era. The people endowed the state with authority and set the limits to that authority. Two constraints flow from this origin: (1) just as the intentions of a settlor who creates a trust, or a donor who makes a gift, or the party to a contract who undertakes certain responsibilities in exchange for agreed-upon rights, or a testator who makes provisions for distributions in a will, govern the construction of the document so here the intentions of the ratifiers of the Constitution govern its construction; and (2) no act of the state is in fact law unless it is consistent with those intentions and thus no such act can be enforced in the courts without first determining that consistency. Thus, is born 'historical argument', and also judicial review which will deploy that form of argument.

II

Historical arguments depend on a determination of the original understanding of the constitutional provision to be construed. At first, one must notice how odd it is that the original understanding in any field of study should govern present behaviour. Certainly no one proposes a historical argument in physics: for example, that we should try to discover what Democritus had in mind when he used the word *atom* so that we could use the term properly when confronted with, say, problems associated with electron spin. Nor is anyone in the arts likely to argue that a particular artist must conceive his problem in terms dictated by his precursors. Indeed, we reserve the epithet 'derivative' for artists who do precisely that. While there are manifestos and schools in the arts and theoretical camps in the sciences, few of their adherents think that the contemporary problems they confront can be definitively resolved by reference to how an earlier artist or scientist would have addressed the problem. When we refer to earlier thinkers, it is more often usually because we are looking for support, not guidance.

The very decision to produce a constitution in writing presupposes a different faith. This faith finds expression in John Adams's view that 'frequent recurrence to the fundamental principles of the constitution . . . [is] absolutely necessary to preserve the advantages of liberty and to maintain a free government. . . . The people have a right to require of their law givers and magistrates an exact and constant observance of them.'[6] Adams asserts that because the people – the framers and ratifiers of the Constitution – intended to bind the government to certain limits and rules they had therefore devised a constitution by means of which those limits and rules could be discerned and enforced. But what was the original understanding of the use to be made of this original understanding? That is, how did the framers and ratifiers intend their intentions to be determined and applied? This is a more difficult question than it might first appear.

We do not have an original commitment by the framers to historical argument; that is, we do not have statements at the Philadelphia convention that demonstrate the expectation or even the hope that the intentions expressed at the convention would later serve as guides to the construction of the Constitution. On the contrary, the Convention voted to keep its proceedings secret and made no provision for lifting this secrecy in the future.

To what source then are we to refer for an authoritative understanding of the 'original intent' to guide us when we construe the Constitution? To statements of members of the convention who proposed a particular provision? To the debate surrounding its adoption on the Convention floor? To earlier language which had been superseded? Or should we look, not to the Constitutional Convention, which we must remember was not authorized to propose a new constitution, but instead to the various ratifying state conventions? James Madison wrote that an appeal to historical argument requires us to 'look . . . not in the General Convention, which proposed, but in the State Conventions, which accepted and ratified the Constitution'.[7] But if to the state conventions, do we look to what they were promised – as, for example, by the *Federalist Papers* – or to what they independently took the various provisions to mean? As Thomas Cooley observed, 'the object of construction, as applied to a written constitution, is to give effect to the intent of the people in adopting it'.[8]

If this method is decided upon, then must each of the thirteen ratifying conventions – or perhaps the first nine, which was the decisive number for ratification – have been in agreement on any point at issue?[9] What would count as agreement, since an up or down vote on the exact construction of a particular provision could not occur in these contexts as it might have in the drafting convention?

Suppose we turn back to the Constitutional Convention. As early as 1838 – two years after the death of James Madison, the last living member of the convention – the Supreme Court announced that construction of the Constitution must rely on 'the meaning and intention of the convention which framed and proposed it for adoption and ratification'.[10] In 1869 the Supreme Court again examined the 'intention of the Convention' when the Court decided that the framers had intended to confer a comprehensive taxing power on Congress. It therefore upheld a federal tax on state-issued banknotes, even though the effect was to drive such notes out of circulation, a context not explicitly considered by the Convention and one, we may speculate, that the state conventions were unlikely to have contemplated with indifference.[11] The Court has since resorted to examination of the debates at the Convention to determine what uniformity is required by the indirect tax provision,[12] to let stand a president's removal of executive officers without congressional consent,[13] to decide whether the treason clause prohibits the imputation of incriminating acts when uncorroborated by two witnesses[14] and to determine the extent to which the Washington DC government could ban handgun possession.[15]

The Court has relied on this sort of historical argument to support its view that congressional districts must have a roughly equal population[16] and its ruling that Congress could not augment the constitutionally required qualifications for membership for justices in its chambers.[17] The list might be expanded considerably, in part, perhaps because garnering an opinion with historical arguments is often considered an expression of good form. But an interesting feature of such reliance by the Court on historical arguments is that in all these cases there is not one instance in which it may be said that the Court has definitively established the intent of the

Convention on any important issue. Usually when this has been attempted it has subsequently been refuted.[18]

Moreover, we face this logical paradox. If the convention intended that their intentions *not* be dispositive, then should we ignore that intention too and apply this 'original intent' of the Constitution after all; if they wished the intentions *to be applied* and their intention was that future generations would not look to this intention, then should we not apply the 'original intent'?

The records of the debates are so scanty that full discussion of almost any point has been lost. More importantly, the convention met without official minutes in an atmosphere that concealed public dissent and put a premium on achieving agreement to a document that was unglossed or unexplained in any way that might disclose or provoke fissures in the coalitions that proposed it. No future sessions were provided for in case ratification failed. Everything was subordinated to the adoption of the Constitution. The debates that were recorded are fragmentary and indicate little more than highly particular or highly general positions that can rarely be said to have been endorsed by the adoption of specific language for which the position had been used as support. It happens, in fact, that even in the brief records we do have, we encounter the phenomenon of delegates urging the adoption of the same language for disconsonant purposes.[19] It is unusual that the debate surrounding the adoption of particular language provides a decisive historical argument for a provision being construed in a particular way. At most research is likely to indicate only the concerns of the more voluble or more forceful members of the Convention. Finally, the debates cannot operate affirmatively to establish the correctness of a particular construction because they can't establish why a coalition of state delegations adopted a particular measure. The debates can sometimes *falsify* a particular reading through recourse to a single exchange (though more often by describing the evolution of a provision through the rejection of various alternatives) but falsification of one reading of the constitutional text does not affirmatively establish the authority of another.

Thus, when called upon to determine the scope of its original jurisdiction, the Court observed that a proposal which would have allocated to the Senate the question of disputes between the states was voted down by the convention.[20] Thus also Justice Brandeis, dissenting from a holding that the president could remove a postmaster without congressional consent, parried the majority's observation that the convention records did not directly answer the matter. 'Nothing', he wrote, 'can be inferred from the silence of the Convention of 1787 on the subject of removal. For the outstanding fact remains that every specific proposal to confer such uncontrollable power upon the President was rejected'.[21]

Similarly, constitutional lawyers have been called upon, in their proper role as citizen-lawyers discussing the Constitution in their communities, to consider the question whether a president may be impeached for acts that are politically repugnant to Congress, though not of constitutional impact. The historical approach to this question might frame the question: 'Did the framers intend the phrase "high crimes and misdemeanors" to include matters of political dispute between the branches?' A study of the debates would seem to reject such an interpretation definitively because language that might have been used to support such a position was put forward by

George Mason at the convention, was the subject of controversy in an exchange between Madison and Mason, and was withdrawn.[22]

But suppose such language had been adopted. Then we would actually have less assurance in determining intent. For while a debate and vote can make clear that a particular provision was *severed* from a rejected meaning, regardless of the delegates' reasons, when a passage was *adopted* we are thrown back on the puzzle of varying and sometimes incompatible intentions left unexpressed or, in the case of trade-offs for votes on other matters, indecisive and embodied in language chosen to satisfy objectives other than clarity. By contrast, when we study the constitutional decisions of the early Congresses and administrations, which were composed of framers and ratifiers of the constitution, we have a surer guide as to the construction of a particular provision. To take up the impeachment question again, it has been suggested that the commission of a crime – perjury arising from a civil dispute, for example – while of no constitutional significance, could nevertheless serve as the predicate for the impeachment of the president.[23] Some doubt is cast on this, however, by the case of Aaron Burr, against whom impeachment proceedings were never tabled by men who had drafted the Constitution and lobbied for its ratification despite Burr's having murdered Alexander Hamilton in a duel.[24]

I am simply describing the topological features of such arguments. I am not questioning the jurisprudential assumptions made by those who employ historical arguments. I am not trying to deprive them of the word 'intent', nor would I rule out any specific sources, including influential collateral sources like the *Federalist Papers*, as useful both in setting the general spirit of specific provisions and, in the way I have suggested, in ruling out particular readings.

But this has seldom been enough for the full-bore historicist in constitutional law. He wants what none of the historical arguments I have drawn can give, and that is the authoritative reading in a particular context. Such scholars have always been a part of our constitutional history; they are a reflection, I think, of both the populist hostility to the elitism of the federal judiciary and the American desire for a certitude that is technological in its freedom from dependence on judgement. It is worth spending a moment on one particular variant of historical argument that promises such certitude. This is the approach that says, with Holmes, 'We ask, not what this man meant, but what those words mean in the mouth of a normal speaker of English, using them in the circumstances in which they were used.'[25] This method, which Contracts scholars quite misleadingly call an 'objective' method – and which constitutional scholars have sometimes called 'original public meaning' rather than 'original intent' – frees us from some of the difficulties of determining intention, difficulties that are enhanced by the paradoxes encountered in a decision by a group said to reflect a certain intent, even though this is likely not shared by most of its members who, in turn, make proposals that are then adopted by yet other groups of decision-makers themselves not necessarily sharing a particular intention. At a stroke all these problems are brushed aside, and with them the negative, asymmetrical qualities of historical argument that can deny and discredit but never affirm. Instead, there is a true meaning, discernible and objective, an object whose contours we may trace by consulting the maps and lithographs of that day. It is an idea that has roots in Spencer Roan and Luther Martin,[26] but in the twentieth century has been principally associated with William Winslow Crosskey, and much later, with Antonin Scalia and Randy Barnett.

Crosskey was by all accounts an unusual, even an eccentric, man. He was, according to Harry Kalven, 'the stuff from which legends are made'[27] and was perhaps not unconscious of his effect. I remember his portrait on the walls of the *Yale Law Journal* office – a balding head over a truculent scowl, his large heavy-set frame crammed into a small officer's chair. He obviously dominated that editorial board as he dominated the photograph. He had been older than the rest of his classmates – thirty when he entered the Yale Law School – because he had taken eight years to graduate from Yale College, interspersing his terms there with periods during which he sold aluminium siding to support his family.

At law school, Crosskey refused to take notes and let it get around that he never read cases in preparation for class. When Charles Clark called on Crosskey one day to recite the facts in a case and the class dissolved in muffled sniggering, Crosskey silenced them by saying, 'Professor Clark, if you can control your class, perhaps we could get somewhere with this case.' Of course, Crosskey excelled as a law student. Decades later Robert Hutchins, Karl Llewellyn and Roscoe Steffen were able to compete with stories chronicling Crosskey's formidable manner and abilities when he was their student.[28]

After Yale, Crosskey clerked for Chief Justice Taft and then went on to a Wall Street practice with Davis, Polk. He was immediately made personal assistant to John W. Davis, and Davis is reported to have said later that Crosskey's brain was the best piece of legal equipment he had ever encountered.[29] In 1935 Crosskey accepted an offer from the University of Chicago Law School where it was thought he might add a note of 'professionalism' to a strongly theoretical faculty. The faculty was shortly disabused of any such notions when his first course, Federal Income and Estate Taxation, resolved into a study of exclusively constitutional issues. For Crosskey was one of those brilliant men who is obsessed by the conviction that life is far simpler than the nitwits running the world perceive it to be. With such iconoclasm it was idle to suppose that he would attempt anything less than a revolution in constitutional scholarship.

As his last task on Wall Street, Crosskey had drafted a lengthy memorandum on the jurisdictional reach of the then-new Securities Act. With lawyerly economy he planned to convert this into his tenure piece at Chicago. The legend is that this initial search for the boundaries of the commerce power lengthened into the investigation that, sixteen years later, resulted in the two volumes we know as *Politics and the Constitution*.

Politics and the Constitution is, I think all agree, a remarkable work. Its central thesis is that the Constitution established a government fully empowered to accomplish the broad charter of the Preamble and not, as has been generally thought, a government of limited enumerated powers.[30] The Supreme Court was to be the final authority on all matters of interpreting state and federal law, but with a sharply circumscribed role regarding the judicial review of congressional acts. The president was endowed with plenary authority to ensure domestic tranquillity just as Congress was empowered to pass all laws necessary and proper in its judgement for the general welfare. It was, in short, the Constitution Franklin Roosevelt would have written in 1935.

How did Crosskey reach these surprising conclusions? Let me give one example. In determining the scope of the commerce power, the Supreme Court has construed the word 'states' in the phrase from Article I to regulate commerce with foreign nations and among the several States and with the Indian tribes to mean 'territorial divisions of the country' and has thus contrived the doctrine of *interstate* commerce. Crosskey argued, with dozens of accompanying citations, that the word 'states' in the Commerce Clause was understood in 1787 to refer to the 'people of the states' and that the term 'commerce' meant 'all gainful activity'. In Crosskey's words, the Commerce Clause was understood in the late eighteenth century as a 'simple and exhaustive catalogue of all the different kinds of commerce to which the people of the United States had access: Commerce, that is, *with the people* of foreign nations, commerce *with the people* of the Indian tribes, and commerce *among the people* of the several states'.[31] Therefore, Crosskey concluded, Congress was granted plenary power to regulate all gainful activity regardless of its scope or character.

Using similar methods, relying on examples of word usage drawn from eighteenth-century newspapers, pamphlets, letters, treatises, diaries, articles and other documents, Crosskey tried to recreate the legal and linguistic context within which the original Constitution was drafted. He expressed scorn for the idea that the Constitution should change through time. 'Did you ever see a *living* document?' he would ask his classes.

How could these meanings have been so utterly lost during the first decades of constitutional construction by the Supreme Court? Crosskey proposed this startling answer: James Madison, converted in old age from the nationalistic Father of the Constitution to a Jeffersonian states' rightist, had tampered with the notes he kept of the constitutional debates and had released them only when all other members of the Convention had died. This deception was advanced by the complicity of Jeffersonian justices on the Supreme Court who, from a date early in Marshall's tenure, began to systematically paint constraining glosses on the true meaning of the constitutional text.

Similarly, the *Federalist Papers*, the chief guide to the historical meaning of the constitutional text, were dismissed by Crosskey as mere political propaganda, designed simply to lure ratification by the reluctant states. Its use thereafter by the Court was a disingenuous, indeed a mendacious, ploy. So it was that the true Constitution became in Crosskey's phrase the 'unknown' Constitution.

What was the reaction to these charges and this wholesale attack on constitutional argument as practised? Initially, the reaction was very favourable. 'This remarkable work sweeps away acres of nonsense that have been written about the Constitution', wrote the eminent historian Arthur Schlesinger Sr. 'It is', he continued (without irony), 'perhaps the most fertile commentary on that document since the *Federalist Papers*.'[32] Arthur Krock reported that among Crosskey's 'earnest students are members of the Supreme Court'.[33] 'For those doubters who find it hard to believe in the fact of actual, intentional distortion of the Constitution', Max Rheinstein wrote, 'Mr. Crosskey produces irrefutable evidence.'[34] And even Arthur Corbin, who had taught us all that the intention of the parties was but a single element in the complex decision whether or not to enforce a disputed contract, approved of the great length Crosskey devoted 'to the language of the time in which the Constitution was written and first interpreted'.[35]

For a year the publication of the first two volumes of *Politics and the Constitution* – two more were projected – was the major event in United States constitutional scholarship. The books were reviewed in thirty-two law reviews and journals; the

University of Chicago Press went into a second printing. Then the pendulum began to return.

A favourable review by Malcolm Sharp in the *Columbia Law Review*[36] was followed by a bewildered notice in the same journal by Irving Brant, Madison's biographer. 'In spite of appalling misrepresentations', Brant wrote, in a placating, if wary, tone, 'there is a vast amount of sound reasoning in Mr. Crosskey's work.'[37] Next came a review by Julius Goebel, a distinguished legal historian. 'Let it be said at once', Goebel began, 'that Mr. Crosskey's performance, measured by even the least exacting of scholarly standards is . . . without merit.' Conceding that 'it is of course possible that what seem to be extraordinary perversions of fact . . . are actually the result not of design but of mere blundering', Goebel launched a devastating thirty-page attack on Crosskey's representation of the state of Anglo-American common law in 1787 – an important, indeed crucial, element in Crosskey's rationale, since many of the terms for which he sought definitions were terms sprung from legal contexts.[38] This was in March of 1954.

In June of that year two more reviews appeared in the *Harvard Law Review*, which had hitherto been silent. The first, by Ernest Brown,[39] proceeded on several fronts. The notion that the Crosskey Constitution could have erupted full-grown without political development was ridiculed; contemporary letters by Washington and Jefferson were quoted to establish the *Federalist Papers* as true reflections of the Convention's understanding. Singularly damning was Brown's use of Crosskey's own method. The words 'among' and 'several' as well as others were examined for their eighteenth-century usage and shown, predictably, to have had several meanings, some of which were compatible with the conventional Constitution and none of which compelled the Crosskey revision.

Most damaging, however, was the review that followed Brown's, a lengthy analysis by Henry Hart of Crosskey's thesis about judicial review. Professor Crosskey, Hart wrote, '[is] a devotee of that technique of interpretation which reaches its apogee of persuasiveness in the triumphant question, "If that's what they meant, why didn't they say so?"' With this remark Hart served notice that he had no intention of adopting the variant of historical argument Crosskey had used, or indeed of relying on originalism in any form. The remainder of the review is revealing for the way in which Hart used a different approach – one I have called 'doctrinal argument'[40] – to attack Crosskey's thesis.

Crosskey had argued that judicial review was a right of courts and, as such, had to be explicitly provided for in the same way that the president has the right to be commander-in-chief, or Congress has the sole right to declare war. Hart replied that judicial review is instead a power merely incident to the judicial process, that is, a necessary means by which the courts discharge their obligation to dispose of a case according to law.[41] As such, a court's decision as to the unconstitutionality of a statute is merely a decision not to give it effect in this and in future cases; it does not purport to control the judgement of Congress or of the president in their discharge of their own functions.[42]

Now compare this approach of Hart's – the derivation of a general principle from the judicial process of case decision, precedent-setting and precedent-following – with Crosskey's approach to the same issue. Crosskey introduces a pamphlet circulated in

Philadelphia when the Convention began discussing the creation of an Equalizing Court to umpire between Congress and the States and to decide appeals brought by Congress against a state for disobedience to federal acts or by a state against Congress for unconstitutionally passing them in the first place. Taking this function to be similar to the present-day functions of the Court, Crosskey contrasts the composition of the proposed Equalizing Court with that actually provided in Article III. 'The Supreme Court is set up in so very different a way', Crosskey writes, 'as, on this basis alone, to make difficult the belief that it was intended to have any such function.' Similarly, Crosskey refers to the various proposals for a Council of Revision and determines that if judicial review had truly been intended, some apparatus less cumbersome than a Supreme Court functioning in a common law mode would have been chosen.

How foreign this is to Hart's approach, which grounds judicial review precisely in the common law method of adjudication and treats it as a necessary by-product. Indeed, in discussing this section of *Politics and the Constitution* Hart says that the principle derived from Crosskey's objections – taking, one might say, a doctrinal approach even to book reviewing – would apply as well to the review of state statutes, regarding which there is not much dispute even in Crosskey.[43] That is, there being no explicit provision empowering the federal courts, including the Supreme Court, to decline to apply state laws that are inconsistent with the federal constitution, the federal judiciary would be compelled to follow state law except where pre-empted by Congress – an absurd result.

Notice once more the difference of methods. Crosskey takes the phrase 'judicial power' and asks whether this phrase, used in its usual way in 1787, assumed the power of judicial review. He answers this rhetorical query by looking at the post-Independence, pre-Convention practices in those states with highly limited constitutional powers. There being few examples of the exercise of judicial review, Crosskey rests his case. But this is where Hart begins. On a different reading of the precedents, Hart concludes that of the nine cases Crosskey discusses at least three are holdings squarely in support of the power of judicial review, a power that is repeatedly asserted and never, in any of the cases, flatly negatived. Read the way one might read precedent, Hart uses Crosskey's cases to buttress a conclusion that the reviewing power was firmly present in the American legal culture of that period, *whether or not* it had yet been used to strike down a statute.

There are many examples of these differing approaches in the review. I will content myself with one more. Crosskey does provide a role for judicial review, albeit a limited one. Courts are to determine the constitutional issue for themselves, regardless of congressional acts, when the matter concerns a provision in the Constitution directly addressed to the judiciary. Article III is one of these, though there are at least two provisions within it addressed to Congress. The Eleventh Amendment is another. The First Amendment is not. And so on.

But beyond these clarities lurk considerable difficulties. The Fourth, Fifth, Sixth, Seventh and Eighth Amendments, Crosskey says, 'taken together' are of a similar 'substance' as Article III, but they are not, by their terms, addressed to judicial competence. Indeed, the prohibitions against unreasonable searches and seizures and against the taking of private property without just compensation would seem to be directed toward executive, not judicial actors. If, by 'substance', one means that these prohibitions are enforced by the judiciary, then the same thing would of course be true of the First, Ninth and Tenth Amendments, which Crosskey excludes.

After exposing other difficulties in Crosskey's prescription, Hart delivers his final assessment of Crosskey's work. 'The root difficulty', Hart writes, 'is not that [Crosskey's analysis] is vague or hard to apply but that it is unintelligible in the profound sense that it is incapable of explication in terms of any principles worthy of the ideals of Constitutional government'.[44] This criticism from a doctrinal point of view amounts to a charge that Crosskey's approach will not function doctrinally, that is, will not generate neutral, general principles for appellate application.

Hart must be right, not just because confinement to a piecemeal slotting in of chosen meanings for specific words is likely to yield an incoherent charter, but because the very method of growth by which principles emerge has been cut off, stunted at the base. Yet creating a generative method for doctrine was not Crosskey's objective. Indeed, he worried that just this process would undermine the application of the original intent that lay behind – and not in front of, as it were – the provisions of the Constitution.

After the Hart review much of the furore around Crosskey subsided. He had promised two more volumes that would vindicate his analyses and further substantiate Madison's perfidy, but advancing years and illness prevented his finishing them. Nothing came of Max Rheinstein's claim only a year before that 'Lawyers will use [Crosskey's book] in argument, judges will have to discuss it, historians will have to test it, politicians will draw upon or inveigh against it'.[45] Crosskey's book has only been cited once in the text of a majority opinion for the Supreme Court and this for a trivial point.[46] It has, with its brilliant and eccentric author, sunk beneath the waves of our constitutional consciousness. Why did this happen? In part it happened because the problem with which Crosskey began in 1937 – the frustration of the New Deal Congress by the Court – was largely solved by the very methods which Crosskey despised and by the institution whose role he wished to limit.

Also, new problems engaged the legal culture, not least those stemming from a case – *Brown* v. *Board of Education of Topeka, Kansas* – handed down at about the same time that Henry Hart's review appeared. In *Brown*, after the Court had requested and received briefs on the question of the 'Original Understanding of the Fourteenth Amendment', it devoted only a single paragraph to the subject in its opinion. The historical arguments were, Chief Justice Warren wrote, 'at best . . . inconclusive'.[47] Crosskey's enterprise, the escape from inconclusiveness, was doomed. He died without fanfare in 1962 in Connecticut, not far from the place of his early triumphs. But the class of argument – a variant of what I have called the historical approach[48] – lives on, promising a renunciation of generations of wrong living and a return to simple rules straightforwardly applied.

Here is Justice Antonin Scalia giving the William Howard Taft Lecture at the University of Cincinnati in which he praises Taft's opinion in *Myers v. United States*.

What attracts my attention about the *Myers* opinion is not its substance but its process. It is a prime example of what, in current scholarly discourse, is known as the 'originalist' approach to constitutional interpretation . . . Now the main danger in judicial interpretation of the Constitution . . . is that judges will mistake their own predilections for the law . . . Non-originalism . . . plays precisely to this weakness . . . Originalism is and does not aggravate the principal weakness of the system, for it establishes a historical criterion that is conceptuality quite separate from the preferences of the judge himself.

I have already discussed the epistemological flaw in this argument – that it assumes that a correspondence between a fact in the world and a constitutional provision to be construed is essential for determining the meaning of the latter – but there are other flaws for historical argument taken on its own terms. One is that, as Henry Monaghan has persuasively argued,[49] the Constitution was not intended to create a perfect society but rather was a political compromise that did not pretend to create a perfect society even for its own age as we know from its provisions to protect slavery, an evil recognized as such by the majority of the founding generation, and as such doctrine and precedent must accompany historical argument. Another flaw in adopting this approach as the only legitimate modality for construing the Constitution is that the framers and ratifiers rather clearly preferred multiple modalities, as has been convincingly demonstrated by Jefferson Powell.[50] In other words, the intention of the framers and ratifiers was not to freeze the Constitution preventing it from coping with the challenges it acknowledgedly did not resolve.

Whether Crosskey's programme and the work of his successors ultimately take over the methods of historical argument[51] will depend on whether more conventional historical arguments can evade this asymmetricality – the ability to negative a particular interpretation but not to establish a single meaning conclusively – without also forsaking its persuasive power. Indeed, conventional historical arguments have sometimes been so powerful that they overrode the construction of the actual texts of a provision completely. This can be seen in the singular and interesting history of the Eleventh Amendment. That text reads:

The judicial power of the United States shall not be construed to extend to any suit in law or equity, commenced or presented against one of the United States by Citizens of another state, or by Citizens of any Foreign State.

The history of the adoption of the amendment is well known. In 1793 the Supreme Court, reading Article III's unamended text literally, had accepted original jurisdiction in *Chisholm* v. *Georgia,* a suit brought against Georgia by two South Carolina citizens to collect a debt.[52] That text reads, 'The judicial Power shall extend to Controversies between a State and Citizens of another State. . . in all Cases affecting Ambassadors, other public Ministers and Consuls, and those in which a state shall be Party, the supreme Court shall have original jurisdiction.' The resultant fury in the states, who feared suits based on Revolutionary War debts and expropriations, was reflected in a bill passed by the Georgia House of Representatives providing that 'any Federal Marshal, or any other person' seeking to execute the mandate in *Chisholm* would be 'guilty of felony, and shall suffer death, without benefit of clergy, by being hanged'.[53]

This outraged, perhaps even unhinged, reaction was not without some justification. Campaigners for the Constitution's ratification, including Hamilton, had given assurances that the states' sovereign immunity would not be abrogated by Article III.[54]

The Court, however, had limited its view to the text alone, a text silent on the matter of immunity, and thus by means of a *textual* argument had reached a result at complete variance with the intentions of the great mass of ratifiers.

At the first meeting of Congress following the decision, the Eleventh Amendment was proposed by an overwhelming vote of both houses and passed, in Justice Frankfurter's phrase, with 'vehement speed'.[55] It was framed precisely to cover the situation in *Chisholm,* in which a citizen of one state had brought an action against a state other than his own in federal court. As quoted earlier, that amendment reads, 'The Judicial power of the United States shall not be construed to extend to any suit in law or equity, commenced or prosecuted against one of the United States by Citizens of another state, or by Citizens or Subjects of any Foreign State.'

Then in 1890, a citizen of Louisiana sued that state in an attempt to recover the interest on state bonds which had been repudiated by a subsequent state constitution.[56] Since the plaintiff was suing his own state he alleged, as Justice Bradley put it, that he was 'not embarrassed by the obstacle of the Eleventh Amendment, inasmuch [as it] only prohibits suits against a state which are brought by the citizens of another state'.[57] 'It is true', Bradley conceded, that 'the amendment does so read'.[58] But the amendment reflects a larger act, he wrote, namely the rejection by the People of the Supreme Court's decision in *Chisholm.* At this point Bradley might simply have stopped and said that, with *Chisholm* out of the way, the original Constitution standing alone did not authorize such a suit in the federal courts. He went further. The people, Bradley reasoned, in rejecting the *Chisholm* majority, were agreeing with the principles of the dissent in that case; therefore, in ratifying the Eleventh Amendment's narrow text the people in fact were adopting much broader views. Can one imagine, Bradley asked in a variation of the rhetorical question posed by the *Chisholm* dissent, what would have been the outcry if the Eleventh Amendment had qualified its prohibition by adding that the US judicial power may nevertheless extend to suits against states brought by their own citizens?[59] And so Bradley construed – no, *construed* is the wrong *word* – *reconstructed* the Eleventh Amendment to govern suits by a corporation created by act of Congress, suits by persons of whatever citizenship in admiralty and suits by a foreign state. In other words, the Eleventh Amendment governed all those situations for which the draftsmen of the amendment were assumed to be too short-sighted to provide. Ever since Bradley's decision in *Hans* v. *Louisiana,* the Court has not hesitated when confronting similar situations to read the Eleventh Amendment in precisely this way.[60]

This example shows a form of historical argument quite distinct from Crosskey's. This variant avoids the pitfalls of the asymmetrical phenomenon I have noted previously because it doesn't attempt to establish a meaning for a particular phrase. It is more forceful yet also fraught with difficulty because it requires us to create the concept from which a particular conception is drawn when the Constitution has given us only the latter. Ronald Dworkin,[61] like Bickel before him,[62] has observed that the Constitution often provides general *concepts* – of equal protection or due process, for example – to which each generation must affix particular *conceptions* – for example, promoting integration in the public schools or providing competent counsel to indigents.[63] This illuminating turn of phrase is, however, the opposite face of the dark, largely featureless side of Bradley's variant of historical argument. Bradley's is a variant that risks an easy elision into a sort of imaginative legal anthropology. There is, for example, Justice Rehnquist's sarcastic charge that

> 'if those responsible for [the Bill of Rights and the Fourteenth Amendment] could have lived to know that their efforts had enshrined in the Constitution the right of commercial vendors of contraceptives to peddle them to unmarried minors through such means as window displays and vending machines located in the men's rooms of truck stops . . . it is not difficult to imagine their reaction'[64]

When actually, it *is* difficult to imagine their reactions, much more difficult than to imagine their reactions to events contemporary with their own lives.

Such imagining is also a variation of historical argument. It too depends on assumptions about intention, but in a peculiar way: that the whole life of an eighteenth-century agrarian society can guide us because of the special nature of its leaders and that we, from our very different lives, can know what those people would have thought in situations within which they would have been very different people. It is easy to see that such arguments are better for dissent than for the Court because they express a particular moral point and are therefore more effective as rhetoric than as decision procedure.

Thus, Justice Antonin Scalia, dissenting from the majority opinion by Justice Kennedy in the historic same-sex marriage case:

> Buried beneath the mummies and straining-to-be-memorable passages of the opinion is a candid and startling assertion. No matter what it was the People ratified, the Fourteenth Amendment protects those rights that the Judiciary, in its 'reasoned judgment', thinks the Fourteenth Amendment ought to protect.[65]

Or this in a First Amendment case:

> What secret knowledge, one must wonder, is breathed into lawyers when they become Justices of this Court, that enables them to discern that a practice which the text of the Constitution does not clearly proscribe, and which our people have regarded as constitutional for 200 years, is in fact unconstitutional? . . . The Court must be living in another world. Day by day, case by case, it is busy designing a Constitution for a country I do not recognize.[66]

Or this in a school prayer case:

> I find it a sufficient embarrassment that our Establishment Clause jurisprudence regarding holiday displays . . . , has come to 'require[e] scrutiny more commonly associated with interior decorators than with the judiciary.' But interior decorating is a rock-hard science compared to psychology practiced by amateurs. A few citations of '[r]esearch in psychology' that have no particular bearing upon the precise issue here . . . cannot disguise the fact that the Court has gone beyond the

realm where judges know what they are doing. The Court's argument that state officials have 'coerced' students to take part in the invocation and benediction at graduation ceremonies is, not to put too fine a point on it, incoherent.[67]

Nevertheless, Justice Scalia was also well aware of the shortcomings of traditional historical argument, so ably dissected by Powell, and by Paul Brest in his essay 'The Misconceived Quest for the Original Understanding'.[68] And so he and others proffered a variant of historical argument designed to parry the usual objections.

They maintained that the 'whole point'[69] of historical argument was to confine itself to the *original public meaning* of the constitutional text. This avoided some of the problems that critics of historical argument like Brest and Powell[70] had identified: the fact that the framers had no authority to adopt the Constitution and thus that their intentions were no more binding than those of a scrivener over the construction of a will; that the intentions of multimember bodies are notoriously elusive, some members voting for the reasons they disclose, some for tactical reasons, some for no reasons at all; that the framers themselves did not intend that their intentions govern the construction of the text. At a single stroke, these penetrating objections were turned aside. This new form of historical argument came to be called 'original public meaning'.[71]

Scalia, however, while anxious to confine his adversaries, was not so enthusiastic about being confined himself. He realized that the text of the Constitution was simply too sparse to provide all the tools necessary for realistic adjudication. And so, to the search for meaning in the words of the text as these were construed at the time of ratification, he appended a study of the understanding of the text by the framers. This is perhaps clearest in his dissent in *Morrison* v. *Olson*,[72] a case in which the Court upheld the independent counsel statute used to investigate President Clinton. Straying into structural argument, he defended this departure with the excuse that the separation of powers was a scheme discussed at length by the framers and reflected in the text that was adopted by the ratifiers.[73]

One can applaud this virtuosity – I happen to think the Independent Counsel statute was unconstitutional and that the Congress rightly let it lapse – but as an example of the move to rehabilitate historical argument by confining it to arguments from the 'original public meaning', it is not.[74]

III

Clio, the muse of history, is customarily depicted holding a parchment scroll, or a book or a set of tablets, and a trumpet. The trumpet promises announcements, verdicts and the tablets suggest that the history that is unfolding has in fact already been written. Both these ideas were challenged in the late twentieth century in ways that are captured by the familiar witticism directed at the Communist leadership of the Soviet Union: the future, it was said, is fixed; it's only the past that keeps changing.[75]

The comrades professed absolute confidence in how history would play out[76] but they had the unsettling habit of rewriting past political events to fit their current policy and personnel preferences. Thus, Old Bolsheviks like Trotsky and Kirov and sinister apparatchiks like Yezhov and other lesser figures like Enukdze were airbrushed out of official photos of past pageants, and the official histories were constantly amended to conform to the present uses to which history was to be put.

Today, however, one might conclude that the joke is on us. Of course, the past keeps changing as our values and perceptions change. Statues that once were objects of reverence are now judged in shame, and hitherto unrecognized causal factors – epidemiological[77] and environmental,[78] for example, or how the epidemiological causes interacted with environmental drivers[79] – are given a salience unrecognized by past historians. At the same time the future written on Clio's tablets, like the shears of the Fates, is remorseless and inexorable. In such a world, how is allegiance to the rule of law to be maintained? New values discredit the law's moral and ethical foundations; new facts defy its efforts to shape behaviour through precedent.

My own view is that past and future are the 'America' of which Locke spoke; they are dream states we can ponder but never visit. Like Major Major's diary in the novel Catch-22, our appointments are scheduled for meetings that can never take place. Condemned to live in the present, it is the common law of constitutional construction that is our surest underpinning. The principal reason we give legitimacy to courts, and to governments enforcing the law, is that we believe that judges and officials believe themselves to be bound by a power they do not wholly create and that they cannot wholly dismiss. Essential to this enterprise of methods that convey this sense is the use of historical argument.[80] We rely on these methods owing to their present value. They allow us to go on. In a democracy of many competing values, that may not be enough to ensure our survival and success, but without a functioning present, constructed from and constructing the past, there can't be a future.

Notes

1 Jeffrey Toobin, 'Our Broken Constitution', *The New Republic*, 9 December 2013.

2 Jonathan R. Macey, 'Originalism as an "Ism"', *Harvard Journal of Law & Public Policy* 19 (1996): 301.

3 M. B. Arneil, 'All the World was America', *John Locke and the American Indian* (Doctoral Dissertation, University College, London, 1992).

4 Grant Gilmore and Philip Bobbitt, *The Ages of American Law*, 2nd edn (2014), at 9.

5 Akhil Amar, *The Words That Made Us: America's Constitutional Conversation* (2021).

6 Quoted in R. Berger, *Government by Judiciary* (1977), 287. See also Massachusetts Constitution of 1780; Murphy notes that these words were 'paraphrased in several other early state constitutions' in 'Book Review', *Yale Law Journal* 87 (1978): 1752, 1763, n. 60.

7 *Writings of James Madison*, ed. G. Hunt (1900), vol. 6, 272. *See also Writings of James Madison*, vol. 9, 71–2, 477. For examples of recourse to the state ratifying conventions, *see Pollack* v. *Farmers Loan and Trust Co.*, 157 U.S. 427, 565 (1865), on the original understanding of 'direct tax'; *Twining* v. *New Jersey*, 211 U.S. 78, 107–10

(1908), on whether 'due process' was understood to include privilege against self-incrimination; *Monaco v. Mississippi*, 292 US. 313, 323–4 (1933), on whether the Constitution bars suits by foreign governments against unconsenting states. See also *Wesberry v. Sanders*, 376 U.S. 1, 15–16 (1964); *Duncan v. Louisiana*, 391 U.S. 145, 174–5 (1967) (J. Harlan and J. Steward, dissenting); *Powell v. McCormack*, 395 U.S. 486, 540–1 (1968).

8 T. Cooley, *Constitutional Limitations*, 8th edn (1927), 124. See also *Bell v. Maryland*, 378 U.S. 226, 288–9 (1964) (J. Goldberg, concurring): 'Our sworn duty to construe the Constitution requires . . . that we read it to effectuate the intent and purpose of the framers'.

9 *See Twinning v. New Jersey*, 211 U.S. 78 (1908).

10 *Rhode Island v. Massachusetts*, 37 U.S. (12 Pet.) 657, 721 (1838).

11 *Veazie Bank v. Fenno*, 75 U.S. (8 Wall) 533, 540–1 (1869).

12 *Knowlton v. Moore*, 178 U.S. 41, 100 (1900).

13 *Myers v. United States*, 272 U.S. 52, 116–18 (1926).

14 *Cramer v. United States*, 325 U.S. 1, 22–6 (1945); Justice Jackson erroneously states that the requirement of two witnesses to the same overt act was an original invention of the Convention of 1878. It originated with the British Treason Trials in 1695: 7 won. III, c. 3.

15 *District of Columbia v. Heller*, 554 U.S. 570, 603–5 (2008).

16 *Wesberry v. Sanders*, 376 U.S. 1, 8–14 (1964).

17 *Powell v. McCormack*, 395 U.S. 486, 532–41 (1969). *See also Gannett Co.* v. *DePasquale*, 44 U.S. 368, 385–91 (1979); *id.* at 418–27 (J. Blackmun, dissenting).

18 A. Bickel, *The Least Dangerous Branch* (1962), 98–110.

19 Madison tells us that George Read of Delaware objected to a draft of the Guaranty Clause which guaranteed Republican government and territory to each state. Read said, '(I)t abetted the idea of distinct states [which] would be a perpetual source of discord. There can be no cure for this evil but in doing away [with] States altogether and uniting them all into one great Society.' J. Madison, *Notes of Debates in the Federal Convention of 1787* (Athens, OH, 1966), 105. Surely, no one would argue that alteration of the draft to delete the term 'territory' means the framers intended to make easy 'doing away [with]' states altogether.

20 *Missouri v. Illinois*, 180 U.S. 208, 223 (1901). It may, however, always be possible that some members may have voted against the rejected proposal because they thought it unnecessary, i.e. that the text unamended would provide for the proposed course.

21 *Myers v. U.S.*, 272 U.S. 52, 294 (1926). For a similar argument, see *Palmore v. United States*, 411 U.S. 389, 412–13 (1973) (J. Douglas, dissenting).

22 *The Records of the Federal Convention of 1787*, ed. M. Farrand (1966), vol. 2, 550.

23 House Rep. 105–830, Impeachment of William Jefferson Clinton (1998).

24 Laurence Tribe and Joshua Matz, *To End a Presidency: The Power of Impeachment* (New York, 2018), 43–4.

25 Holmes, 'The Theory of Legal Interpretation', *Harvard Law Review* 12 (1899): 417–18.

26 See *Branch Historical Papers* (June 1908), vol. 2, 51–2, 56–7, for criticism by Roane of Marshall's historical arguments in *Martin* v. *Hunter's Lessee*. *See* argument of counsel in *McCulloch v. Maryland*, 17 U.S. (4 Wheat.) 315, 372–4 (1819), for Martin's view that Congress has no implied power to charter a bank because 'the scheme of the framers intended to leave nothing to implication'.

27 Kalven, 'Our Man From Wall Street', *University of Chicago Law Review* 35 (1968): 229.

28 Ibid.

29 Gregory, 'William Winslow Crosskey—As I Remember Him', *University of Chicago Law Review* 35 (1968): 243, 244.

30 See Calvin Johnson, *Righteous Anger at the Wicked States: The Meaning of the Founders' Constitution* (Cambridge, 2005).

31 W. Crosskey, *Politics and the Constitution in the History of the United States* (1953), 77.

32 Rheinstein, 'Book Review', *University of Chicago Law School Record* 2 (1953): 6 (quoting Schlesinger).

33 Krock, 'Book Review', *University of Chicago Law School Record* 3 (1954): 8.

34 Rheinstein, 'Book Review', 6.

35 Corbin, 'Book Review', *University of Chicago Law School Record* 2 (1953): 14, *see also* Corbin, 'Book Review', *Yale Law Journal* 62 (1953): 1137.

36 Sharp, 'Book Review', *Columbia Law Review* 54 (1954): 439.

37 Brant, 'Book Review', *Columbia Law Review* 54 (1954): 443, 450.

38 Goebel, 'Book Review', *Columbia Law Review* 54 (1954): 450–1.

39 Brown, 'Book Review', *Harvard Law Review* 67 (1954): 1439.

40 Philip Bobbitt, 'Constitutional Law and Interpretation', in *A Companion to Philosophy of Law and Legal Theory*, 2nd edn (2010).

41 Hart, 'Book Review', *Harvard Law Review* 67 (1954): 1456, 1457.

42 Ibid., 1458.

43 Ibid., 1461.

44 Ibid., 1474.

45 Rheinstein, 'Book Review', 16.

46 *Michelin Tire Corp.* v. *Wages, Tax Comm'r*, 423 U.S. 276, 290–1 (1976). The Court later questioned even the slight reliance on *Michelin*, see *Dept. of Revenue* v. *Ass'n. of Wash. Stevedoring Cos.*, 435 U.S. 734, 760 n.26 (1978).

47 347 U.S. 483, 489 (1954).

48 It is clear that Crosskey recognizes his approach as such a 'variant'. See, e.g. his criticism of the Fairman article: '[E]ntirely apart from questions of the adequacy, and of the handling, of the evidence which Mr. Fairman presents, it is to be remembered that a recurrence to evidence of the sort he presents, is illegitimate in the case of a provision, like the first section of the Fourteenth Amendment, which is clear in itself, or clear when read in the light of the prior law. It is doubly illegitimate when it is remembered that most of what the first section of that amendment requires, was also required by Amendments II–VIII. Mr. Fairman apparently forgets that the ultimate question is not what the legislatures meant, any more than it is what Congress or the more immediate framers of the amendment means.' *Cf.*, Holmes, 'The Theory of Legal Interpretation', 417. See also Crosskey, *Politics and the Constitution*, 1381.

49 Henry Monaghan, 'Our Perfect Constitution', *New York University Law Review* 56 (1981): 353.

50 H. Jefferson Powell, 'The Original Understanding of Original Intent', *Harvard Law Review* 98 (1984): 885.

51 Which is how it looks at present. See the influential essay Randy E. Barnett, 'An Originalism for Non-Originalists', *Loyola Law Review* 45 (1999): 611.

52 *Chisholm* v. *Georgia*, 2 U.S. (2 Dall.) 419 (1793).

53 G. Gunther, *Constitutional Law Cases and Materials*, 9th edn (1975), 49.

54 *The Federalist, No. 81* (A. Hamilton) (Bourne ed., 1937), 119, 125–6.

55 *Larson* v. *Domestic & Foreign Commerce Corp.*, 377 U.S. 682, 708 (1949) (J. Frankfurter, dissenting).

56 *Hans* v. *Louisiana*, 134 U.S. 1 (1890).

57 *Hans* v. *Louisiana*, at 10.

58 See, e.g. *Principality of Monaco* v. *Mississippi*, 292 U.S. 313 (1934); but this does not apply to suits by sister states or by the United States. See *North Dakota* v. *Minnesota*, 263 U.S. 365, 372–3 (1923); *United States* v. *Mississippi*, 380 U.S. 128, 140–1 (1965).

59 134 U.S. at 15.

60 See *Edelman* v. *Jordan*, 415 U.S. 651 (1974) and cases cited therein.

61 R. Dworkin, 'The Jurisprudence of Richard Nixon', *New York Review of Books*, 4 May 1972, 27.

62 Bickel, 'The Original Understanding and the Segregation Decision', *Harvard Law Review* 69 (1955): 1.

63 Jack Balkin, 'Framework Originalism and the Living Constitution', *Northwestern Law Review* 103 (2009): 549. For a similar idea, he uses to rehabilitate historical argument, construing 'original meaning' [concept] with 'original expected application' [conception] at 552.

64 *Carey* v. *Population Services International*, 431 U.S. 678, 717 (1977) (J. Rehnquist, dissenting).

65 *Obergefell* v. *Hodges*, 135 S. Ct. 2584, 2628 (J. Scalia, dissenting).

66 *Bd. Of City Comm'rs* v. *Umbehr*, 518 U.S. 668, 688–89, 711 (1996) (J. Scalia, dissenting).

67 *Lee* v. *Weisman*, 505 U.S. 577, 636 (1992) (J. Scalia, dissenting) (citations omitted) (quoting *American Jewish Congress* v. *Chicago*, 827 F. 2nd 120, 129 (7th Cir. 1987) (J. Easterbrook, dissenting)).

68 *Boston University Law Review* 60 (1980): 204.

69 3 Hearings on the Nomination of the Honorable Neil M. Gorsuch to Be an Associate Justice of the Supreme Court of the United States Before the S. Comm. On the Judiciary, 115th Cong. 9 (2017) (statement of Lawrence B. Solum, Professor, Georgetown University Law Center, https://www.judiciary.senate.gov/imo/media/doc/03-23-17%20Solum%20Testimony.pdf [https://perma.cc/UP9D-CKUT).

70 'The Original Understanding of Original Intent', *Harvard Law Review* 98 (1984): 885.

71 487 U.S. 654 (1988).

72 See John Yoo, 'Scalia: What Were the Founding Fathers Thinking? http://www.newsweek.com/scalia-founding-fathers-thinking-426513; John Yoo, 'Antonin Scalia and the Conservative Revolution', https://www.aei.org/society-and-culture/antonin-scalia-and-the-conservative-revolution/.

73 Although Randy Barnett, a distinguished Originalist who certainly ought to know, credits Justice Scalia with being 'Perhaps the first defender to shift the theory from its previous forms on the intentions of the framers of the Constitution to the original public meaning of the text at the time of its enactment', it certainly bears a family resemblance to Crosskey's method of historical argument. Barrett at 9, *infra*.

74 For an outstanding example of recent constitutional scholarship using history, see Amar, *The Words That Made Us*, n. 5 *supra*.

75 Erin Blakemore, 'How Photos Became a Weapon in Stalin's Great Purge', https://www.history.com/news/josef-stalin-great-purge-photo-retouching.

76 'The Future Is Ours', *Political Statement from the Communist Party of Britain Marxist-Leninist, 14th Congress*, London, April 2006, https://www.cpbml.org.uk/about/what-we-stand/the-future-is-ours.

77 'Pandemics That Changed History', 21 December 2020, https://www.history.com/topics/middle-ages/pandemics-timeline.

78 E. LeR. Ladurie, *Times of Feast, Times of Famine: A History of Climate since the Year 1000* (New York, 1988); Sam White, *A Cold Welcome: The Little Ice Age and Europe's Encounter with North America* (New York, 2017).

79 'How Colonization's Death Toll May Have Affected Earth's Climate', 31 January 2019, https://www.history.com/news/climate-change-study-colonization-death-farming-collapse.

80 Though there are other competing modalities that also contribute to legitimacy, e.g. prudence, ethos, doctrine, structure and text. Indeed, the use of history alone, either by giving its precedence over the other forms of argument or by using it to deny their legitimacy, would ultimately undermine the entire enterprise of constitutional construction.

12

Learning from military history

Jeremy Black

This chapter will explore the ways in which historical reflection on the nature of war can deepen our understanding of the challenges of military conflict and the difficulties of attaining the political objective for which violence is employed. It will begin with the concept of the so-called Revolution in Military Affairs (RMA), which was much in vogue during the 1990s following the development of precision-guided munitions and stealth technologies. I will argue that the RMA was not in fact a revolution, and did not alter the fundamental nature of war, forcing a paradigm shift as was argued at the time, which, in practice, has remained consistent throughout human history.

The RMA reflected the fusion of a technological confidence based on the apparent potential of new weaponry with the misleading historical concept of development through a series of revolutionary changes. The two were linked in an understanding of war as primarily the product of material culture. Thus, the move from one form of weaponry or of a related technology, for example, in communications, to another apparently described capability, explained effectiveness and established a new paradigm that determined success. Indeed, there was teleology and determinism at stake. This is an aspect of the role of modernization theory in military history and vice versa.

Academic theories in the humanities and social sciences gain traction not because of any inherent intellectual merit but because they are readily usable and very useful. The 'pull' dimension, the usefulness of a thesis and, more especially, its usefulness in a particular context is one that can be approached in materialist terms, whether filling textbooks and lecture slots or advancing academic careers, but also with reference to the value of an argument at a specific moment. Indeed, from that perspective, it is the unoriginal thesis that generally does best, as 'thinking within the box' or, at least, a similar box, helps to make a proposition readily digestible. The 'push' dimension is an aspect of the same factors, of material and ideological import. The key one is the ability to appear cutting-edge but in terms that are in practice somewhat predictable.

And so with the idea of an early-modern military revolution, a proposition that drew heavily on already established ideas and literatures of modernization and, eventually, globalization. These ideas had a long genesis, but the key origin was that of progress as measured in and by social development, an approach that put to one side religious notions of time as leading towards a millenarian outcome. If Montesquieu, Smith and Robertson are all key names in this intellectual project, it was in practice one of a longer pedigree, with notions of improvability in human life accompanied by that of development. These ideas lent themselves to nineteenth-century interest in scientific formulation and application. Darwinism is part of the mix, as evolutionary ideas provided metaphors and concepts, notably what was to be termed functionalism, in the shape of serving goals necessary for survival and therefore strength.

These ideas affected new developing sciences such as sociology, geopolitics and anthropology, and were brought into academic history through a shared concern with modernity and therefore modernization. Rational choice was seen as being at play, from biological preference to economic and political practice, but there were different emphases; some (following Durkheim) stressed the constraints on action, while others (with following Weber) stressed the power of contingency. There was a parallel with geographical ideas of determinism or 'possibilism'. Weber's approach to modernity led him to define it in terms of rationality and standardization, with motivation in terms of instrumental behaviour as opposed to traditional action. Weber also linked the prudent rationality related to capitalism with Protestantism. Taken into American thought by Talcott Parsons, Weber was the forbear of what was to be called the Structural-Functional approach, and modernization theory became a key tool in the social sciences, a theory emphasizing rational abstract principles and an abandonment of past practices. Key texts included Walt Rostow's *Politics and the Stages of Growth* (1971) and Francis Fukuyama's *The End of History and the Last Man* (1992), the latter a work propounded around the means, goals and modernity of liberal democracy and free-market capitalism. In the 1960s, and again in the 1990s, modernization was regarded as a form of global New Deal, able to create a new world order, and information and theory were deployed accordingly.[1]

Modernization theory, however, was often advanced with insufficient attention to practicalities, let alone reality, as with the failure to understand Vietnamese society. As a related, but separate point, the attempt to produce 'modern', quantifiable criteria of military success fell afoul of the ability of the Viet Cong and North Vietnamese to soak up heavier casualties and to defy American equations of success with their emphasis on quantification.[2] It would be easy to draw a line between these (and other) modernization writers and the proponents of, and even more response to, the thesis of a military revolution, with Geoffrey Parker in particular offering a parallel account to Fukuyama. While that is apposite, there are other elements of modernization theory that should first be addressed. A key one was that of secularization, as against analysis, means and goal of development. Durkheim, Weber and many others argued that modernization meant a decline in religious practice and significance, and this approach affected a broad tranche of writing in the social sciences and humanities, as well as discussion of historical change.[3] The cult of reason, understood as inherently secular, with faith banished to the private sphere, meant that the present necessarily understood the past better than the latter did: reason could reveal the prospectus to a better future and a better-understood past.

A circularity in thought and selectivity in evidence were inherent to this process, and both, indeed, were very much to be seen in the work by the proponents of a military revolution. As far as the first was concerned functions were presented in a quasi-automatic fashion, with needs and drives readily ascribed to states, and effects ascribed to functions while those functions were defined by the effects they produced.[4]

I

A key aspect of the cult of a modern reason, in terms of secularism and of other elements, is a total failure not only to understand the military cultures of the past (and even arguably the present) but also to appreciate the nature of development. Failing to perceive the values of the past and to understand its practices understandably leads to a neglect of key factors in the evaluation of proficiency, capability and success, both individual and collective. Honour is misleadingly disparaged as conservative if not redundant, and practices of aristocratic officership are misunderstood. A more informed comment can be found in the work of Gregory Hanlon,[5] and it is instructive that his new book makes scant mention of the military revolution, a thesis that is presented as 'argued to an indecisive end'.[6]

'Revolution' was a term in more than fashion in the twentieth century, reflecting not only political commitment but also that it became the standard way to describe and explain structural change. This practice owed much to the industrial revolution, a term first used in 1799, but popularized by Arnold Toynbee in 1881, with significant capitals. This term was much applied thereafter, and was to be the basis for subsequent revolutions, as with the Agricultural Revolution.[7] It was not therefore surprising that the term was deployed in military history. There were precursors, but the most influential argument was advanced in 1955 by Michael Roberts in a work published in 1956[8] that liberally employed the idea of fundamental change and the term 'military revolution', and closed with a clear affirmation of transformation: 'By 1660, the modern art of war had come to birth. Mass armies, strict discipline, the control of the state, the submergence of the individual had already arrived' and so on, culminating with 'The road lay open, broad and straight, to the abyss of the twentieth century'. With its failure to grasp the nature of pre-1560 or post-1660 warfare, its neglect of navies and the global dimension, its failure to understand the requirements of command and its simplification and misreading of modern warfare, this was a disappointing piece, a classic instance indeed of footnotes rather than foresight; but it was given publicity, not least in Sir George Clark's *War and Society in the Seventeenth Century* (1958).

Parker was far more impressive with his inclusion of the naval dimension, his wider-ranging chronology and his engagement with the world scale. Initially Parker focused on the Spanish dimension, but he broadened out with his hugely influential *The Military Revolution: Military Innovation and the Rise of the West, 1500-1800* (1988). That work deserves a careful reading as does the perceptive criticism by a number of scholars including Bert Hall, Kelly DeVries and David Parrott. It is particularly instructive that Parker addressed the global question, employing 'the Military Revolution of the sixteenth century'[9] to in effect explain both the rise (and multipolarity) of the West and why it was to provide the most successful of the 'gunpowder empires' to employ a term probed by William H. McNeill. The strengths of Parker's work can be qualified empirically, not least, but not only, by questioning the idea of a three-century revolution, or by reference to the limitations of Western success, the nature of late medieval circumstances, the importance of the post-1660 period and, despite the brilliance of the footnotes, to the selection and deployment of evidence.

There are also, which is the intention of this note, debatable assumptions in terms of theses of modernization, and the characterization of capability. Parker's emphasis on particular notions of proficiency, and his embrace of the proposition of change that is fundamental because described as revolutionary, and described as revolutionary because fundamental, fits within a practice of historical writing that increasingly looks very much that of a particular period. Alluding earlier to Fukuyama was deliberate because there are instructive parallels between the mindsets represented in these two works. Each appears qualified at the very least by the more varied presentation of modern warfare that the subsequent three decades were to offer. Parker very much takes modernization theory on board: 'the Muslim states . . . could no longer meet and defeat the expanding repertory of innovations developed by their Christian adversaries, because the Westernization of war also required replication of the economic and social structures and infrastructures, in particular the machinery of resource-mobilization and modern finance, on which the new techniques depended',[10] which doubtless explains why the United States was invariably successful in the Islamic world over the last two decades, as well as Israel in Lebanon. Instead, it is the specificity of conflict and individual conflicts and the multivalent character of war, that emerge; and the language of modernity, modernization and revolution is misleading as an account, narrative and/or analytical, or this phenomenon.

Thus contemporary debates have a strong and still insistent historical and contextual perspective, although it is one that most practitioners seek to ignore both those who consider military history and those who write on the present. Instead, they cite Clausewitz in an attempt to discern timeless characteristics of conflict.

At the same time, ironically, there was, and is, generally a focus on technology. That, however, was, and is, to put one aspect of military activity to the fore and to do so in a decontextualized fashion that did not assess adequately, or sometimes at all, the contexts of such conflict. This was particularly so of the dynamics involved in tasking, the key measure of effectiveness and achievement. Indeed, ironically, one of the classic lessons from military history became that of the relationship between proficiency in terms of weaponry and failure in terms of outcomes and tasking. That was a lesson that was often unwelcome both to military figures and to their political allies/masters. Indeed, that very reluctance became an aspect of military history that deserved attention but that scholars proved unwilling to address adequately. In particular, there was a focus on debating theorists, notably Clausewitz, rather than addressing key practical, methodological, conceptual and historiographical problems in learning from the past, and notably so with counter-insurgency. Here there was not the developmental slant seen in work on technology nor, indeed, the variant advanced in some discussion of insurgency, and particularly that of the impact of the revolutionary theorist, propagandist or practitioner of the moment, for example, Mao Zedong or Che Guevara.

Consideration of the theses of insurgency underlines the extent to which the standard approach of focusing on training by and for military is insufficient, and, frequently, indeed, inadequate as an approach to learning from military history. While important, that is made even more questionable due to the importance of political issues in both tasking and implementation. Thus the process of learning from military history becomes an aspect of the 'history wars' in which the past is contested. This is frequently done through the shorthand of historical analogy by phrasing. Thus Vietnam or Suez or Munich is a key aspect of debate, with the first used to debate counter-insurgency. It is at this level that it is necessary to add to the consideration of military history because it tends to be the aspect of the learning process that is underplayed.

And yet it is important to see how politicians frame discussion. When, for example, in February 2020, Matthew Hancock, the British secretary of state for health, referred to the Maginot Line in terms of the folly of relying on a stoppage of travel as a means to prevent the spread of coronavirus, he was, of course, not interested in the idea that the Maginot Line (like the anti-ship guns at Singapore that allegedly pointed in the wrong direction) worked by confining the likely direction of attack, only for the overall strategy to fail because of problems in handling the mobile stage of the campaign. Similarly, with the Vietnam War, it is not helpful in terms of public debate to suggest that, while tactically and operationally problematic for the Americans, the intervention ended with the United States allied to China, with the spread of Communism restricted in South-East Asia, with Indonesia securely in the Western camp, with the Viet Cong shattered and with the North Vietnamese both greatly weakened by the struggle and now committed in Cambodia and facing Chinese hostility.

These points can be contested, but they underline the extent to which 'learning from military history' involves inherently political, and, for many, therefore, problematic, questions about goals, policies and strategies, questions that the military deliberately seek to avoid both in military education and in presenting a role to the public. These questions can be further amplified if the consideration of military history is taken into broader currents of issues in the public sphere. That might appear to be a learning process that has little to do with applicability for policy, but that would be a misleading view because these very constructions affect the parameters of public debate and thus an aspect of the applicability of strategic assumptions.

This conspectus of methodological problems helps explain the attraction of answers, of which the most seductive, as already mentioned, are those of technology. That answer serves important military, economic, political and popular constituencies; and does so in a manner that works in terms of a modern culture fascinated with material culture. In practical terms, this can be a case of 'Get me the weapons and I will get you the war that makes them work', only for it to be discovered that this rarely works that way, and certainly less so in the longer term beyond the initial campaign. Indeed, friction really arises not so much as usually understood within campaigns (and generally then for operational reasons), but more within conflicts as a whole, and then essentially because the strategic paradigms have altered.

II

What then does history teach and how should statesmen and military practitioners think about war? Why teach military history? Military history serves a variety of purposes, including institutional education, academic scholarship, popular interest, commercial opportunity and collective myth-making. All and each needs to be considered when the subject is evaluated, and to judge one by the standards of another is not necessarily helpful, and can be positively misleading. The question why teach military history might seem to shrink the options to the educational process, but that is not, however, in practice the case, for teaching, understood in the widest sense, embraces the question of the nature and sustaining of civic militarism, and also overlaps with the issue of commercial opportunity. To approach the subject in another perspective, one that draws heavily on the role and resonance of civic militarism, there is also the question of the point of reference. The question, 'Why teach military history?' can be approached in the abstract, but it really depends on the country and society that is in the forefront. The issue is different, or, at least appears very different, in Sweden or Israel, Spain or Estonia, Ireland or South Korea. As a reminder of the variety of social contexts and needs, in many states, indeed, the teaching of military history is an aspect not simply of civic patriotism, but also of a wider social engagement that can owe something to conscription, as in Finland, Israel and Switzerland. In these cases, as also more generally, the teaching of military history fulfils pedagogic purposes but also helps in fostering the engagement of the civilian soldier, including the civilian reservist. Thus, morale, as widely conceived, plays a role in the reasons for teaching military history, and also in the content and tone of the teaching.

Conscription can be unrelated to immediate threats, the case, for example, of Switzerland, but, usually, this is not the position. Thus, the teaching of military history, whether professional, educational or civic, is an aspect of a threat environment, and the assessment of value has to take note of this context. That, indeed, helps explain the role of military history in America's culture wars, as its downplaying is associated with a downplaying or alteration of the threat environment, and vice versa.

The prominence of the threat environment is also the case with societies, such as contemporary Iran and Myanmar, where the politics of paranoia are crucial to the mobilization of enforced consent on behalf of the government. In some states, moreover, such as Turkey, Pakistan and, to a lesser extent, Brazil, the military present themselves as crucial to national integrity and identity.

Considering these and other cases serve to underline the unusual, not to say eccentric, character of Western commitment both to intellectual independence and to academic and educational detachment from public politics. Indeed, on the world case, the pressure of public politics on education will probably become more salient as China rises in relative importance, not least as an economic-political model. This underlines the need to appreciate the diversity of national cultures within which military affairs are considered, with the teaching of military history presented as an aspect of the politics of these cultures.

The teaching of military history in the United States, by far the world's leading military power, is currently a matter of controversy. This is not least due to the widely repeated charge that this teaching is being downplayed by the 'politically correct'. Indeed, it is widely argued that they are preventing the appointment of military historians in American universities and marginalizing the subject as a whole. Is this true? Does it matter? Is military history desirable, a 'politically correct' view, or, indeed, from 'non-politically-correct' dimension and the specific perspective of military change, not least technological change, the so-called Revolution in Military Affairs (RMA) and its sequel 'Transformation', relevant? Does military history have a future?

The last is the key issue, both for the United States and more generally, but let us first address the question of whether the subject is being deliberately downplayed or discarded. Once one moves from the easy polemic of press discussion, it is possible to see this in two lights. On the one hand, the problems facing military history are not unique to the subject but are part of a wider issue that involves the range of subjects that were central to the teaching of history prior to the 1960s. Thus, this is as much a question of constitutional history, of legal history, of diplomatic history, of ecclesiastical history, and of high political history, as much as of military history.

Indeed, constitutional history and pre-1900 diplomatic history have fared considerably worse than military history, not least because they do not have the support offered by the military academies and by widespread public interest from outside higher education, each of which ensures that military history is buoyant, whatever the situation in the universities. To a limited extent, professional interest in the law operates in a similar fashion.

The sense of a wider issue of shifts in the nature and understanding of history that are also relevant to other sub-disciplines is not one that most military historians tend to grasp, as they generally have the tunnel vision common to most subject specialists. Nevertheless, this wider issue needs addressing, not least because of the extent to which this is an aspect of a more wholesale marginalization of the longer-term continuity of American history. In part, this reflects a jettisoning of a historical tradition that looks back towards colonial days, the struggle for independence, and the early decades of the republic, a tradition sometimes, inaccurately, referred to as the 'dead white men' approach.

In its place has come an emphasis on more recent decades, and on social forces and movements, as the agents of change. The same process can be seen at work in Britain, although there, as in the United States, it generally fails to make sufficient allowance for other factors that have moulded recent history including not only economic trends, fiscal policy and high politics but also the impact of war. Thus, for example, the Second World War had more of a consequence for twentieth-century American developments and was more central to them than civil rights; this was the case not simply as far as America's international position was concerned but also with reference to its development as both state and society. War had even more traumatic consequences for the internal development of France and Russia, Germany and Japan.

An emphasis on social forces as the causes and agents of change can misleadingly make military history appear redundant or simply the expression of social developments. This, incidentally, is an approach that helps those on the Left who see 'peoples' warfare' as bound to prevail over regular, professional forces, an approach that is of limited validity, but one that flourished during the period of so-called wars of national liberation, and was powerfully advanced in the United States by particular readings of the Vietnam War. The terrorism/insurrection in Iraq was seen by some in the same light, but it is necessary to note, first, the military perspective – that insurrections do not necessarily succeed, and, second, the political point that, by any standards, many of these movements were and are highly undesirable.

The relative diminution of military history thus reflects wider currents including those in both society and in historical scholarship. In the former case, it is pertinent to note the degree to which the individualism, hedonism and atomization of society associated with both 1960s and post-1960s values sapped general adherence to collectivist solutions and commitments. Thus, conscription, and the accompanying mental attitudes and social patterns, no longer commanded support, and, in part, this is relevant to the context of military history, at least compared to the 1950s.

In the case of historical scholarship, it is possible when discussing the relative decline of military history to point both to the rise of social history and cultural studies, and to the influence on historical work of perspectives derived from other social sciences including anthropology and collective psychology. This process is not restricted to the United States, which indicates that locating the issue solely in terms of America's culture wars is inadequate. It requires a broader contextualization that is alive to the interaction of American and international developments.

Turning more specifically to the history of war, there is a tension between military history as understood by many, but by no means all, of those who are interested in the subject, and the history of war. For many, particularly, but not only, in the non-academic world, this is a subject that should be about fighting, about battles and campaigns, troops and weapons. This operational dimension is indeed important, and military history should not be demilitarized, but it is not the complete subject. Indeed, part of the tension in the discussion of military history, not least among specialists, revolves not so much around its neglect, but, instead, is in terms of how the subject is treated. Here, it is necessary to note differences among military historians. The operational historians, sometimes unfairly, but frequently all too accurately, referred to in terms of drum and trumpet history, are indeed neglected within the academy, but those looking at wider dimensions, such as the staples of war and society, and war and the state, are generally assured of an audience.

This is further the case because the 'history' in these cases is as much explored by sociologists, anthropologists and political scientists, as by those seen more conventionally as historians. In part, therefore, the discussion of military history today is a case of tensions among military historians and about the character of such history. This debate is not always explicit, but, in practice, exists not simply in terms of the content of the subject, but also of the way in which topics are pursued and presented, as well as of the powerful issues of patronage and appointment, and publication strategies. These latter issues are difficult to discuss, but are nonetheless important for that. Indeed, this can lend a shadowboxing character to public debate, with vague remarks about general attitudes when, in practice, it is the views of a small number of individuals operating in particular institutions that are crucial and at issue. Those of publishers are also particularly important, because, if the major presses do not publish military history, then it seems to lack scholarly weight. This makes it far more difficult for academics in this field to obtain posts in leading universities, and there is no doubt that that is a factor in the politics and culture of appointments; not least because of the American habit of validating opinions and individuals by their labels, as if a book or person was necessarily better because published by, or at, Yale than Oklahoma.

It is easier to probe questions about the appropriateness of the standard approach to military history, because this moves us from the more shadowy world of patronage. This approach is characterized by a fascination with technology, both definition of capability and an explanation of change, and by a focus on the Western way of war. The West dominates attention not simply because it is indeed important, but because it is seen as setting global standards for effectiveness. This, however, is an aspect of a misleading tendency to dismiss non-Western military history as primitive, a tendency that makes it more difficult to devise an appropriate doctrine for waging war with such powers.

These fundamental parameters of the subject are, in turn, linked to other issues. The fascination with technology and, more generally, with the material culture of war, contributes to a presentation of military history in terms of revolutionary developments, rather than of incrementalism, understood in general in terms of an evolutionary change based on trial and error. This is mistaken, as incrementalism is crucial, not least in terms of the response to allegedly revolutionary developments. The latter have to be grasped, a response defined, and the response embedded in terms of procurement and training. These responses involve what may be seen as cultural dimensions and these repay attention in a subject that is frequently overly oriented towards battle, whether operational or in terms of the experience of war. A response open to cultural dimensions, is also less overly determined, not least in terms of the habitual emphasis on the material aspects of war. More generally, this serves as a reminder that the subject is far from 'closed' or 'done'.

The treatment of war in universities can be mocked by focusing on some research topics that are indeed far removed from fighting, and, more seriously, by asking whether an emphasis on civilians, atrocities, or the memorialization of war, all three of which play a major role in the literature, has been pushed too far. These are relevant points, and some of the war and society literature indeed tells us far more about society than it does about war, and more about victims than about fighting. I note this tension in the discussion of military history by colleagues in my own university.

Nevertheless, in terms of conflict, it is also clear that victory is obtained when one of the sides is persuaded that it has lost, and this involves more than just fighting. The cultural dimension is also present in the shape of very different responses to loss and suffering. Current conflicts around the world serve as an abrupt reminder that victory and defeat, suffering and loss, have very different meanings in particular contexts, and success in such conflict, in part, depends on an accurate perception of these contrasts.

Far from being ignored, war also plays a crucial role in international relations studies, not least those on the rise and fall of great powers. Again, there is scarcely any sense that the subject is ignored from this perspective. It can, however, be treated in an overly reductionist fashion, as in the tendency to ascribe likely, if not inevitable, results to more powerful economies. This was seen in Paul Kennedy's influential *The Rise and Fall of the Great Powers: Economic Change and Military Conflict from 1500 to 2000* (1988), which encapsulated a widespread tendency.

There is an undoubted lack of interest in most American universities in military history. This is particularly true of the Ivys, in several of which the serious neglect of the subject contrasts pointedly with the impressive memorials to the many who lost their life in war. This is the case, for example, with Yale and its powerful presentation of loss in the First World War. This lack of interest is also true of the University of California system. Furthermore, a number of universities that were noted for the subject have lost relevant posts, as with Florida State, or have become less dynamic, as with Hawaii Pacific. There are a number of universities with important programmes, but there is a problem at the senior level, as John Lynn has pointed out: many of the best and the brightest did not go to graduate school in the United States in the 1970s and 1980s, those who did rarely chose military history, and, of those, few chose American military history. Thus, there is a lack of suitable senior applicants comparable to those in other fields, such as early-modern European military; but student interest lies precisely in modern American military. So the profession faces a major crisis here.

This, of course, matters. Military history is a key element of military studies, a point to which I will turn later, and it is unsatisfactory that these are at best spottily developed in the American education system. I was once asked by a student at Chapel Hill why it mattered, and I replied that if he became a politician it would be of great value if he understood the potential and problems of war. More generally, this point might be made about public opinion as a whole.

III

As the study of war matters, so it is obviously desirable. The question is whether military history as an aspect of this study is relevant, and if so why, and thus how. This idea of relevance was strongly challenged, directly and indirectly, by the belief in the RMA. This was advanced strongly in the 1990s and early 2000s as a description of changes in American military capability, and as a prospectus for fresh change. It is instructive to consider the RMA as it indicates the tension sometimes discerned between (new) doctrine and historical perspectives, and was earlier employed within the military to deny the value of military history. Integral to the RMA were a number of concepts each rich in acronyms and jargon. The common focus is on smart doctrine: operational planning and practice, in order to take advantage of a new generation of weapons and the possibilities posed by advances in information technology. The emphasis on precise information as a means, as well as a tool, of conflict, relates to its use in order to locate forces accurately, as well as to destroy enemy units with semi-automated weapons. Accurate targeting is required if precision weaponry is to be effective. This, in turn, entails 'information dominance', in order to deny such a capability to opponents. The RMA also calls for 'network-centric warfare': a focus on the new capability of information systems, rather than on traditional practices and structures of command and control. The concept thus linked developments in weapon systems with a doctrine that meshed with theories of modernization that rest on the adoption of technological systems. In the language of the RMA, weaponry is designed to ensure what are termed dominant manoeuvre, precision engagements, full-dimensional protection, focused logistics and information warfare.

Broader requirements were also served by this creation of a belief that total victory can be ensured through a specific type of High Intensity Conflict. These tasks and assumptions can be discussed, without any suggestion of prioritization, in terms of liberal internationalism, the particular requirements of American foreign policy and the growing disjuncture between highly ambitious Western goals and a widespread reluctance to risk casualties. Liberal internationalism became part of the New World order that followed the collapse of the Soviet Union, with the argument, fed in particular by the atrocities in Rwanda in 1994 and Bosnia in 1995, that there was a duty to intervene in order to prevent humanitarian disasters. Such intervention presupposed success, and relied on the notion of a clear capability gap between the two sides. Indeed, from the humanitarian perspective, the forces of good had to be successful in order to avoid the suffering that would result from a difficult conquest. This concept helped explain the difficulties faced by Anglo-American representatives when discussing Iraqi casualties during and after the war of 2003.

From the perspective of American foreign policy, the RMA also apparently explained how policy goals could be fulfilled, as this policy rested in part on a military underpinning, and in particular on how best to forestall threats. The need to be able to respond to more than one threat simultaneously, was regarded as particularly necessary, and the force multiplication apparently offered by the RMA was especially important in this context. In short, the RMA made American foreign policy possible: it contributed not only to strategic concerns but also to foreign policy interests around the world. Looked at more critically, the RMA aided in a militarization of this policy in which, furthermore, the views of allies were of limited significance.

The value of the RMA as an analysis can be debated, not least the extent to which current conflicts apparently qualify its applicability. However, the key issue here is whether the RMA made military history redundant by moving warmaking forward to a new plane, as was claimed. The answer is no, for aside from the point that the RMA can be historicized by reference to other real or supposed revolutions in military affairs, an approach on which there is a useful literature, the claim that the RMA made history redundant clashes with other approaches. It is not so much that there are unchanging realities in war, though that is the theme of a literature, as, rather, that military history throws light on the variety of military trajectories in the world as different societies have responded in contrasting ways to the opportunities and problems of their situation. This can be seen further if the emphasis in military development is placed on changes in 'tasking', in short on the goals and functions of the military, rather than a focus on capability, in particular on weaponry. Understanding the contrasting rationales of militaries, and how they rest on different strategic cultures is important because this provides a way to understand the military drives of opponents. This is particularly important for the West as force projection has become so important since the close of the Cold War.

Military history thus has a direct value as an aspect of understanding strategic culture, which now is a key concept in military studies with military history proving a key aspect in these studies. Military history is also important as the repository of experience and thus the background of training. Experience is particularly important, because war, at the tactical, operational or strategic level, is about the management of risk. Experience helps define the understanding of risk. Furthermore, when two powers begin a war, each generally assumes that it can win, and at least one is wrong. History helps explain victory and defeat and also shows that the balance between them was frequently very narrow. At the tactical level, staff rides are a valuable part of training, while operational exercises can indicate principles of manoeuvrist warfare, such as concentration and defeating opponents in detail (separately).

This is a continuing process. A handbook for the Nonresident Seminar Syllabus of the Strategy and Policy Division of the College of Distance Education of the United States Naval War College noted: 'The overall purpose of the National Security Decision Making Course is to educate military officers and U.S. government civilians in the effective development and command of armed forces within the constraints of national resources.' The case studies have included Theory and Prototype Studies; The Classical Prototype: Athens vs. Sparta; The American Revolution and Maritime Theory; Policy and Strategy in a Revolutionary Era: Europe 1792-1815; Limited War and Escalation Control: The Wars of German Unification; The Russo-Japanese War and Modern Naval Strategic Thought; World War II: The United States, The Grand Alliance, and Global War; The Cold War, Containment and Korea; Limited War in a Revolutionary Setting: The Vietnam Conflict; Limited War in a Global Setting: The Gulf War; Strategies and Policies of Terrorism; and Retrospect and Prospect: The Terror War, the latter two reflecting the response of military educators to the issue of the moment, and the need to make historical courses relevant.

More generally, the need to make historical courses relevant can be seen with a stress on the history of joint warfare. Such operations, and associated doctrine, planning, command structures and procurement, became more important from the 1980s and, even more, 1990s, leading to a more integrated sense of military power, as well as to a questioning of former boundaries between tactical, operational and strategic perspectives and activities. For example, the shift in the strategic nuclear role from air power to submarines in the United States and Britain led in the 1960s to a reconsideration of the doctrine and history of air power in terms of a greater emphasis on joint operations.

The reconceptualization of military power indicates the interplay of 'real world' experience in the reformulation of doctrine, a process that also alters the parameters of historical relevance. Thus, American interest in cooperating with local forces, seen in Afghanistan in 2001, led the Army Command and General Staff College Press to publish in 2002 *Compound Warfare. That Fatal Knot*, a collection produced by its Combat Studies Institute on regulars and irregulars fighting in concert. The preface declared, 'knowing how the dynamics of compound warfare have affected the outcome of past conflicts will better prepare us to meet both present crises and future challenges of a similar nature.'

Reference to history is also widespread elsewhere. For example, in December 2000, Alain Richard, the French minister of defence, declared, 'the place of history is fundamental in the formation of officers, in order to illuminate their actions and their role in society', and, in 1994, the Ministry of Defence had been responsible for the foundation of a Centre d'études d'histoire de la Défense, based at Vincennes from 1995. In Germany and Japan, however, defeat and humiliation in the 'last war', and concern about being accused of being militaristic, have lessened professional interest, rather than stimulating it.

A more specific cause for historical debate was provided by the extent to which history was used to provide a frame of reference for debating military options. Thus, before the Iraq War of 2003, there was much reference in Britain to the 1956 invasion of Egypt, the Suez Crisis. In this, as in many other cases, 'history' served as a box from which words and images could be pulled for citation. This was seen, moreover, as the frame of reference offered by outside commentators (sometimes well-informed and often not) for American military activities in Iraq from 2003 moved from being the rapid success of the Gulf War of 1991 to the intractable commitment of the Vietnam War. In turn, in 2007, President George W. Bush cited the chaos in Southeast Asia that followed American withdrawal in 1973 as a reason for continuing to persist in Iraq. Compared to this questionable (although a speech is not the place for an informed debate), part of the value of military history is that it should offer the possibility of a more sophisticated usage of references, not least in terms of the public debate.

Claims that a historical perspective on war is irrelevant are misguided, although, as discussion of the RMA indicates, they reflect a powerful impulse within modern American military culture that draws on a wider practice in the West. For at least a quarter-millennium, it has been customary to emphasize the importance of an approach, insight or development by stressing its novel character and consequences; and the search for them has been an important aspect of Western intellectual culture.

This emphasis on innovation has had multiple advantages, and to argue that military history should abandon its focus on the new and revolutionary might seem counter-intuitive, especially if cutting-edge technology is regarded as the great force multiplier. Military realities, however, are both too complex and too dependent on previous experiences to make a focus on change, let alone revolutionary change, helpful. An emphasis on continuities captures the role of limitations, especially of Western tactical, operational and strategic military effectiveness and limitations with regard to non-Western environments, although, of course, continuity does not imply an absence of change. Such an understanding, of both continuity and change, underlines the crucial value of a historical approach.

Second, aside from the last point, what else does military history offer modern-day statesmen and military practitioners? Bullet points would include:

1. The contingent nature of capability advantages, and notably so in light of the degree to which anti-tactics, anti-operations and anti-strategies exist and/or rapidly develop.
2. That the world is not an isotropic surface, equal in all points, and thus readily open to particular technologies.
3. That the past has to be understood not as a template, but as a thinking tool, and notably so about the role of non-linear change.
4. That related to these points, it can be highly misleading to focus on the methods of the leading power in the system, as its goals and capabilities will be inherently different.
5. That most military participants are not even second-level powers, however the levels are assessed; but that that does not mean that they lack potential and notably so on their own turf.
6. That there is a tendency to underplay the role of civil conflict when considering military goals and means.
7. That, linked to that, there is a widespread disinclination, and notably so in the West, to see that policing agencies are a key element in military capability.

8. That the last point is related to a reading of strategy as much more than a practice of operationalization.

9. That the prioritizations of goals, tasks and means that are central to strategy are not only inherently political but also necessarily contingent.

10. That the latter characteristic leads to a process in which history should not be used to set the pattern.

11. Instead, history emerges in part as an analytical device, even rhetorical tool, in discussing prioritization and, more particularly, in assessing the practicalities of what are variously advanced as goals, tasks and means, not least in considering the interacting relationships between these facets.

12. That the historian can offer particular insights on the various strategic cultures at play across the world, both at state level and within states; and that this concept helps in the assessment of the threat and opportunity perceptions of other players, and, crucially, how one's own intentions and actions will be understood by others.

13. That the more strategic culture is advanced as a conceptual tool in understanding the motivation, pursuit and impact of conflict, the more history takes on value, because strategic culture is very much a presentist meditation on the lasting impact of persistent factors. Moreover, the concept of strategic culture directs attention to beliefs, ideas and assumptions, and in a fashion that relates to far more than the formal pursuit of strategy.

This list could, and should, be extended, and readers are invited to do so. What is more germane is to return to the question about how to think about war. A frequent canard is to argue that those who have not fought cannot think about war, which is unhelpful as

1. many in the military have only experienced particular types of conflict;

2. the ability to kill or to risk being killed is no guide to operational, let alone strategic, skillsets;

3. politicians have a duty to try to understand the issues involved in war.

Moreover, politicians, whether in democratic or in authoritarian societies, have a public interface, and it is best if they understand what they are trying to justify/elicit support for, and, in particular, grasp the risks involved, and the possible timetables. This is made more important because of the evidence that concerns even disaffection on Home Fronts play a role in affecting capability. Moreover, this is even more the case in modern contexts when troops are in easy contact with their families through social media. Morale has always been an issue but has become more so ever since the collapse of empires that began in 1917.

Indeed, this dependence on the military effort on a broad understanding of capability is one that emerges as a major lesson. In the 1910s, this included not only the demise of the governing systems in Russia, Austria and Germany but also the role of the military in the Chinese revolution, and, in the early 1920s, in the transformation of the Turkish/Ottoman Empire. It would be ironic, indeed, if, while the agenda of the present is focused increasingly on the consequences of great-power confrontation between America and China, in practice, the major use of the military across the world hinged on insurrection and/or suppression. Moreover, as during the Cold War, the great-power confrontation will relate to this issue. Again, however, that very phrase carries the message of this piece. 'As during the Cold War' does not mean that the course of events will be the same, nor that, say, 'Suez' or 'Vietnam' will be useful as guides other than to the uncertainties of outcome. When two powers go to war, generally both think they can win, and at least one is always wrong, and often both.

Notes

1   M. E. Latham, *Modernisation as Ideology: American Social Science and 'Nation Building' in the Kennedy Era* (Chapel Hill, NC, 2000) and *The Right Kind of Revolution: Modernisation, Development, and U.S. Foreign Policy from the Cold War to the Present* (Ithaca, NY, 2011); N. Gilman, *Mandarins of the Future: Modernization Theory in Cold War America* (Baltimore, MD, 2003); D. C. Engerman, 'American Knowledge and Global Power', *Diplomatic History* 31 (2007): 599–622.

2   G. A. Gaddis, *No Sure Victory: Measuring U.S. Army Effectiveness and Progress in the Vietnam War* (New York, 2011).

3   For a critique, J. C. D. Clark, 'Secularisation and Modernisation: The Failure of a "Grand Narrative"', *Historical Journal* 55 (2012): 161–94.

4   A. Hawkins, 'Modernity and the Victorians', unpublished paper. I am grateful to Angus Hawkins for providing me with a copy.

5   See, in particular, G. Hanlon, *Italy 1636: Cemetery of Armies* (Oxford, 2016).

6   G. Hanlon, *European Military Rivalry, 1500-1750: Fierce Pageant* (Abingdon, 2020), xvii.

7   J. D. Chambers and G. E. Mingay, *The Agricultural Revolution* (London, 1966).

8   M. Roberts, *The Military Revolution, 1560-1660* (Belfast, 1956).

9   G. Parker, 'In Defense of *The Military Revolution*', in *The Military Revolution Debate*, ed. C. J. Rogers (Boulder, CO, 1995), 356.

10 Ibid., 355.

13

Beware of war

Lessons from the past

Margaret MacMillan

Among the many effects of the Covid-19 pandemic, this generation may gain a sense of humility about its own capacity to foresee and deal with huge catastrophes and their challenges. If we had a tendency to look at the past and shake our heads over how incompetent and short-sighted those leaders in the last century were who led much of the world into two world wars or botched the peace-making at the end, our own fitful and chaotic responses to a pandemic that experts had long been predicting should give us both a greater sense of the difficulties of decision-making and a willingness to learn some useful lessons for the future. Reviewing the past is never going to provide rules about human affairs or a clear set of policy prescriptions, but it can give us useful and instructive comparisons and, equally important, warnings on how to avoid costly blunders.

We may think, at least those of us living in the fortunate prosperous and peaceful parts of the world, that a major war is not among those events we need fear. In recent years it has become commonplace to talk of the long peace since 1945, perhaps with a certain smugness. That ignores the dozens of wars that have gone on and continue to go on around the world, many of which are fuelled by the peace-loving nations. It also ignores the long and inglorious history of war and the extent to which it has been deeply intertwined in human society throughout recorded history.

Ignorance of history can be dangerous just as ignoring warnings of foul weather – or possible pandemics – can be. True, some societies revere and rely, perhaps too much, on the examples from their pasts. Classical Chinese civilization, much as the ancient Greeks, assumed that a golden age had once existed and that humanity had declined from that ever since. Reverence for the wisdom of the elders and established tradition served, as the nineteenth century demonstrated all too clearly, to handicap China's leaders and intellectuals as they faced the dual challenges of the collapse of the Qing dynasty and the aggressive imperialist West. Those among the elite who dared to suggest that China might learn from the outsiders risked losing their status or even their lives.

The converse, to believe that the past has nothing to teach us and that what is new is best, can be equally constraining and dangerous. In 2002, when the war on terror was in its early stages, a senior White House aide reproved a journalist for the *New York Times* for being stuck in the 'reality-based community', in other words caring about evidence. 'That's not the way the world really works anymore', the aide continued.

> We're an empire now, and when we act, we create our own reality. And while you're studying that reality – judiciously, as you will – we'll act again, creating other new realities, which you can study too, and that's how things will sort out. We're history's actors . . . and you, all of you, will be left to just study what we do.[1]

I

Great powers can too easily fall into the trap of thinking that superior power, from economic to armed forces armed with the latest weapons, can overwhelm the smaller and weaker, perhaps even deterring them from defiance in the first place. France and the United States made the same calculation with Indochina in the 1950s and 1960s as Great Britain had with the two tiny South African republics in the war of 1899–1902 and in all cases had a rude awakening. The powers faced determined peoples fighting for their homelands who showed an unexpected ability to organize themselves and to improvise. In the South African Wars the local Afrikaners used their superior knowledge of the land and guerrilla warfare to inflict defeat after defeat on the cumbersome British army.[2] In both the insurgency in Iraq and the Soviet and NATO wars in Afghanistan, booby traps using simple technology and explosives inflicted heavy casualties on the much-better equipped foreigners.[3]

A sour joke circulating in Washington in the mid-1960s when the war in Vietnam was already problematic had an early computer crunching all the data about the two sides. The United States led, of course, in all measurable categories. When the computer was asked when the United States would beat North Vietnam the answer came that it already had. The Soviet Union made a similar calculation about relative strengths when it invaded Afghanistan in 1979 and found, as the United States did, that it was involved in a costly war without end and one that was increasingly unpopular with its own people. The Bush administration was sufficiently confident of victory in 2001 that it was already turning its attention to Saddam Hussein's regime in Iraq.[4]

In most cases the great powers had also failed to inform themselves sufficiently about the histories and attitudes of their enemies. Robert McNamara, secretary of defence in the Kennedy and Johnson administrations, spent much of the rest of his life trying to work out what had gone wrong with the American intervention in Vietnam. The Americans had made the fundamental mistake, he said, of assuming the Vietnamese were just like them. 'Our misjudgements of friend and foe alike reflected our profound ignorance of the history, culture, and politics of the people in the area and the personalities and habits of their leaders.'[5] On the eve of the coalition's invasion of Iraq neither Bush nor Blair – and it was true of much of their senior leadership – showed curiosity about the land and the people they were about to occupy. The State Department prepared a full and detailed briefing book on the future of Iraq. The Pentagon did not want to know about it and nor would the vice president, Dick Cheney, or the secretary of defence, Donald Rumsfeld, allow senior and experienced State Department staff to serve on the body being run out of the Pentagon to administer Iraq after the war.[6] When a reluctant Blair was persuaded to meet several of the UK's leading Iraq experts, he showed little interest in what they had to tell him.[7] Once things started to fall apart for the coalition with the spread of resistance and civil war among the Iraqis top generals sent for copies of T. E. Lawrence's *Seven Pillars of Wisdom* in a belated attempt to try to understand what they were embroiled in.

Given the ignominious outcome of the Iraq adventure and the recent equally ignominious withdrawal of NATO forces from Afghanistan as well as the continuing wars elsewhere it is curious that Western intellectuals and academic institutions show so little interest in understanding the dynamics of war and the challenges of making peace. While potential hot spots around the world are increasing if anything – those involving Ethiopia and its neighbours, Russia and the Baltics, Ukraine and Crimea, or along the Indo-Chinese border – the centres for the study of war, especially in North America, are underfunded with retirements often not replaced and students discouraged from studying war as a subject. That partly reflects a distaste for the subject as well as competition from new and interesting fields of study, in social and cultural history for example, but also a misplaced sense that our societies do not need to know about war because they have become peaceable, that wars today are in far-off places, fought by people who are not like us. Is that complacency justified?

At the start of the last century, we should remember, Europeans, perhaps a majority, prided themselves on the great achievements the continent had made since the end of the Napoleonic Wars almost a century before. The industrial revolution, the great leaps forward in science and technology and rapid urbanization had transformed the ways people lived and produced a population that was on average significantly better off and better educated. More European nations collectively dominated the rest of the world either through direct rule or through the power of European economies and finance. While there had been the wars of Italian and German unification in the heart of the continent those had been short, limited in their scope and had apparently produced clear and lasting results. The Europeans of 1914 largely assumed that their continent was going to continue its progress to even more prosperity and in peace. War was so improbable, the great Austrian writer Stefan Zweig recalled, that to his parents' generation it was no more likely than ghosts or witches.[8] True there were crises, a whole series from 1905 onwards, which led to threats of war against each other by the powers but deterrence had apparently worked and conferences of ambassadors had met to hammer out agreements. When tensions started to mount after the assassination of the Archduke at Sarajevo, Europeans, including many of their leaders, assumed that the familiar pattern would occur: bluster and ostentatious preparations for war followed by the inevitable peaceful settlement. Only in 1914 that did not work.

While historians will continue to argue, over what or who was responsible for the Great War, whether the reckless determination of Austria-Hungary to destroy Serbia, the equally reckless provocations of the Serbs, Germany's blank cheque of support for Austria-Hungary, Russia's determination to act as the protector of Serbia, France's encouragement of Russia or even Britain's failure to make its position clear or to work more actively for peace, the first lesson today's world should draw is that accidents can happen, especially when those involved are complacent about their ability to deal with every challenge. And we should never underestimate the role played by inattention. In the summer of 1914 the French leadership and the French public were gripped, not by the unfolding crisis in the centre of Europe, but by the trial of Mme Caillaux who had shot the editor of *Le Figaro* who was leading a campaign against her husband, Joseph Caillaux, the prime minister. A further unfortunate coincidence was the scandal had obliged him to resign, thus removing from office a man who had worked for Franco-German understanding. In Britain, which was a strong force for peace on the continent, the Asquith government and the media were deeply concerned about the deepening crisis over Irish Home Rule and the growing unrest and divisions in Ireland which were threatening to infect the British army and British society itself. Alarmists were wondering if there would be civil war.[9]

Another sort of accident is that which places in power those who either actively pursue war or do not want or know how to stop it. After the events of 11 September 2001, a different American president would almost have certainly wanted to bring the Taliban government down in Afghanistan but might not have made the decision to wage war on Saddam Hussein in Iraq. The younger Bush and the hawks around him had long wanted the excuse to get rid of a regime they abhorred. In 1914 the hereditary principle meant that on the thrones of three of the key powers were men who were unable to resist the pressures from their closest advisers to sign the mobilization orders which moved Europe beyond the point of no return. (While Britain was also a monarchy, its rulers had long since ceded their power to parliament.) The emperor Franz Joseph of Austria-Hungary was old, ailing and isolated, and focused, as he had always been, on preserving the dynasty at whatever cost. It was a supreme irony that the one man, his heir the archduke, who might have been able to persuade him not to move against Serbia had been assassinated in Sarajevo. In Germany Wilhelm II was fearful of war but even more afraid of being considered a coward by his beloved army and in Russia, Nicholas II was finally persuaded to give in and sign the orders by the argument that if he backed down in the face of Germany's and Austria-Hungary's aggression his dynasty might fall.[10] By comparison in 1962 the young president John F. Kennedy found the fortitude during the Cuban Missile Crisis to withstand the strong pressures coming from different quarters and in particular from the military who were for taking action despite the risk of escalation to nuclear exchanges with the Soviet Union. The crushing and open failure of the Bay of Pigs invasion of Cuba the previous year, when Cuban exiles with American military backing wrongly thought they could easily overthrow Castro, contributed to Kennedy's scepticism about what his own generals were telling him. As important, perhaps, he had just read Barbara Tuchman's *The Guns of August* which showed how mistakes and miscalculations had contributed to the outbreak of the First World War.[11]

II

Analogies, such as the one Kennedy made, can be helpful in thinking about a current situation and thinking through possible options. They can also be traps if they are treated as an established truth and a sure guide. The appeasement analogy, which held that the democracies failed to stop the aggressors such as Nazi Germany or Fascist Italy in the 1930s while there was still time, was thrown reproachfully at Kennedy by some of his military in the Cuban Missile Crisis but he was right to resist it. Eden made the same mistake with Nasser over the latter's seizing of the Suez Canal. Nasser was not Hitler, not in terms of power or of ambition and it would have been wiser to negotiate than to resort, in this case unsuccessfully, to military power. The appeasement analogy again helped to lure the Americans into Vietnam when, as George Kennan pointed out, American interests and the future of democracy were not at stake as they been in the 1930s. George Ball, who probably understood Asia as well as anyone in the government, argued against escalation in the Johnson administration by pointing to another analogy, that of the French failure in Indochina. Choosing the right analogy for the circumstances is crucial.[12]

It is also a mistake to assume that history will repeat itself. A recent book by Michael Neiburg shows how the Roosevelt administration and most of the American establishment assumed at the outbreak of hostilities in Europe in 1939 that the war would follow the pattern of the First.[13] In the widely accepted scenario, the German attack in the West would blunt itself on France's defences and the powerful French armies, resulting in a stalemate like that of 1914–18, while at sea the British would again impose an effective blockade which would ultimately undermine Germany's capacity to fight. That combination of French military power on land and British at sea was to be the shield for the Western hemisphere, making it unlikely that the United States would have to involve itself again. The United States would remain safe and gradually build up its military strength in the Pacific to counter the threat from Japan. As Neiberg shows the sudden defeat of France in the summer of 1940 and the expected defeat of Britain created consternation and panic in Washington and in public opinion across the country. In what was to cause endless problems later on, the Roosevelt administration decided to recognize the Vichy regime in the hopes that it might eventually swing around against Germany.

There is a further peril too which can affect leaders especially in moments of crisis and that is a longing to end the intolerable uncertainty and pressures, come what may. In 1914 the German chancellor Theobald von Bethmann Hollweg made some last, perhaps half-hearted, attempts to mediate between Russia and Austria-Hungary, but by the end of July he was increasingly sidelined by the German military. 'The control', he was reported to have remarked, 'has slipped out of the hands of responsible monarchs and statesmen so that the mad European war would happen without the rulers or their people wanting it.' The next day, 1 August, as German mobilization started, he simply said, 'If the iron dice must roll, may God help us.'[14] Franz Conrad von Hötzendorf, the chief of the General Staff of Germany's ally, Austria-Hungary, wrote with equal resignation, 'It will be a hopeless struggle, but it must be pursued, because so old a Monarchy and so glorious an army cannot go down ingloriously.'[15] In late 1941, as the Japanese government was moving towards its fatal decision to wage war on the

United States and the European empires, Tojo Hideki, the prime minister, said it was like jumping off a cliff with one's eyes closed. 'There are times when we must have the courage to do extraordinary things.'[16]

What also affected Japanese decision-making was the knowledge that if they were to take on their key adversary, the United States, they had only a limited time in which to do it. The Americans were gearing up for war and with their resources and population would outmatch the Japanese within two years. In July 1914, the German military were making similar calculations. If the Russia intended to wage war on Germany, and most of the senior leadership assumed it did, the Russians would not have the edge in numbers and equipment over Germany or the railway network adequate to move significant forces to their common frontiers until 1917. It therefore made a sort of sense for Germany to wage war while it still had a hope of success just as it did for Japan in the Second World War.

In 1962 Khrushchev took a giant gamble by moving nuclear weapons to Cuba, so close to the continental United States. Fyodor Burlatsky, who was close to him, later described the 'irrational reasons' why Khrushchev, a 'risky man', did so despite knowing that the Americans were almost certain to respond. These reasons included Khrushchev's wish to see the Soviet Union treated as an equal superpower with the United States and his almost obsessive fixation with how many American bases, in Turkey for example, were close to the Soviet Union while the Soviets had none on land near the United States.[17] Kennedy and ultimately Khrushchev himself fortunately found the inner resources and fortitude to stop on the edge of the precipice. Nevertheless the world came dangerously close to a nuclear war. Both sides went on to high alert as the crisis deepened and a single mistake or rash decision could have triggered a chain reaction. At the height of the crisis Soviet missiles targeted on major American cities were prepared for launching while Soviet long-range bombers were sent to their forward bases. The American air force was put on to a fifteen-minute alert and the commander of the Strategic Air Command, responsible for the planes carrying nuclear bombs and a leading hawk, took the initiative to order the final level of alert before war itself for bases in the United States and around the world. Since he deliberately sent out his message by radio without encrypting it the Soviets were able to pick it up.[18]

The most critical decision of all was the one that was not taken on 27 October when tensions were at their height. Four Soviet submarines, armed with nuclear torpedoes, had arrived in the waters near Cuba as Kennedy's 'quarantine', enforced by the American navy, was in effect. Communications with Moscow were by now highly erratic, but the Soviet crews could hear American broadcasts and realized how close their country was to war. As the American vessels harassed the underwater Soviet by dropping grenades, one commander decided to fire his torpedoes. 'We will die', he said, 'but we will sink them all – we will not become the shame of the fleet.' By a fortunate coincidence he had on board Vasili Arkhipov, a senior officer who outranked him and who refused to approve the order. After the end of the Cold War, Arkhipov became known as the man who had saved the world.[19]

Memories of the crisis faded and, as can happen too often after a peril is avoided, the attention of those making policies and decisions turned to other matters. While a hot line was set up between the White House and the Kremlin to ensure that the leaders of the superpowers could communicate rapidly when needed, weaknesses in command and control of nuclear weapons remained. Once the Cold War ended, it became more widely known that the world had only narrowly averted a nuclear war on this occasion and again in 1983 in the aftermath of the Soviet blunder in shooting down Korean Airline flight 007. Many of the documents from 1962 from both sides were released and, as important, the remaining participants, American, Soviet and Cuban, met in a series of conferences and exchanged recollections. Where the Americans had always assumed that the Soviet command and control system of their nuclear weapons was like theirs – in theory controlled tightly from the very top – they now learned that Soviet theatre commanders, those in the Caribbean, for example, could have launched nuclear weapons on their own initiative. In fact when the American protocols are examined more closely there was nothing to stop bomber pilots, for example, patrolling the edges of the Soviet Empire to decide on their own to attack. The movie *Dr Strangelove*, where a mad general decides to attack the Soviet Union, was not the satire it seemed.[20] Equally frightening, as we now know, were the unforced mistakes such as the shooting down of KAL007 or earlier, in 1979, the technician mistakenly putting a training tape into the computers of the North American Air Defence Command so that for a few terrifying minutes a real attack seemed to be underway.[21] As the British historian A. J. P. Taylor once wisely remarked great events do not always have great causes.

III

One of the difficulties in looking back from results to causes, as historians so often do, is that we run the risk of assuming that because we know so much of what was going on and so many of the relevant factors, those making decisions in the past also had that knowledge. More that they had the time and the capacity to assess volumes of information and weigh one possibility against another. Crises do not work like that. Time often gets telescoped and the cacophony of different voices, demanding, warning or simply trying to convey new pieces of information grows. What is striking in the accounts of the Cuban Missile Crisis is what pressure those at the heart of events in Moscow and Washington were working under. 'I know *I* felt ten years older afterwards', said George Ball, then the US under secretary of state. Tiredness, stress, demands on the politicians from the military to strike first or lose the advantage, intense arguments how to approach the other side and the growing apprehension that next day might be their last day on earth heightened the risk of hasty or poor decisions. McNamara, the secretary of defence, who had always insisted on what he saw as calm and rational deliberations, said of the atmosphere in those crucial days: 'There were deep differences of opinion among us, and very strong feelings about Cuba, and the fact is that we weren't going through an unemotional, orderly and comprehensive analytical decisionmaking process.'[22]

The Cuban Missile Crisis and the later one of 1983 are also good reminders of how easy it is to misjudge others once they are conceived as deadly and determined enemies. The temptation, which the leaders of many powers have fallen into over the centuries, is to assume that you know what the other is planning and then interpret all words and actions to fit an ominous scenario. Since the 1890s, for example, Russia's strategists had fixed on a conflict with the Dual Alliance of Germany and Austria-Hungary as being inevitable and consequently interpreted what took place in those countries as evidence of their malign intentions. In 1912 when, yet again, the government of Austria-Hungary failed to get from its parliament increases in the military budget, the Russians concluded that this was a charade to conceal a real increase in spending.[23]

Michael Howard, the great historian of war, who spent a lot of time in Washington during the Cold War, found that American strategists held a simplistic and unshakeable view of the enemy. 'The Soviet Union', he said, 'was seen in the USA as a force of cosmic evil whose policy and intentions could be divined simply by multiplying Marxists dogma by Soviet military capacity.' When he suggested that a knowledge of the many times Russia had been invaded would help to explain its insecurity or that reading Dostoevsky and Tolstoy would give better idea than Marx or Lenin of the Russian character, his views were dismissed with polite incredulity.[24] The Soviets came no closer to understanding Americans. Dobrynin initially saw the world through Soviet lenses. He and his colleagues believed that a war between socialism and capitalism was inevitable. 'My mind', he said of himself as a young diplomat in the 1950s, 'was clogged by the long years of Stalinism, by our own ideological blindness, by our deep-seated beliefs and perceptions, which led to our misconstruing all American intentions as inherently aggressive.'[25]

One of the most dangerous moments of the Cold War came with the Soviet shooting down of KAL007 on 1 September 1983, when the Soviets followed the wrong scenario. President Reagan went on American television a few days later to accuse the Soviet Union of a crime against humanity and of flouting 'the moral precepts which guide human relations among people everywhere.' The Soviet leadership which was well aware that the action had been a mistake responded with equal vehemence. The experienced Anatoly Dobrynin, the long-serving Soviet ambassador in Washington from the Kennedy to the Reagan administrations, thought both sides had gone 'slightly crazy' in their handling of the incident. The Soviets were already jumpy as a result of the election of conservative hawkish leaders in the West from Ronald Reagan to Margaret Thatcher and orders had gone out from Moscow at the start of 1981 to Soviet agents in the West to find evidence of Western plans for a nuclear first strike on the Soviet Union. While many agents were sceptical that the West was planning an attack they did not want to risk their careers by saying so. Under pressure from above to produce results the agents funnelled back to Moscow every possible scrap of possible evidence – for example, a new British pamphlet on civil defence – and every rumour. In what Dobrynin called 'a paranoid interpretation' it all seemed to add up. That in turn produced more demands from Moscow for information which the agents duly supplied.[26] Then early in 1983 Reagan announced his plans for the Strategic Defence Initiative, which would in theory provide protection for the United States against the Soviet Union, thus leaving the Americans free to attack the latter with impunity. (The Americans had no intention of doing that and were later startled to discover the Soviet fears.) The scheme, which came to be known as Star Wars, was wildly optimistic and experts on both sides thought it unlikely ever to succeed, but it left the Soviets shaken and still more worried. In the febrile days after KAL007's destruction, the Soviet establishment, from the intelligence agencies to the government they advised, became convinced that the United States and its allies were on the verge of a nuclear first strike and contemplated doing their own. By one of those unfortunate coincidences that mark human affairs NATO was conducting long-planned troop exercises in West Germany culminating in a test, known as Able Archer, of NATO's command and control in the event of an escalation to nuclear war initiated by the Soviets and their allies. Fortunately word reached the West that the Soviets were seriously worried and were starting preparations of their own and the exercise was wound down early.[27]

Governments can equally make mistakes about allies. Premier Nikita Khrushchev was stunned, for example, when he discovered during the Cuban Missile Crisis that Cuba's leader, Fidel Castro, was prepared to risk all-out nuclear war rather than see his revolution in Cuba fail. During the Vietnam War, the Americans never appreciated the force of nationalism among both the South and the North Vietnamese. They assumed that Ngo Dinh Diem, the president of the South they put in office in 1955 and whom they connived at removing in a coup in 1963, was simply out for himself and his family whereas he was, in his own way, a proud patriot who did not relish being told by foreigners how to fight the forces of the North and their Viet Cong allies. The Americans also assumed that the costs of the war would become too high for the North without grasping how far the leaders of the North were prepared to go.

IV

Understanding and learning from how individuals or powerful groups have come to make bad decisions in the past also needs to take into account what the British historian James Joll once called the 'unspoken assumptions',[28] the things we usually do not need to articulate because we all share the same system of values and beliefs or what the Germans call the *Zeitgeist*. Before the First World War the landed upper classes of Europe, whose members tended to dominate politics, the civil service and the military, valued the martial virtues as physical bravery, discipline and a willingness to die for one's country or ruler. War was seen as a test of a nation's moral fibre and of those who fought in it. And the misapplication of Darwin's ideas about the natural world to the human meant that war came to be seen as an inevitable part of the struggle between nations and victory as the survival of the fittest. Indeed those who were not prepared to fight did not deserve to survive.

Even if they did not share the view of war as a necessary and indeed a good thing, European statesmen and those who advised them still thought of it as a usable tool, which, like many earlier wars such as the Napoleonic, could be kept under control and brought to an end when a clear victory had been achieved. In the military schools and academies of the nineteenth and early twentieth centuries they studied the great decisive battles of the past, from Cannae to Sedan, and in the chancelleries of Europe they remembered the treaties that brought wars firmly and conclusively to an end. They might have done better to study the wars of attrition such as the Thirty Years in seventeenth-century Europe which dragged on until both sides were exhausted or the many settlements in that war and others such as the War of the Austrian Succession between 1740 and 1748 which helped to prepare the way for the Seven Years War.[29]

With the confidence that came from the great leaps forward in science and technology in the course of the nineteenth century, European military thinkers persuaded themselves that they were discovering the laws of war so that they could ensure victory as long as they had a preponderance of the right sort of resources and the correct plans. As they looked at their world they could find evidence to support that hope. Military force had played a big role in the building of the big European empires, and a modernizing Japan was acquiring territories in Asia through conquest in the decades before 1914. In Europe Bismarck's use of war to defeat Prussia's enemies and make possible the state of Germany offered a powerful example. And just before 1914, the Balkan states had fought successfully to acquire territory from their old ruler, the Ottoman Empire. The Balkan Wars, which had threatened to draw in the great powers, also raised tensions in Europe so that the prospect of a major war became more real.

As they contemplated the possibility, the leadership, both civil and military, in the major powers made two key assumptions: that a future war could only be won by the offensive with decisive battles and that it would be short. By 1914 all the war plans of the powers were based on the assumption that they would attack.[30] Even Russia, whose geography and history were a demonstration of the power of the defence, had stopped updating its plans to retreat into its vast spaces in the face of an offensive war by Germany, Austria-Hungary or both. Germany had developed a detailed plan, known as the Schlieffen after an earlier chief of the General Staff, on the assumption that it would have to fight a two-front war against France and its ally Russia. While for a time the General Staff kept alive plans for a war against only one of its enemies, it had let these lapse by 1914, with the result that there was little chance of limiting the war to one front. With their focus on the decisive battle which would, in theory, bring the enemy to concede defeat, most of Europe's military leaders also counted on a short war and had given little thought as to what they would do if the enemy refused to concede and fought on. As a fellow officer who was critical of Schlieffen's ideas said, 'You cannot carry away the armed strength of a great Power like a cat in a bag.'[31] As early as September 1914, when its armies had won a series of victories over the Allies in France the German high command realized there were no plans for what to do if the Allies refused to concede and the war dragged on into the winter. Their Austrian allies were as unprepared. They had not thought to stockpile winter clothing for their troops, with the result that soldiers on the eastern front had only paper socks to protect their feet. The civilian leaders on all sides were equally incapable of imagining a struggle that lasted more than a few months. Governments failed to stockpile and use effectively essential raw materials for the war effort and skilled labour was allowed to enlist or conscripted so that the factories producing essential war materiel were operating at less than their full capacity. The stalemate that developed forced the military, the governments and their societies to make painful and difficult adjustments.

Yet there had been warnings enough before 1914 of what might happen when industrialized societies with great resources and productive capacities and with their peoples motivated by nationalism and prepared to endure considerable suffering went to war. The German Confederation had won the battle of Sedan in

1870 and forced the French government to surrender, but the French nation fought on for another year. Ivan Bloch, the Polish-Russian financier, published a massive study in 1898 which argued with a wealth of evidence that future wars were likely to be fought on a huge scale and develop into stalemates, draining and ultimately destroying the societies which fought in them. The military to whose attention his arguments came dismissed them as nonsense.[32] There had been demonstrations too of the increasing power of the defence, thanks to more rapid firing, longer range and more accurate infantry and artillery weapons and thanks too to the ordinary spade and barbed wire. Well-dug-in and well-armed troops could inflict disproportionate casualties on attackers as they did in all the major wars from the American Civil War onwards. Europe's military thinkers were aware of this, but that did not alter their faith in the attack. Some of the evidence was explained away by the fact that, in a number of the conflicts before 1914, the combatants had not had the privilege of European training and European military traditions. The American Civil War after all was fought largely by civilians and many of the officers such as General Grant had had a chequered career before the war. The Russo-Turkish war of the late 1870s was between the most backward of the European powers and an Asian one. The Balkan Wars of 1912 and 1913, it was held, could scarcely be considered modern wars. To overcome the power of the defence soldiers would have to be better trained and filled with a spirit of attack and a willingness to die. In a rare admission that sometimes non-European powers got it right the costly Japanese attacks on the Russians at Port Arthur were used to show that, in the end, the Japanese had better morale and were able to absorb larger losses to achieve victory. That capacity to ignore or explain away inconvenient evidence is still with us.[33]

The costly stalemate of the First World War shook but did not eradicate the view that war could be profitable or indeed that it could end in a clear decision. Germany and Japan initiated the Second World War to expand their territory and dominance. That they failed in the end at vast cost to themselves and their enemies helped to produce renewed attempts to limit and outlaw war. The United Nations was intended to, as its Charter says, 'maintain international peace and security'. Yet during the Cold War its two leading powers, the United States and the Soviet Union, regarded war with each other as a possibility and their military continued to make plans for fighting it. With the advent of the hydrogen bomb in the 1950s and improvements in the means of delivery, the superpowers had the ability to inflict massive destruction at the cost of millions of deaths on each other, megadeaths as they came to be known in American military circles. In the early 1960s a top-level meeting of scientists and the military suggested that the United States consider developing 1,000-megaton bombs, which could be 're-evaluated for their possible military use'.[34] The bomb that was dropped on Hiroshima killing an estimated 130,000 people was between 15 and 20 kilotons. During the Cuban Missile Crisis, the Chief of Staff of the US Air Force, General Curtis LeMay, who had been at that meeting, accused Kennedy of appeasement and urged an invasion of Cuba which almost certainly would have led the Soviets to retaliate. In the aftermath of the crisis the superpowers took significant steps towards limiting the arms race but as memories faded both sides began to build their nuclear arsenals again. Even when the stockpiles grew to such absurd heights that each side was running out of significant targets, strategists on both sides continued to talk confidently about a winnable war.

While the world with a good deal of luck managed to escape a war between its superpowers, nevertheless wars have continued to be fought, one on average every year since 1945. Nationalist leaders in the European empires turned to wars of national liberation when more peaceful options seemed unlikely to succeed. As the French and then the American war in Indochina showed, democracies, for all their superior power, had difficulties in sustaining wars against ruthless and determined enemies that were unpopular at home. That was a lesson that NATO in Afghanistan and the coalition forces in Iraq would have done well to heed. Civil wars too have torn apart fragile states as differences have been magnified and played upon by unscrupulous leaders. Have the gains been worth it? In the former Yugoslavia, the wars of the 1990s left a truncated Serbia, a Bosnia divided into ethnic cantons, a weak and divided Kosovo. While a few of those who instigated the wars and the concomitant atrocities have been punished, the price has largely been paid by the civilians who were murdered or forced to flee and those who still live in a state of uneasy tension.

We have also seen wars made deliberately by great powers on weaker ones, whether, as in the case of Russia with Ukraine to seize coveted territory, or in that of the United States and its allies to bring about regime change. The results, as the long history of war should have warned, have not always been what was expected. A fundamental truth about war is that it cannot easily be controlled. The tsar helped to take Russia into the First World War to preserve his regime. The war ended tsarist rule forever and cost Nicholas his life and those of his family. As von Clausewitz famously said, war has its own logic. Watching Hitler start the Second World War from his place of exile in the Netherlands, Wilhelm II, not generally known for his insight, predicted, 'It will run away with him, as it ran away with me.'[35]

V

Given what is at stake, it is also striking how often peoples or states will enter wars without any clear definition of what victory might look like or what they would like to achieve or acquire. President George W. Bush's administration announced a war on terror after the terrorist attacks of 11 September 2001, but who or what the enemy was was never firmly established. Al Qaeda and Osama bin Laden for sure and the Taliban government of Afghanistan which had protected him but after that who or what? Daesh, Boko Haram, domestic terrorists even? And with a war on a concept rather than a physical enemy what does victory mean? NATO initially went into Afghanistan in 2001 to overthrow the Taliban. Over the years the aims grew to include the building of democratic institutions, economic development, women's education and the eradication of opium production. Similarly, in Iraq, the goal of getting rid of Saddam Hussein's regime expanded into rooting out the Ba'ath, ending Sunni dominance and creating a whole new society which reached its point of absurdity when keen young advisers arrived from Washington with the goal of making Baghdad drivers obey traffic lights.

As wars go on and the costs mount, war aims often shift and expand. Germany entered the First World War to support its ally and to secure its own position in the centre of Europe. Just over a month after the start of the war and inspired by the early victories, Bethmann Hollweg, the chancellor, envisaged the annexation of parts of France and Belgium and the reduction of both to client states, as well as the acquisition of Allied colonies in order to build a large empire in Central Africa. By 1917, the military dictatorship of Generals Hindenburg and Ludendorff, which had taken over the government, was thinking of a vast German empire to the east taking in parts of Russia. The Allies' war aims underwent a similar expansion, from diminishing or destroying Germany's power, to acquiring its colonies and carving up the territory of its Ottoman ally.

In addition, in what is another common pattern in war, as victory seemed nearer in the summer of 1918, the Allies found the glue that had held them together started to dissolve. Even during the darkest days of the war, there had been profound disagreements over strategy, between those who thought the Western Front the key to winning the war and those who wanted to strike at Germany's weaker partners in the east or over the issue of a single Allied command. It was also clear that British-French colonial rivalry, briefly submerged in the Entente Cordiale, had never gone away and, as the war's end approached, the competition to stake out claims in the Ottoman Empire grew more acute. Italian claims and, until 1917, Russian ones also strained alliance solidarity. The entry of the United States into the war added a new complication. The European allies needed American money, resources and manpower but did not want to cede leadership in formulating the peace to President Woodrow Wilson, who had an alarming tendency to talk about a peace without indemnities or other punitive measures and who was not prepared to see colonies parcelled out among the victors. While many in Europe hoped for a better international order and shared Wilson's hopes for a league of nations to enforce peace, the British and French leadership did not want to see American influence grow any greater than it already was. When the Germans appealed directly to Wilson for an armistice in November 1918, the British and French governments were alarmed and irritated by his assumption that he could speak for them. On the other hand, they were pleased to see the war ending before even more American troops arrived to give the United States an even greater say in Europe's affairs.

Given the social and political upheavals after the First World War and the large range of issues to be settled, it was probably impossible to get peace settlements at the end of the First World War that would have satisfied even a majority of participants. In the wreckage of empires, the newly emerging states had an appetite for land that often could only be satiated at the expense of their neighbours. Over time, German public opinion, much influenced by the propaganda emanating from the military and the Foreign Office, came to think that Germany had not started nor lost the war and that therefore its treaty of Versailles was unjustly punitive and unfair.[36] Italians, although on the winning side, came to think they had been cheated out of territory by a 'mutilated peace'. The French felt that they had conceded much and yet still faced a powerful Germany on their eastern borders, while the British turned away in part from the continent and its problems. Many Americans came to the conclusion that Wilson should never have taken their country into the war in the first place, a sentiment which served to strengthen isolationism in the 1930s as the world slid towards another war.

Wars can start because someone or some group wants them but they can also start as a result of miscalculations, even mistakes. The fighting rarely goes as predicted, goals shift and alliances form and dissolve. Ending them is often difficult. Too often wars do not end tidily with peace re-established. Rather they leave a residue of disappointment, disillusionment or the longing for revenge that helps to create the conditions for future wars. The First World War did not lead directly to the Second; rather, it created the conditions which made possible the outbreak of conflict in Europe in 1939 and in the Far East in 1941. The ending of the Cold War has helped to make possible the hostility of Russia to the West and the hubris of the United States which led it into its costly adventures in Afghanistan and Iraq. That in turn has exacerbated divisions among the Western powers and eased the rise of China to regional and global power. We face a future that looks set to be turbulent. All the more reason, therefore, that those in positions of power and influence should ponder the many lessons and warnings of the past and take the prospect of wars seriously. Some of the weapons today are the same as in previous centuries, from machetes to simple rifles; others are high technology such as drones and autonomous weapons systems. Yet the challenges for human beings remain the same from how to gauge as correctly as possible what your enemy is planning to do to being clear what it is you hope to achieve by a war. The costs of getting it wrong, however, are higher than ever.

Notes

1   Ron Suskind, 'Faith, Certainty and the Presidency of George W. Bush', *New York Times Magazine*, 17 October 2004.
2   See Bill Nasson, *The South African War 1899-1902* (London, 1999).
3   Andrew Bacevich, *America's War for the Greater Middle East: A Military History* (New York, 2016); Russia (Federation), General'nyĭ shtab, Lester W. Grau, and Michael A. Gress, *The Soviet-Afghan War: How a Superpower Fought and Lost* (Lawrence, KS, 2002), especially chapter 3; Carter Malkasian, *The American War in Afghanistan: A History* (New York, 2021).
4   James Mann, *Rise of the Vulcans: The History of Bush's War Cabinet* (New York, 2004).
5   Robert S. McNamara, *In Retrospect: The Tragedy and Lessons of Vietnam* (New York, 1995), 321–2.
6   Thomas Ricks, *Fiasco: The American Military Adventure in Iraq* (New York, 2006).
7   Jonathan Steele, 'Guys, I'm Afraid We Haven't Got a Clue ...', *Guardian*, 21 January 2008.
8   Stefan Zweig, *The World of Yesteryear* (London, 2009), 26.
9   For a sample of the debates about the war's origins see Christopher Clark, *The Sleepwalkers: How Europe War in 1914* (London, 2012); Margaret MacMillan, *The War That Ended Peace: The Road to 1914* (New York, 2013); Annika Mombauer, *The Origins of the First World War: Controversies and Consensus* (London, 2013).
10 MacMillan, *The War That Ended Peace*, chapters 19 and 20.
11 Max Hastings, *Abyss: The Cuban Missile Crisis 1962* (forthcoming September 2022).

12 Yuen Foong Khong, *Analogies at War: Korea, Munich, Dien Bien Phu, and the Vietnam Decisions of 1965* (Princeton, NJ, 1992).

13 Michael S. Neiberg, *When France Fell: The Vichy Crisis and the Fate of the Anglo-American Alliance* (Cambridge, MS, 2021).

14 MacMillan, *The War That Ended Peace*, 520.

15 Ibid., 610.

16 Margaret MacMillan, *War How Conflict Shaped Us* (London, 2020), 57.

17 James G. Blight and David A. Welch, *On the Brink: Americans and Soviets Reexamine the Cuban Missile Crisis* (New York, 1989), 235–6.

18 Ibid., 75.

19 Rodric Braithwaite, *Armageddon and Paranoia: The Nuclear Confrontation* (London, 2019), 324–8; *The Man Who Saved the World*, pbs.org (2012).

20 Braithwaite, *Armageddon and Paranoia*, 324–9; Eric Schlosser, *Command and Control: The Story of Nuclear Weapons and the Illusion of Safety* (London, 2014), 297–301.

21 Eric Schlosser, *Command and Control: Nuclear Weapons, The Damascus Accident and the Illusion of Safety* (New York, 2013).

22 Blight and Welch, *On the Brink*, 51.

23 MacMillan, *The War That Ended Peace*, 363.

24 Michael Howard, *Captain Professor* (London, 2006).

25 Anatoly Dobrynin, *In Confidence: Moscow's Ambassador to Six Cold War Presidents* (New York, 2015), 26.

26 Christopher Andrew, *The Sword and the Shield: The Mitrokhin Archive and the Secret History of the KGB* (London, 1999), 213–14.

27 Taylor Downing, *1983: Reagan, Andropov, and a World on the Brink* (New York, 2018); for a critical assessment see Vojtech Mastny, 'How Able Was "Able Archer"?' *Journal of Cold War Studies* 11, no. 1 (2009): 108–23.

28 J. Joll, *1914: The Unspoken Assumptions: An Inaugural Lecture Delivered 25 April 1968 at the London School of Economics* (London, 1968).

29 Cathal Nolan, *The Allure of Battle: A History of How Wars Have Been Won and Lost* (New York, 2017).

30 Hew Strachan, *The First World War*. Vol. 1 *To Arms* (Oxford, 2001); Richard F. Hamilton and Holger Herwig, *War Planning 1914* (Cambridge, 2010).

31 MacMillan, *The War That Ended Peace*, 351.

32 Ibid., 327.

33 Jack Snyder, *The Ideology of the Offensive: Military Decision Making and the Disasters of 1914* (Ithaca, NY, 1984).

34 Braithwaite, *Armageddon and Paranoia*, 286.

35 MacMillan, *The War That Ended Peace*, 645.

36 Holger H. Herwig, 'Clio Deceived: Patriotic Self-Censorship in Germany after the Great War', *International Security* 12, no. 2 (Fall 1987): 5–44.

14

Serving history hot

On contemporary history

Charlie Laderman

During the first week of October 2020, President Donald Trump was diagnosed with coronavirus. That same week, as the world was grappling with the latest wave of the pandemic, renewed violence broke out between Azerbaijan and Armenia over the disputed Nagorno-Karabakh region, threatening a wider conflict that might suck in Turkey, Russia and Iran. Concurrently, the United States also announced its determination to re-impose all United Nations sanctions on Tehran, as it sought to ratchet up pressure on the Iranian regime over its nuclear programme. In the South China Sea, tensions were escalating between the United States and China amid fears of a war over Taiwan. As I sat down to write this chapter at the end of that week, amid this sea of international crises, a joke was doing the rounds on social media that, rather than becoming specialists on decades, centuries and whole eras, future historians of 2020 would need to become specialists in one day, such was the rapidity with which contemporaries felt the international political landscape was shifting beneath them.

As the world becomes more complex and crisis-ridden, it is natural for humans to comb over the recent past, searching for trends and developments that might have led us to this point. Yet the recent past is a period that the vast majority of professional historians shy away from, in both their research and teaching. As the esteemed military historian and astute analyst of contemporary international politics Michael Howard lamented in his inaugural lecture as Regius Chair of Modern History in 1981, there has long been an 'academic snobbery that disdains the history of the recent past precisely because it relates so obviously to the present'.[1] This was certainly the experience of R. W. Seton-Watson, the Balkan specialist and one of the most perceptive contemporary historians of the early twentieth century, who recalled that his own study of recent events was regarded by his colleagues as an '[un]worthy subject for the true historian's pen' because of its 'incompatibility with the detachment and calm of academic life'.[2] In the early twenty-first century that same 'academic snobbery' that dismisses contemporary history as not being 'true' history persists. There are certainly clear pitfalls in writing the first draft of history. But if historians seeking to chronicle their own times, while maintaining their scholarly standards, face acute challenges, that does not mean they should shirk the responsibility of attempting to do so.

I

Contemporary history has its own rich history. Indeed, for Thucydides, it was the only true form of history. His history of *The Peloponnesian War* was based 'partly on what I saw myself, partly on what others saw for me.'[3] For Thucydides, history had a social purpose. In writing what, as far as we are aware, was the first systematic analysis of the causes and conduct of a war, he intended to record 'events which happened in the past and human beings being what they are, will at some other time and in much the same ways, be repeated in the future.'[4] This perception of history as fundamentally intertwined with the present was echoed in Cicero's admonition that 'to be ignorant of what occurred before you were born is to remain always a child. For what is the worth of human life, unless it is woven into the life of our ancestors by the records of history?'[5]

The classical conception of history as essential to understanding and acting in the contemporary world reverberated across the ages. It was captured by Nicolo Machiavelli's observation that 'prudent men are wont to say that he who would foresee what has to be should reflect on what has been.'[6] A similar sense that the purpose of history was to inform and invigorate an understanding of the present was reflected in the late Victorian, British historian Sir John Seeley's dictum that 'history is the school of statesmanship' and his contemporary Edward Augustus Freeman's declaration that 'history is past politics and politics is present history.'[7] Freeman was adamant that the ancient and modern should not be artificially divided, as there was an essential 'unity of history.'[8] Consequently, Freeman maintained, 'the past and present are alike realities', imbuing those historians who immerse themselves in a period with a historical consciousness that enables them to perceive patterns across historical epochs.[9]

Yet around the same time, in central Europe, historians were questioning whether this close connection between history and contemporary affairs was an appropriate basis for scholarship. In Germany, professional historians were determined to differentiate their scientific methods from those of amateur chroniclers and journalists. Drawing on the writings of Leopold von Ranke, widely regarded as the father of 'scientific' history, they aimed to reconstruct the past, free from the influence of an author's subjective biases, by presenting documentary evidence and allowing it to speak for itself.[10] Inspired by Ranke's statement in his *History of the Latin and German Peoples* that he intended to write 'what actually happened', rather than of 'judging the past, of instructing the present for the benefit of future ages', they sought to divorce the writing of history completely from contemporary affairs and political passions.[11] Yet while Ranke advised scholars to approach their archival sources without having their perspective clouded by personal prejudices, he did not necessarily regard it as possible for a scholar to write about the past without being influenced by their present-day surroundings. Indeed, in the same section from *History of the Latin and German Peoples* referenced earlier, Ranke declared: 'I know to what extent I have fallen short of my aim. One tries, one strives, but in the end it is not attained.'[12] In other works, particularly his account of the early-nineteenth-century Serbian Revolution against Ottoman rule, Ranke embraced the link between history and contemporary affairs. In his inaugural address as a Professor in Berlin in 1836, which explored the relationship between history and politics, he declared: 'A knowledge of the past is imperfect without an acquaintance with the present; there is no understanding of the present without a knowledge of earlier times. The one gives to the other its hand; neither can exist or be perfect without the other.'[13] And as he mused late in life, a historian's 'personal development requires that great events complete their course before his eyes, that others collapse, that new forms be attempted'.[14]

Yet Ranke's more limited statement that he was writing history as 'what actually happened', once lifted from its specific context, took on a broader meaning and became a dictum for many in Germany and beyond, particularly in the United States where many of the first generation of academic historians had received their doctoral training in German institutions. The prevailing sentiment within academic history departments across much of the Atlantic world was that the writing of history should not be coloured by contemporary politics. Consequently, it was felt that a number of decades needed to pass before an event could be reviewed in its appropriate context and with access to as many of the necessary documents as possible. This was reflected in the pages of the leading historical journals of the nineteenth century. The *Historical Review* announced that it would reject 'contributions arguing still burning questions with reference to present controversy', the *Historische Zeitschrift* wanted no 'discussion of unresolved problems of current politics' and *Revue Historique* declared its intention to 'avoid contemporary controversies'.[15]

This dispassionate commitment to ensuring the historical craft was not sullied by contemporary controversies faced a profound challenge with the outbreak of the First World War. Across the combatant nations, historians responded to the call for patriotic service, and many drew on their research and writing skills to help mobilize their nations for war. A number of them published treatises on contemporary history and edited collections of documents as part of government propaganda initiatives designed to vindicate the pre-war and wartime records of their nations and to denigrate those of their opponents.

The deployment of contemporary history to buttress national diplomacy would take on new forms after 1918 due to the dispute over the war's origins. In order to combat the 'war guilt' clause in the Versailles Treaty, the new Weimar government published a substantial, if selective, tranche of documents from the German archives, covering the period from the nation's unification to 1914. As a result, the British and French governments responded with their own published collections of documents to support their positions. As part of this 'documentary moment' that followed the end of the war, a number of official and private national institutions emerged, committed to the liberal vision that greater openness and access to government proceedings would help pacify international relations. These institutions, including the Hoover Institution of War, Revolution and Peace in the United States, the Imperial War Museum in London and the French Ministry of Public Instruction's Bibliotheque de Documentation Internationale Contemporaine, served as repositories for primary sources and centres for the publication of contemporary history secondary sources.[16] The ready availability of published government sources and private papers of participants led to an outpouring of publications on the contemporary history of the war and its origins.

Nevertheless, across much of Western Europe, there remained, at that time, no formal requirement for government departments to make their records available for public access. It was only in 1958 that the Public Records Act in the UK mandated that material needed to be made open to the public when it was fifty years old, unless there were special provisions that prevented it. Even this legislation did not necessarily mean that Cabinet papers would be released into the public domain. In the early 1960s, most official First World War archives in Britain were still closed to historians, while it remained unclear when material relating to the origins, and conduct, of the Second World War would be made available for public access.[17]

II

In this context, historians remained divided over the intellectual respectability of contemporary history. In 1964, one of the most prominent and popular historians of the era, Barbara Tuchman, pondered the question, 'Can History be Served up Hot?' in a *New York Times* column and declared herself sceptical. Tuchman suggested the 'contemporary has no perspective; everything is in the foreground and appears the same size', meaning 'little matters loom big, and great matters are sometimes missed because their outlines cannot be seen'. For Tuchman, contemporary historians could be split into two camps. There were the 'Onlookers', like Thucydides, who 'set out to chronicle an episode of their own age . . . and shape it into a historical narrative with character and validity of its own'. And then there were the 'Active Participants or Axe-Grinders', among whom one of the most notable was Winston Churchill, whose histories of the 'World Crisis' and 'Second World War' had done so much to shape contemporary perspectives on those conflicts. While insiders attempted 'a genuine history of events they have known', their 'accounts are inevitably weighted, some subtly and imperceptibly, sometimes crudely, by the requirements of the role in which they wish themselves to appear'. What the participant 'gains in intimacy through personal acquaintance', he or she ultimately 'sacrifices in detachment'. As a result, Tuchman asked, 'are we now in possession of history when we have these accounts in hand?' Only 'in the sense that we are in possession of wine when the first pressing of the grapes is in hand'. A contemporary account, according to Tuchman, 'has not fermented, and it has not aged'. Only temporal 'distance [could] confer a kind of removal that cools the judgement and permits a juster appraisal than is possible to a contemporary'.[18]

That same year, the British academic Geoffrey Barraclough published his *Introduction to Contemporary History*. Barraclough came late to the subject. His background was in medieval history, but in 1957 he had been appointed Research Professor of International History at the University of London and also the director of the Royal Institute of International Affairs. In his primer, Barraclough set out to demonstrate that 'recent' history was not only legitimate but an essential subject for scholarship. Those who possessed a historical perspective could appreciate when fundamental ruptures occurred. Concepts like 'watershed' and 'turning point' abound in Barraclough's study. Through possessing a unique outlook on the world, it was 'the business of the historian', according to Barraclough, to 'look back over events from a distance, to take a wider view than contemporaries, to correct their perspectives and to draw attention to developments whose long-term bearing they could not have expected to see'. But too many historians had abdicated this responsibility. As a result, they were 'in danger of being frozen forever in the patterns of thought of the years 1933-1945'.[19]

Rather than adopting the traditional historical approach of starting in the past and moving forwards, emphasizing causality, Barraclough argued that contemporary historians should begin in the present and work backwards. Barraclough's definition of his field of study was thus succinct but wide-ranging: 'Contemporary history begins when the problems which are actual in the world today first take visible shape'.[20] For Barraclough, from his position in Britain in the early 1960s, the principal issues were 'the changed position of Europe in the world, the emergence of the United States and the Soviet Union as "superpowers," the breakdown (or transformation) of old imperialisms, British, French and Dutch, the resurgence of Asia and Africa, the readjustments of relations between white and coloured [*sic*] peoples, the strategic or thermonuclear revolution'.[21] It was these developments, in tandem, that had constituted a transformation from the 'modern' to the 'post-modern', or contemporary, world.

While cognizant that these shifts had not occurred simultaneously and had progressed at various speeds, Barraclough believed that the final decade of the nineteenth century witnessed a series of technical, industrial, social and geopolitical revolutions, inaugurating 'the transition from a European to a global pattern of international politics' and heralding the start of the contemporary age.[22] Self-consciously channelling, and globalizing, John F. Kennedy's declaration in his inaugural address that the 'torch has been passed to a new generation', one 'born in this century, tempered by war, disciplined by a hard and bitter peace', Barraclough, on the one hand, located the origins of contemporary history well before 1939 and, on the other, extended its scope right up to his own day. Historians, both at the time and since, have quibbled with Barraclough's characterization of what constituted the contemporary. Notably, Barraclough's 'wider view' gave him no greater insight than most of his contemporaries into the future prospects of Soviet Communism, an ideology that he believed was here to stay. Nor did he fully appreciate the continued potency of religion to shape human societies, intimating that it would dwindle in significance and thus failing to anticipate the full force of its resurgence as a revolutionary force across much of the world in the late twentieth and early twenty-first centuries.[23] Yet the larger significance of Barraclough's work was less in how he categorized the phenomena that made his own era distinct and more in how he extended the parameters of what constituted contemporary history, both temporally and geographically.

'Whoever wishes to write history, Martin Luther once said, must have the heart of a lion' and 'Geoffrey Barraclough is one of the bravest of the brave' for taking on 'the kind of subject which in this age of the narrow specialist few historians would dare to tackle', declared a reviewer in the *New York Times*. The review's author was Walter Laqueur, a refugee from Nazi Germany and the first director of the Wiener Library for the Study of the Holocaust and Genocide. Laqueur applauded Barraclough for making a 'very sensible case for the writing of contemporary history, which is not, as so many historians believe, a newfangled notion, a subject of doubtful provenance and uncertain academic standing'. Rather, 'almost all great historians from Thucydides to Ranke wrote contemporary history without any doubts or qualms of conscience'.

Where Laqueur took issue with Barraclough was in declaring the 'end of the European age which extended from 1492 to 1947 and with it the end of the predominance of the old European scale of values', to be replaced by a new era 'in which the chief impulses will come from outside Europe (and the Americas)'. In doing so, Laqueur believed, Barraclough had 'moved from the realm of contemporary history to that of noble fantasy'. Laqueur noted that 'Europe has been written off many times before but it has shown a surprising power of recovery'. He was concerned that Barraclough's study would contribute to the already 'fashionable neglect' of recent European history in the United States. Laqueur bemoaned that there was 'at this moment not a single journal devoted to present-day Europe' and appealed for 'some Columbus in reverse to initiate a crash program for the rediscovery of that neglected and, I still think, most promising of continents'.[24]

The following year, Laqueur himself would move to help fill this void. Together with George L. Mosse, a fellow German-born émigré from Nazi Germany, Laqueur established the *Journal of Contemporary History*. In its initial issue, the editors declared that, although there were many subjects in contemporary history that needed exploration, 'since resources are limited and the central problems of contemporary European history are still inadequately studied', their new journal would focus on that continent. While the regional focus of the editors contrasted with Barraclough's more global perspective, together they were helping to revive the study of contemporary history. Having lamented the previous year about academic attitudes to its study, Laqueur now believed a transformation had taken place. He and Mosse asserted in their opening credo that 'the idea that contemporary history could not and should not be written, prevalent between, roughly, the last third of the nineteenth century and the end of the second world war, no longer has many vigorous proponents'.[25]

That view was echoed by the doyen of liberal historians, Arthur Schlesinger Jr., in an address to the 1966 American Historical Association that was subsequently published in *The Atlantic*. Having recently served in, and then chronicled in a bestselling account, the John F. Kennedy administration, Schlesinger was one of the era's most celebrated practitioners of contemporary history. He recalled that on the eve of the Second World War, 'an American professor who carried a course of lectures up to his own time was deemed rash and unorthodox', but now 'only the most austere scholars object to attempts to write a serious account of the very recent past'. Schlesinger attributed this 'surprising acceptance' of contemporary history as a legitimate topic for scholarly study primarily to the 'acceleration of the rate of change', so that the 'present' becomes the 'past' 'more swiftly than ever before'. This was supplemented by the duty of the historian to sate the public desire for information: 'history, as a relevant form of knowledge, finds itself pressed into the service of crisis' to help address the most acute policy problems of the day.

Less salubriously, the 'morbid and often sick appetite for inside stories, sensational speculation, and prurient gossip' had also 'enlarged the market for contemporary history' and 'diminished the inhibitions, which once restrained academic historians from pronouncing judgement until their dramatis personae were safely dead'. Nevertheless despite, or perhaps because of, this public curiosity for the unseemly and scandalous, leaders had recognized that there was now pressure on them to open their manuscript collections as soon as possible. Whereas John Adams had denied access to his papers for decades, and Herbert Hoover had recently signified his intention to keep his papers closed for a generation, Franklin D. Roosevelt, about whom Schlesinger had written a largely laudatory study, 'in leaving his papers to the National Archives and providing for their early accessibility, to students, set a salutary example'. Consequently, Schlesinger envisaged all future presidents 'making papers available to scholars as speedily as prudent standards of security and discretion permit – or the alternative presumption will be that the deponent has something to hide'.[26]

In Britain, too, the onus was now on policymakers to allow access to government proceedings more rapidly. In 1967, further legislation cut the period of closure to thirty years, sparking a spate of publications on appeasement, and five years later the records of the Second World War and the immediate aftermath were thrown open for research, precipitating a flood of publications on these periods too. In time, many other democratic nations would adopt similar policies based around this 'thirty-year rule'. Unprecedented access to sources from Western European and North American archives seemed to confirm Schlesinger's declaration that 'contemporary history in the late twentieth century is thus no longer, I submit, a personal whim or passing fashion' but had a vital role that was fully recognized by the historical profession at large. Schlesinger noted approvingly that 'few colleges now would hesitate to offer courses which start with the Second World War and end with yesterday's newspaper'.[27]

III

Yet it was not so easy to shake the ostensibly Rankean notion that historians must strive for objectivity and that this was incompatible with studying the recent past. By 1990, shortly after the fall of the Berlin Wall, the dean of Cold War historians John Lewis Gaddis was telling a meeting of the National Council for History Education that the idea had again become established in American schools and colleges that 'the writing and teaching of history should stop well short of the present' and the principal reason for this was 'the fear of controversy'. The 'failure to teach the history of our own times' was the 'single greatest impediment to the effective teaching of history', according to Gaddis. It 'not only leaves our students ill-equipped to deal with the present and the future; it also ensures that they will have little interest in, and therefore little knowledge of, the history of other times either'.[28] In Britain, too, the educator and contemporary historian Anthony Seldon observed that there was 'something inherently, indeed insanely, wrong in a nation's education system that turns out young men and women lacking even a rudimentary knowledge of the nation's recent past'. This absence in school curricula and university courses was matched by a relative dearth in coverage of these contemporary topics in academic journals. As the historian Kristina Spohr has demonstrated in her survey of the principal historical journals between 1990 and 2005, 'the tendency of virtually ignoring "the more recent past" is widely spread'.[29]

Yet at the same time, the wider public continued to clamour for accounts of the recent past. Walter Laqueur noted in the pages of the *Journal of Contemporary History*, as the publication approached its twenty-fifth anniversary just as the Cold War was coming to a close, that 'interest in contemporary history, in any case, is greater than ever before and it is more widely published, studied and read'. The issue 'is that much of this interest is bypassing the academic profession'.[30]

It has proven difficult to dispel many of the traditional concerns about writing history 'while it is still smoking'. There, of course, remain valid critiques of contemporary history, particularly when it is simply a case of following the latest news story. As Laqueur noted, that professional historians should not try to 'compete with the sensationalism and journalistic approach (in the pejorative sense) goes without saying; he or she cannot turn history into a chain of anecdotes concerning a few colourful individuals'.[31] In doing so, Laqueur was echoing the sentiments of the Oxford philosopher of history R. G. Collingwood, who remarked back in 1924 that it was 'only after close and prolonged reflection that we begin to see why things happened as they did, and to write history instead of newspapers'.

Yet Collingwood was also conscious that 'we can never see the bones of historical fact till the flesh has dropped off them and by then it is too late', because historians, rather than drawing on their own memories and experiences, were forced to rely on 'stories handed down to us which may have been, and indeed almost always are, falsified by the passions of their authors'.[32] As the British diplomatic historian Llewelyn Woodward stated, reflecting on his own experience of living through the First World War, 'the writer of contemporary history has an advantage over scholars investigating earlier periods' in being able to 'remember the impression events left on him at the time' and can potentially 'consult other contemporaries and check their recollections with his own'.[33] Or as Alexis de Tocqueville remarked, in relation to the French Revolution, what contemporaries 'know better than does posterity are the movements of opinion, the popular inclinations of their times, the vibrations of which they can still sense in their minds and hearts'.[34]

This brings its own challenges. Collingwood suggested that 'contemporary history embarrasses a writer not only because he knows too much, but also because what he knows is too undigested, too unconnected, too atomic'.[35] These are, as the American political historian Kevin M. Kruse noted in the immediate aftermath of Donald Trump's 2016 election victory, just some of 'the pitfalls of writing the first draft of history'.[36] But while the potential for embarrassment should imbue a contemporary historian with humility, it does not invalidate their craft. Indeed, as Schlesinger maintained, 'the contemporary historian acquires an indispensable function, if only to improve the record for the historian of the future'. There was 'a technical necessity to rescue and preserve evidence for future historians'. Yet the role of contemporary historian was not confined to preserving artefacts for the purpose of those who came after. The writing of contemporary history, at its best, could 'be more exacting in its standards – of evidence, of precision, of judgement, of responsibility – than the history of the past; for contemporary history involves the writing of history in face of the only people who can contradict it, that is, the actual participants'.[37]

To draw these comparisons between contemporary and more distant forms of history is not to suggest universities and schools should prioritize the study of the former at the expense of utterly neglecting the latter. As Michael Howard made clear in his Regius lecture, 'the range of the historical profession must be universal' and 'in the eyes of the scholar, as in the eyes of God, all ages are of equal significance'. Scholars must continue to stress to those responsible for deciding what history is studied in higher education institutions that 'the past is a vast chain, every link of which must be kept in good repair' and 'the links that lie chronologically or geographically near us can claim no special priority from the professional historian'.[38]

Indeed, the most adept contemporary historians possess what the former director of the Institute of Contemporary British History Peter Catterall called a 'hinterland'. They require a knowledge that goes beyond just knowing about the events of the recent past and instead encompasses the larger human experience because, as Catterall observed, 'separating the contemporary artificially from history diminishes both'.[39] The purpose of contemporary history must be to situate the recent past within broader trends and currents. Unless a historian took this broad perspective, as the pioneering French historian of the Annales school, Fernand Braudel, observed, they risked having their 'eye caught by anything which moves quickly or glitters' and would be incapable of ascertaining whether 'what one is witnessing is the rise of a new movement, the tail end of an old one, an echo from the very distant past, or a monotonously recurring phenomenon'.[40] This was what the Harvard global historian David Armitage recently described as 'the long view', a perspective necessary 'to distinguish what is temporary or contingent from what is enduring and cumulative among our current global discontents'.[41]

The 'long view' requires a level of detachment because, as Braudel's fellow founding father of the *Annales* school, March Bloch, once warned, 'when the passions of the past blend with the prejudices of the present, human reality is reduced to a picture in black and white'.[42] Yet Bloch also recognized that 'the faculty of understanding the living is, in very truth, the master quality of the historian'. While 'misunderstanding of the present is the inevitable consequence of ignorance of the past', it was equally true that a 'man may wear himself out just as fruitlessly in seeking to understand the past, if he is totally ignorant of the present'.[43] Without knowledge of both, it is impossible for an analyst to truly appreciate 'our current global discontents' or 'the problems which are actual in the world today'.

IV

Historians retain a responsibility, particularly if they are receiving public money and providing publicly funded education, to help their contemporaries understand the trends and developments that have shaped the modern world. As the German scholar Friedrich Schiller declared back in 1789 it was the duty of the intellectual to 'select from the stream of events those that exercise an essential, unmistakeable, and easily comprehensible influence on the present shape of the world and the situation of the contemporary generation'.[44] If historians do not study the recent past, then others will interpret it for a broader public, who thirst for this knowledge. Contemporary history would become a branch of journalism or political science. Both have their place, but historians offer a way of taking a broad, long-range perspective on contemporary events.

Archival documents, of course, remain the foundational building blocks of history and the basis for historical narratives. Yet even when analysing periods that are close at hand, for which many of the principal document collections remain classified, there are still ways to deploy historical tools and techniques to uncover the contemporary record. Kristina Spohr, whose own work has drawn on recently declassified material, both from the newly opened archives of Eastern European nations and those released from Western collections, to help provide a fuller insight into the immediate post–Cold War world, has demonstrated cogently that these written documents alone are insufficient to recover the full diplomatic history of the period. In order to do so, a historian cannot be confined by 'Rankean rules of historicism: "temporal" (and implicitly ideological) distance and the use of traditional (written sources)' but must move beyond this 'methodological conservatism' and consider other types of sources, encompassing a range of multimedia, magazine and newspaper archives, in addition to government documents. Like Schlesinger before her, Spohr noted this was a necessity given 'the reality of the growing speed in which things have been changing'. If this was the case for Schlesinger in the mid-late 1960s, it is even more the case since the 1990s. The velocity at which history happens also has important ramifications for how it can be captured. In the age of the internet and social media, it is even more critical that contemporary historians help to preserve source material that might otherwise fall through the cracks of time.[45]

When the public perceives that the pace of historical change has quickened precipitously the role of the contemporary historian becomes increasingly significant. In *The History Boys*, the playwright Alan Bennett has Irwin, a history teacher in a 1980s English grammar school who ultimately becomes a public historian and political advisor, muse that, 'looking back, immediately in front of us is dead ground: we don't see it, and because we don't see it this means that there is no period so remote as the recent past'. Consequently, 'one of the historian's jobs is to anticipate what our perspective of that period will be'.[46] Most political or diplomatic historians, even those who identify as contemporary historians, are more comfortable providing that perspective when studying 'closed' periods of history – those with clear origins, points of rupture and ends, such as the Cold War and Gulf Wars or the tenure of a particular president or prime minister – than those where the outcome remains open.

Yet our sense of when historical epochs start and stop is constantly in flux. Soon after the Al Qaeda terrorist attacks of 11 September 2001, John Lewis Gaddis proclaimed the end of the 'the post-Cold War era', a period for which 'we have never had a good name' but which 'began with the collapse of one structure, the Berlin Wall on November 9 1989, and ended with the collapse of another, the World Trade Center's Twin Towers'.[47] It could be that the Covid-19 pandemic will constitute another watershed in global history, though contemporary analysts are already debating whether it will fundamentally transform international politics, accelerate existing trends or cement the existing order.[48] In order to contribute to that discussion, and to ascertain which of these developments are what Braudel would have characterized as 'crests of foam' carried by the 'tides of history', a 'long view' historical perspective is necessary.[49] To fully understand what are essentially evolutionary trends and what are truly revolutionary forces will, of course, require time. Yet if historians are to be most useful in helping their contemporaries to resolve 'the problems which are actual in the world today', and in enhancing the record for future historians, then they must be prepared to evaluate them even before all the sources are available and at the risk of personal embarrassment. In short, they must be willing to write about history before it cools.

Notes

1 Michael Howard, *The Lessons of History* (Oxford, 1991), 17.
2 R. W. Seton-Watson, 'A Plea for the Study of Contemporary History', *History* 14 (1929): 4.
3 Thucydides, *The Peloponnesian War*, trans. R. Crawley (1910; New York, 1951), 1.1.22-23.
4 Thucydides, *The Peloponnesian War*, trans. R. Warner (New York, 1985), 1.22, 48.
5 Cicero, *Brutus – Orator*, trans. G. L. Hendrickson and H. M. Hubbell (Cambridge, MA, 1939), 394–5.
6 Quoted in Benjamin Frankel, *Roots of Realism* (London, 1996), 220.
7 Both quoted in John L. Herkless, 'Seeley and Ranke', *The Historian* 43, no. 1 (1980): 4.
8 E. A. Freeman, *The Unity of History* (London, 1872).
9 Quoted in 'Edward Augustus Freedman: Making History', Alex Bremner and Jonathan Conlin in Conversation with Diarmaid MacCulloch, *British Academy Review* 27 (2016): 25–9, https://www.thebritishacademy.ac.uk/documents/1607/BritishAcad emyReview27.pdf.
10 Andreas D. Boldt, 'Leopold von Ranke on Irish History and the Irish Nation', *Cogent Arts & Humanities* 4, no. 1 (2017): 1–19.
11 Quoted in Gertrude Himmelfarb, *The New History and the Old: Essays and Reappraisals* (Cambridge, MA, 2004), 17.
12 Quoted in Felix Gilbert, 'Historiography: What Ranke Meant', *The American Scholar* 56, no. 3 (1987): 393–7, At 394.
13 Quoted in 'Leopold von Ranke', *Proceedings of the American Academy of Arts and Sciences* 22 (May–December 1886): 542–58, at 549.
14 Leopold von Ranke, *The Secret of World History: Selected Writings on the Art and Science of History*, ed. James Wines (New York, 1981), 261.
15 All quotes in 'Editorial Note', *Journal of Contemporary History* 1, no. 1 (1966): iv.
16 Katharina Rietzler, 'The War as History: Writing the Economic and Social History of the First World War', *Diplomatic History* 38, no. 4 (2014): 826–39.
17 Ian F. W. Beckett, 'Great Britain', in Dennis Showalter, *Researching World War I: A Handbook* (Westport, CT, 2003), 79.
18 Barbara Tuchman, 'Can History be Served Up Hot?' *New York Times*, 8 March 1964, 1.
19 This quotation also includes Barraclough's suggested edits to page 27 of his original *Introduction to Contemporary History* (London, 1964) that he wanted to make for a revised 1967 edition but which were declined by his publishers, as noted in Kristina Spohr Readman, 'Contemporary History in Europe: From Mastering National Pasts to the Future of Writing the World', *Journal of Contemporary History* 46, no. 3 (2011): 506.
20 Barraclough, *Introduction to Contemporary History*, 20.
21 Ibid., 9.
22 Ibid., 18.

23   For an incisive analysis see Bruce Mazlish, 'Revisiting Barraclough's Contemporary History', *New Global Studies* 2, no. 3 (2008): 6.

24   Walter Laqueur, 'The World and the West', *New York Times*, 2 May 1965, BR12.

25   'Editorial Note', *Journal of Contemporary History* (1966): iii.

26   Arthur Schlesinger, Jr, 'On the Writing of Contemporary History', *The Atlantic*, March 1967, Issue - https://www.theatlantic.com/magazine/archive/1967/03/on-the-writing -of-contemporary-history/305731/.

27   Ibid.

28   John Lewis Gaddis, 'The Nature of Contemporary History',, Occasional Paper, National Council for History Education, Inc. (Westlake, OH, 1990), https://files.eric .ed.gov/fulltext/ED368608.pdf.

29   Readman, 'Contemporary History in Europe', 506–30 (tables on 510–11).

30   Walter Laqueur, 'Introduction', *Journal of Contemporary History* 25, no. 2/3 (1990): 163–7.

31   Ibid., 163–7.

32   R. G. Collingwood, *Speculum Mentis, or The Map of Knowledge* (Oxford, 1924), 236.

33   Llewelyn Woodward, 'The Study of Contemporary History',, *Journal of Contemporary History* 1, no. 1 (1966): 1–13.

34   Quoted in Arthur M. Schlesinger, *A Thousand Days: John F. Kennedy in the White House* (New York, 2002), ix.

35   Collingwood, *Speculum Mentis*, 236.

36   Kevin M. Kruse, 'The Pitfalls of Writing the First Draft of History', *Process: A Blog for American History*, 30 November 2016, http://www.processhistory.org/the-pitfalls-of -writing-the-first-draft-of-history/.

37   Schlesinger, Jr, 'On the Writing of Contemporary History',.

38   Howard, *The Lessons of History*, 16.

39   Peter Catterall, 'What (If Anything) Is Distinctive about Contemporary History?' *Journal of Contemporary History* 32, no. 4 (1997): 449–50.

40   Quoted in John Lewis Gaddis, *On Contemporary History: An Inaugural Lecture Delivered before the University of Oxford on 18 May 1993* (Oxford, 1995) 22.

41   David Armitage, 'Why Politicians Need Historians', *The Guardian*, 7 October 2014.

42   Marc Bloch, *The Historian's Craft: Reflections on the Nature and Uses of History and the Techniques and Methods of Those Who Write It*, trans. Peter Putnam (New York, 1953), 140.

43   Ibid., 43.

44   Quoted in Gordon A. Craig, 'The Historian and the Study of International Relations',, Presidential Address, American Historical Association, 28–30 December 1982, https://www.historians.org/about-aha-and-membership/aha-history-and-archives/ presidential-addresses/gordon-a-craig.

45   Readman, 'Contemporary History in Europe', 506–30, at 524–4.

46   Alan Bennett and Nicholas Hytner, *The History Boys: The Film* (London, 2006), 72.

47   John Lewis Gaddis, 'Setting Right a Dangerous World',, *The Chronicle of Higher Education*, 11 January 2002.

48   See in particular Hal Brands and Francis J. Gavin, *COVID-19 and World Order: The Future of Conflict, Competition and Cooperation* (Baltimore, MD, 2020) and 'How the World Will Look After the Coronavirus Pandemic', *Foreign Policy*, 20 March 2020, https://foreignpolicy.com/2020/03/20/world-order-after-coroanvirus-pandemic/.

49   Fernand Braudel, *The Mediterranean and the Mediterranean World in the Age of Phillip II*, Vol. 1 (London, 1972), 21.

15

When reason replaces wisdom

How the neglect of history and statesmanship has diminished political science

Steven F. Hayward

When a student asked Winston Churchill in the late 1950s how an aspiring young person should prepare for a life in politics, Churchill answered unhesitatingly: 'Study history. In history lies all the secrets of statecraft.' Yet history is one thing students of politics or public administration won't study much today in any serious way, beyond narrow legislative or institutional history for a policy specialty. At the root of this slow abandoning of historical perspectives on politics is the divorce of history from politics at our universities starting more than a century ago. This divorce has been a disaster for both political education and political practice ever since. It has impoverished history and denigrated the idea that *statesmanship* – a concept once frequently used without apology or embarrassment in academic literature about politics – can be understood seriously and intelligibly.

It is barely recalled today that until the late nineteenth century, history and politics were considered a single academic discipline, as vitally related approaches to the same phenomena of human action, if not unified at the deepest level. Academic treatment of history and politics was usually combined more generally with economics and law, reflecting the older neoclassical view of the unity of the 'humane' or 'moral sciences'. It was typical to find joint departments of history and politics in Anglo-American colleges. Hence a curriculum of study in politics integrated extensive historical reading, starting with Thucydides, Herodotus, Plutarch and other classical and early modern authors. A good example of this older mode can be found in what is thought to be the first American textbook on politics, written in 1795 by Prof John Daniel Gros of Columbia (though still called Kings College at the time). It bore the capacious title typical of the times: *Natural Principles of Rectitude, for the Conduct of Man in All States and Situations of Life, Demonstrated and Explained in a Systematic Treatise on Moral Philosophy: Comprehending the Law of Nature—Ethics—Natural Jurisprudence— General Economy—Politics—and the Law of Nations*. Only 456 pages! Peter Odegard, chairman of UC Berkeley's political science department in the 1950s and early 1960s, remarked about this approach to political education in his 1951 presidential address to the American Political Science Association (APSA):

> If one is to argue that such training is a poor preparation for practical politics, at least he must admit that it did not seriously handicap Jefferson and Madison, Hamilton, and other practical politicians, who became the architects of democratic government and the modern world. Indeed, one may well ask whether the Declaration of Independence, the Constitution, or the Federalist Papers could have been written except by men trained in this way. We might well ask ourselves also where in America we are today preparing the Jeffersons, the James Wilsons, the James Madisons or Alexander Hamiltons that our world so sorely needs?[1]

Harvard's iconoclastic political scientist Edward Banfield offered his own pungent version of this challenge, asking, 'Would anyone maintain that in the Convention of 1787 the Founders would have reached a better result with the assistance of a staff of model builders?'[2]

To be sure, historical perspectives can still be found in corners of modern political science, but in attenuated form. In a supreme irony, political scientists today sometimes produce better biographies and accounts of historical episodes than historians do. But these are generally regarded as outside the 'mainstream' of the discipline. The devaluing of history for purposes of political insight is not a new story. The distinguished political scientist Aaron Wildavsky reflected on his graduate education at Yale with the observation that 'in 1955 the Yale University political science department was fast becoming a hotbed of vile and amoral behaviorism, not to say an emporium of hyperfactualism and vulgar empiricism . . . [H]istory was out of style and political theory [was] a subject fit only for unscientific dilettantes'.[3]

Nothing in the intervening years since Wildavsky wrote this has redeemed history as a serious component of political science. There are several reasons for the great divorce of history from politics. A complete analysis is not possible in the scope of this essay, but a few central issues should still command our attention today. One reason for the separation was organizational, in particular the increasing emphasis on academic specialization as Anglo-American universities embraced the new model of the German research university. More important, though, was the simultaneous playing out of the Enlightenment-inspired idea that only empirical or 'scientific' knowledge was true knowledge – in short, positivism. The academic transformation of 'politics' into 'political *science*' provides one clue for the marginalization of history in the discipline, as the social science revolution swept all before it – including history. Prior to the social science revolution, both politics and history were understood as arts rather than sciences – both in theory and in practice. The modern disposition about scientific politics was best summed up in Friedrich Engels's phrase, 'The government of men is replaced by the administration of things.' Much of modern political science aims willy-nilly to replace the statesman with the bureaucrat, and substitute science (supposedly) for ambition. If political problems are reduced chiefly to material factors to be treated 'scientifically' or technically, there is little further need for historical study.

In another respect the divorce of history from politics represents the failure of history to become 'scientific' in the same way that the study of politics did. The social science revolution was more successful in political science than history for the simple reason that political phenomena can be counted more easily (such as votes in elections, to take the simplest example, along with other things than can be illuminated through statistical regression models), while history is closer to poetry than mathematics. Not for lack of trying on the part of history. It is mostly forgotten today that in the second half of the nineteenth century, many leading historians were casting about for an applied 'natural science of history' that would be the full equal of other natural sciences and the emerging social sciences. Henry Thomas Buckle wrote as early as 1857 in his *History of Civilization in England* that 'I entertain little doubt that before another century has elapsed, the chain of evidence will be complete, and it will be as rare to find an historian who denies the undeviating regularity of the moral world, as it is now to find a philosopher who denies the regularity of the material world'. J. B. Bury, author of *The Idea of Progress* (1913), thought history could, and should, seek to become 'a science, no more and no less'. Even Lord Acton thought that 'ultimate history' might eventually be discovered.[4] While scientific administration would hold the key to 'the new science of politics', the key to unlocking the explanatory power of 'the new science of history' looked to be economic determinism for starters. There was a highly fertile cross-pollination between Germanic-style historicism and economics in the late nineteenth century that had a powerful influence on history for a generation. 'Almost every historian of that generation', Henry Steele Commager wrote, 'felt that he was on the verge of some discovery that should do for history what Darwin had done for nature.'[5]

If a precise and mechanical science of historical causation could be developed, history would rival scientific politics for explanatory and above all *predictive* power. Although history as an academic discipline has embraced social science methodology to a large extent (culminating in the enthusiasm for 'cliometrics' in the 1970s), the idea of a rigorously applied scientific history has proven as elusive as earthquake prediction, and quietly abandoned. Today academic history is going through something of an identity crisis, with the number of undergraduate majors in the discipline plummeting while its academic practitioners descend further into esoteric or narrow investigations that have little appeal or importance beyond a tenure review committee. One sign of this identity crisis can be seen in the fact that Harvard classifies history as a 'social science', while Yale places history in the humanities.

Another clue comes from this curious fact about biographies of major historical figures: The general reading public can't get enough of them. Biographies, especially of presidents and figures from the American Founding but also generals and major business leaders, have not only rocketed to the top of the bestseller lists, but even spawned Broadway musicals. And yet very few of them are written by academic historians any more, unlike the 1950s and 1960s when leading academics such as Arthur Schlesinger Jr., Arthur Link and James Macgregor Burns produced multivolume works on American presidents. Academic historians today still write often about presidents, but usually confine themselves to a narrow aspect rather than a synoptic biography, that is, 'President X and Civil Rights', or 'President Y and Latin American

Policy'. Instead, today bestselling biographies tend to be written by journalists or professional non-academic writers like Ron Chernow (George Washington, Andrew Hamilton, Ulysses S. Grant and J.P. Morgan), James Grant (Bernard Baruch), Doris Kearns Goodwin (Franklin D. Roosevelt and Abraham Lincoln) or David McCulloch (John Adams, Harry Truman). There are some exceptions such as Yale's David Blight, author of recent biography of Frederick Douglass, but these tend to be exceptions that prove the rule. The few academic historians like Blight who have written popular biographies tend to be older, and withdrawn from the mainstream of academic history, like Douglas Brinkley, H. W. Brands, Andrew Roberts, Julian T. Jackson, Joseph Ellis and the recently deceased Jean Edward Smith.

What can explain this relative neglect of popular biography among academic historians? It may in part be the result of the corrosive envy too often present in academia. (A recent example from a different field might be some of the churlish criticism directed at Harvard's Steven Pinker for his bestseller *Enlightenment Now*, much of which consisted of complaints that Pinker is a mere showman, rather than offering a substantive critique of specific aspects of his admittedly capacious book.) Academic historians will whisper sotto voce that publishing a history popular with the general reading public is most likely to be counted against you in university history departments at tenure and promotion time – one of the uglier aspects of academic life that mostly goes unremarked. But more likely what explains this 'market failure', as economists would call it, is the tide of academic trends towards fine-grained social history and away from biography as well as diplomatic, military, and 'meta-history' (as sweeping narratives are now sometimes stigmatized). It is not necessary to charge that academic history has succumbed too much to Marxist-inspired frameworks that explain history primarily as the result of material or other sub-rational forces to the exclusion of individual human choice to understand this ultimate 'town-versus-gown' split. The popularity of biography and old-fashioned narrative with the general public reflects the general citizen's common-sense perception of the purely human things – perceptions that go a long way towards informing their attitudes – and voting preferences. A discipline of history that ignores this is dooming itself to boutique status. Most market failures have a way of correcting themselves over time, even at universities. The precipitous decline in undergraduate history majors might eventually provide a market signal strong enough to cause the discipline to have some second thoughts and make course corrections.

I

On the surface, political science may be thought more successful than history in achieving some of the original promise of social science, and hence reason to regard history with benign neglect. It produces empirical findings and regression models that often qualify or refute commonly held misperceptions (usually spread by the news media) about public opinion, voting behaviour and election outcomes. But as a predictive science, it has fared no better than history. The list of intelligence failures by the CIA and other governmental organizations that represent supposedly expert techniques is legendary. Beyond specific questions such as estimating whether Iraq circa 2002 had extensive caches of weapons of mass destruction, or how long it would take the Taliban to conquer Afghanistan in 2021, the failure on larger, more important questions is even worse. Philip Tetlock points out in *Expert Political Judgment* that there was virtually no expert at any point in the 1980s in American or European universities or intelligence agencies who predicted the imminent demise of the Soviet Union, and notes that 'experts' (and historians!) remain locked in vigorous argument today about the primary causes of why it happened. There were few, and perhaps no, political scientists who predicted Donald Trump's rise and electoral victory in 2016, and few who perceived the underlying 'populist' shifts in public opinion that brought about Trump and the Brexit vote in Britain. The shock of these unexpected events has generated a rush of scholarly concern about the future of democracy itself, but there is no clear consensus on how to assess the risks. (The lack of consensus on this issue is probably a good thing for now, but is beyond the scope of this enquiry.) As James Q. Wilson once admonished social scientists: 'Stop trying to predict the future; you can't even predict the past!'

Perhaps a deliberate attempt at reunifying history and political science would reinvigorate both fields. The political philosopher Harry V. Jaffa wrote that 'political science, properly so-called, would have at its heart the study of the speeches and deeds of statesmen'. The first objection to this more history-based disposition is the simple fact that historians and biographers disagree sharply about their subjects of inquiry, and, unlike a regression analysis, there can be no recourse to replication or data quality verification. The candid observer might well go beyond attributing different conclusions to subjective ideological or methodological commitments and wonder whether the descent of academic history into esoterica has made many historians and biographers simply incompetent at politically relevant treatments.

Aside from that provocation, a second objection against the charge of the self-desiccation of history is that history should hardly be blamed for neglecting what political science itself has shoved to the margins: the idea that statesmanship can be understood intelligibly. A long-range review of political science finds that the term 'statesman' and its correlates ('statesmanship' and 'statecraft') appeared regularly in academic literature without irony or scare quotes as recently as the 1970s but has gradually disappeared from use. Arnold Wolfers's 1949 essay in *World Politics*, 'Statesmanship and Moral Choice', was widely cited and included in reading lists for the next twenty-five years at least, as were many similar articles. By degrees, however, the idea of statesmanship, and especially its indispensable virtue, prudence, began to disappear for both ideological and methodological reasons (the concept is 'unscientific'). By the mid-1970s, Herbert Storing wrote that 'statesmanship is not much respected . . . [it] is almost un-American. The word has an elitist and obsolete ring'. Carnes Lord observed in 2002: 'In the eyes of most political scientists, the cognitive status of statecraft differs little from the cognitive status of witchcraft.' More recently Daniel Stid of the Hewlett-Packard Foundation echoed Storing and Lord: 'Nowadays, Americans rarely speak of statesmanship. Many even become uncomfortable when the concept is invoked – it strikes them as a fussy, hopelessly gendered notion from a bygone era.'[6] And thus the term has nearly disappeared from academic journals.

As with the defects and omissions of academic history charged earlier, there are reasonable objections to statesmanship as an intelligible concept for political science. The first is that the idea is too dependent on subjective or contestable factors, that is, our partisan or ideological inclinations. The plainspoken or cynical version of this objection was succinctly put by the early-twentieth-century Speaker of the House Thomas Reed, who quipped that 'A statesman is a politician who is safely dead'. And even Abraham Lincoln, in his thoughtful eulogy of his 'beau ideal of a statesman', Henry Clay, pointed out that 'Taking a prominent part, as he did, in all the great political questions of his country for the last half century, *the wisdom of his course on many, is doubted and denied by a large portion of his countrymen*' (emphasis added.) In other words, a person may have a substantial effect on a nation's course – think of Franklin Roosevelt and the New Deal, or Margaret Thatcher's many sweeping domestic policy changes in Britain in the 1980s – while informed opinion remains divided as to the wisdom of these accomplishments. In addition to these reasonable disagreements, there is the additional dimension, the plain fact that even the most successful political leader usually falls short of all their main ambitions – an ineluctable fact best expressed in Enoch Powell's melancholy remark that 'all political lives end in failure'.

But this is a feeble objection in the end, for the simple reason that the consequential impacts of certain political figures can neither be denied nor be reduced to mere chance or necessity, or to sub-rational material forces that supersede or determine all human choice. Were that the case, we would sooner or later have seen arise political organizations that dispensed with singular executive power altogether.

A second objection to statesmanship as an intelligible category of systematic study is that it is thought to be dependent on contingent events, especially crises, usually involving war or foreign relations. But the idea needn't be tied to such extraordinary international events. Certain aspects of more routine governmental ambitions can reveal useful truths. A comparison of how Lyndon Johnson, Ronald Reagan, Margaret Thatcher, Bill Clinton and Barack Obama handled proposed enactments or reforms of social welfare entitlement programmes can provide instructive lessons for future practitioners.

Still, Isaiah Berlin explains the general problem well in his essay on 'The Concept of Scientific History':

> When historians assert particular propositions like 'Lenin played a crucial role in making the Russian revolution', or 'Without Churchill Britain would have been defeated in 1940', the rational grounds for such assertions, whatever their degree of plausibility, are not identical with generalizations of the type, 'Such men, in such conditions, usually affect events in this fashion' for which the evidence may be exceedingly feeble; for we do not test the propositions solely – or indeed generally – by their logical links with such general propositions (or explanation sketches), but rather in terms of their coherence with our picture of a specific situation. To analyze this type of knowledge into a finite collection of general and particular, categorical and hypothetical, propositions, is not practicable.[7]

On the other hand, Berlin used the term 'statesman' throughout in his essay on 'Political Judgment'. If history could not treat statesmanship consistently, it did not mean that it was also beyond the reach of political science, and in fact what Berlin called 'political judgment' was a modern version of what the classics and early moderns called *prudence* – the indispensable virtue of the statesman that relates means to ends. While Berlin purposely avoided using the term 'prudence' (or the debased modern substitute term, 'pragmatism') he used the term 'practical wisdom' in the same sense Aristotle used it. There's an old joke that an academic is someone who sees something in practice and wonders if it will work in theory, and 'practical' in its ordinary use connotes a skill or craft one might learn as an apprentice or in a training programme. But Berlin said the political leaders he thought displayed true practical wisdom were possessed of 'genius', which is not a term we would use for a plumber, carpenter or fix-it man.

II

Meanwhile, the perception that modern political science has grown detached from civic education and actual political life, and thereby failing its early modern aspirations as an applied science, has been around for a long time. One remark from Harvard graduate Robert F. Kennedy in the early 1960s, when he was attorney general of the United States, ought to be seen as an early fire bell about the growing incompetence of academic political science as a civic educator: 'I majored in Government at Harvard and never learned anything which helped me in practical political situations or in overseas travel thereafter. How can universities answer this problem?' David Ricci's spirited 1984 challenge to the discipline, *The Tragedy of Political Science: Politics, Scholarship, and Democracy* (1984), lamented that the 'tyranny of the scientific method' had led the discipline to abdicate its role as a conscious teacher of civic responsibility, character development and moral values. While Ricci's critique was not well received in the discipline, it did not go away, and keeps recurring in new forms every few years.

In 2000, an email from a pseudonymous 'Mr. Perestroika' circulated to a group of seventeen political scientists on the eve of the annual convention of the APSA 'went viral' (before that term was in common use, let alone the existence of social media that is the primary driver of 'viral' phenomena today), becoming an overnight sensation that became known as the 'perestroika movement'.[8] This 'raucous rebellion', as it was described, came chiefly from the left end of the ideological spectrum of the discipline, but many of its specific challenges about methodological narrowness and rigidity were wholly compatible with conservative critiques. Among the specific challenges that the 'perestroika movement' issued was asking a variation of Philip Tetlock's question previously mentioned – why were none of the elaborate models of leading Western universities able to detect the vulnerability and decline of the Soviet Union in its terminal decade (with the additional wrinkle of noting that in fact some academics in the developing world actually did perceive something significant was happening)?

The irony of the 'perestroika movement' is evident: it fared no better than the original 'perestroika' in the Soviet Union. Still, the unease inside political science continues to surface as a subject of concern, while the response is typically to hunker down further into narrow methodological and subject-area specialization. Harvard's Joseph Nye observed in 2009:

> Scholars are paying less attention to questions about how their work relates to the policy world, and in many departments a focus on policy can hurt one's career. Advancement comes faster for those who develop mathematical models, new methodologies or theories expressed in jargon that is unintelligible to policymakers. A survey of articles published over the lifetime of the American Political Science Review found that about one in five dealt with policy prescription or criticism in the first half of the century, while only a handful did so after 1967. Editor Lee Sigelman observed in the journal's centennial issue that 'if "speaking truth to power" and contributing directly to public dialogue about the merits and demerits of various courses of action were still numbered among the functions of the profession, one would not have known it from leafing through its leading journal.'[9]

One remedy for this detachment was the founding of graduate programmes in public policy or administration, whose deliberate focus was on training cadres of public sector professionals. These new disciplines – think of them as applied political science with a side order of management training – had the virtue of teaching technical expertise in service of practical public aims, but also represented merely a narrower re-founding of the original progressive promise of solving social problems with scientific expertise, and shunting off to the side the fact that, as Edward Banfield put it, 'Social problems are at bottom political; they arise from differences of opinion and interest and, except in trivial instances, are difficulties to be coped with (ignored, got around, put up with, exorcised by the arts of rhetoric, etc.) rather than puzzles to be solved.'[10]

Even less satisfying has been the effort to reduce or revive statesmanship through 'leadership' studies of various kinds, which on close inspection turn out to be little more than applied psychology and organizational theory (when they rise to that level of rigour). In other words, 'leadership' as a formal category represents the attempt to get beyond the problem of subjective opinion about what constitutes statesmanship by converting the question into a matter of mere technique. Put even more simply: leadership attempts to solve problems and direct action through value-neutral technique, while statesmanship always involves choices among contested principles (often deeply moral in character) of right action that will never command unanimous agreement. Leadership studies have their value, though more so for the world of commerce than politics, as the political world cannot escape the realm of opinion and reasonable differences about judgement and action. Carnes Lord, Aristotle scholar and national security practitioner (as a one-time member of the National Security Council in the White House), pours chill water on the idea:

> Leadership. . . is a fundamentally apolitical concept, ignoring central concerns of political leadership such as power and authority. And because it assumes that leadership is a quality that can be exercised in any field of human endeavor, it tends to downplay the need for political leadership and its special requirements.

In particular, it downplays the need for political leaders to have any specialized knowledge of political phenomena.[11]

'Leadership' as a value-neutral technique is no more suitable for statesmanship than quantitative regressions models.

III

To summarize the dilemma as Isaiah Berlin presents it: on the one hand, we have a quality that is not 'practicable' to study or teach in the conventional sense, but on the other hand 'practical wisdom' is the highest quality in a political leader, much to be hoped for and celebrated. Although Churchill, a figure Berlin highly admired, urged aspiring participants in political life to study history, he wrote that 'genius, *though it might be armed*, cannot be acquired, either by reading or by experience' (emphasis added). If a precise 'science of statesmanship' is impossible, how might we 'arm' the disposition to approach the idea with respect?

No new gimmicks or techniques will suffice, but taking seriously an idea that receives wide lip service, but no follow-through, at many universities today would be a step in the right direction: reviving the liberal arts as they were once understood and taught. The aforementioned Peter Odegard, in his 1951 address to the APSA, said: 'To reconcile the legitimate demand for specialized training with the equally urgent need for a liberal education is a central problem of higher education in the United States.' Among Odegard's recommendations that the APSA adopt as requirements for undergraduate and graduate students in political science were:

- Two full-year courses – taken successively if possible – although not necessarily so – in the humanities, fine arts and music.
- Two full-year courses in history and social sciences outside the field of the student's major.
- One full-year course dealing with selected problems in American civilization.
- Two full-year courses in a modern foreign language or languages – unless the student can pass a proficiency test in at least one foreign language.

Such a course of study would be 'a small step toward restoring to political science the scientific, cultural and humane foundation that it had in the beginning. Only along some such road can we hope to recover a sense of the unity of knowledge without which our highly specialized sciences become sterile and dangerous'.[12]

Of course these kinds of capacious programmes of study are found almost nowhere today except for a handful of small liberal arts colleges that have held out against the tides. But perhaps a practice from our most elite business schools might be emulated. Although graduate education in business – the MBA – has become increasingly quantitative owing to the prominence of finance today, Harvard, which founded the first graduate school of business (in the humanities!) over a century ago, still employs the case method, wherein students are presented with real circumstances requiring analysis and decision by a responsible person or persons. In other words, history. (While the case method is clearly borrowed from legal education, ironically the Harvard Business School initially modelled itself after the French *Ecole des Sciences Politique* – the Institute of Political Studies.)

We fortunately have a few examples of this imaginative mode still in existence that ought to be more widely emulated, such as Graham Allison and Philip Zelikow's *Essence of Decision: Explaining the Cuban Missile Crisis*, a classic from the moment of its first publication in 1971 that skilfully blended current academic models of international relations with a wider angle view that demonstrated the limitations of such theoretical frameworks. As a teaching tool *Essence of Decision* has few peers.

Maybe more such peers can be produced with deliberate effort. Why not systematic case studies about the crises, key issues and decisions of 'statesmen'? There are limitless topics that could be recommended for dissertations for both history and political science graduate programmes. President Kennedy's handling of the Cuban Missile Crisis is considered a major success of prudent statecraft; how about a companion study of the Bay of Pigs invasion, which was a fiasco? (Likewise Roberta Wohlstetter and Thomas Schelling's *Pearl Harbor: Warning and Decision* is a classic analysis of a major failure that is likely disappearing from graduate reading lists.)

Needless to say, the American 'war on terror' since 2001 will be a major focus of study for many years to come, though sometimes the passage of time (along with the access to complete records) is necessary to reach solid conclusions. Other episodes with seemingly little contemporary resonance might paradoxically produce wisdom not obvious on the surface. Was Churchill right to have rejected the offer of Italian mediation in May 1940? Likewise, his decision to attack the French fleet at Oran in July 1940? Should Lincoln have embraced the Crittenden Compromise in 1860 and thereby avoided (or postponed) the Civil War? Was it a mistake for President Bill Clinton to have rejected compromise offers from Republican senators on health care in 1993 and 1994? For that matter, was it a mistake for Franklin Roosevelt to have decided to exclude universal health coverage from the Social Security Act in 1935?

The parade of useful case studies – of failures as well as decisions regarded as correct or successful – is abundant and can deepen our understanding of the complexities of ruling far better than a hundred new regression models. It is not necessary to re-fight or settle the old and stale methodological arguments about the fact-value distinction for an older mode of inquiry to prove its usefulness.

Notes

1	Peter H. Odegard, 'Variations on a Familiar Theme', *American Political Science Review* 45, no. 4 (1951): 965.

2	Edward Banfield, 'Policy Science as Metaphysical Madness', in *Here the People Rule: Selected Essays* (New York, 1985), 146. Isaiah Berlin offered a similar reflection in his classic essay 'Political Judgment': 'In theory, no doubt, such laws [of empirical history] should have been discoverable, but in practice this looked less promising. If I am a statesman faced with an agonising choice of possible courses of action in a critical situation, will I really find it useful—even if I can afford to wait that long for the answer—to employ a team of specialists in political science to assemble for me from past history all kinds of cases analogous to my situation, from which I or they must then abstract what these cases have in common, deriving from this exercise relevant laws of human behaviour? The instances for such induction – or for the construction of hypotheses intended to systematise historical knowledge -would, because human experience is so various, not be numerous; and the dismissal even from these instances of all that is unique to each, and the retention only of that which is common, would produce a very thin, generalized residue, and one far too unspecific to be of much help in a practical dilemma.'

3 Aaron Wildavsky, *The Revolt Against the Masses, and Other Essays on Politics and Public Policy* (New York, 1971), viii.
4 Buckle and Bury cited in Isaiah Berlin, 'The Concept of Scientific History', in *Concepts & Categories* (Oxford, 1980), 103–42; Lord Acton, 'The Study of History', in *Essays in the Study and Writing of History* (Indianapolis, IN, 1985), 504–52.
5 Henry Steele Commager, *The American Mind: An Interpretation of American Thought and Character Since the 1880s* (New York, 1950), 290.
6 Daniel Stid, 'A Time for Statesmanship', *National Affairs*, Summer 2021, 139.
7 Berlin, 'The Concept of Scientific History', 138.
8 The episode eventually produced a book, *Perestroika!: The Raucous Rebellion in Political Science*, ed. Kristen Renwick Monroe (New Haven, 2005).
9 Joseph S. Nye, Jr., 'Scholars on the Sidelines', *Washington Post*, 13 April 2009.
10 Banfield, 'Policy Science as Metaphysical Madness', 146.
11 Carnes Lord, 'Bringing Prudence Back In: Leadership, Statecraft, and Political Science', in *Tempered Strength: Studies in the Nature and Scope of Prudential Leadership*, ed. Ethan Fishman (Lanham, MD, 2002), 71.
12 Odegard, 'Variations on a Familiar Theme', 970–1.

Select Bibliography

Bobbitt, Philip, *The Shield of Achilles: War, Peace and the Course of History* (New York, 2002).

Brands, Hal and Jeremi Suri (eds.), *The Power of the Past: History and Statecraft* (Washington, DC, 2016).

Brands, Hal and William Inboden, 'Wisdom Without Tears: Statecraft and the Uses of History', *Journal of Strategic Studies* 41, no. 7 (2018): 916–46.

Collingwood, R. G., *An Autobiography* (Oxford, 1939).

Collingwood, R. G., *The Idea of History*, edited by Jan van der Dussen (Oxford, 1993).

Collingwood, R. G., *The Principles of History: And Other Writings in Philosophy of History*, edited by W. H. Dray and W. J. van der Dussen (Oxford, 1999).

Gaddis, John Lewis, *The Landscape of History: How Historians Map the Past* (Oxford, 2004).

Polybius, *The Rise of the Roman Empire*, translated by Ian Scott-Kilvert (London, 1979).

Thucydides, *The War of the Peloponnesians and the Athenians*, edited by Jeremy Wynott (Cambridge, 2013).

Index

Note: Page numbers followed by 'n' refer to notes.

Printed in Great Britain
by Amazon

46002526R00150